STOCK TRADER'S ALMANAC 2013

Jeffrey A. Hirsch & Yale Hirsch

WILEY

John Wiley & Sons, Inc.

www.stocktradersalmanac.com

Published by John Wiley & Sons, Inc., Hoboken, New Jersey
Published simultaneously in Canada

Editor in Chief	Jeffrey A. Hirsch
Editor at Large	Yale Hirsch
Director of Research	Christopher Mistal
Production Editor	Melissa Lopez

For general information about our other products and services, please contact our Customer Care Department within the United States at 800-762-2974, outside the United States at 317-572-3993 or fax 317-572-4002.

Wiley also publishes its books in a variety of electronic formats. Some content that appears in print may not be available in electronic books. For more information about Wiley products, visit our Web site at www.wiley.com.

ISBN: 978-1-118-15987-3 (cloth)
ISBN: 978-1-118-22610-0 (ebk)
ISBN: 978-1-118-23944-5 (ebk)
ISBN: 978-1-118-26408-9 (ebk)
10 9 8 7 6 5 4 3 2 1

Printed in China

This Forty-Sixth Edition is respectfully dedicated to:

Jordan L. Kimmel

An active user of the Almanac since the early 1990s, we first met Jordan back in 1997 as he was honing his now widely recognized and respected Magnet® Stock Selection Process. One of the early adopters of "quantitative screening" for stocks, he did not listen when others told him you could not successfully blend value, growth, and momentum together. His tenacity, research, and dedication have paid off. The American Association of Individual Investors ranks the Magnet® Simple #1 over the last 3- and 5-year periods, and #2 over the last 10 years as we go to press.

As important as market returns are, character also counts. We have known Jordan personally and worked together over the last 15 years. One of the things Jordan has focused on over the past several years is combining "what-to-buy" with "when-to-buy." In 2012 we joined forces with Jordan, combining the insights of the Almanac with the Magnet process.

INTRODUCTION TO THE FORTY-SIXTH EDITION

We are pleased and proud to introduce the Forty-Sixth Edition of the *Stock Trader's Almanac*. The *Almanac* provides you with the necessary tools to invest successfully in the twenty-first century.

J. P. Morgan's classic retort, "Stocks will fluctuate," is often quoted with a wink-of-the-eye implication that the only prediction one can make about the stock market is that it will go up, down, or sideways. Many investors agree that no one ever really knows which way the market will move. Nothing could be further from the truth.

We discovered that while stocks do indeed fluctuate, they do so in well-defined, often predictable patterns. These patterns recur too frequently to be the result of chance or coincidence. How else do we explain that since 1950 all the gains in the market were made during November through April, compared to a loss May through October? (See page 48.)

The *Almanac* is a practical investment tool. It alerts you to those little-known market patterns and tendencies on which shrewd professionals enhance profit potential. You will be able to forecast market trends with accuracy and confidence when you use the *Almanac* to help you understand:

- How our presidential elections affect the economy and the stock market—just as the moon affects the tides. Many investors have made fortunes following the political cycle. You can be sure that money managers who control billions of dollars are also political cycle watchers. Astute people do not ignore a pattern that has been working effectively throughout most of our economic history.

- How the passage of the Twentieth Amendment to the Constitution fathered the January Barometer. This barometer has an outstanding record for predicting the general course of the stock market each year, with only seven major errors since 1950, for a 88.7% accuracy ratio. (See page 16.)

- Why there is a significant market bias at certain times of the day, week, month, and year.

Even if you are an investor who pays scant attention to cycles, indicators, and patterns, your investment survival could hinge on your interpretation of one of the recurring patterns found within these pages. One of the most intriguing and important patterns is the symbiotic relationship between Washington and Wall Street. Aside from the potential profitability in seasonal patterns, there's the pure joy of seeing the market very often do just what you expected.

The *Stock Trader's Almanac* is also an organizer. Its wealth of information is presented on a calendar basis. The *Almanac* puts investing in a business framework and makes investing easier because it:

- Updates investment knowledge and informs you of new techniques and tools.
- Is a monthly reminder and refresher course.
- Alerts you to both seasonal opportunities and dangers.
- Furnishes a historical viewpoint by providing pertinent statistics on past market performance.
- Supplies forms necessary for portfolio planning, record keeping, and tax preparation.

The WITCH icon signifies THIRD FRIDAY OF THE MONTH on calendar pages and alerts you to extraordinary volatility due to the expiration of equity and index options and index futures contracts. Triple-witching days appear during March, June, September, and December.

The BULL icon on calendar pages signifies favorable trading days based on the S&P 500 rising 60% or more of the time on a particular trading day during the 21-year period January 1991 to December 2011.

A BEAR icon on calendar pages signifies unfavorable trading days based on the S&P falling 60% or more of the time for the same 21-year period.

Also, to give you even greater perspective, we have listed next to the date of every day that the market is open the Market Probability numbers for the same 21-year period for the Dow (D), S&P 500 (S) and NASDAQ (N). You will see a "D," "S," and "N" followed by a number signifying the actual Market Probability number for that trading day, based on the recent 21-year period. On pages 121–128 you will find complete Market Probability Calendars, both long-term and 21-year for the Dow, S&P, and NASDAQ, as well as for the Russell 1000 and Russell 2000 indices.

Other seasonalities near the ends, beginnings, and middles of months—options expirations, around holidays, and other significant times—as well as all FOMC Meeting dates are noted for *Almanac* investors' convenience on the weekly planner pages. All other important economic releases are provided in the Strategy Calendar every month in our e-newsletter, *Almanac Investor*, available at our website *www.stocktradersalmanac.com*.

As a reminder to long time *Almanac* readers, the ten years of monthly Daily Dow Point Changes have moved from their respective *Almanac* pages to the Databank section toward the rear of this book. We continue to rely on the clarity of this presentation to observe market tendencies. In response to newsletter subscriber feedback, we include our well-received Monthly Vital Stats on the *Almanac* pages.

The Notable Events on page 6 provides a handy list of major events of the past year that can be helpful when evaluating things that may have moved the market. Over the past few years, our research had been restructured to flow better with the rhythm of the year. This has also allowed us more room for added data. Again, we have included historical data on the Russell 1000 and Russell 2000 indices. The Russell 2K is an excellent proxy for small and mid caps, which we have used over the years, and the Russell 1K provides a broader view of large caps. Annual highs and lows for all five indices covered in the *Almanac* appear on pages 149–151 and we've tweaked the Best & Worst section.

In order to cram in all the new material, we had to cut some of our Record Keeping section. We have converted many of these paper forms into computer spreadsheets for our own internal use. As a service to our faithful readers, we are making these forms available at our website *www.stocktradersalmanac.com*.

Post-presidential election year perspectives can be found on pages 24, 30, 32, 34, 52, and 74. The Dow has posted full-year gains in only 9 of 19 post-election years when a sitting president had just completed his re-election bid (page 24). More bear markets and negative market action have plagued Republican administrations in the post-election year, whereas the midterm year has been worse under Democrats since 1953 (page 32). Election year campaigning rarely allows time for incumbent administrations to deal with challenging issues. More times than not, difficult tasks are not begun until after the Inaugural Ball, which frequently impacts the market negatively (page 34). Democratic administrations have enjoyed the greatest market gains while purchasing power has held up better under Republican administrations (page 52). The best scenario for all investors has been a Democrat in the White House and Republican control of Congress with average gains of 19.5% (page 74).

Sector seasonalities include several consistent shorting opportunities and appear on pages 92–96. In response to many reader inquiries about how and what to trade when implementing the Best Months Switching Strategies, we detail some simple techniques, including a sampling of tradable mutual funds and ETFs on page 32.

We are constantly searching for new insights and nuances about the stock market and welcome any suggestions from our readers.

Have a healthy and prosperous 2013!

NOTABLE EVENTS

2011

Jun 22	President Obama announces Afghanistan troop withdrawal timeline
Jul 22	Two sequential terrorist attacks kill 77 in Norway
Aug 2	President Obama signs Debt plan to avoid default
Aug 22	Gold trades to new all-time high of $1894
Aug 28	Tropical Storm Irene hits New York
Sep 21	Fed Announces Operation Twist
Sep 30	Federal Budget Deficit $1.3 trillion, tie 2nd highest
Oct 3	October slays another bear market
Oct 20	Muammar al-Qaddafi killed
Oct 21	U.S. Troop withdrawal from Iraq announced
Oct 31	World population officially reaches 7 billion
Nov 15	Federal government debt reaches $15 trillion
Dec 21	ECB extends $643 billion in 3-year loans
Dec 28	Iran threatens closure of Straits of Hormuz

2012

Jan 23	Europe bans Iranian oil imports, effective July 1
Feb 9	U.S. states reach $25 billion mortgage fraud settlement with country's largest loan servicers
Feb 29	Apple Inc market cap exceeds $500 billion
Feb 29	ECB extends $712 billion in 3-year loans
Mar 4	Putin re-elected to President of Russia
Mar 6	Lehman Brothers emerges from largest corporate bankruptcy in history
Mar 9	Greece completes largest debt restructuring in history, to receive additional $130 billion in aid
Apr 12	Defying international pressure, N. Korea launches rocket
May 10	JPMorgan Discloses $2 billion trading loss
May 18	Facebook IPO's at $38 and flops
May 30	10-year Treasury bond yields fall to 60-yr low
May 30	Romney reaches delegate count for nomination

2013 OUTLOOK

By our reckoning there was a mild bear market in 2011, although the S&P 500 just barely missed the widely accepted 20% decline from its late April high to its October low. S&P and NASDAQ failed to recoup their losses last year, but the Dow did gain 5.5% to keep its streak of no losing pre-election years since 1939.

Seasonality has been on track since September 2009. Last year unfolded in near text-book fashion. The catalyst for last year's decline was persistent European debt concerns and, at press time, they are mounting again and pressuring markets. Slowing growth in emerging markets, a historically weak post-election year track record, the expiration of tax cuts, and unemployment benefits at yearend is likely to make for an exciting three-ring circus in D.C. after Election Day and plague stocks in 2013. Markets do not like uncertainty.

Unless a full-blown bear market occurs in 2012 or the market slogs along into the New Year, market gains will be harder to come by in 2013 than they have since the March 2009 bottom. A more likely scenario is that seasonal and economic softness gives way as the presidential election approaches and some resolution in Europe coincides with at least the hint of an easing move from the Bernanke Fed.

If things look good for Obama, October is likely to be stronger. If Romney wins, expect a bigger move in November. Either way, there have been only two losses in the last seven months of election years for the S&P 500 since 1952. Also on the bright side for 2012, the DJIA has averaged 9% in years when a sitting president was running for reelection—win or lose.

Full-year 2013 is another story. Markets are likely to come under pressure as whoever the president is will have tall orders to remedy the economy, the deficit, and the dysfunc-tional government. The easy economic data and corporate results comparisons of the past few years will be gone. Foreign hot spots and diplomatic issues will also require renewed attention from the White House once the campaigning and/or inaugural balls are over. Central banking will remain accommodative, but there is little more they can do. After the yearend rally and positive 2012, we are concerned that the next major bear market will occur in the 2013–2014 period.

— *Jeffrey A. Hirsch, June 1, 2012*

THE 2013 STOCK TRADER'S ALMANAC

CONTENTS

DIRECTORY OF TRADING PATTERNS AND DATABANK

STRATEGY PLANNING AND RECORD SECTION

2013 STRATEGY CALENDAR
(Option expiration dates circled)

	MONDAY	TUESDAY	WEDNESDAY	THURSDAY	FRIDAY	SATURDAY	SUNDAY
JANUARY	31	1 JANUARY New Year's Day	2	3	4	5	6
	7	8	9	10	11	12	13
	14	15	16	17	(18)	19	20
	21 Martin Luther King Day	22	23	24	25	26	27
FEBRUARY	28	29	30	31	1 FEBRUARY	2	3
	4	5	6	7	8	9	10
	11	12	13 Ash Wednesday	14 ♥	(15)	16	17
	18 Presidents' Day	19	20	21	22	23	24
MARCH	25	26	27	28	1 MARCH	2	3
	4	5	6	7	8	9	10 Daylight Saving Time Begins
	11	12	13	14	(15)	16	17 St. Patrick's Day
	18	19	20	21	22	23	24
	25	26 Passover	27	28	29 Good Friday	30	31 Easter
APRIL	1 APRIL	2	3	4	5	6	7
	8	9	10	11	12	13	14
	15 Tax Deadline	16	17	18	(19)	20	21
	22	23	24	25	26	27	28
MAY	29	30	1 MAY	2	3	4	5
	6	7	8	9	10	11	12 Mother's Day
	13	14	15	16	(17)	18	19
	20	21	22	23	24	25	26
JUNE	27 Memorial Day	28	29	30	31	1 JUNE	2
	3	4	5	6	7	8	9
	10	11	12	13	14	15	16 Father's Day
	17	18	19	20	(21)	22	23
	24	25	26	27	28	29	30

Market closed on shaded weekdays; closes early when half-shaded.

2013 STRATEGY CALENDAR

(Option expiration dates circled)

MONDAY	TUESDAY	WEDNESDAY	THURSDAY	FRIDAY	SATURDAY	SUNDAY	
1 JULY	2	3	4 Independence Day	5	6	7	JULY
8	9	10	11	12	13	14	
15	16	17	18	(19)	20	21	
22	23	24	25	26	27	28	
29	30	31	1 AUGUST	2	3	4	AUGUST
5	6	7	8	9	10	11	
12	13	14	15	(16)	17	18	
19	20	21	22	23	24	25	
26	27	28	29	30	31	1 SEPTEMBER	SEPTEMBER
2 Labor Day	3	4	5 Rosh Hashanah	6	7	8	
9	10	11	12	13	14 Yom Kippur	15	
16	17	18	19	(20)	21	22	
23	24	25	26	27	28	29	
30	1 OCTOBER	2	3	4	5	6	OCTOBER
7	8	9	10	11	12	13	
14 Columbus Day	15	16	17	(18)	19	20	
21	22	23	24	25	26	27	
28	29	30	31 🎃	1 NOVEMBER	2	3 Daylight Saving Time Ends	NOVEMBER
4	5 Election Day	6	7	8	9	10	
11 Veterans' Day	12	13	14	(15)	16	17	
18	19	20	21	22	23	24	
25	26	27	28 Thanksgiving Chanukah	29	30	1 DECEMBER	DECEMBER
2	3	4	5	6	7	8	
9	10	11	12	13	14	15	
16	17	18	19	(20)	21	22	
23	24	25 Christmas	26	27	28	29	
30	31	1 JANUARY New Year's Day	2	3	4	5	

JANUARY ALMANAC

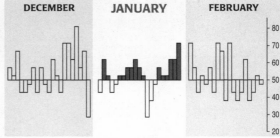

JANUARY								FEBRUARY						
S	M	T	W	T	F	S		S	M	T	W	T	F	S
		1	2	3	4	5							1	2
6	7	8	9	10	11	12		3	4	5	6	7	8	9
13	14	15	16	17	18	19		10	11	12	13	14	15	16
20	21	22	23	24	25	26		17	18	19	20	21	22	23
27	28	29	30	31				24	25	26	27	28		

Market Probability Chart above is a graphic representation of the S&P 500 Recent Market Probability Calendar on page 124.

◆ January Barometer predicts year's course with .758 batting average (page 16) ◆ 12 of last 15 post-presidential election years followed January's direction ◆ Every down January on the S&P since 1950, *without exception*, preceded a new or extended bear market, a flat market, or a 10% correction (page 42) ◆ S&P gains January's first five days preceded full-year gains 84.6% of the time, 11 of last 15 post-presidential years followed first five days' direction (page 14) ◆ November, December, and January constitute the year's best three-month span, a 4.3% S&P gain (pages 44 & 147) ◆ January NASDAQ powerful 2.9% since 1971 (pages 56 & 148) ◆ "January Effect" now starts in mid-December and favors small-cap stocks (pages 104 & 108) ◆ 2009 has the dubious honor of the worst S&P 500 January on record.

January Vital Statistics

	DJIA		S&P 500		NASDAQ		Russell 1K		Russell 2K	
Rank	6		5		1		4		2	
Up	41		39		28		22		19	
Down	22		24		14		12		15	
Average % Change	1.1%		1.1%		2.9%		1.2%		1.8%	
Post-Election Year	0.3%		0.4%		2.0%		1.1%		1.5%	
Best & Worst January										
	% Change		% Change		% Change		% Change		% Change	
Best	1976	14.4	1987	13.2	1975	16.6	1987	12.7	1985	13.1
Worst	2009	–8.8	2009	–8.6	2008	–9.9	2009	–8.3	2009	–11.2
Best & Worst January Weeks										
Best	1/9/76	6.1	1/2/09	6.8	1/12/01	9.1	1/2/09	6.8	1/9/87	7.0
Worst	1/24/03	–5.3	1/28/00	–5.6	1/28/00	–8.2	1/28/00	–5.5	1/4/08	–6.5
Best & Worst January Days										
Best	1/17/91	4.6	1/3/01	5.0	1/3/01	14.2	1/3/01	5.3	1/21/09	5.3
Worst	1/8/88	–6.9	1/8/88	–6.8	1/2/01	–7.2	1/8/88	–6.1	1/20/09	–7.0
First Trading Day of Expiration Week: 1980–2012										
Record (#Up–#Down)	23–10		21–12		20–13		20–13		20–13	
Current streak	U3		U3		U3		U3		U1	
Avg % Change	0.15		0.15		0.19		0.12		0.20	
Options Expiration Day: 1980–2012										
Record (#Up–#Down)	16–17		17–16		18–15		17–16		18–15	
Current streak	U2		U2		D3		U2		U1	
Avg % Change	–0.12		–0.10		–0.16		–0.12		–0.13	
Options Expiration Week: 1980–2012										
Record (#Up–#Down)	17–16		14–19		18–15		14–19		17–16	
Current streak	U2		U1		U1		U1		U1	
Avg % Change	–0.20		–0.10		0.25		–0.11		0.21	
Week After Options Expiration: 1980–2012										
Record (#Up–#Down)	17–16		20–13		18–15		20–13		22–11	
Current streak	D4		U1		U1		U1		U2	
Avg % Change	–0.01		0.19		0.09		0.16		0.18	
First Trading Day Performance										
% of Time Up	58.7		49.2		57.1		44.1		47.1	
Avg % Change	0.25		0.15		0.18		0.14		0.06	
Last Trading Day Performance										
% of Time Up	58.7		63.5		66.7		61.8		76.5	
Avg % Change	0.24		0.27		0.31		0.36		0.28	

Dow & S&P 1950–April 2012, NASDAQ 1971–April 2012, Russell 1K & 2K 1979–April 2012.

20th Amendment made "lame ducks" disappear.
Now, "As January goes, so goes the year."

DECEMBER 2012/JANUARY 2013

Last Trading Day of the Year, NASDAQ Down 11 of last 12
NASDAQ Was Up 29 Years in a Row 1971–1999

MONDAY

D 38.1
S 28.6
N 47.6

31

Those that forget the past are condemned to repeat its mistakes, and those that mis-state the past should be condemned.
— Eugene D. Cohen (Letter to the Editor Financial Times 10/30/06)

New Years Day (Market Closed)

TUESDAY

1

If we did all the things we are capable of doing, we would literally astound ourselves.
— Thomas Alva Edison (American inventor, 1093 patents, 1847–1931)

Small Caps Punished First Trading Day of Year
Russell 2000 Down 14 of Last 23, But Up Last 4

WEDNESDAY

D 66.7
S 42.9
N 61.9

2

[A contrarian's opportunity] If everybody is thinking alike, then somebody isn't thinking.
— General George S. Patton, Jr. (U.S. Army field commander WWII, 1885–1945)

Second Trading Day of the Year, Dow Up 14 of Last 19
Santa Claus Rally Ends (Page 112)

THURSDAY

D 66.7
S 61.9
N 66.7

3

The universal line of distinction between the strong and the weak is that one persists, while the other hesitates, falters, trifles and at last collapses or caves in.
— Edwin Percy Whipple (American essayist, 1819–1886)

FRIDAY

D 47.6
S 52.4
N 52.4

4

Entrepreneurs who believe they're in business to vanquish the competition are less successful than those who believe their goal is to maximize profits or increase their company's value.
— Kaihan Krippendorff (Business consultant, strategist, author, The Art of the Advantage, The Strategic Learning Center, b. 1971)

SATURDAY

5

January Almanac Investor Seasonalities: See Pages 92, 94 and 96

SUNDAY

6

JANUARY'S FIRST FIVE DAYS: AN EARLY WARNING SYSTEM

The last 39 up First Five Days were followed by full-year gains 33 times for an 84.6% accuracy ratio and a 13.6% average gain in all 39 years. The five exceptions include flat 1994 and four related to war. Vietnam military spending delayed start of 1966 bear market. Ceasefire imminence early in 1973 raised stocks temporarily. Saddam Hussein turned 1990 into a bear. The war on terrorism, instability in the Mideast, and corporate malfeasance shaped 2002 into one of the worst years on record. The 23 down First Five Days were followed by 12 up years and 11 down (47.8% accurate) and an average gain of 0.2%.

In 9 of the last 15 Post-Election Years the S&P 500 posted a loss for January's First Five Days. Six were followed by full-year losses averaging −11.1%. 1993 rebounded 7.1% after the sluggish 1992 economy. 1985 followed the trend of no losing "fifth" years (page 129). 2005 was flat with the Dow down 0.6%. Six Post-Election First Five Days showed gains. Only 1973 was a loser at the start of the major bear caused by Vietnam, Watergate, and the Arab Oil Embargo. The other four years gained 22.8% on average.

THE FIRST-FIVE-DAYS-IN-JANUARY INDICATOR

	Chronological Data				Ranked By Performance		
	Previous Year's Close	January 5th Day	5-Day Change	Year Change	Rank		5-Day Change	Year Change
1950	16.76	17.09	2.0%	21.8%	1	1987	6.2%	2.0%
1951	20.41	20.88	2.3	16.5	2	1976	4.9	19.1
1952	23.77	23.91	0.6	11.8	3	1999	3.7	19.5
1953	26.57	26.33	−0.9	−6.6	4	2003	3.4	26.4
1954	24.81	24.93	0.5	45.0	5	2006	3.4	13.6
1955	35.98	35.33	−1.8	26.4	6	1983	3.3	17.3
1956	45.48	44.51	−2.1	2.6	7	1967	3.1	20.1
1957	46.67	46.25	−0.9	−14.3	8	1979	2.8	12.3
1958	39.99	40.99	2.5	38.1	9	2010	2.7	12.8
1959	55.21	55.40	0.3	8.5	10	1963	2.6	18.9
1960	59.89	59.50	−0.7	−3.0	11	1958	2.5	38.1
1961	58.11	58.81	1.2	23.1	12	1984	2.4	1.4
1962	71.55	69.12	−3.4	−11.8	13	1951	2.3	16.5
1963	63.10	64.74	2.6	18.9	14	1975	2.2	31.5
1964	75.02	76.00	1.3	13.0	15	1950	2.0	21.8
1965	84.75	85.37	0.7	9.1	16	2004	1.8	9.0
1966	92.43	93.14	0.8	−13.1	17	2012	1.8	??
1967	80.33	82.81	3.1	20.1	18	1973	1.5	−17.4
1968	96.47	96.62	0.2	7.7	19	1972	1.4	15.6
1969	103.86	100.80	−2.9	−11.4	20	1964	1.3	13.0
1970	92.06	92.68	0.7	0.1	21	1961	1.2	23.1
1971	92.15	92.19	0.04	10.8	22	1989	1.2	27.3
1972	102.09	103.47	1.4	15.6	23	2011	1.1	−0.003
1973	118.05	119.85	1.5	−17.4	24	2002	1.1	−23.4
1974	97.55	96.12	−1.5	−29.7	25	1997	1.0	31.0
1975	68.56	70.04	2.2	31.5	26	1980	0.9	25.8
1976	90.19	94.58	4.9	19.1	27	1966	0.8	−13.1
1977	107.46	105.01	−2.3	−11.5	28	1994	0.7	−1.5
1978	95.10	90.64	−4.7	1.1	29	1965	0.7	9.1
1979	96.11	98.80	2.8	12.3	30	2009	0.7	23.5
1980	107.94	108.95	0.9	25.8	31	1970	0.7	0.1
1981	135.76	133.06	−2.0	−9.7	32	1952	0.6	11.8
1982	122.55	119.55	−2.4	14.8	33	1954	0.5	45.0
1983	140.64	145.23	3.3	17.3	34	1996	0.4	20.3
1984	164.93	168.90	2.4	1.4	35	1959	0.3	8.5
1985	167.24	163.99	−1.9	26.3	36	1995	0.3	34.1
1986	211.28	207.97	−1.6	14.6	37	1992	0.2	4.5
1987	242.17	257.28	6.2	2.0	38	1968	0.2	7.7
1988	247.08	243.40	−1.5	12.4	39	1990	0.1	−6.6
1989	277.72	280.98	1.2	27.3	40	1971	0.04	10.8
1990	353.40	353.79	0.1	−6.6	41	2007	−0.4	3.5
1991	330.22	314.90	−4.6	26.3	42	1960	−0.7	−3.0
1992	417.09	418.10	0.2	4.5	43	1957	−0.9	−14.3
1993	435.71	429.05	−1.5	7.1	44	1953	−0.9	−6.6
1994	466.45	469.90	0.7	−1.5	45	1974	−1.5	−29.7
1995	459.27	460.83	0.3	34.1	46	1998	−1.5	26.7
1996	615.93	618.46	0.4	20.3	47	1988	−1.5	12.4
1997	740.74	748.41	1.0	31.0	48	1993	−1.5	7.1
1998	970.43	956.04	−1.5	26.7	49	1986	−1.6	14.6
1999	1229.23	1275.09	3.7	19.5	50	2001	−1.8	−13.0
2000	1469.25	1441.46	−1.9	−10.1	51	1955	−1.8	26.4
2001	1320.28	1295.86	−1.8	−13.0	52	2000	−1.9	−10.1
2002	1148.08	1160.71	1.1	−23.4	53	1985	−1.9	26.3
2003	879.82	909.93	3.4	26.4	54	1981	−2.0	−9.7
2004	1111.92	1131.91	1.8	9.0	55	1956	−2.1	2.6
2005	1211.92	1186.19	−2.1	3.0	56	2005	−2.1	3.0
2006	1248.29	1290.15	3.4	13.6	57	1977	−2.3	−11.5
2007	1418.30	1412.11	−0.4	3.5	58	1982	−2.4	14.8
2008	1468.36	1390.19	−5.3	−38.5	59	1969	−2.9	−11.4
2009	903.25	909.73	0.7	23.5	60	1962	−3.4	−11.8
2010	1115.10	1144.98	2.7	12.8	61	1991	−4.6	26.3
2011	1257.64	1271.50	1.1	−0.003	62	1978	−4.7	1.1
2012	1257.60	1280.70	1.8	??	63	2008	−5.3	−38.5

Based on S&P 500

JANUARY

January's First Five Days Act as an "Early Warning" (Page 14)

MONDAY
7

D 52.4
S 42.9
N 52.4

Big money is made in the stock market by being on the right side of major moves. I don't believe in swimming against the tide.
— Martin Zweig (Fund manager, *Winning on Wall Street*)

TUESDAY
8

D 33.3
S 47.6
N 52.4

There are two kinds of people who lose money: those who know nothing and those who know everything.
— Henry Kaufman (German-American economist, b. 1927, to Robert Lenzner in Forbes 10/19/98 who added, "With two Nobel Prize winners in the house, Long-Term Capital clearly fits the second case.")

January Ends "Best Three-Month Span" (Pages 44, 56,147 and 148)

WEDNESDAY
9

D 52.4
S 52.4
N 66.7

We are nowhere near a capitulation point because it's at that point where it's despair, not hope, that reigns supreme, and there was scant evidence of any despair at any of the meetings I gave.
— David Rosenberg (Economist, Merrill Lynch, *Barron's* 4/21/2008)

THURSDAY
10

D 52.4
S 52.4
N 52.4

The fear of capitalism has compelled socialism to widen freedom, and the fear of socialism has compelled capitalism to increase equality.
— Will and Ariel Durant

FRIDAY
11

D 52.4
S 57.1
N 57.1

There is a perfect inverse correlation between inflation rates and price/earnings ratios . . . When inflation has been very high . . . P/E has been [low].
— Liz Ann Sonders (Chief Investment Strategist Charles Schwab, June 2006)

SATURDAY
12

SUNDAY
13

THE INCREDIBLE JANUARY BAROMETER (DEVISED 1972): ONLY SEVEN SIGNIFICANT ERRORS IN 62 YEARS

Devised by Yale Hirsch in 1972, our January Barometer states that as the S&P 500 goes in January, so goes the year. The indicator has registered **only seven major errors since 1950 for an 88.7% accuracy ratio**. Vietnam affected 1966 and 1968; 1982 saw the start of a major bull market in August; two January rate cuts and 9/11 affected 2001; the anticipation of military action in Iraq held down the market in January 2003; 2009 was the beginning of a new bull market following the second worst bear market on record; and the Fed saved 2010 with QE2 (*Almanac Investor* newsletter subscribers receive full analysis of each reading as well as its potential implications for the full year.)

Including the eight flat-year errors (less than +/- 5%) yields a 75.8% accuracy ratio. A full comparison of all monthly barometers for the Dow, S&P, and NASDAQ in our February 6, 2012 blog post at *blog.stocktradersalmanac.com* details January's market forecasting prowess. Bear markets began or continued when Januarys suffered a loss *(see page 42)*. Full years followed January's direction in 12 of the last 15 post-presidential election years. *See pages 18 and 22 for more January Barometer items.*

AS JANUARY GOES, SO GOES THE YEAR

	Market Performance In January					January Performance By Rank			
	Previous Year's Close	January Close	January Change	Year Change		Rank	Year	January Change	Year's Change
1950	16.76	17.05	1.7%	21.8%		1	1987	13.2%	2.0% flat
1951	20.41	21.66	6.1	16.5		2	1975	12.3	31.5
1952	23.77	24.14	1.6	11.8		3	1976	11.8	19.1
1953	26.57	26.38	−0.7	−6.6		4	1967	7.8	20.1
1954	24.81	26.08	5.1	45.0		5	1985	7.4	26.3
1955	35.98	36.63	1.8	26.4		6	1989	7.1	27.3
1956	45.48	43.82	−3.6	2.6 flat		7	1961	6.3	23.1
1957	46.67	44.72	−4.2	−14.3		8	1997	6.1	31.0
1958	39.99	41.70	4.3	38.1		9	1951	6.1	16.5
1959	55.21	55.42	0.4	8.5		10	1980	5.8	25.8
1960	59.89	55.61	−7.1	−3.0 flat		11	1954	5.1	45.0
1961	58.11	61.78	6.3	23.1		12	1963	4.9	18.9
1962	71.55	68.84	−3.8	−11.8		13	2012	4.4	??
1963	63.10	66.20	4.9	18.9		14	1958	4.3	38.1
1964	75.02	77.04	2.7	13.0		15	1991	4.2	26.3
1965	84.75	87.56	3.3	9.1		16	1999	4.1	19.5
1966	92.43	92.88	0.5	−13.1 X		17	1971	4.0	10.8
1967	80.33	86.61	7.8	20.1		18	1988	4.0	12.4
1968	96.47	92.24	−4.4	7.7 X		19	1979	4.0	12.3
1969	103.86	103.01	−0.8	−11.4		20	2001	3.5	−13.0 X
1970	92.06	85.02	−7.6	0.1 flat		21	1965	3.3	9.1
1971	92.15	95.88	4.0	10.8		22	1983	3.3	17.3
1972	102.09	103.94	1.8	15.6		23	1996	3.3	20.3
1973	118.05	116.03	−1.7	−17.4		24	1994	3.3	−1.5 flat
1974	97.55	96.57	−1.0	−29.7		25	1964	2.7	13.0
1975	68.56	76.98	12.3	31.5		26	2006	2.5	13.6
1976	90.19	100.86	11.8	19.1		27	1995	2.4	34.1
1977	107.46	102.03	−5.1	−11.5		28	2011	2.3	−0.003 flat
1978	95.10	89.25	−6.2	1.1 flat		29	1972	1.8	15.6
1979	96.11	99.93	4.0	12.3		30	1955	1.8	26.4
1980	107.94	114.16	5.8	25.8		31	1950	1.7	21.8
1981	135.76	129.55	−4.6	−9.7		32	2004	1.7	9.0
1982	122.55	120.40	−1.8	14.8 X		33	1952	1.6	11.8
1983	140.64	145.30	3.3	17.3		34	2007	1.4	3.5 flat
1984	164.93	163.41	−0.9	1.4 flat		35	1998	1.0	26.7
1985	167.24	179.63	7.4	26.3		36	1993	0.7	7.1
1986	211.28	211.78	0.2	14.6		37	1966	0.5	−13.1 X
1987	242.17	274.08	13.2	2.0 flat		38	1959	0.4	8.5
1988	247.08	257.07	4.0	12.4		39	1986	0.2	14.6
1989	277.72	297.47	7.1	27.3		40	1953	−0.7	−6.6
1990	353.40	329.08	−6.9	−6.6		41	1969	−0.8	−11.4
1991	330.22	343.93	4.2	26.3		42	1984	−0.9	1.4 flat
1992	417.09	408.79	−2.0	4.5 flat		43	1974	−1.0	−29.7
1993	435.71	438.78	0.7	7.1		44	2002	−1.6	−23.4
1994	466.45	481.61	3.3	−1.5 flat		45	1973	−1.7	−17.4
1995	459.27	470.42	2.4	34.1		46	1982	−1.8	14.8 X
1996	615.93	636.02	3.3	20.3		47	1992	−2.0	4.5 flat
1997	740.74	786.16	6.1	31.0		48	2005	−2.5	3.0 flat
1998	970.43	980.28	1.0	26.7		49	2003	−2.7	26.4 X
1999	1229.23	1279.64	4.1	19.5		50	1956	−3.6	2.6 flat
2000	1469.25	1394.46	−5.1	−10.1		51	2010	−3.7	12.8 X
2001	1320.28	1366.01	3.5	−13.0 X		52	1962	−3.8	−11.8
2002	1148.08	1130.20	−1.6	−23.4		53	1957	−4.2	−14.3
2003	879.82	855.70	−2.7	26.4 X		54	1968	−4.4	7.7 X
2004	1111.92	1131.13	1.7	9.0		55	1981	−4.6	−9.7
2005	1211.92	1181.27	−2.5	3.0 flat		56	1977	−5.1	−11.5
2006	1248.29	1280.08	2.5	13.6		57	2000	−5.1	−10.1
2007	1418.30	1438.24	1.4	3.5 flat		58	2008	−6.1	−38.5
2008	1468.36	1378.55	−6.1	−38.5		59	1978	−6.2	1.1 flat
2009	903.25	825.88	−8.6	23.5 X		60	1990	−6.9	−6.6
2010	1115.10	1073.87	−3.7	12.8 X		61	1960	−7.1	−3.0 flat
2011	1257.64	1286.12	2.3	−0.003 flat		62	1970	−7.6	0.1 flat
2012	1257.60	1312.41	4.4	??		63	2009	−8.6	23.5 X

X = major error   Based on S&P 500

JANUARY

First Trading Day of January Expiration Week, Dow Up 15 of Last 20

MONDAY
D 52.4
S 57.1
N 57.1
14

Sometimes the best investments are the ones you don't make.
— Donald Trump (Real estate mogul and entrepreneur, *Trump: How to Get Rich*, 2004)

TUESDAY
D 61.9
S 61.9
N 52.4
15

Nothing gives one person so much advantage over another as to remain always cool and unruffled under all circumstances.
— Thomas Jefferson (3rd U.S. President, 1743–7/4/1826)

January Expiration Week Horrible Since 1999, Dow Down 9 of Last 14

WEDNESDAY
D 57.1
S 57.1
N 66.7
16

I don't believe in intuition. When you get sudden flashes of perception, it is just the brain working faster than usual.
— Katherine Anne Porter (American author, 1890–1980)

THURSDAY
D 33.3
S 52.4
N 61.9
17

The whole problem with the world is that fools and fanatics are always so certain of themselves, but wiser people so full of doubts.
— Bertrand Russell (British mathematician and philosopher, 1872–1970)

January Expiration Day, Dow Down 10 of Last 14 With Big Losses
Off 2.1% in 2010, Off 2.0% in 2006 and 1.3% in 2003

FRIDAY
D 28.6
S 28.6
N 33.3
18

If investing is entertaining, if you're having fun, you're probably not making any money. Good investing is boring.
— George Soros (Financier, philanthropist, political activist, author and philosopher, b. 1930)

SATURDAY
19

SUNDAY
20

JANUARY BAROMETER IN GRAPHIC FORM SINCE 1950

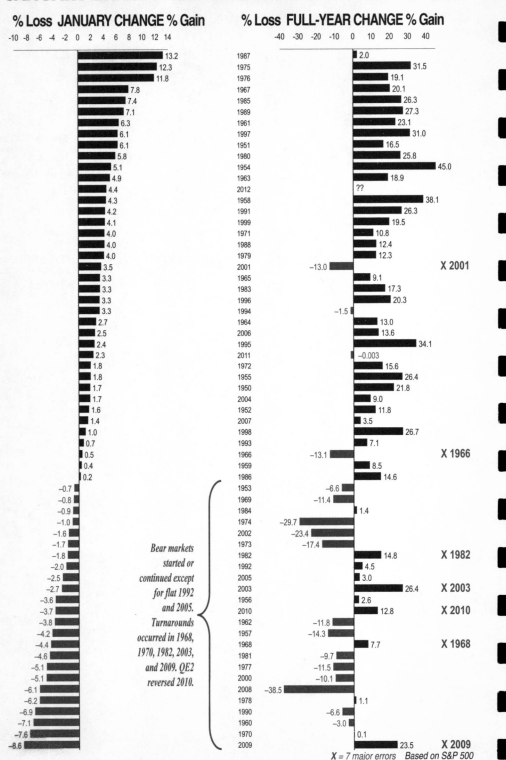

% Loss JANUARY CHANGE % Gain

-10 -8 -6 -4 -2 0 2 4 6 8 10 12 14

13.2
12.3
11.8
7.8
7.4
7.1
6.3
6.1
6.1
5.8
5.1
4.9
4.4
4.3
4.2
4.1
4.0
4.0
4.0
3.5
3.3
3.3
3.3
3.3
2.7
2.5
2.4
2.3
1.8
1.8
1.7
1.7
1.6
1.4
1.0
0.7
0.5
0.4
0.2
-0.7
-0.8
-0.9
-1.0
-1.6
-1.7
-1.8
-2.0
-2.5
-2.7
-3.6
-3.7
-3.8
-4.2
-4.4
-4.6
-5.1
-5.1
-6.1
-6.2
-6.9
-7.1
-7.6
-8.6

Bear markets started or continued except for flat 1992 and 2005. Turnarounds occurred in 1968, 1970, 1982, 2003, and 2009. QE2 reversed 2010.

% Loss FULL-YEAR CHANGE % Gain

-40 -30 -20 -10 0 10 20 30 40

Year	Value	
1987	2.0	
1975	31.5	
1976	19.1	
1967	20.1	
1985	26.3	
1989	27.3	
1961	23.1	
1997	31.0	
1951	16.5	
1980	25.8	
1954	45.0	
1963	18.9	
2012	??	
1958	38.1	
1991	26.3	
1999	19.5	
1971	10.8	
1988	12.4	
1979	12.3	
2001	−13.0	X 2001
1965	9.1	
1983	17.3	
1996	20.3	
1994	−1.5	
1964	13.0	
2006	13.6	
1995	34.1	
2011	−0.003	
1972	15.6	
1955	26.4	
1950	21.8	
2004	9.0	
1952	11.8	
2007	3.5	
1998	26.7	
1993	7.1	
1966	−13.1	X 1966
1959	8.5	
1986	14.6	
1953	−6.6	
1969	−11.4	
1984	1.4	
1974	−29.7	
2002	−23.4	
1973	−17.4	
1982	14.8	X 1982
1992	4.5	
2005	3.0	
2003	26.4	X 2003
1956	2.6	
2010	12.8	X 2010
1962	−11.8	
1957	−14.3	
1968	7.7	X 1968
1981	−9.7	
1977	−11.5	
2000	−10.1	
2008	−38.5	
1978	1.1	
1990	−6.6	
1960	−3.0	
1970	0.1	
2009	23.5	X 2009

X = 7 major errors   Based on S&P 500

JANUARY

Martin Luther King Jr. Day (Market Closed)

MONDAY
21

Civility is not a sign of weakness, and sincerity is always subject to proof. Let us never negotiate out of fear. But let us never fear to negotiate.
— John F. Kennedy (35th U.S. President, Inaugural Address 1/20/1961, 1917–1963)

TUESDAY
D 33.3
S 38.1
N 38.1
22

If I owe a million dollars I am lost. But if I owe $50 billion the bankers are lost.
— Celso Ming (Brazilian journalist)

WEDNESDAY
D 47.6
S 47.6
N 52.4
23

The future now belongs to societies that organize themselves for learning. What we know and can do holds the key to economic progress.
— Ray Marshall (b. 1928) and Marc Tucker (b. 1939) (*Thinking for a Living: Education and the Wealth of Nations*, 1992)

THURSDAY
D 42.9
S 57.1
N 61.9
24

A person's greatest virtue is his ability to correct his mistakes and continually make a new person of himself.
— Yang-Ming Wang (Chinese philosopher, 1472–1529)

FRIDAY
D 61.9
S 52.4
N 42.9
25

The principles of successful stock speculation are based on the supposition that people will continue in the future to make the mistakes that they have made in the past.
— Thomas F. Woodlock (Wall Street Journal editor & columnist, quoted in *Reminiscences of a Stock Operator*, 1866–1945)

SATURDAY
26

February Almanac Investor Seasonalities: See Pages 92, 94 and 96

SUNDAY
27

February Almanac Investor Seasonalities: See Pages 92, 94 and 96

FEBRUARY ALMANAC

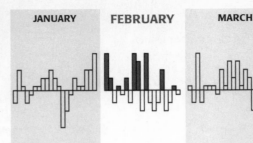

◆ February is the weak link in "Best Six Months" (pages 44, 48, & 147) ◆ RECENT RECORD: S&P up 6, down 8, average change −1.5% last 14 years ◆ Worst NASDAQ month in post-presidential election years average loss 4.4%, up 2, down 10 (page 157), #11 Dow, up 6, down 9 and #12 S&P, up 6, down 9 (pages 153 & 155) ◆ Day before Presidents' Day weekend S&P down 16 of 20, 11 straight 1992–2002, day after down 7 of last 11 (see page 86 & 133) ◆ Many technicians modify market predictions based on January's market.

February Vital Statistics

	DJIA		S&P 500		NASDAQ		Russell 1K		Russell 2K	
Rank	8		11		9		11		7	
Up	36		34		22		20		19	
Down	27		29		20		14		15	
Average % Change	0.04%		−0.1%		0.5%		0.10%		1.0%	
Post-Election Year	−1.6%		−2.0%		−4.4%		−2.2%		−2.4%	
Best & Worst February										
	% Change		% Change		% Change		% Change		% Change	
Best	1986	8.8	1986	7.1	2000	19.2	1986	7.2	2000	16.4
Worst	2009	−11.7	2009	−11.0	2001	−22.4	2009	−10.7	2009	−12.3
Best & Worst February Weeks										
Best	2/1/08	4.4	2/6/09	5.2	2/4/00	9.2	2/6/09	5.3	2/1/91	6.6
Worst	2/20/09	−6.2	2/20/09	−6.9	2/9/01	−7.1	2/20/09	−6.9	2/20/09	−8.3
Best & Worst February Days										
Best	2/24/09	3.3	2/24/09	4.0	2/11/99	4.2	2/24/09	4.1	2/24/09	4.5
Worst	2/10/09	−4.6	2/10/09	−5.0	2/16/01	−4.9	2/10/09	−4.8	2/10/09	−4.7
First Trading Day of Expiration Week: 1980–2012										
Record (#Up–#Down)	20–13		23–10		18–15		23–10		19–14	
Current streak	U1		U3		U3		U3		U3	
Avg % Change	0.29		0.24		0.01		0.21		0.05	
Options Expiration Day: 1980–2012										
Record (#Up–#Down)	16–17		14–19		13–20		15–18		14–19	
Current streak	U3		U3		D1		U3		D1	
Avg % Change	−0.07		−0.15		−0.30		−0.15		−0.11	
Options Expiration Week: 1980–2012										
Record (#Up–#Down)	20–13		17–16		17–16		16–17		20–13	
Current streak	U3		U3		U3		U3		U3	
Avg % Change	0.35		0.11		−0.05		0.11		0.13	
Week After Options Expiration: 1980–2012										
Record (#Up–#Down)	14–19		15–18		18–15		15–18		17–16	
Current streak	U1		U1		U1		U1		D5	
Avg % Change	−0.38		−0.28		−0.24		−0.23		−0.16	
First Trading Day Performance										
% of Time Up	61.9		61.9		71.4		67.6		67.6	
Avg % Change	0.15		0.16		0.37		0.22		0.41	
Last Trading Day Performance										
% of Time Up	50.8		57.1		54.8		58.8		58.8	
Avg % Change	0.01		−0.004		−0.05		−0.05		0.12	

Either go short, or stay away the day before Presidents' Day.

JANUARY/FEBRUARY

MONDAY
D 66.7
S 52.4
N 81.0
28

No other country can substitute for the U.S. The U.S. is still No. 1 in military, No. 1 in economy, No. 1 in promoting human rights and No. 1 in idealism. Only the U.S. can lead the world. No other country can.
— Senior Korean official (to Thomas L. Friedman *NY Times* Foreign Affairs columnist, 2/25/2009)

TUESDAY
D 61.9
S 61.9
N 71.4
29

There's nothing wrong with cash. It gives you time to think.
— Robert Prechter, Jr. (*Elliott Wave Theorist*)

FOMC Meeting (2 Days)

WEDNESDAY
D 57.1
S 61.9
N 52.4
30

Buy when you are scared to death; sell when you are tickled to death.
— Market Maxim (*The Cabot Market Letter*, April 12, 2001)

"January Barometer" 88.7% Accurate (Page 16)
Almanac Investor Subscribers Emailed Official Results (See Insert)

THURSDAY
D 66.7
S 71.4
N 61.9
31

Today's generation of young people holds more power than any generation before it to make a positive impact on the world.
— William J. Clinton (42nd U.S. President, Clinton Global Initiative, b. 1946)

First Day Trading in February, Dow and S&P Up 9 of Last 10
NASDAQ Up 8 Years in a Row

FRIDAY
D 71.4
S 71.4
N 81.0
1

The most valuable executive is one who is training somebody to be a better man than he is.
— Robert G. Ingersoll (American lawyer and orator, "the Great Agnostic," 1833–1899)

SATURDAY
2

SUNDAY
3

HOT JANUARY INDUSTRIES BEAT S&P NEXT 11 MONTHS

The S&P 500 in January tends to predict the market's direction for the year. In turn, Standard & Poor's top 10 industries in January outperform the index over the next 11 months.

Our friend Sam Stovall, chief investment strategist at S&P, has crunched the numbers over the years. He calls it the "January Barometer Portfolio," or JBP. Since 1970, a portfolio of the top 10 S&P industries during January has beaten the S&P 500 itself—and performed even better in years when January was up.

The JBP went on to outperform the S&P 500 during the remaining 11 months of the year 69% of the time, 14.3% to 6.7%, on average. When the S&P 500 is up in January, a top-10 industries portfolio increases the average portfolio gain to 18.6% for the last 11 months of the year vs. 11.8% for the S&P. For more of Sam's Sector Watch, click on "Free Trial" at *http://www.marketscope.com*.

AS JANUARY GOES, SO GOES THE YEAR
FOR TOP-PERFORMING INDUSTRIES
January's Top 10 Industries vs. S&P 500 Next 11 Months

	11 Month % Change		S&P Jan	After S&P Up in January		After S&P Down in January	
	Portfolio	S&P	%	Portfolio	S&P	Portfolio	S&P
1970	-4.7	-0.3	-7.6			-4.7	-0.3
1971	23.5	6.1	4.0	23.5	6.1		
1972	19.7	13.7	1.8	19.7	13.7		
1973	5.2	-20.0	-1.7			5.2	-20.0
1974	-29.2	-30.2	-1.0			-29.2	-30.2
1975	57.3	22.2	12.3	57.3	22.2		
1976	16.3	8.1	11.8	16.3	8.1		
1977	-9.1	-9.6	-5.1			-9.1	-9.6
1978	7.3	6.5	-6.2			7.3	6.5
1979	21.7	8.1	4.0	21.7	8.1		
1980	38.3	20.4	5.8	38.3	20.4		
1981	5.0	-6.9	-4.6			5.0	-6.9
1982	37.2	18.8	-1.8			37.2	18.8
1983	17.2	13.9	3.3	17.2	13.9		
1984	-5.0	-1.1	-0.9			-5.0	-1.1
1985	28.2	20.8	7.4	28.2	20.8		
1986	18.1	19.4	0.2	18.1	19.4		
1987	-1.5	-8.9	13.2	-1.5	-8.9		
1988	18.4	10.4	4.0	18.4	10.4		
1989	16.1	22.1	7.1	16.1	22.1		
1990	-4.4	-3.3	-6.9			-4.4	-3.3
1991	35.7	19.4	4.2	35.7	19.4		
1992	14.6	4.7	-2.0			14.6	4.7
1993	23.7	7.2	0.7	23.7	7.2		
1994	-7.1	-4.6	3.3	-7.1	-4.6		
1995	25.6	30.9	2.4	25.6	30.9		
1996	5.4	16.5	3.3	5.4	16.5		
1997	4.7	23.4	6.1	4.7	23.4		
1998	45.2	25.4	1.0	45.2	25.4		
1999	67.9	14.8	4.1	67.9	14.8		
2000	23.6	-5.3	-5.1			23.6	-5.3
2001	-13.1	-16.0	3.5	-13.1	-16.0		
2002	-16.2	-22.2	-1.6			-16.2	-22.2
2003	69.3	29.9	-2.7			69.3	29.9
2004	9.9	7.1	1.7	9.9	7.1		
2005	20.7	5.7	-2.5			20.7	5.7
2006	-0.3	10.8	2.5	-0.3	10.8		
2007	-5.5	2.1	1.4	-5.5	2.1		
2008	-27.1	-34.5	-6.1			-27.1	-34.5
2009	38.7	35.0	-8.6			38.7	35.0
2010	9.2	17.1	-3.7			9.2	17.1
2011	0.6	2.0	2.3	0.6	2.0		
2012			4.4				
Averages	14.3%	6.7%		18.6%	11.8%	7.9%	-0.9%

FEBRUARY

Live beyond your means; then you're forced to work hard, you have to succeed.
— Edward G. Robinson (American actor)

Bear markets don't act like a medicine ball rolling down a smooth hill. Instead, they behave like a basketball bouncing down a rock-strewn mountainside; there's lots of movement up and sideways before the bottom is reached.
— Daniel Turov (*Turov on Timing, Barron's* May 21, 2001, b. 1947)

Week Before February Expiration Week, NASDAQ Down 9 of Last 12, 2010 Up 2.0%, 2011 Up 1.5%

What counts more than luck, is determination and perseverance. If the talent is there, it will come through. Don't be too impatient.
— Fred Astaire (The report from his first screen test stated, "Can't act. Can't sing. Balding. Can dance a little.")

Methodology is the last refuge of a sterile mind.
— Marianne L. Simmel (Psychologist)

The usual bull market successfully weathers a number of tests until it is considered invulnerable, whereupon it is ripe for a bust.
— George Soros (Financier, philanthropist, political activist, author and philosopher, b. 1930)

MARKET BEHAVIOR AFTER SITTING PRESIDENT WINS AND LOSSES

For 46 annual editions of this *Almanac* we have had to look ahead six to eighteen months and try to anticipate what the stock market will do in the year to come. Predictable effects on the economy and stock market from quadrennial presidential and biennial congressional elections have steered us well over the years. Also, bear markets lasting about a year on average tended to consume the first year of Republican and second of Democratic terms (page 32).

Prognosticating was tougher in the 1990s during the greatest bull cycle in history. Being bullish and staying bullish was the best course. Bear markets were few and far between and when they did come, were swift and over in a few months. Market timers and fundamentalists, as a result, did not keep pace with the momentum players. The market has come back to earth the last thirteen years and many of these patterns have reemerged.

Since the inception of the Dow Jones Industrial Average in 1896 there have been 19 presidential elections that a sitting president was running for reelection. The Dow posted gains in 9 of these 19 post-election years. In 1933, the Dow soared 66.7% for its best post-election ever, after President Hoover lost his reelection bid during the worst bear market in history that brought the blue chip average down 86% from April 1930 to July 1932. Hoover was the only sitting president running for reelection to lose the office when the market was down. The Dow posted only one other post-election year gain (1993) when a sitting president was not reelected.

Wilson won after the Republican Party split in two in 1912. Carter won after the Watergate scandal. Roosevelt and Clinton won elections during bad economies. Reagan ousted Carter following the late 1970s stagflation and the Iran hostage crisis.

War dampened market returns in 1917, 1937, and 1941. McKinley was shot and died in office in 1901. The Civil Rights Act and Cold War machinations hurt stocks in 1957. 1973 was rocked by Watergate, Vietnam, the Yom Kippur War and OPEC. Hurricanes and setbacks in Iraq made 2005 the Dow's first loss in a "fifth" year since 1885, though S&P and NASDAQ were up.

A struggling economy, European financial and political duress, ongoing foreign military operations, and a divided Republican party make handicapping this November's winner difficult at press time. Prospects for 2013 improve should the market decline in 2012.

POST-ELECTION MARKETS WHEN SITTING PRESIDENT WINS REELECTION

Democrats		Dow %	Republicans		Dow %
Wilson	1917	−21.7	McKinley	1901	−8.7
F. Roosevelt	1937	−32.8	T. Roosevelt	1905	38.2
F. Roosevelt	1941	−15.4	Coolidge	1925	30.0
F. Roosevelt	1945	26.6	Eisenhower	1957	−12.8
Truman	1949	12.9	Nixon	1973	−16.6
Johnson	1965	10.9	Reagan	1985	27.7
Clinton	1997	22.6	G. W. Bush	2005	−0.6

WHEN SITTING PRESIDENT IS OUSTED

Succeeding Democrats			Succeeding Republicans		
Wilson	1913	−10.3	Reagan	1981	−9.2
F. Roosevelt	1933	66.7			
Carter	1977	−17.3			
Clinton	1993	13.7			

First Trading Day of February Expiration Week Dow Down 5 of Last 8

MONDAY

D 57.1
S 42.9
N 42.9

11

The man who can master his time can master nearly anything.
— Winston Churchill (British statesman, 1874–1965)

TUESDAY

D 57.1
S 71.4
N 57.1

12

Banking establishments are more dangerous than standing armies; and that the principle of spending money to be paid by posterity, under the name of funding, is but swindling futurity on a large scale.
— Thomas Jefferson (3rd U.S. President, 1743–7/4/1826, 1816 letter to John Taylor of Caroline)

Ash Wednesday

WEDNESDAY

D 61.9
S 66.7
N 57.1

13

Today's Ponzi-style acute fragility and speculative dynamics dictate that he who panics first panics best.
— Doug Noland (Prudent Bear Funds, *Credit Bubble Bulletin*, 10/26/07)

Valentine's Day ♥

THURSDAY

D 38.1
S 38.1
N 52.4

14

To change one's life: Start immediately. Do it flamboyantly. No exceptions.
— William James (Philosopher, psychologist, 1842–1910)

Day Before Presidents' Day Weekend, S&P Down 16 of Last 21
February Expiration Day, Dow Down 7 of Last 13

FRIDAY

D 66.7
S 71.4
N 57.1

15

It is better to be out wishing you were in, than in wishing you were out.
— Albert W. Thomas (Trader, investor, *Over My Shoulder*, mutualfundmagic.com, *If It Doesn't Go Up, Don't Buy It!*, b. 1927)

SATURDAY

16

SUNDAY

17

THE THIRD YEAR OF DECADES

Graphic presentation reveals that "third" years have a mixed record. But since the market rose from the ashes in 1933, only 1973—in the wake of Watergate, Vietnam, Mideast Turmoil, and an Oil Embargo—posted a substantial loss. Third years that follow strong election years have not fared well, dimming 2013's prospects.

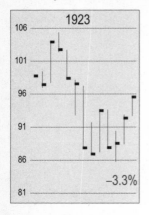

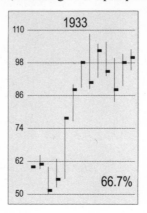

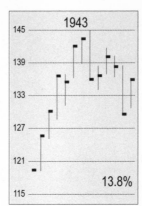

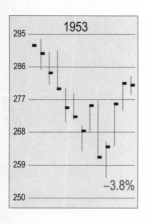

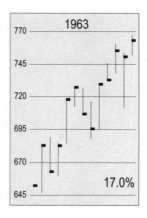

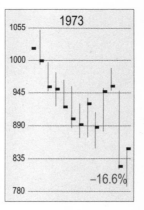

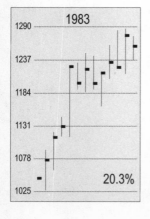

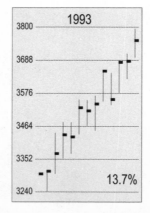

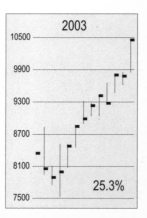

Based on Dow Jones Industrial Average monthly ranges and closing prices.

FEBRUARY

Presidents' Day (Market Closed)

MONDAY

18

If I had eight hours to chop down a tree, I'd spend six sharpening my axe.
— Abraham Lincoln (16th U.S. President, 1809–1865)

Day After Presidents Day, S&P Down 7 of Last 12

TUESDAY

D 47.6
S 42.9
N 38.1

19

A government which robs Peter to pay Paul can always depend on the support of Paul.
— George Bernard Shaw (Irish dramatist, 1856–1950)

WEDNESDAY

D 33.3
S 38.1
N 47.6

20

There are no secrets to success. Don't waste your time looking for them. Success is the result of perfection, hard work, learning from failure, loyalty to those for whom you work, and persistence.
— General Colin Powell (Chairman, Joint Chiefs 1989–1993, secretary of state 2001–2005, *NY Times*, 10/22/2008, b. 1937)

Week After February Expiration Week, Dow Down 10 of Last 14

THURSDAY

D 47.6
S 42.9
N 42.9

21

Financial markets will find and exploit hidden flaws, particularly in untested new innovations—and do so at a time that will inflict the most damage to the most people.
— Raymond F. DeVoe, Jr. (Market strategist Jesup & Lamont, *The DeVoe Report*, 3/30/07)

FRIDAY

D 52.4
S 61.9
N 57.1

22

The first human who hurled an insult instead of a stone was the founder of civilization.
— Sigmund Freud (Austrian neurologist, psychiatrist, "father of psychoanalysis," 1856–1939)

SATURDAY

23

March Almanac Investor Seasonalities: See Pages 92, 94 and 96

SUNDAY

24

MARCH ALMANAC

MARCH						
S	M	T	W	T	F	S
					1	2
3	4	5	6	7	8	9
10	11	12	13	14	15	16
17	18	19	20	21	22	23
24	25	26	27	28	29	30
31						

APRIL						
S	M	T	W	T	F	S
	1	2	3	4	5	6
7	8	9	10	11	12	13
14	15	16	17	18	19	20
21	22	23	24	25	26	27
28	29	30				

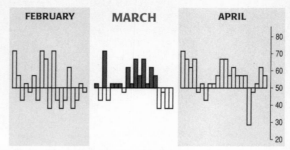

Market Probability Chart above is a graphic representation of the S&P 500 Recent Market Probability Calendar on page 124.

◆ Mid-month strength and late-month weakness are most evident above ◆ RECENT RECORD: S&P 19 up, 10 down, average gain 1.3%, fourth best ◆ Rather turbulent in recent years with wild fluctuations and large gains and losses ◆ March has been taking some mean end-of-quarter hits (page 134), down 1469 Dow points March 9–22, 2001 ◆ Last three or four days Dow a net loser 14 out of last 23 years ◆ NASDAQ hard hit in 2001, down 14.5% after 22.4% drop in February ◆ Fourth worst NASDAQ month during post-presidential election years average loss 0.7%, up 4, down 6.

March Vital Statistics

	DJIA		S&P 500		NASDAQ		Russell 1K		Russell 2K	
Rank	5		4		6		5		6	
Up	41		41		27		23		25	
Down	22		22		15		11		9	
Average % Change	1.1%		1.2%		0.8%		1.1%		1.3%	
Post-Election Year	0.2%		0.4%		−0.7%		0.4%		0.8%	
	Best & Worst March									
	% Change		% Change		% Change		% Change		% Change	
Best	2000	7.8	2000	9.7	2009	10.9	2000	8.9	1979	9.7
Worst	1980	−9.0	1980	−10.2	1980	−17.1	1980	−11.5	1980	−18.5
	Best & Worst March Weeks									
Best	3/13/09	9.0	3/13/09	10.7	3/13/09	10.6	3/13/09	10.7	3/13/09	12.0
Worst	3/16/01	−7.7	3/6/09	−7.0	3/16/01	−7.9	3/6/09	−7.1	3/6/09	−9.8
	Best & Worst March Days									
Best	3/23/09	6.8	3/23/09	7.1	3/10/09	7.1	3/23/09	7.0	3/23/09	8.4
Worst	3/2/09	−4.2	3/2/09	−4.7	3/12/01	−6.3	3/2/09	−4.8	3/27/80	−6.0
	First Trading Day of Expiration Week: 1980–2012									
Record (#Up–#Down)	21–12		21–12		14–19		19–14		16–17	
Current streak	U1		U1		D5		D5		D5	
Avg % Change	0.14		0.01		−0.36		−0.05		−0.39	
	Options Expiration Day: 1980–2012									
Record (#Up–#Down)	18–15		20–13		16–17		18–15		15–17	
Current streak	D1		U2		D1		U2		D1	
Avg % Change	0.06		0.01		−0.03		0.01		−0.06	
	Options Expiration Week: 1980–2012									
Record (#Up–#Down)	22–10		21–12		19–14		20–13		17–16	
Current streak	U1		U1		U1		U1		U1	
Avg % Change	0.86		0.70		−0.05		0.63		0.10	
	Week After Options Expiration: 1980–2012									
Record (#Up–#Down)	15–18		12–21		18–15		12–21		17–16	
Current streak	D1		D1		U7		D1		D1	
Avg % Change	−0.21		−0.08		0.17		−0.08		0.15	
	First Trading Day Performance									
% of Time Up	66.7		63.5		61.9		58.8		64.7	
Avg % Change	0.15		0.15		0.22		0.11		0.18	
	Last Trading Day Performance									
% of Time Up	41.3		39.7		64.3		47.1		82.4	
Avg % Change	−0.11		−0.01		0.17		0.09		0.38	

Dow & S&P 1950–April 2012, NASDAQ 1971–April 2012, Russell 1K & 2K 1979–April 2012.

March has Ides and St. Patrick's Day;
Begins bullishly, then fades away.

FEBRUARY/MARCH

MONDAY
D 33.3
S 38.1
N 52.4
25

The biggest change we made was the move to a boundary-less company. We got rid of the corner offices, the bureaucracy, and the not-invented-here syndrome. Instead we got every mind in the game, got the best out of all our people.
— Jack Welch (retiring CEO of General Electric, *Business Week*, September 10, 2001)

TUESDAY
D 42.9
S 42.9
N 47.6
26

Let me end my talk by abusing slightly my status as an official representative of the Federal Reserve. I would like to say to Milton [Friedman]: regarding the Great Depression, you're right; we did it. We're very sorry. But thanks to you, we won't do it again.
— Ben Bernanke (Fed Chairman 2006–, 11/8/02 speech as Fed Govenor)

WEDNESDAY
D 42.9
S 52.4
N 52.4
27

There is no one who can replace America. Without American leadership, there is no leadership. That puts a tremendous burden on the American people to do something positive. You can't be tempted by the usual nationalism.
— Lee Hong-koo (South Korean prime minister 1994–1995 and ambassador to U.S. 1998–2000, *NY Times* 2/25/2009)

THURSDAY
D 42.9
S 47.6
N 42.9
28

I sold enough papers last year of high school to pay cash for a BMW.
— Michael Dell (Founder Dell Computer, *Forbes*)

First Trading Day in March, Dow Down 4 of Last 6, −4.2% in 2009, 1996–2006 Up 9 of 11

FRIDAY
D 57.1
S 52.4
N 52.4
1

In investing, the return you want should depend on whether you want to eat well or sleep well.
— J. Kenfield Morley

SATURDAY
2

SUNDAY
3

MARKET CHARTS OF POST-PRESIDENTIAL ELECTION YEARS

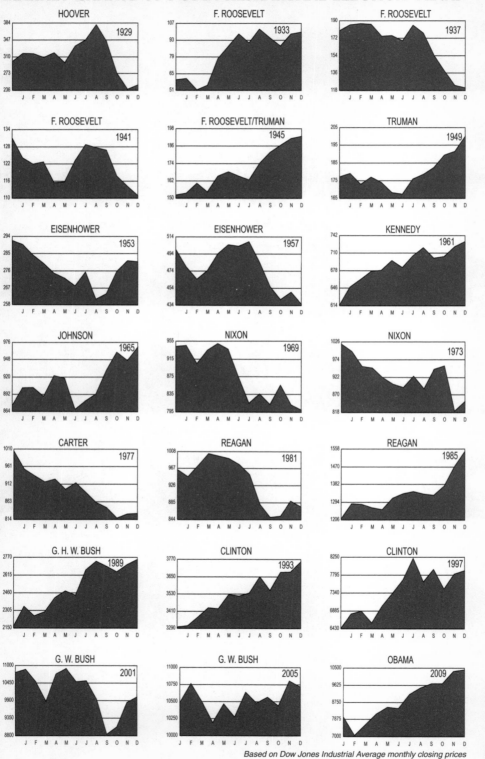

Based on Dow Jones Industrial Average monthly closing prices

MARCH

MONDAY 4

D 52.4
S 42.9
N 38.1

Knowing others is intelligence; knowing yourself is true wisdom. Mastering others is strength; mastering yourself is true power.
— Lau Tzu (Shaolin monk, founder of Taoism, circa 6th–4th century B.C.)

March Historically Strong Early in the Month (Pages 28 and 134)

TUESDAY 5

D 61.9
S 71.4
N 71.4

A generation from now, Americans may marvel at the complacency that assumed the dollar's dominance would never end.
— Floyd Norris (Chief financial correspondent, NY Times, 2/2/07)

WEDNESDAY 6

D 42.9
S 42.9
N 42.9

Nothing will improve a person's hearing more than sincere praise.
— Harvey Mackay (Pushing the Envelope, 1999)

THURSDAY 7

D 57.1
S 52.4
N 47.6

Government is like fire—useful when used legitimately, but dangerous when not.
— David Brooks (*NY Times* columnist, 10/5/07)

Dow Down 1469 Points March 9–22 in 2001

FRIDAY 8

D 42.9
S 52.4
N 42.9

Always grab the reader by the throat in the first paragraph, sink your thumbs into his windpipe in the second, and hold him against the wall until the tag line.
— Paul O'Neil (Marketer, *Writing Changes Everything*)

SATURDAY 9

Daylight Saving Time Begins

SUNDAY 10

POST-ELECTION YEAR PERFORMANCE BY PARTY

From the table on page 130 it is clear that during the first two years of a president's term market performance lags well behind the later two. After a president wins the election the first two years are spent pushing through as much policy as possible. Frequently the market, economy, and country experience bear markets, recessions, and war. Conversely, as presidents and their parties get anxious about holding onto power they begin to prime the pump in the third year, fostering bull markets, prosperity, and peace.

There is a dramatic difference in market performance under the two parties in post-election and midterm years the last fifteen administrations. Since 1953 there have been nineteen confirmed bull and bear markets. Only six bear markets have bottomed in the pre-election or election year and nine tops have occurred in these years; the bulk of the declines were relegated to the post-election and midterm years. However, more bear markets and negative market action have plagued Republican administrations in the post-election year whereas the midterm year has been worse under Democrats.

Republicans have mostly taken over after foreign entanglements and personal transgressions during boom times and administered tough action right away, knocking the market down: 1953 (Korea), 1969 (Vietnam), 1981 (Iran hostage crisis), and 2001 (Lewinsky affair). Democrats have usually reclaimed power after economic duress or political scandal during leaner times and addressed more favorable policy moves the first year, buoying the market: 1961 (recession), 1977 (Watergate), 1993 (recession), and 2009 (financial crisis).

MARKET ACTION UNDER REPUBLICANS & DEMOCRATS SINCE 1953
Annual % Change in Dow Jones Industrial Average[1]

4-Year Cycle Beginning		REPUBLICANS Post-Election Year	Mid-Term Year	Pre-Election Year	Election Year	Totals
1953*	Eisenhower (R)	−3.8	44.0	20.8	2.3	
1957	Eisenhower (R)	−12.8	34.0	16.4	−9.3	
1969*	Nixon (R)	−15.2	4.8	6.1	14.6	
1973	Nixon (R)***	−16.6	−27.6	38.3	17.9	
1981*	Reagan (R)	−9.2	19.6	20.3	−3.7	
1985	Reagan (R)	27.7	22.6	2.3	11.8	
1989	G. H. W. Bush (R)	27.0	−4.3	20.3	4.2	
2001*	G. W. Bush (R)	−7.1	−16.8	25.3	3.1	
2005	G. W. Bush (R)	−0.6	16.3	6.4	−33.8	
	Total % Gain	**−10.6**	**92.6**	**156.2**	**7.1**	**245.3**
	Average % Gain	**−1.2**	**10.3**	**17.4**	**0.8**	**6.8**
	# Up	2	6	9	6	23
	# Down	7	3	0	3	13
	DEMOCRATS					
1961*	Kennedy (D)**	18.7	−10.8	17.0	14.6	
1965	Johnson (D)	10.9	−18.9	15.2	4.3	
1977*	Carter (D)	−17.3	−3.1	4.2	14.9	
1993*	Clinton (D)	13.7	2.1	33.5	26.0	
1997	Clinton (D)	22.6	16.1	25.2	−6.2	
2009*	Obama (D)	18.8	11.0	5.5		
	Total % Gain	**67.4**	**−3.6**	**100.6**	**53.6**	**218.0**
	Average % Gain	**11.2**	**−0.6**	**16.8**	**10.7**	**9.5**
	# Up	5	3	6	4	18
	# Down	1	3	0	1	5
	BOTH PARTIES					
	Total % Gain	**56.8**	**89.0**	**256.8**	**60.7**	**463.3**
	Average % Gain	**3.8**	**5.9**	**17.1**	**4.3**	**7.8**
	# Up	7	9	15	10	41
	# Down	8	6	0	4	18

*Party in power ousted, **Death in office, ***Resigned, D—Democrat, R—Republican, [1]Based on annual close

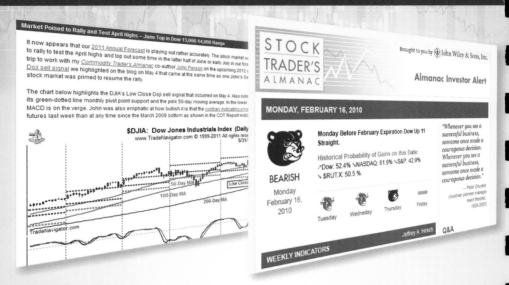

Monday Before March Triple Witching, Dow Up 18 of Last 25

MONDAY
11

D 61.9
S 52.4
N 47.6

A statistician is someone who can draw a straight line from an unwarranted assumption to a foregone conclusion.
— Anonymous

TUESDAY
12

D 57.1
S 47.6
N 47.6

The reading of all good books is indeed like a conversation with the noblest men of past centuries, in which they reveal to us the best of their thoughts.
— René Descartes (French philosopher, mathematician & scientist, 1596–1650)

Bullish Cluster Highlights March's "Sweet Spot"

WEDNESDAY
13

D 47.6
S 61.9
N 66.7

Capitalism without bankruptcy is like Christianity without hell.
— Frank Borman (CEO Eastern Airlines, April 1986)

THURSDAY
14

D 61.9
S 52.4
N 47.6

The investor who concentrated on the 50 stocks in the S&P 500 that are followed by the fewest Wall Street analysts wound up with a rousing 24.6% gain in [2006 versus] 13.6% [for] the S&P 500.
— Rich Bernstein (Chief Investment Strategist, Merrill Lynch, *Barron's* 1/8/07)

March Triple Witching Day Mixed Last 12 Years
Dow Down 3 of Last 4

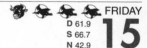

FRIDAY
15

D 61.9
S 66.7
N 42.9

People do not change when you tell them they should; they change when they tell themselves they must.
— Michael Mandelbaum (Johns Hopkins foreign policy specialist, *NY Times*, 6/24/2009, b. 1946)

SATURDAY
16

St. Patrick's Day ♣

SUNDAY
17

POST-ELECTION YEARS: PAYING THE PIPER

Politics being what it is, incumbent administrations during election years try to make the economy look good to impress the electorate and tend to put off unpopular decisions until the votes are counted. This produces an American phenomenon—the Post-Election Year Syndrome. The year begins with an Inaugural Ball, after which the piper must be paid, and we Americans have often paid dearly in the past 99 years.

Victorious candidates rarely succeed in fulfilling campaign promises of "peace and prosperity." In the past 25 post-election years, three major wars began: World War I (1917), World War II (1941), and Vietnam (1965); four drastic bear markets started in 1929, 1937, 1969, and 1973; 9/11, recession, and continuing bear markets in 2001 and 2009; less severe bear markets occurred or were in progress in 1913, 1917, 1921, 1941, 1949, 1953, 1957, 1977, and 1981. Only in 1925, 1985, 1989, 1993, and 1997 were Americans blessed with peace and prosperity.

THE RECORD SINCE 1913

1913	Wilson (D)	Minor bear market.
1917	Wilson (D)	World War I and a bear market.
1921	Harding (R)	Post-war depression and bear market.
1925	Coolidge (R)	Peace and prosperity. Hallelujah!
1929	Hoover (R)	Worst market crash in history until 1987.
1933	Roosevelt (D)	Devaluation, bank failures, Depression still on but market strong.
1937	Roosevelt (D)	Another crash, 20% unemployment rate.
1941	Roosevelt (D)	World War II and a continuing bear.
1945	Roosevelt (D)	Post-war industrial contraction, strong market precedes 1946 crash.
1949	Truman (D)	Minor bear market.
1953	Eisenhower (R)	Minor post-war (Korea) bear market.
1957	Eisenhower (R)	Major bear market.
1961	Kennedy (D)	Bay of Pigs fiasco, strong market precedes 1962 crash.
1965	Johnson (D)	Vietnam escalation. Bear came in 1966.
1969	Nixon (R)	Start of worst bear market since 1937.
1973	Nixon, Ford (R)	Start of worst bear market since 1929.
1977	Carter (D)	Bear market in blue chip stocks.
1981	Reagan (R)	Bear strikes again.
1985	Reagan (R)	No bear in sight.
1989	Bush (R)	Effect of 1987 Crash wears off.
1993	Clinton (D)	S&P up 7.1%, next year off 1.5%.
1997	Clinton (D)	S&P up 31.0%, next year up 26.7%.
2001	Bush, GW (R)	9/11, recession, bear market intensifies.
2005	Bush, GW (R)	Flat year, narrowest range, Dow off −0.6%.
2009	Obama (D)	Financial crisis, bear bottom, Dow up 18.8%.

Republicans took back the White House following foreign involvements under Democrats in 1921 (WWI), 1953 (Korea), 1969 (Vietnam), and 1981 (Iran); and scandal in 2001. Bear markets occurred in these post-election years. Democrats recaptured power after domestic problems under Republicans: in 1913 (GOP split), 1933 (Crash and Depression), 1961 (recession), 1977 (Watergate), 1993 (sluggish economy), and 2009 (financial crisis). Post-election years have been better under Democrats (page 32).

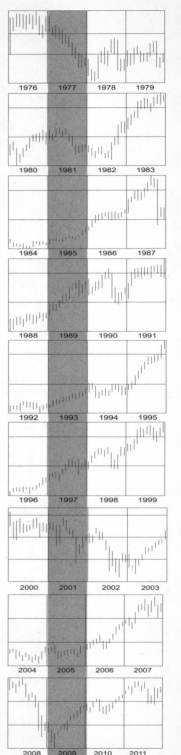

Graph shows Post-Election years screened
Based on Dow Jones industial average monthly ranges

MONDAY
D 57.1
S 57.1
N 61.9
18

Show me a good phone receptionist and I'll show you a good company.
— Harvey Mackay (*Pushing the Envelope*, 1999)

*Week After Triple Witching, Dow Down 16 of Last 25, 2000 Up 4.9%,
2007 Up 3.1%, 2009 Up 6.8%, 2011 Up 3.1%, Up 6 of Last 9*

TUESDAY
D 57.1
S 66.7
N 61.9
19

There is always plenty of capital for those who can create practical plans for using it.
— Napoleon Hill (Author, *Think and Grow Rich*, 1883–1970)

FOMC Meeting (2 Days)

WEDNESDAY
D 66.7
S 52.4
N 66.7
20

*Whatever method you use to pick stocks . . . , your ultimate success or failure will depend on your ability to
ignore the worries of the world long enough to allow your investments to succeed. It isn't the head but the
stomach that determines the fate of the stockpicker.*
— Peter Lynch (Fidelity Investments, *Beating the Street*, 1994)

THURSDAY
D 38.1
S 61.9
N 57.1
21

You know a country is falling apart when even the government will not accept its own currency.
— Jim Rogers (Financier, *Adventure Capitalist*, b. 1942)

March Historically Weak Later in the Month (Pages 28 and 134)

FRIDAY
D 57.1
S 57.1
N 61.9
22

*The generally accepted view is that markets are always right—that is, market prices tend to discount future
developments accurately even when it is unclear what those developments are. I start with the opposite point of
view. I believe that market prices are always wrong in the sense that they present a biased view of the future.*
— George Soros (1987, Financier, philanthropist, political activist, author and philosopher, b. 1930)

SATURDAY
23

SUNDAY
24

HOW TO TRADE BEST MONTHS SWITCHING STRATEGIES

Our Best Months Switching Strategies found on pages 48, 50, 58, and 60 are simple and reliable with a proven 62-year track record. Thus far we have failed to find a similar trading strategy that even comes close over the past six decades. And to top it off, the strategy has only been improving, since we first discovered it in 1986.

Exogenous factors and cultural shifts must be considered. "Backward" tests that go back to 1925 or even 1896 and conclude that the pattern does not work are best ignored. They do not take into account these factors. Farming made August the best month from 1900–1951. Since 1987 it is the second worst month of the year for the Dow and S&P. Panic caused by financial crisis in 2007–2008 caused every asset class aside from U.S. Treasuries to decline substantially. But the bulk of the major decline in equities in the worst months of 2008 was sidestepped using these strategies.

Our Best Months Switching Strategy will not make you an instant millionaire, as other strategies claim they can do. What it will do is steadily build wealth over time with half the risk (or less) of a "buy and hold" approach.

A sampling of tradable funds for the Best and Worst Months appears in the table below. These are just a starting point and only skim the surface of possible trading vehicles available to take advantage of these strategies. Your specific situation and risk tolerance will dictate a suitable choice. If you are trading in a tax-advantaged account, such as a company sponsored 401(k) or Individual Retirement Account (IRA), your investment options may be limited to what has been selected by your employer or IRA administrator. But if you are a self-directed trader with a brokerage account, then you likely have unlimited choices (perhaps too many).

TRADABLE BEST AND WORST MONTHS SWITCHING STRATEGY FUNDS

Best Months		Worst Months	
Exchange Traded Funds (ETF)		**Exchange Traded Funds (ETF)**	
Symbol	**Name**	**Symbol**	**Name**
DIA	SPDR Dow Jones Industrial Average	SHY	iShares 1–3 Year Treasury Bond
SPY	SPDR S&P 500	IEI	iShares 3–7 Year Treasury Bond
QQQ	PowerShares QQQ	IEF	iShares 7–10 Year Treasury Bond
IWM	iShares Russell 2000	TLT	iShares 20+ Year Treasury Bond
Mutual Funds		**Mutual Funds**	
Symbol	**Name**	**Symbol**	**Name**
VWNDX	Vanguard Windsor Fund	VFSTX	Vanguard Short-Term Investment-Grade Bond Fund
FMAGX	Fidelity Magellan Fund	FBNDX	Fidelity Investment Grade Bond Fund
AMCPX	American Funds AMCAP Fund	ABNDX	American Funds Bond Fund of America
FKCGX	Franklin Flex Cap Growth Fund	FKUSX	Franklin U.S. Government Securities Fund
SECEX	Rydex Large Cap Core Fund	SIUSX	Rydex U.S. Intermediate Bond Fund

Generally speaking, during the Best Months you want to be invested in equities that offer similar exposure to the companies that constitute the Dow, S&P 500, and NASDAQ indices. These would typically be large-cap growth and value stocks as well as technology concerns. Reviewing the holdings of a particular ETF or mutual fund and comparing them to the index members is an excellent way to correlate.

During the Worst Months, switch into Treasury bonds, money market funds, or a bear/short fund. **Grizzly Short** (GRZZX) and **AdvisorShares Active Bear** (HDGE) are two possible choices. Money market funds will be the safest, but are likely to offer the smallest return, while bear/short funds offer potentially greater returns, but more risk. If the market moves sideways or higher during the Worst Months, a bear/short fund is likely to lose money. Treasuries offer a combination of decent returns with limited risk. In the *2013 Commodity Trader's Almanac*, a detailed study of 30-year Treasury bonds covers their seasonal tendency to advance during summer months as well as a correlating ETF trade.

Additional Worst Month possibilities include precious metals and the companies that mine them. **SPDR Gold Shares** (GLD), **Market Vectors Gold Miners** (GDX), and **ETF Securities Physical Swiss Gold** (SGOL) are a few well recognized names available from the ETF universe. Gold's seasonal price tendencies are also covered in the *2013 Commodity Trader's Almanac*.

Become an *Almanac Investor*

Almanac Investor subsribers receive specific buy and sell recommendations, based upon the Best Months Switching Strategies, online and via email. Sector Index Seasonalities, found on page 92, are also put into action throughout the year with ETF recommendations. Buy limits, stop losses, and auto-sell price points for the majority of seasonal trades are delivered directly to your inbox. Visit *www.stocktradersalmanac.com,* or see the insert for details and a special offer for new subscribers.

MONDAY
D 33.3
S 38.1
N 42.9
25

You have to keep digging, keep asking questions, because otherwise you'll be seduced or brainwashed into the idea that it's somehow a great privilege, an honor, to report the lies they've been feeding you.
— David Halberstam (Amercian writer, war reporter, 1964 Pulitzer Prize, 1934–2007)

Passover

TUESDAY
D 52.4
S 47.6
N 42.9
26

Keep me away from the wisdom which does not cry, the philosophy which does not laugh and the greatness which does not bow before children.
— Kahlil Gibran (Lebanese-born American mystic, poet and artist, 1883–1931)

Start Looking for the Dow and S&P MACD SELL Signal (Pages 48 and 50)
Almanac Investor Subscribers Emailed When It Triggers (See Insert)

WEDNESDAY
D 57.1
S 38.1
N 47.6
27

Cannot people realize how large an income is thrift?
— Marcus Tullius Cicero (Great Roman Orator, Politician, 106–43 B.C.)

Last Trading Day of March, Dow Down 15 of Last 23
Russell 2K Up 13 of 18, NASDAQ Up Last 12 Day Before Good Friday

THURSDAY
D 33.3
S 38.1
N 57.1
28

Those heroes of finance are like beads on a string, when one slips off, the rest follow.
— Henrik Ibsen (Norwegian playwright, 1828–1906)

Good Friday (Market Closed)

FRIDAY
29

Everything possible today was at one time impossible. Everything impossible today may at some time in the future be possible.
— Edward Lindaman (Apollo space project, president Whitworth College, 1920–1982)

April Almanac Investor Seasonalities: See Pages 92, 94 and 96

SATURDAY
30

Easter

SUNDAY
31

APRIL ALMANAC

	APRIL								MAY					
S	M	T	W	T	F	S		S	M	T	W	T	F	S
	1	2	3	4	5	6					1	2	3	4
7	8	9	10	11	12	13		5	6	7	8	9	10	11
14	15	16	17	18	19	20		12	13	14	15	16	17	18
21	22	23	24	25	26	27		19	20	21	22	23	24	25
28	29	30						26	27	28	29	30	31	

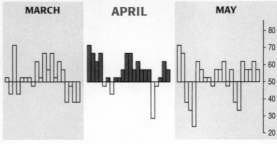

Market Probability Chart above is a graphic representation of the S&P 500 Recent Market Probability Calendar on page 124.

◆ April is still the best Dow month (average 2.0%) since 1950 (page 44) ◆ April 1999 first month ever to gain 1000 Dow points, 856 in 2001, knocked off its high horse in 2002 down 458, 2003 up 488 ◆ Up seven straight, average gain 3.6% ◆ Prone to weakness after mid-month tax deadline ◆ Stocks anticipate great first quarter earnings by rising sharply before earnings are reported, rather than after ◆ Rarely a dangerous month, recent exceptions are 2002, 2004, and 2005 ◆ "Best Six Months" of the year end with April (page 48) ◆ Post-election year Aprils solid since 1953 (Dow 1.9%, S&P 1.6%, NASDAQ 2.4%) ◆ End of April NASDAQ strength (pages 125 & 126).

April Vital Statistics

	DJIA		S&P 500		NASDAQ		Russell 1K		Russell 2K	
Rank	1		2		3		3		3	
Up	41		43		27		22		22	
Down	22		20		15		12		12	
Average % Change	2.0%		1.5%		1.5%		1.6%		1.8%	
Post-Election Year	1.9%		1.6%		2.4%		2.7%		2.5%	
Best & Worst April										
		% Change		% Change		% Change		% Change		% Change
Best	1978	10.6	2009	9.4	2001	15.0	2009	10.0	2009	15.3
Worst	1970	−6.3	1970	−9.0	2000	−15.6	2002	−5.8	2000	−6.1
Best & Worst April Weeks										
Best	4/11/75	5.7	4/20/00	5.8	4/12/01	14.0	4/20/00	5.9	4/3/09	6.3
Worst	4/14/00	−7.3	4/14/00	−10.5	4/14/00	−25.3	4/14/00	−11.2	4/14/00	−16.4
Best & Worst April Days										
Best	4/5/01	4.2	4/5/01	4.4	4/5/01	8.9	4/5/01	4.6	4/9/09	5.9
Worst	4/14/00	−5.7	4/14/00	−5.8	4/14/00	−9.7	4/14/00	−6.0	4/14/00	−7.3
First Trading Day of Expiration Week: 1980–2012										
Record (#Up–#Down)	21–12		19–14		18–15		18–15		14–19	
Current streak	U3		D2		D2		D2		U1	
Avg % Change	0.25		0.18		0.18		0.17		0.07	
Options Expiration Day: 1980–2012										
Record (#Up–#Down)	23–10		22–11		19–14		22–11		21–12	
Current streak	U2		U2		D1		U2		U2	
Avg % Change	0.25		0.20		−0.03		0.18		0.21	
Options Expiration Week: 1980–2012										
Record (#Up–#Down)	27–6		24–9		22–11		22–11		25–8	
Current streak	U1		U1		D2		U1		U1	
Avg % Change	1.18		0.94		1.00		0.91		0.86	
Week After Options Expiration: 1980–2012										
Record (#Up–#Down)	22–11		22–11		24–9		22–11		22–11	
Current streak	U3		U3		U6		U3		U3	
Avg % Change	0.40		0.37		0.63		0.37		0.84	
First Trading Day Performance										
% of Time Up	60.3		63.5		47.6		61.8		50.0	
Avg % Change	0.18		0.15		−0.12		0.19		−0.06	
Last Trading Day Performance										
% of Time Up	50.8		55.6		66.7		55.9		67.6	
Avg % Change	0.10		0.09		0.17		0.08		0.13	

Dow & S&P 1950–April 2012, NASDAQ 1971–April 2012, Russell 1K & 2K 1979–April 2012.

April "Best Month" for Dow since 1950; Day-before-Good Friday gains are nifty.

APRIL

First Trading Day in April, Dow Up 15 of Last 18
Day After Easter, Worst Post-Holiday (Page 86)

MONDAY
D 76.2
S 71.4
N 57.1
1

Bill [Gates] isn't afraid of taking long-term chances. He also understands that you have to try everyhting because the real secret to innovation is failing fast.
— Gary Starkweather (Inventor of laser printer in 1969 at Xerox, *Fortune*, July 8, 2002)

TUESDAY
D 66.7
S 66.7
N 57.1
2

Corporate guidance has become something of an art. The CFO has refined and perfected his art, gracefully leading on the bulls with the calculating grace and cunning of a great matador.
— Joe Kalinowski (I/B/E/S)

WEDNESDAY
D 52.4
S 61.9
N 76.2
3

Early in March (1960), Dr. Arthur F. Burns called on me . . . Burns' conclusion was that unless some decisive action was taken, and taken soon, we were heading for another economic dip which would hit its low point in October, just before the elections.
— Richard M. Nixon (37th U.S. President, Six Crises, 1913–1994)

THURSDAY
D 66.7
S 66.7
N 57.1
4

But how do we know when irrational exuberance has unduly escalated asset values, which then become subject to unexpected and prolonged contractions as they have in Japan over the past decade?
— Alan Greenspan (Fed Chairman 1987–2006, 12/5/96 speech to American Enterprise Institute, b. 1926)

FRIDAY
D 42.9
S 47.6
N 38.1
5

Discipline always makes hard work easy.
— Jordan Kimmel (Portfolio manager Magnet AE Fund, b. 1958)

SATURDAY
6

SUNDAY
7

THE DECEMBER LOW INDICATOR: A USEFUL PROGNOSTICATING TOOL

When the Dow closes below its December closing low in the first quarter, it is frequently an excellent warning sign. Jeffrey Saut, managing director of investment strategy at Raymond James, brought this to our attention a few years ago. The December Low Indicator was originated by Lucien Hooper, a *Forbes* columnist and Wall Street analyst back in the 1970s. Hooper dismissed the importance of January and January's first week as reliable indicators. He noted that the trend could be random or even manipulated during a holiday-shortened week. Instead, said Hooper, "Pay much more attention to the December low. If that low is violated during the first quarter of the New Year, watch out!"

Eighteen of the 32 occurrences were followed by gains for the rest of the year—and 16 full-year gains—after the low for the year was reached. For perspective we've included the January Barometer readings for the selected years. Hooper's "Watch Out" warning was absolutely correct, though. All but two of the instances since 1952 experienced further declines, as the Dow fell an additional 10.9% on average when December's low was breached in Q1.

Only three significant drops occurred (not shown) when December's low was not breached in Q1 (1974, 1981, and 1987). Both indicators were wrong only five times, and nine years ended flat. If the December low is not crossed, turn to our January Barometer for guidance. It has been virtually perfect, right nearly 100% of these times (view the complete results at *www.stocktradersalmanac.com*).

YEARS DOW FELL BELOW DECEMBER LOW IN FIRST QUARTER

Year	Previous Dec Low	Date Crossed	Crossing Price	Subseq. Low	% Change Cross-Low	Rest of Year % Change	Full Year % Change	Jan Bar
1952	262.29	2/19/52	261.37	256.35	−1.9%	11.7%	8.4%	1.6%[2]
1953	281.63	2/11/53	281.57	255.49	−9.3	−0.2	−3.8	−0.7[3]
1956	480.72	1/9/56	479.74	462.35	−3.6	4.1	2.3	−3.6[1, 2, 3]
1957	480.61	1/18/57	477.46	419.79	−12.1	−8.7	−12.8	−4.2
1960	661.29	1/12/60	660.43	566.05	−14.3	−6.7	−9.3	−7.1
1962	720.10	1/5/62	714.84	535.76	−25.1	−8.8	−10.8	−3.8
1966	939.53	3/1/66	938.19	744.32	−20.7	−16.3	−18.9	0.5[1]
1968	879.16	1/22/68	871.71	825.13	−5.3	8.3	4.3	−4.4[1, 2, 3]
1969	943.75	1/6/69	936.66	769.93	−17.8	−14.6	−15.2	−0.8
1970	769.93	1/26/70	768.88	631.16	−17.9	9.1	4.8	−7.6[2, 3]
1973	1000.00	1/29/73	996.46	788.31	−20.9	−14.6	−16.6	−1.7
1977	946.64	2/7/77	946.31	800.85	−15.4	−12.2	−17.3	−5.1
1978	806.22	1/5/78	804.92	742.12	−7.8	0.01	−3.1	−6.2[3]
1980	819.62	3/10/80	818.94	759.13	−7.3	17.7	14.9	5.8[2]
1982	868.25	1/5/82	865.30	776.92	−10.2	20.9	19.6	−1.8[1, 2]
1984	1236.79	1/25/84	1231.89	1086.57	−11.8	−1.6	−3.7	−0.9[3]
1990	2687.93	1/15/90	2669.37	2365.10	−11.4	−1.3	−4.3	−6.9[3]
1991	2565.59	1/7/91	2522.77	2470.30	−2.1	25.6	20.3	4.2[2]
1993	3255.18	1/8/93	3251.67	3241.95	−0.3	15.5	13.7	0.7[2]
1994	3697.08	3/30/94	3626.75	3593.35	−0.9	5.7	2.1	3.3[2, 3]
1996	5059.32	1/10/96	5032.94	5032.94	NC	28.1	26.0	3.3[2]
1998	7660.13	1/9/98	7580.42	7539.07	−0.5	21.1	16.1	1.0[2]
2000	10998.39	1/4/00	10997.93	9796.03	−10.9	−1.9	−6.2	−5.1
2001	10318.93	3/12/01	10208.25	8235.81	−19.3	−1.8	−7.1	3.5[1]
2002	9763.96	1/16/02	9712.27	7286.27	−25.0	−14.1	−16.8	−1.6
2003	8303.78	1/24/03	8131.01	7524.06	−7.5	28.6	25.3	−2.7[1, 2]
2005	10440.58	1/21/05	10392.99	10012.36	−3.7	3.1	−0.6	−2.5[3]
2006	10717.50	1/20/06	10667.39	10667.39	NC	16.8	16.3	2.5
2007	12194.13	3/2/07	12114.10	12050.41	−0.5	9.5	6.4	1.4[2]
2008	13167.20	1/2/08	13043.96	7552.29	−42.1	−32.7	−33.8	−6.1
2009	8149.09	1/20/09	7949.09	6547.05	−17.6	31.2	18.8	−8.6[1, 2]
2010	10285.97	1/22/10	10172.98	9686.48	−4.8	13.8	11.0	−3.7[1, 2]
				Average Drop	**−10.9%**			

[1] *January Barometer wrong* [2] *December Low Indicator wrong* [3] *Year Flat*

APRIL

MONDAY
D 47.6
S 52.4
N 52.4

8

A day will come when all nations on our continent will form a European brotherhood...A day will come when we shall see...the United States of Europe...reaching out for each other across the seas.
— Victor Hugo (French novelist, playwright, *Hunchback of Notre Dame* and *Les Misérables*, 1802–1885)

April is the Best Month for the Dow, Average 2.0% Gain Since 1950

TUESDAY
D 47.6
S 42.9
N 42.9

9

When everbody thinks alike, everyone is likely to be wrong.
— Humphrey B. Neill (Investor, analyst, author, *Art of Contrary Thinking* 1954, 1895–1977)

WEDNESDAY
D 66.7
S 52.4
N 57.1

10

Don't be overly concerned about your heirs. Usually, unearned funds do them more harm than good.
— Gerald M. Loeb (E.F. Hutton, *The Battle for Investment Survival*, predicted 1929 Crash, 1900–1974)

April is 2nd Best Month for S&P, 3rd Best for NASDAQ (Since 1971)

THURSDAY
D 61.9
S 52.4
N 52.4

11

The "canonical" market peak typically features rich valuations, rising interest rates, often a reasonably extended and "flattish" period...despite marginal new highs...and finally, an abrupt reversal in leadership...to a preponderance of new lows ...with the reversal often occurring over a period of just a week or two.
— John P. Hussman, Ph.D. (Hussman Funds, 5/22/06)

FRIDAY
D 71.4
S 57.1
N 57.1

12

We're not believers that the government is bigger than the business cycle.
— David Rosenberg (Economist, Merrill Lynch, *Barron's* 4/21/2008)

SATURDAY
13

SUNDAY
14

DOWN JANUARYS: A REMARKABLE RECORD

In the first third of the twentieth century, there was no correlation between January markets and the year as a whole (page 24). Then, in 1972 Yale Hirsch discovered that the 1933 "lame duck" Amendment to the Constitution changed the political calendar, and the January Barometer was born. Its record has been quite accurate (page 16).

Down Januarys are harbingers of trouble ahead, in the economic, political, or military arenas. Eisenhower's heart attack in 1955 cast doubt on whether he could run in 1956—a flat year. Two other election years with down Januarys were also flat (1984 and 1992). Twelve bear markets began, and ten continued into second years with poor Januarys. 1968 started down, as we were mired in Vietnam, but Johnson's "bombing halt" changed the climate. Imminent military action in Iraq held January 2003 down before the market triple-bottomed in March. After Baghdad fell, pre-election and recovery forces fueled 2003 into a banner year. 2005 was flat, registering the narrowest Dow trading range on record. 2008 was the worst January on record and preceded the worst bear market since the Great Depression. A negative reading in 2010 preceded a 16% April-July correction, which was quickly reversed by QE2.

Unfortunately, bull and bear markets do not start conveniently at the beginnings and ends of months or years. Though some years ended higher, **every down January since 1950 was followed by a new or continuing bear market, a 10% correction or a flat year. Down Januarys were followed by substantial declines averaging** *minus* **13.9%,** providing excellent buying opportunities later in most years.

FROM DOWN JANUARY S&P CLOSES TO LOW NEXT 11 MONTHS

Year	January Close	% Change	11-Month Low	Date of Low	Jan Close to Low %	% Feb to Dec	Year % Change	
1953	26.38	−0.7%	22.71	14-Sep	−13.9%	−6.0%	−6.6%	bear
1956	43.82	−3.6	43.42	14-Feb	−0.9	6.5	2.6	FLAT/bear
1957	44.72	−4.2	38.98	22-Oct	−12.8	−10.6	−14.3	Cont. bear
1960	55.61	−7.1	52.30	25-Oct	−6.0	4.5	−3.0	bear
1962	68.84	−3.8	52.32	26-Jun	−24.0	−8.3	−11.8	bear
1968	92.24	−4.4	87.72	5-Mar	−4.9	12.6	7.7	−10%/bear
1969	103.01	−0.8	89.20	17-Dec	−13.4	−10.6	−11.4	Cont. bear
1970	85.02	−7.6	69.20	26-May	−18.6	8.4	0.1	Cont. bear/FLAT
1973	116.03	−1.7	92.16	5-Dec	−20.6	−15.9	−17.4	bear
1974	96.57	−1.0	62.28	3-Oct	−35.5	−29.0	−29.7	Cont. bear
1977	102.03	−5.1	90.71	2-Nov	−11.1	−6.8	−11.5	bear
1978	89.25	−6.2	86.90	6-Mar	−2.6	7.7	1.1	Cont. bear/bear
1981	129.55	−4.6	112.77	25-Sep	−13.0	−5.4	−9.7	bear
1982	120.40	−1.8	102.42	12-Aug	−14.9	16.8	14.8	Cont. bear
1984	163.42	−0.9	147.82	24-Jul	−9.5	2.3	1.4	Cont. bear/FLAT
1990	329.07	−6.9	295.46	11-Oct	−10.2	0.4	−6.6	bear
1992	408.79	−2.0	394.50	8-Apr	−3.5	6.6	4.5	FLAT
2000	1394.46	−5.1	1264.74	20-Dec	−9.3	−5.3	−10.1	bear
2002	1130.20	−1.6	776.76	9-Oct	−31.3	−22.2	−23.4	bear
2003	855.70	−2.7	800.73	11-Mar	−6.4	29.9	26.4	Cont. bear
2005	1181.27	−2.5	1137.50	20-Apr	−3.7	5.7	3.0	FLAT
2008	1378.55	−6.1	752.44	20-Nov	−45.4	−34.5	−38.5	Cont. bear
2009	825.88	−8.6	676.53	9-Mar	−18.1	35.0	23.5	Cont. bear
2010	1073.87	−3.7	1022.58	2-Jul	−4.8	17.1	12.8	−10%/no bear
		Totals			−334.4%	−1.1%	−96.2%	
		Average			−13.9%	−0.05%	−4.0%	

Income Tax Deadline, *Generally Bullish, Dow Down Only Five Times Since 1981*
Monday Before Expiration, Dow Up 17 of Last 24, Down 4 of Last 8

MONDAY
D 71.4
S 66.7
N 42.9
15

Taxes are what we pay for civilized society.
— Oliver Wendell Holmes Jr. (U.S. Supreme Court Justice 1902–1932, "The Great Dissenter," inscribed above IRS HQ entrance, 1841–1935)

April Prone to Weakness After Tax Deadline (Pages 36 and 134)

TUESDAY
D 61.9
S 66.7
N 52.4
16

The government would not look fondly on Caesar's Palace if it opened a table for wagering on corporate failure. It should not give greater encouragement for Goldman Sachs [et al] to do so.
— Roger Lowenstein (Financial journalist and author, *End of Wall Street*, NY Times OpEd 4/20/2010, b. 1954)

WEDNESDAY
D 57.1
S 57.1
N 52.4
17

The symbol of all relationships among such men, the moral symbol of respect for human beings, is the trader.
— Ayn Rand (Russian-born American novelist and philosopher, from Galt's Speech, *Atlas Shrugged*, 1957, 1905–1982)

THURSDAY
D 66.7
S 61.9
N 61.9
18

When Paris sneezes, Europe catches cold.
— Prince Klemens Metternich (Austrian statesman, 1773–1859)

April Expiration Day Dow Up 13 of Last 16,
2007 Up 1.2%, 2008 Up 1.8%; 2001, 2005 and 2010 –1.0%+

FRIDAY
D 61.9
S 57.1
N 57.1
19

Life is like riding a bicycle. You don't fall off unless you stop peddling.
— Claude D. Pepper (U.S. Senator Florida 1936–1951, 1900–1989)

SATURDAY
20

SUNDAY
21

TOP PERFORMING MONTHS PAST 62⅓ YEARS: STANDARD & POOR'S 500 AND DOW JONES INDUSTRIALS

Monthly performance of the S&P and the Dow are ranked over the past 62⅓ years. NASDAQ monthly performance is shown on page 56.

April, November, and December still hold the top three positions in both the Dow and the S&P. March has reclaimed the fourth spot on the S&P. Two disastrous Januarys in 2008 and 2009 knocked January into fifth. This, in part, led to our discovery in 1986 of the market's most consistent seasonal pattern. You can divide the year into two sections and have practically all the gains in one six-month section and very little in the other. September is the worst month on both lists. (See "Best Six Months" on page 48.)

MONTHLY % CHANGES (JANUARY 1950 TO APRIL 2012)

Standard & Poor's 500					Dow Jones Industrials				
Month	Total % Change	Avg. % Change	# Up	# Down	Month	Total % Change	Avg. % Change	# Up	# Down
Jan	69.6%	1.1%	39	24	Jan	66.4%	1.1%	41	22
Feb	−7.4	−0.1	34	29	Feb	2.8	0.04	36	27
Mar	74.2	1.2	41	22	Mar	68.1	1.1	41	22
Apr	95.2	1.5	43	20	Apr	124.2	2.0	41	22
May	14.1	0.2	35	27	May	1.0	0.02	31	31
Jun	−4.5	−0.1	32	30	Jun	−22.9	−0.4	28	34
Jul	57.8	0.9	33	29	Jul	72.1	1.2	38	24
Aug	−2.4	−0.04	34	28	Aug	−4.8	−0.1	35	27
Sep*	−35.4	−0.6	27	34	Sep	−53.1	−0.9	24	38
Oct	49.2	0.8	37	25	Oct	32.5	0.5	37	25
Nov	93.3	1.5	40	22	Nov	93.3	1.5	41	21
Dec	105.8	1.7	47	15	Dec	105.9	1.7	44	18
% Rank					**% Rank**				
Dec	105.8%	1.7%	47	15	Apr	124.2%	2.0%	41	22
Apr	95.2	1.5	43	20	Dec	105.9	1.7	44	18
Nov	93.3	1.5	40	22	Nov	93.3	1.5	41	21
Mar	74.2	1.2	41	22	Jul	72.1	1.2	38	24
Jan	69.6	1.1	39	24	Mar	68.1	1.1	41	22
Jul	57.8	0.9	33	29	Jan	66.4	1.1	41	22
Oct	49.2	0.8	37	25	Oct	32.5	0.5	37	25
May	14.1	0.2	35	27	Feb	2.8	0.04	36	27
Aug	−2.4	−0.04	34	28	May	1.0	0.02	31	31
Jun	−4.5	−0.1	32	30	Aug	−4.8	−0.1	35	27
Feb	−7.4	−0.1	34	29	Jun	−22.9	−0.4	28	34
Sep*	−35.4	−0.6	27	34	Sep	−53.1	−0.9	24	38
Totals	509.5%	8.1%			**Totals**	485.5%	7.8%		
Average		0.67%			**Average**		0.65%		

*No change 1979

Anticipators, shifts in cultural behavior, and faster information flow have altered seasonality in recent years. Here is how the months ranked over the past 15⅓ years (184 months), using total percentage gains on the S&P 500: April 36.6, March 28.0, December 26.8, October 26.2, November 20.3, May 5.2, July 3.1, January −3.3, June −8.4, September −13.3, February −14.0, August −22.2.

During the last 15⅓ years, front-runners of our Best Six Months may have helped push October into the number-four spot. May has improved to the number-six spot. January has declined in seven of the last thirteen years. Sizable turnarounds in "bear killing" October were a common occurrence from 1998 to 2007. Recent big Dow losses in the period were: August 1998 (SE Asia crisis), off 15.1%; September 2001 (9/11 attack), off 11.1%; September 2002 (Iraq war drums), off 12.4%; October 2008, off 14.1%; and February 2009 (financial crisis), off 11.7%.

April 1999 First Month Ever to Gain 1000 Dow Points

MONDAY
D 52.4
S 57.1
N 61.9
22

Politics ought to be the part-time profession of every citizen who would protect the rights and privileges of free people and who would preserve what is good and fruitful in our national heritage.
— Dwight D. Eisenhower (34th U.S. President, 1890–1969)

TUESDAY
D 61.9
S 57.1
N 57.1
23

Knowledge born from actual experience is the answer to why one profits; lack of it is the reason one loses.
— Gerald M. Loeb (E.F. Hutton, *The Battle for Investment Survival*, predicted 1929 Crash, 1900–1974)

WEDNESDAY
D 42.9
S 28.6
N 52.4
24

If you torture the data long enough, it will confess to anything.
— Darrell Huff (*How to Lie With Statistics*, 1954)

THURSDAY
D 52.4
S 47.6
N 42.9
25

Whoso would be a man, must be a non-conformist ... Nothing is at last sacred but the integrity of your own mind.
— Ralph Waldo Emerson (American author, poet and philosopher, *Self-Reliance*, 1803–1882)

FRIDAY
D 52.4
S 52.4
N 61.9
26

Capitalism works because it encourages and rewards those who successfully take risks, adapt to change, and develop profitable opportunities.
— Henry Blodget (former stock analyst, NY Times Op-Ed 12/20/06, *The Wall Street Self-Defense Manual*)

SATURDAY
27

May Almanac Investor Seasonalities: See Pages 92, 94 and 96

SUNDAY
28

MAY
ALMANAC

MAY						
S	M	T	W	T	F	S
		1	2	3	4	
5	6	7	8	9	10	11
12	13	14	15	16	17	18
19	20	21	22	23	24	25
26	27	28	29	30	31	

JUNE						
S	M	T	W	T	F	S
						1
2	3	4	5	6	7	8
9	10	11	12	13	14	15
16	17	18	19	20	21	22
23	24	25	26	27	28	29
30						

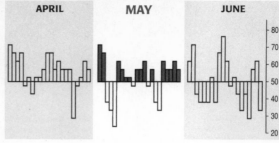

Market Probability Chart above is a graphic representation of the S&P 500 Recent Market Probability Calendar on page 124.

◆ "May/June disaster area" between 1965 and 1984 with S&P down 15 out of 20 Mays ◆ Between 1985 and 1997 May was the best month with 13 straight gains, gaining 3.3% per year on average, up 7, down 7 since ◆ Worst six months of the year begin with May (page 48) ◆ A $10,000 investment compounded to $674,073 for November–April in 62 years compared to a $1,024 loss for May–October ◆ Dow Memorial Day week record: up 12 years in a row (1984–1995), down nine of the last 16 years ◆ Since 1953 post-presidential election year Mays rank high, #4 Dow, #2 S&P, and #1 NASDAQ.

May Vital Statistics

	DJIA	S&P 500	NASDAQ	Russell 1K	Russell 2K
Rank	9	8	5	6	5
Up	31	35	24	22	21
Down	31	27	17	11	12
Average % Change	0.02%	0.2%	0.9%	1.1%	1.5%
Post-Election Year	1.3%	1.7%	3.4%	3.4%	4.7%
Best & Worst May					
	% Change	% Change	% Change	% Change	% Change
Best	1990 8.3	1990 9.2	1997 11.1	1990 8.9	1997 11.0
Worst	2010 −7.9	1962 −8.6	2000 −11.9	2010 −8.1	2010 −7.7
Best & Worst May Weeks					
Best	5/29/70 5.8	5/2/97 6.2	5/17/02 8.8	5/2/97 6.4	5/14/10 6.3
Worst	5/25/62 −6.0	5/25/62 −6.8	5/7/10 −8.0	5/7/10 −6.6	5/7/10 −8.9
Best & Worst May Days					
Best	5/27/70 5.1	5/27/70 5.0	5/30/00 7.9	5/10/10 4.4	5/10/10 5.6
Worst	5/28/62 −5.7	5/28/62 −6.7	5/23/00 −5.9	5/20/10 −3.9	5/20/10 −5.1
First Trading Day of Expiration Week: 1980–2011					
Record (#Up–#Down)	21–11	21–11	17–15	20–12	16–16
Current streak	D1	D1	D1	D1	D1
Avg % Change	0.21	0.20	0.14	0.16	−0.04
Options Expiration Day: 1980–2011					
Record (#Up–#Down)	14–18	17–15	15–17	17–15	15–17
Current streak	D1	D1	D1	D1	D1
Avg % Change	−0.13	−0.14	−0.14	−0.13	−0.04
Options Expiration Week: 1980–2011					
Record (#Up–#Down)	17–15	16–16	16–16	15–17	17–15
Current streak	D3	D3	D3	D3	D3
Avg % Change	0.14	0.10	0.27	0.10	−0.07
Week After Options Expiration: 1980–2011					
Record (#Up–#Down)	17–15	19–13	21–11	19–13	23–9
Current streak	D2	D1	D1	D1	U3
Avg % Change	−0.08	0.06	0.06	0.08	0.20
First Trading Day Performance					
% of Time Up	58.7	58.7	61.9	55.9	61.8
Avg % Change	0.22	0.24	0.33	0.28	0.33
Last Trading Day Performance					
% of Time Up	62.9	64.5	73.2	60.6	72.7
Avg % Change	0.23	0.31	0.26	0.30	0.42

Dow & S&P 1950–April 2012, NASDAQ 1971–April 2012, Russell 1K & 2K 1979–April 2012.

May's new pattern, a smile or a frown,
Odd years UP and even years DOWN.

MONDAY

D 66.7
S 61.9
N 71.4

29

We will have to pay more and more attention to what the funds are doing. They are the ones who have been contributing to the activity, especially in the high-fliers.
— Humphrey B. Neill (Investor, analyst, author, *NY Times* 6/11/1966, 1895–1977)

End of "Best Six Months" of the Year (Pages 44, 48, 50 and 147)

TUESDAY

D 47.6
S 57.1
N 66.7

30

Explosive growth of shadow banking was about the invisible hand having a party, a non-regulated drinking party, with rating agencies handing out fake IDs.
— Paul McCulley (Economist, bond investor, PIMCO, coined "shadow banking" in 2007, *NY Times* 4/26/2010, b. 1957)

First Trading Day in May, Dow Up 12 of Last 15
FOMC Meeting (2 Days)

WEDNESDAY

D 71.4
S 71.4
N 71.4

1

"Sell in May and go away." However, no one ever said it was the beginning of the month.
— John L. Person (Professional trader, author, speaker, *Commodity Trader's Almanac*, nationalfutures.com, 6/19/2009, b. 1961)

THURSDAY

D 71.4
S 66.7
N 61.9

2

With respect to trading Sugar futures, if they give it away for free at restaurants you probably don't want to be trading it.
— John L. Person (Professional trader, author, speaker, *Commodity Trader's Almanac*, nationalfutures.com, 2/22/2011 TradersExpo, b. 1961)

FRIDAY

D 33.3
S 38.1
N 57.1

3

All there is to investing is picking good stocks at good times and staying with them as long as they remain good companies.
— Warren Buffett (CEO Berkshire Hathaway, investor & philanthropist, b. 1930)

SATURDAY

4

SUNDAY

5

"BEST SIX MONTHS": STILL AN EYE-POPPING STRATEGY

Our Best Six Months Switching Strategy consistently delivers. Investing in the Dow Jones Industrial Average between November 1st and April 30th each year and then switching into fixed income for the other six months has produced reliable returns with reduced risk since 1950.

The chart on page 147 shows November, December, January, March, and April to be the top months since 1950. Add February, and an excellent strategy is born! These six consecutive months gained 14,654.27 Dow points in 62 years, while the remaining May through October months lost 1,654.97 points. The S&P gained 1,477.55 points in the same best six months versus a loss of 97.71 points in the worst six.

Percentage changes are shown along with a compounding $10,000 investment. The November–April $674,073 gain overshadows May–October's $1,024 loss. (S&P results were $499,148 to $5,204.) Just three November–April losses were double-digit: April 1970 (Cambodian invasion), 1973 (OPEC oil embargo) and 2008 (financial crisis). Similarly, Iraq muted the Best Six and inflated the Worst Six in 2003. When we discovered this strategy in 1986, November–April outperformed May–October by $88,163 to minus $1,522. Results improved substantially these past 26 years, $585,910 to $498. A simple timing indicator triples results (page 50).

	SIX-MONTH SWITCHING STRATEGY			
	DJIA % Change May 1–Oct 31	Investing $10,000	DJIA % Change Nov 1–Apr 30	Investing $10,000
1950	5.0%	$10,500	15.2%	$11,520
1951	1.2	10,626	−1.8	11,313
1952	4.5	11,104	2.1	11,551
1953	0.4	11,148	15.8	13,376
1954	10.3	12,296	20.9	16,172
1955	6.9	13,144	13.5	18,355
1956	−7.0	12,224	3.0	18,906
1957	−10.8	10,904	3.4	19,549
1958	19.2	12,998	14.8	22,442
1959	3.7	13,479	−6.9	20,894
1960	−3.5	13,007	16.9	24,425
1961	3.7	13,488	−5.5	23,082
1962	−11.4	11,950	21.7	28,091
1963	5.2	12,571	7.4	30,170
1964	7.7	13,539	5.6	31,860
1965	4.2	14,108	−2.8	30,968
1966	−13.6	12,189	11.1	34,405
1967	−1.9	11,957	3.7	35,678
1968	4.4	12,483	−0.2	35,607
1969	−9.9	11,247	−14.0	30,622
1970	2.7	11,551	24.6	38,155
1971	−10.9	10,292	13.7	43,382
1972	0.1	10,302	−3.6	41,820
1973	3.8	10,693	−12.5	36,593
1974	−20.5	8,501	23.4	45,156
1975	1.8	8,654	19.2	53,826
1976	−3.2	8,377	−3.9	51,727
1977	−11.7	7,397	2.3	52,917
1978	−5.4	6,998	7.9	57,097
1979	−4.6	6,676	0.2	57,211
1980	13.1	7,551	7.9	61,731
1981	−14.6	6,449	−0.5	61,422
1982	16.9	7,539	23.6	75,918
1983	−0.1	7,531	−4.4	72,578
1984	3.1	7,764	4.2	75,626
1985	9.2	8,478	29.8	98,163
1986	5.3	8,927	21.8	119,563
1987	−12.8	7,784	1.9	121,835
1988	5.7	8,228	12.6	137,186
1989	9.4	9,001	0.4	137,735
1990	−8.1	8,272	18.2	162,803
1991	6.3	8,793	9.4	178,106
1992	−4.0	8,441	6.2	189,149
1993	7.4	9,066	0.03	189,206
1994	6.2	9,628	10.6	209,262
1995	10.0	10,591	17.1	245,046
1996	8.3	11,470	16.2	284,743
1997	6.2	12,181	21.8	346,817
1998	−5.2	11,548	25.6	435,602
1999	−0.5	11,490	0.04	435,776
2000	2.2	11,743	−2.2	426,189
2001	−15.5	9,923	9.6	467,103
2002	−15.6	8,375	1.0	471,774
2003	15.6	9,682	4.3	492,060
2004	−1.9	9,498	1.6	499,933
2005	2.4	9,726	8.9	544,427
2006	6.3	10,339	8.1	588,526
2007	6.6	11,021	−8.0	541,444
2008	−27.3	8,012	−12.4	474,305
2009	18.9	9,526	13.3	537,388
2010	1.0	9,621	15.2	619,071
2011	−6.7	8,976	10.5	684,073
Average/Gain	**0.3%**	**($1,024)**	**7.5%**	**$674,073**
# Up/Down	**37/25**		**48/14**	

48

MONDAY

D 42.9
S 33.3
N 47.6

6

The wisdom of the ages is the fruit of freedom and democracy.
— Lawrence Kudlow (Economist, 24th Annual Paulson SmallCap Conference, Waldorf Astoria NYC, 11/8/01)

TUESDAY

D 33.3
S 23.8
N 33.3

7

Today we deal with 65,000 more pieces of information each day than did our ancestors 100 years ago.
— Dr. Jean Houston (A founder of the Human Potential Movement, b. 1937)

WEDNESDAY

D 71.4
S 61.9
N 76.2

8

Anyone who believes that exponential growth can go on forever in a finite world is either a madman or an economist.
— Kenneth Ewart Boulding (Economist, activist, poet, scientist, philosopher, cofounder General Systems Theory, 1910–1993)

THURSDAY

D 66.7
S 57.1
N 57.1

9

The worst trades are generally when people freeze and start to pray and hope rather than take some action.
— Robert Mnuchin (Partner Goldman Sachs)

Friday Before Mother's Day, Dow Up 11 of Last 18

FRIDAY

D 61.9
S 52.4
N 38.1

10

The only function of economic forecasting is to make astrology look respectable.
— John Kenneth Galbraith (Canadian/American economist and diplomat, 1908–2006)

SATURDAY

11

Mother's Day

SUNDAY

12

MACD-TIMING TRIPLES "BEST SIX MONTHS" RESULTS

Using the simple MACD (Moving Average Convergence Divergence) indicator developed by our friend Gerald Appel to better time entries and exits into and out of the Best Six Months (page 48) period nearly triples the results. Several years ago, Sy Harding enhanced our Best Six Months Switching Strategy with MACD triggers, dubbing it the "best mechanical system ever." In 2006, we improved it even more, quadrupling the results with just four trades every four years (page 60).

Our *Almanac Investor Newsletter* (see insert) implements this system with quite a degree of success. Starting October 1, we look to catch the market's first hint of an uptrend after the summer doldrums, and beginning April 1, we prepare to exit these seasonal positions as soon as the market falters.

In up-trending markets, MACD signals get you in earlier and keep you in longer. But if the market is trending down, entries are delayed until the market turns up, and exit points can come a month earlier.

The results from applying the simple MACD signals are astounding. Instead of $10,000 gaining $674,073 over the 62 recent years when invested only during the Best Six Months (page 48), the gain nearly tripled to $1,878,557. The $1,024 loss during the worst six months expanded to a loss of $6,723.

Impressive results for being invested during only 6.3 months of the year on average! For the rest of the year, consider money markets, bonds, puts, bear funds, covered calls, or credit call spreads. See page 36 for more executable trades employing ETFs and mutual funds.

Updated signals are e-mailed to our *Almanac Investor eNewsletter* subscribers as soon as they are triggered. Visit *www.stocktradersalmanac.com*, or see the insert for details and a special offer for new subscribers.

SIX-MONTH SWITCHING STRATEGY+TIMING

	DJIA % Change May 1–Oct 31*	DJIA Investing $10,000	DJIA % Change Nov 1–Apr 30*	DJIA Investing $10,000
1950	7.3%	$10,730	13.3%	$11,330
1951	0.1	10,741	1.9	11,545
1952	1.4	10,891	2.1	11,787
1953	0.2	10,913	17.1	13,803
1954	13.5	12,386	16.3	16,053
1955	7.7	13,340	13.1	18,156
1956	−6.8	12,433	2.8	18,664
1957	−12.3	10,904	4.9	19,579
1958	17.3	12,790	16.7	22,849
1959	1.6	12,995	−3.1	22,141
1960	−4.9	12,358	16.9	25,883
1961	2.9	12,716	−1.5	25,495
1962	−15.3	10,770	22.4	31,206
1963	4.3	11,233	9.6	34,202
1964	6.7	11,986	6.2	36,323
1965	2.6	12,298	−2.5	35,415
1966	−16.4	10,281	14.3	40,479
1967	−2.1	10,065	5.5	42,705
1968	3.4	10,407	0.2	42,790
1969	−11.9	9,169	−6.7	39,923
1970	−1.4	9,041	20.8	48,227
1971	−11.0	8,046	15.4	55,654
1972	−0.6	7,998	−1.4	54,875
1973	−11.0	7,118	0.1	54,930
1974	−22.4	5,524	28.2	70,420
1975	0.1	5,530	18.5	83,448
1976	−3.4	5,342	−3.0	80,945
1977	−11.4	4,733	0.5	81,350
1978	−4.5	4,520	9.3	88,916
1979	−5.3	4,280	7.0	95,140
1980	9.3	4,678	4.7	99,612
1981	−14.6	3,995	0.4	100,010
1982	15.5	4,614	23.5	123,512
1983	2.5	4,729	−7.3	114,496
1984	3.3	4,885	3.9	118,961
1985	7.0	5,227	38.1	164,285
1986	−2.8	5,081	28.2	210,613
1987	−14.9	4,324	3.0	216,931
1988	6.1	4,588	11.8	242,529
1989	9.8	5,038	3.3	250,532
1990	−6.7	4,700	15.8	290,116
1991	4.8	4,926	11.3	322,899
1992	−6.2	4,621	6.6	344,210
1993	5.5	4,875	5.6	363,486
1994	3.7	5,055	13.1	411,103
1995	7.2	5,419	16.7	479,757
1996	9.2	5,918	21.9	584,824
1997	3.6	6,131	18.5	693,016
1998	−12.4	5,371	39.9	969,529
1999	−6.4	5,027	5.1	1,018,975
2000	−6.0	4,725	5.4	1,074,000
2001	−17.3	3,908	15.8	1,243,692
2002	−25.2	2,923	6.0	1,318,314
2003	16.4	3,402	7.8	1,421,142
2004	−0.9	3,371	1.8	1,446,723
2005	−0.5	3,354	7.7	1,558,121
2006	4.7	3,512	14.4	1,782,490
2007	5.6	3,709	−12.7	1,556,114
2008	−24.7	2,793	−14.0	1,338,258
2009	23.8	3,458	10.8	1,482,790
2010	4.6	3,617	7.3	1,591,034
2011	−9.4	3,277	18.7	1,888,557
Average	**−1.2%**		**9.3%**	
# Up	**32**		**53**	
# Down	**30**		**9**	
62-Year Gain (Loss)		**($6,723)**		**$1,878,557**

MACD generated entry and exit points (earlier or later) can lengthen or shorten six-month periods.

Monday After Mother's Day, Dow Up 14 of Last 18
Monday Before May Expiration, Dow Up 20 of Last 25, Average Gain 0.4%

MONDAY

D 52.4
S 52.4
N 52.4

13

A "tired businessman" is one whose business is usually not a successful one.
— Joseph R. Grundy (U.S. Senator Pennsylvania 1929–1930, businessman, 1863–1961)

TUESDAY

D 52.4
S 47.6
N 42.9

14

A weak currency is the sign of a weak economy, and a weak economy leads to a weak nation.
— H. Ross Perot (American businessman, *The Dollar Crisis*, 2-time 3rd-party presidential candidate 1992 & 1996, b. 1930)

WEDNESDAY

D 57.1
S 57.1
N 52.4

15

War is God's way of teaching Americans geography.
— Ambrose Bierce (Writer, satirist, Civil War hero, *The Devil's Dictionary*, 1842–1914?)

THURSDAY

D 52.4
S 57.1
N 61.9

16

There is no great mystery to satisfying your customers. Build them a quality product and treat them with respect. It's that simple.
— Lee Iacocca (American industrialist, Former Chrysler CEO, b. 1924)

May Expiration Day, Dow Down 14 of Last 23, Average Loss 0.2%

FRIDAY

D 57.1
S 61.9
N 66.7

17

Age is a question of mind over matter. If you don't mind, it doesn't matter.
— Leroy Robert "Satchel" Paige (Negro League and Hall of Fame Pitcher, 1906–1982)

SATURDAY

18

SUNDAY

19

MARKET FARES BETTER UNDER DEMOCRATS
DOLLAR HOLDS UP UNDER REPUBLICANS

Does the market perform better under Republicans or Democrats? The market surge under Reagan and Bush I after Vietnam, OPEC, and Iran inflation helped Republicans even up the score in the 20th century vs. the Democrats, who benefited when Roosevelt came in following an 89.2% drop by the Dow. However, under Clinton, the Democrats took the lead again. Both parties were more evenly matched in the last half of the 20th century. Under Obama, the Dow has gained 28.5% while the dollar has lost 5.8%.

THE STOCK MARKET UNDER REPUBLICANS AND DEMOCRATS

Republican Eras		% Change	Democratic Eras		% Change
1901–1912	12 Years	48.3%	1913–1920	8 Years	29.2%
1921–1932	12 Years	−24.5%	1933–1952	20 Years	318.4%
1953–1960	8 Years	121.2%	1961–1968	8 Years	58.3%
1969–1976	8 Years	2.1%	1977–1980	4 Years	−3.0%
1981–1992	12 Years	247.0%	1993–2000	8 Years	236.7%
2001–2008	8 Years	−12.1%	2009–2012*	4 Years*	28.5%
Totals	**60 Years**	**382.1%**	**Totals**	**52 Years***	**668.3%**
Average Annual Change		**6.4%**	**Average Annual Change**		**13.0%**

Based on Dow Jones Industrial Average on previous year's Election Day or day before when closed
*Through May 18, 2012

A $10,000 investment compounded during Democratic eras would have grown to $359,447 in 52* years. The same investment during 60 Republican years would have appreciated to $77,175. After lagging for many years, performance under the Republicans improved under Reagan and Bush. Under Clinton Democratic performance surged ahead. Under Bush II Republicans lost ground.

DECLINE OF THE DOLLAR UNDER REPUBLICANS AND DEMOCRATS

Republican Eras		Loss in Purch. Power	Value of Dollar	Democratic Eras		Loss in Purch. Power	Value of Dollar
1901–1912	12 Years	−23.6%	$0.76	1913–1920	8 Years	−51.4%	$0.49
1921–1932	12 Years	+46.9%	$1.12	1933–1952	20 Years	−48.6%	$0.25
1953–1960	8 Years	−10.2%	$1.01	1961–1968	8 Years	−15.0%	$0.21
1969–1976	8 Years	−38.9%	$0.62	1977–1980	4 Years	−30.9%	$0.15
1981–1992	12 Years	−41.3%	$0.36	1993–2000	8 Years	−18.5%	$0.12
2001–2008	8 Years	−20.0%	$0.29	2009–2012**	4 Years**	−5.8%	$0.11

The Republican Dollar declined to $0.29 in 60 years.   **The Democratic Dollar declined to $0.11 in 52 years**.**

Based on average annual Consumer Price Index 1982–1984 = 100
** Through May 18, 2012

Adjusting stock market performance for loss of purchasing power reduced the Democrats' $359,447 to $42,956 and the Republicans' $77,175 to $22,344. Republicans may point out that all four major wars of the 20th century began while the Democrats were in power. Democrats can counter that the 46.7% increase in purchasing power occurred during the Depression and was not very meaningful to the 25% who were unemployed.

For the record, there have been 14 recessions and 18 bear markets under the Republicans and 7 recessions and 16 bear markets under the Democrats.

MAY

MONDAY
D 52.4
S 47.6
N 42.9
20

Investors operate with limited funds and limited intelligence, they don't need to know everything. As long as they understand something better than others, they have an edge.
— George Soros (Financier, philanthropist, political activist, author and philosopher, b. 1930)

TUESDAY
D 57.1
S 57.1
N 71.4
21

Wall Street's graveyards are filled with men who were right too soon.
— William Peter Hamilton (Editor, *Wall Street Journal, The Stock Market Barometer*, 1922, 1867–1929)

WEDNESDAY
D 38.1
S 38.1
N 47.6
22

If I have seen further, it is by standing upon the shoulders of giants
— Sir Isaac Newton (English physicist, mathematician, Laws of Gravity, letter to Robert Hooke 2/15/1676, 1643–1727)

THURSDAY
D 33.3
S 33.3
N 42.9
23

Governments last as long as the under-taxed can defend themselves against the over-taxed.
— Bernard Berenson (American art critic, 1865–1959)

Friday Before Memorial Day Tends to Be Lackluster with Light Trading, Dow Down 7 of Last 12, Average –0.3%

FRIDAY
D 52.4
S 61.9
N 52.4
24

Being uneducated is sometimes beneficial. Then you don't know what can't be done.
— Michael Ott (Venture capitalist)

SATURDAY
25

June Almanac Investor Seasonalities: See Pages 92, 94 and 96

SUNDAY
26

JUNE ALMANAC

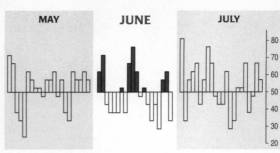

JUNE	JULY
S M T W T F S	S M T W T F S
1	1 2 3 4 5 6
2 3 4 5 6 7 8	7 8 9 10 11 12 13
9 10 11 12 13 14 15	14 15 16 17 18 19 20
16 17 18 19 20 21 22	21 22 23 24 25 26 27
23 24 25 26 27 28 29	28 29 30 31
30	

Market Probability Chart above is a graphic representation of the S&P 500 Recent Market Probability Calendar on page 124.

◆ The "summer rally" in most years is the weakest rally of all four seasons (page 70) ◆ Week after June Triple-Witching Day Dow down 20 of last 22 (page 76) ◆ RECENT RECORD: S&P up 10, down 7, average loss 0.4%, ranks tenth ◆ Stronger for NASDAQ, average gain 1.2% last 17 years ◆ Watch out for end-of-quarter "portfolio pumping" on last day of June, Dow down 15 of last 21, NASDAQ down 6 of last 7 ◆ Post-presidential election year Junes: #9 S&P, #8 NASDAQ, Dow weaker, ranks #10 ◆ June ends NASDAQ's Best Eight Months.

June Vital Statistics

	DJIA		S&P 500		NASDAQ		Russell 1K		Russell 2K	
Rank	11		10		7		10		8	
Up	28		32		23		19		20	
Down	34		30		18		14		13	
Average % Change	−0.4%		−0.1%		0.7%		0.1%		0.3%	
Post-Election Year	−1.2%		−0.7%		0.8%		0.3%		1.1%	
Best & Worst June										
	% Change		% Change		% Change		% Change		% Change	
Best	1955	6.2	1955	8.2	2000	16.6	1999	5.1	2000	8.6
Worst	2008	−10.2	2008	−8.6	2002	−9.4	2008	−8.5	2010	−7.9
Best & Worst June Weeks										
Best	6/7/74	6.4	6/2/00	7.2	6/2/00	19.0	6/2/00	8.0	6/2/00	12.2
Worst	6/30/50	−6.8	6/30/50	−7.6	6/15/01	−8.4	6/15/01	−4.2	6/9/06	−4.9
Best & Worst June Days										
Best	6/28/62	3.8	6/28/62	3.4	6/2/00	6.4	6/10/10	3.0	6/2/00	4.2
Worst	6/26/50	−4.7	6/26/50	−5.4	6/29/10	−3.9	6/4/10	−3.5	6/4/10	−5.0
First Trading Day of Expiration Week: 1980–2011										
Record (#Up−#Down)	17–15		19–13		14–18		17–15		12–19	
Current streak	U1		U1		D1		D3		D1	
Avg % Change	0.01		−0.08		−0.24		−0.09		−0.32	
Options Expiration Day: 1980–2011										
Record (#Up−#Down)	19–13		20–12		18–14		20–12		18–14	
Current streak	U2		U3		D1		U3		U3	
Avg % Change	−0.08		0.010		−0.04		−0.03		−0.03	
Options Expiration Week: 1980–2011										
Record (#Up−#Down)	18–14		16–16		13–19		14–18		14–18	
Current streak	U2		U2		D1		D1		U2	
Avg % Change	−0.11		−0.13		−0.35		−0.19		−0.32	
Week After Options Expiration: 1980–2011										
Record (#Up−#Down)	10–22		16–16		18–14		16–16		15–17	
Current streak	D13		D9		U1		D7		U1	
Avg % Change	−0.46		−0.17		0.11		−0.14		−0.13	
First Trading Day Performance										
% of Time Up	53.2		51.6		58.5		57.6		63.6	
Avg % Change	0.16		0.14		0.18		0.12		0.21	
Last Trading Day Performance										
% of Time Up	53.2		50.0		65.9		48.5		66.7	
Avg % Change	0.02		0.06		0.25		−0.06		0.33	

Dow & S&P 1950–April 2012, NASDAQ 1971–April 2012, Russell 1K & 2K 1979–April 2012.

Last Day of June not hot for the Dow;
Down 15 of 21, WOW!

Memorial Day (Market Closed)

Never tell people how to do things. Tell them what to do and they will surprise you with their ingenuity.
— General George S. Patton, Jr. (U.S. Army field commander WWII, 1885–1945)

Day After Memorial Day, Dow Up 18 of Last 26

TUESDAY
D 52.4
S 57.1
N 52.4
28

The authority of a thousand is not worth the humble reasoning of a single individual.
— Galileo Galilei (Italian physicist and astronomer, 1564–1642)

Memorial Day Week Dow Down 9 of Last 16, Up 12 Straight 1984–1995

WEDNESDAY
D 52.4
S 57.1
N 61.9
29

A senior European diplomat said he was convinced that the choice of starting a war this spring was made for political as well as military reasons. [The President] clearly does not want to have a war raging on the eve of his presumed reelection campaign.
— Reported by Steven R. Weisman (*NY Times* 3/14/03)

THURSDAY
D 71.4
S 61.9
N 76.2
30

Another factor contributing to productivity is technology, particularly the rapid introduction of new microcomputers based on single-chip circuits. . . . The results over the next decade will be a second industrial revolution.
— Yale Hirsch (Creator of Stock *Trader's Almanac, Smart Money Newsletter* 9/22/1976, b. 1923)

Start Looking for NASDAQ MACD Sell Signal (Page 58)
Almanac Investor Subscribers Emailed When It Triggers (See Insert)

FRIDAY
D 52.4
S 57.1
N 66.7
31

If you have an important point to make, don't try to be subtle or clever. Use a pile driver. Hit the point once. Then come back and hit it again. Then hit it a third time—a tremendous whack.
— Winston Churchill (British statesman, 1874–1965)

SATURDAY
1

SUNDAY
2

TOP PERFORMING NASDAQ MONTHS PAST 41⅓ YEARS

NASDAQ stocks continue to run away during three consecutive months, November, December, and January, with an average gain of 6.4% despite the slaughter of November 2000, down 22.9%, December 2000, −4.9%, December 2002, −9.7%, November 2007, −6.9%, January 2008, −9.9%, November 2008, −10.8%, January 2009, −6.4%, and January 2010, −5.4%. Solid gains in November and December 2004 offset January 2005's 5.2% Iraq-turmoil-fueled drop.

You can see the months graphically on page 148. January by itself is impressive, up 2.9% on average. April, May, and June also shine, creating our NASDAQ Best Eight Months strategy. What appears as a Death Valley abyss occurs during NASDAQ's bleakest four months: July, August, September, and October. NASDAQ's Best Eight Months seasonal strategy using MACD timing is displayed on page 58.

MONTHLY % CHANGES (JANUARY 1971 TO APRIL 2011)

	NASDAQ Composite*					Dow Jones Industrials			
Month	Total % Change	Avg. % Change	# Up	# Down	Month	Total % Change	Avg. % Change	# Up	# Down
Jan	123.2%	2.9%	28	14	Jan	56.7%	1.3%	27	15
Feb	19.1	0.5	22	20	Feb	8.4	0.2	24	18
Mar	34.8	0.8	27	15	Mar	46.9	1.1	28	14
Apr	63.1	1.5	27	15	Apr	93.2	2.2	26	16
May	37.5	0.9	24	17	May	14.4	0.4	21	20
Jun	28.6	0.7	23	18	Jun	−5.7	−0.1	20	21
Jul	0.8	0.02	20	21	Jul	28.6	0.7	22	19
Aug	3.2	0.1	22	19	Aug	−7.5	−0.2	23	18
Sep	−27.7	−0.7	22	19	Sep	−49.2	−1.2	14	27
Oct	24.8	0.6	22	19	Oct	21.1	0.5	25	16
Nov	62.6	1.5	26	15	Nov	49.3	1.2	27	14
Dec	83.7	2.0	24	17	Dec	69.6	1.7	29	12
% Rank					**% Rank**				
Jan	123.2%	2.9%	28	14	Apr	93.2%	2.2%	26	16
Dec	83.7	2.0	24	17	Dec	69.6	1.7	29	12
Apr	63.1	1.5	27	15	Jan	56.7	1.3	27	15
Nov	62.6	1.5	26	15	Nov	49.3	1.2	27	14
May	37.5	0.9	24	17	Mar	46.9	1.1	28	14
Mar	34.8	0.8	27	15	Jul	28.6	0.7	22	19
Jun	28.6	0.7	23	18	Oct	21.1	0.5	25	16
Oct	24.8	0.6	22	19	May	14.4	0.4	21	20
Feb	19.1	0.5	22	20	Feb	8.4	0.2	24	18
Aug	3.2	0.1	22	19	Jun	−5.7	−0.1	20	21
Jul	0.8	0.02	20	21	Aug	−7.5	−0.2	23	18
Sep	−27.7	−0.7	22	19	Sep	−49.2	−1.2	14	27
Totals	**453.7%**	**10.8%**			**Totals**	**325.8%**	**7.8%**		
Average		**0.90%**			**Average**		**0.65%**		

Based on NASDAQ composite; prior to February 5, 1971, based on National Quotation Bureau indices.

For comparison, Dow figures are shown. During this period, NASDAQ averaged a 0.90% gain per month, 38 percent more than the Dow's 0.65% per month. Between January 1971 and January 1982, NASDAQ's composite index doubled in twelve years, while the Dow stayed flat. But while NASDAQ plummeted 77.9% from its 2000 highs to the 2002 bottom, the Dow only lost 37.8%. The Great Recession and bear market of 2007–2009 spread its carnage equally across Dow and NASDAQ. Recent market moves are increasingly more correlated.

JUNE

First Trading Day in June, Dow Up 18 of Last 24, 2008/2010 –1.1%, 2011 –2.2%

MONDAY

D 71.4
S 61.9
N 61.9

3

There's a lot of talk about self-esteem these days. It seems pretty basic to me. If you want to feel good about yourself, you've got to do things that you can be proud of.
— Osceola McCarty (American author, *Simple Wisdom for Rich Living*, 1908–1999)

TUESDAY

D 52.4
S 71.4
N 81.0

4

Whenever a well-known bearish analyst is interviewed [Cover story] in the financial press, it usually coincides with an important near-term market bottom.
— Clif Droke (Clifdroke.com, 11/15/04)

WEDNESDAY

D 47.6
S 42.9
N 52.4

5

We prefer to cut back exposure on what's going against us and add exposure where it's more favorable to our portfolio. This way, we're always attempting to tilt the odds in our favor. This is the exact opposite of a long investor that would average down. Averaging down is a very dangerous practice.
— John Del Vecchio & Brad Lamensdorf (Portfolio managers Active Bear ETF, 5/10/12 *Almanac Investor Interview*)

June Ends NASDAQ's "Best Eight Months" (Pages 56, 58 and 148)

THURSDAY

D 47.6
S 38.1
N 42.9

6

We were fairly arrogant, until we realized the Japanese were selling quality products for what it cost us to make them.
— Paul A. Allaire (former Chairman of Xerox)

FRIDAY

D 47.6
S 38.1
N 33.3

7

It is totally unproductive to think the world has been unfair to you. Every tough stretch is an opportunity.
— Charlie Munger (Vice-Chairman Berkshire Hathaway, 2007 Wesco Annual Meeting, b. 1924)

SATURDAY

8

SUNDAY

9

GET MORE OUT OF NASDAQ'S "BEST EIGHT MONTHS" WITH MACD TIMING

NASDAQ's amazing eight-month run from November through June is hard to miss on pages 56 and 148. A $10,000 investment in these eight months since 1971 gained $377,596 versus a loss of $3,196 during the void that is the four-month period July–October (as of May 18, 2012).

Using the same MACD timing indicators on the NASDAQ as is done for the Dow (page 50) has enabled us to capture much of October's improved performance, pumping up NASDAQ's results considerably. Over the 41 years since NASDAQ began, the gain on the same $10,000 more than doubles to $930,665, and the loss during the four-month void increases to $7,305. Only four sizeable losses occurred during the favorable period, and the bulk of NASDAQ's bear markets were avoided, including the worst of the 2000–2002 bear. See page 36 for more executable trades employing ETFs and mutual funds.

Updated signals are e-mailed to our monthly newsletter subscribers as soon as they are triggered. Visit *www.stocktradersalmanac.com,* or see insert for details and a special offer for new subscribers.

BEST EIGHT MONTHS STRATEGY + TIMING

MACD Signal Date	Worst 4 Months July 1–Oct 31* NASDAQ	% Change	Investing $10,000	MACD Signal Date	Best 8 Months Nov 1–June 30* NASDAQ	% Change	Investing $10,000
22-Jul-71	109.54	−3.6	$9,640	4-Nov-71	105.56	24.1	$12,410
7-Jun-72	131.00	−1.8	9,466	23-Oct-72	128.66	−22.7	9,593
25-Jun-73	99.43	−7.2	8,784	7-Dec-73	92.32	−20.2	7,655
3-Jul-74	73.66	−23.2	6,746	7-Oct-74	56.57	47.8	11,314
11-Jun-75	83.60	−9.2	6,125	7-Oct-75	75.88	20.8	13,667
22-Jul-76	91.66	−2.4	5,978	19-Oct-76	89.45	13.2	15,471
27-Jul-77	101.25	−4.0	5,739	4-Nov-77	97.21	26.6	19,586
7-Jun-78	123.10	−6.5	5,366	6-Nov-78	115.08	19.1	23,327
3-Jul-79	137.03	−1.1	5,307	30-Oct-79	135.48	15.5	26,943
20-Jun-80	156.51	26.2	6,697	9-Oct-80	197.53	11.2	29,961
4-Jun-81	219.68	−17.6	5,518	1-Oct-81	181.09	−4.0	28,763
7-Jun-82	173.84	12.5	6,208	7-Oct-82	195.59	57.4	45,273
1-Jun-83	307.95	−10.7	5,544	3-Nov-83	274.86	−14.2	38,844
1-Jun-84	235.90	5.0	5,821	15-Oct-84	247.67	17.3	45,564
3-Jun-85	290.59	−3.0	5,646	1-Oct-85	281.77	39.4	63,516
10-Jun-86	392.83	−10.3	5,064	1-Oct-86	352.34	20.5	76,537
30-Jun-87	424.67	−22.7	3,914	2-Nov-87	328.33	20.1	91,921
8-Jul-88	394.33	−6.6	3,656	29-Nov-88	368.15	22.4	112,511
13-Jun-89	450.73	0.7	3,682	9-Nov-89	454.07	1.9	114,649
11-Jun-90	462.79	−23.0	2,835	2-Oct-90	356.39	39.3	159,706
11-Jun-91	496.62	6.4	3,016	1-Oct-91	528.51	7.4	171,524
11-Jun-92	567.68	1.5	3,061	14-Oct-92	576.22	20.5	206,686
7-Jun-93	694.61	9.9	3,364	1-Oct-93	763.23	−4.4	197,592
17-Jun-94	729.35	5.0	3,532	11-Oct-94	765.57	13.5	224,267
1-Jun-95	868.82	17.2	4,140	13-Oct-95	1018.38	21.6	272,709
3-Jun-96	1238.73	1.0	4,181	7-Oct-96	1250.87	10.3	300,798
4-Jun-97	1379.67	24.4	5,201	3-Oct-97	1715.87	1.8	306,212
1-Jun-98	1746.82	−7.8	4,795	15-Oct-98	1611.01	49.7	458,399
1-Jun-99	2412.03	18.5	5,682	6-Oct-99	2857.21	35.7	622,047
29-Jun-00	3877.23	−18.2	4,648	18-Oct-00	3171.56	−32.2	421,748
1-Jun-01	2149.44	−31.1	3,202	1-Oct-01	1480.46	5.5	444,944
3-Jun-02	1562.56	−24.0	2,434	2-Oct-02	1187.30	38.5	616,247
20-Jun-03	1644.72	15.1	2,802	6-Oct-03	1893.46	4.3	642,746
21-Jun-04	1974.38	−1.6	2,757	1-Oct-04	1942.20	6.1	681,954
8-Jun-05	2060.18	1.5	2,798	19-Oct-05	2091.76	6.1	723,553
1-Jun-06	2219.86	3.9	2,907	5-Oct-06	2306.34	9.5	792,291
7-Jun-07	2541.38	7.9	3,137	1-Oct-07	2740.99	−9.1	724,796
2-Jun-08	2491.53	−31.3	2,155	17-Oct-08	1711.29	6.1	769,009
15-Jun-09	1816.38	17.8	2,539	9-Oct-09	2139.28	1.6	781,313
7-Jun-10	2461.19	18.6	3,011	4-Nov-10	2577.34	7.4	839,130
1-Jun-11	2769.19	−10.5	2,695	7-Oct-11	2479.35	12.1	940,665
18-May-12	2778.79						

As of 5/18/2012, MACD Sell Signal not triggered at press time

41-Year Loss ($7,305)   **41-Year Gain $930,665**

MACD-generated entry and exit points (earlier or later) can lengthen or shorten eight-month periods.

JUNE

MONDAY
D 47.6
S 38.1
N 28.6
10

We always live in an uncertain world. What is certain is that the United States will go forward over time.
— Warren Buffett (CEO Berkshire Hathaway, investor & philanthropist, CNBC 9/22/2010, b. 1930)

TUESDAY
D 42.9
S 52.4
N 47.6
11

A man isn't a man until he has to meet a payroll.
— Ivan Shaffer (*The Stock Promotion Game*)

2008 Second Worst June Ever, Dow –10.2%, S&P –8.6%,
Only 1930 Was Worse, NASDAQ –9.1%, June 2002 –9.4%

WEDNESDAY
D 42.9
S 38.1
N 38.1
12

Markets are constantly in a state of uncertainty and flux and money is made by discounting the obvious and betting on the unexpected.
— George Soros (Financier, philanthropist, political activist, author and philosopher, b. 1930)

THURSDAY
D 66.7
S 66.7
N 52.4
13

Successful innovation is not a feat of intellect, but of will.
— Joseph A. Schumpeter (Austrian-American economist, *Theory of Economic Development*, 1883–1950)

FRIDAY
D 76.2
S 76.2
N 66.7
14

I went to a restaurant that serves "breakfast at any time." So I ordered French toast during the Renaissance.
— Steven Wright (Comedian, b. 1955)

SATURDAY
15

Father's Day

SUNDAY
16

TRIPLE RETURNS, FEWER TRADES: BEST 6 + 4-YEAR CYCLE

We first introduced this strategy to *Almanac Investor* newsletter subscribers in October 2006. Recurring seasonal stock market patterns and the four-year Presidential Election/Stock Market Cycle (page 130) have been integral to our research since the first Almanac 46 years ago. Yale Hirsch discovered the Best Six Months in 1986 (page 48), and it has been a cornerstone of our seasonal investment analysis and strategies ever since.

Most of the market's gains have occurred during the Best Six Months, and the market generally hits a low point every four years in the first (post-election) or second (midterm) year and exhibits the greatest gains in the third (pre-election) year. This strategy combines the best of these two market phenomena, the Best Six Months and the four-year cycle, timing entries and exits with MACD (pages 50 and 58).

We've gone back to 1949 to include the full four-year cycle that began with post-election year 1949. Only four trades every four years are needed to nearly triple the results of the Best Six Months. Buy and sell during the post-election and midterm years and then hold from the midterm MACD seasonal buy signal sometime after October 1 until the post-election MACD seasonal sell signal sometime after April 1, approximately 2.5 years: better returns, less effort, lower transaction fees, and fewer taxable events. See page 36 for more executable trades employing ETFs and mutual funds.

FOUR TRADES EVERY FOUR YEARS		
	Worst Six Months	Best Six Months
Year	May–Oct	Nov–April
Post-election	Sell	Buy
Midterm	Sell	Buy
Pre-election	Hold	Hold
Election	Hold	Hold

BEST SIX MONTHS+TIMING+4-YEAR CYCLE STRATEGY

	DJIA % Change May 1–Oct 31*	Investing $10,000	DJIA % Change Nov 1–Apr 30*	Investing $10,000
1949	3.0%	$10,300	17.5%	$11,750
1950	7.3	$11,052	19.7	$14,065
1951		$11,052		$14,065
1952		$11,052		$14,065
1953	0.2	$11,074	17.1	$16,470
1954	13.5	$12,569	35.7	$22,350
1955		$12,569		$22,350
1956		$12,569		$22,350
1957	−12.3	$11,023	4.9	$23,445
1958	17.3	$12,930	27.8	$29,963
1959		$12,930		$29,963
1960		$12,930		$29,963
1961	2.9	$13,305	−1.5	$29,514
1962	−15.3	$11,269	58.5	$46,780
1963		$11,269		$46,780
1964		$11,269		$46,780
1965	2.6	$11,562	−2.5	$45,611
1966	−16.4	$9,666	22.2	$55,737
1967		$9,666		$55,737
1968		$9,666		$55,737
1969	−11.9	$8,516	−6.7	$52,003
1970	−1.4	$8,397	21.5	$63,184
1971		$8,397		$63,184
1972		$8,397		$63,184
1973	−11.0	$7,473	0.1	$63,247
1974	−22.4	$5,799	42.5	$90,127
1975		$5,799		$90,127
1976		$5,799		$90,127
1977	−11.4	$5,138	0.5	$90,578
1978	−4.5	$4,907	26.8	$114,853
1979		$4,907		$114,853
1980		$4,907		$114,853
1981	−14.6	$4,191	0.4	$115,312
1982	15.5	$4,841	25.9	$145,178
1983		$4,841		$145,178
1984		$4,841		$145,178
1985	7.0	$5,180	38.1	$200,491
1986	−2.8	$5,035	33.2	$267,054
1987		$5,035		$267,054
1988		$5,035		$267,054
1989	9.8	$5,528	3.3	$275,867
1990	−6.7	$5,158	35.1	$372,696
1991		$5,158		$372,696
1992		$5,158		$372,696
1993	5.5	$5,442	5.6	$393,455
1994	3.7	$5,643	88.2	$740,482
1995		$5,643		$740,482
1996		$5,643		$740,482
1997	3.6	$5,846	18.5	$877,471
1998	−12.4	$5,121	36.3	$1,195,993
1999		$5,121		$1,195,993
2000		$5,121		$1,195,993
2001	−17.3	$4,235	15.8	$1,384,960
2002	−25.2	$3,168	34.2	$1,858,616
2003		$3,168		$1,858,616
2004		$3,168		$1,858,616
2005	−0.5	$3,152	7.7	$2,001,729
2006	4.7	$3,300	−31.7	$1,367,181
2007		$3,300		$1,367,181
2008		$3,300		$1,367,181
2009	23.8	$4,085	10.8	$1,514,738
2010	4.6	$4,273	8.2**	$1,749,523
Average	**−1.0%**		**9.7%**	
# Up	**16**		**28**	
# Down	**16**		**4**	
63-Year Gain (Loss)		**($5,727)**		**$1,647,124**

* MACD and 2.5-year hold lengthen and shorten six-month periods ** As of 5/18/2012

Monday of Triple Witching Week, Dow Down 9 of Last 15

MONDAY
D 52.4
S 61.9
N 61.9
17

Anytime there is change there is opportunity. So it is paramount that an organization get energized rather than paralyzed.
— Jack Welch (GE CEO, *Fortune*)

TUESDAY
D 52.4
S 47.6
N 38.1
18

No one ever claimed that managed care was either managed or cared.
— Anonymous

Triple Witching Week Often Up in Bull Markets and Down in Bears (Page 76)
FOMC Meeting (2 Days)

WEDNESDAY
D 52.4
S 52.4
N 52.4
19

In business, the competition will bite you if you keep running; if you stand still, they will swallow you.
— William Knudsen (Former President of GM)

THURSDAY
D 42.9
S 42.9
N 42.9
20

It isn't the incompetent who destroy an organization. It is those who have achieved something and want to rest upon their achievements who are forever clogging things up.
— Charles E. Sorenson (Danish-American engineer, officer, director of Ford Motor Co. 1907–1950, helped develop 1st auto assembly line, 1881–1968)

June Triple Witching Day, Dow Mixed Down 7 of Last 14,
Average Loss 0.4%

FRIDAY
D 33.3
S 33.3
N 28.6
21

Of a stock's move, 31% can be attributed to the general stock market, 12% to the industry influence, 37% to the influence of other groupings, and the remaining 20% is peculiar to the one stock.
— Benjamin F. King (*Market and Industry Factors in Stock Price Behavior, Journal of Business*, January 1966)

SATURDAY
22

SUNDAY
23

FIRST MONTH OF QUARTERS IS THE MOST BULLISH

We have observed over the years that the investment calendar reflects the annual, semiannual, and quarterly operations of institutions during January, April, and July. The opening month of the first three quarters produces the greatest gains in the Dow Jones Industrials and the S&P 500. NASDAQ's record differs slightly.

The fourth quarter had behaved quite differently, since it is affected by year-end portfolio adjustments and presidential and congressional elections in even-numbered years. Since 1991, major turnarounds have helped October join the ranks of bullish first months of quarters. October transformed into a bear-killing-turnaround month, posting some mighty gains in nine of the last 14 years, 2008 was a significant exception. (See pages 152–160.)

After experiencing the most powerful bull market of all time during the 1990s, followed by the ferocious bear market early in the millennium, we divided the monthly average percentage changes into two groups: before 1991 and after. Comparing the month-by-month quarterly behavior of the three major U.S. averages in the table, you'll see that first months of the first three quarters perform best overall. Nasty sell-offs in April 2000, 2002, 2004, and 2005, and July 2000–2002 and 2004, hit the NASDAQ hardest. The bear market of October 2007–March 2009, which more than cut the markets in half, took a toll on every first month except April. October 2008 was the worst month in a decade. January was also a difficult month in 2008, 2009, and 2010. (See pages 152–160.)

Between 1950 and 1990, the S&P 500 gained 1.3% (Dow, 1.4%) on average in first months of the first three quarters. Second months barely eked out any gain, while third months, thanks to March, moved up 0.23% (Dow, 0.07%) on average. NASDAQ's first month of the first three quarters averages 1.67% from 1971–1990, with July being a negative drag.

DOW JONES INDUSTRIALS, S&P 500, AND NASDAQ
AVERAGE MONTHLY % CHANGES BY QUARTER

	DJIA 1950–1990			S&P 500 1950–1990			NASDAQ 1971–1990		
	1st Mo	2nd Mo	3rd Mo	1st Mo	2nd Mo	3rd Mo	1st Mo	2nd Mo	3rd Mo
1Q	1.5%	−0.01%	1.0%	1.5%	−0.1%	1.1%	3.8%	1.2%	0.9%
2Q	1.6	−0.4	0.1	1.3	−0.1	0.3	1.7	0.8	1.1
3Q	1.1	0.3	−0.9	1.1	0.3	−0.7	−0.5	0.1	−1.6
Tot	**4.2%**	**−0.1%**	**0.2%**	**3.9%**	**0.1%**	**0.7%**	**5.0%**	**2.1%**	**0.4%**
Avg	**1.40%**	**−0.04%**	**0.07%**	**1.30%**	**0.03%**	**0.23%**	**1.67%**	**0.70%**	**0.13%**
4Q	*−0.1%*	*1.4%*	*1.7%*	*0.4%*	*1.7%*	*1.6%*	*−1.4%*	*1.6%*	*1.4%*
	DJIA 1991–April 2012			S&P 500 1991–April 2012			NASDAQ 1991–April 2012		
1Q	0.3%	0.2%	1.2%	0.4%	−0.2%	1.3%	2.2%	−0.3%	0.8%
2Q	2.6	0.8	−1.2	1.9	0.9	−0.7	1.3	1.0	0.4
3Q	1.3	−0.8	−0.9	0.6	−0.6	−0.4	0.5	0.1	0.2
Tot	**4.2%**	**0.2%**	**−0.9%**	**2.9%**	**0.1%**	**0.2%**	**4.0%**	**0.9%**	**1.4%**
Avg	**1.40%**	**0.05%**	**−0.30%**	**0.97%**	**0.03%**	**0.06%**	**1.33%**	**0.28%**	**0.47%**
4Q	*1.7%*	*1.7%*	*1.8%*	*1.6%*	*1.2%*	*1.9%*	*2.5%*	*1.5%*	*2.6%*
	DJIA 1950–April 2012			S&P 500 1950–April 2012			NASDAQ 1971–April 2012		
1Q	1.1%	0.04%	1.1%	1.1%	−0.1%	1.2%	2.9%	0.5%	0.8%
2Q	2.0	0.02	−0.4	1.5	0.2	−0.1	1.5	0.9	0.7
3Q	1.2	−0.1	−0.9	0.9	−0.04	−0.6	0.02	0.1	−0.7
Tot	**4.3%**	**−0.04%**	**−0.2%**	**3.5%**	**0.1%**	**0.5%**	**4.4%**	**1.5%**	**0.8%**
Avg	**1.43%**	**−0.01%**	**−0.07%**	**1.17%**	**0.02%**	**0.18%**	**1.47%**	**0.49%**	**0.27%**
4Q	*0.5%*	*1.5%*	*1.7%*	*0.8%*	*1.5%*	*1.7%*	*0.6%*	*1.5%*	*2.0%*

MONDAY
D 42.9
S 42.9
N 42.9
24

Regardless of current economic conditions, it's always best to remember that the stock market is a barometer and not a thermometer.
— Yale Hirsch (Creator of *Stock Trader's Almanac*, b. 1923)

TUESDAY
D 38.1
S 28.6
N 38.1
25

The years teach much which the days never know.
— Ralph Waldo Emerson (American author, poet and philosopher, *Self-Reliance*, 1803–1882)

Week After June Triple Witching, Dow Down 13 in a Row and 20 of Last 22
Average Loss Since 1990, 1.2%

WEDNESDAY
D 52.4
S 57.1
N 61.9
26

You get stepped on, passed over, knocked down, but you have to come back.
— 90-year old Walter Watson (MD, *Fortune*, 11/13/2000)

THURSDAY
D 52.4
S 61.9
N 71.4
27

Laws are like sausages. It's better not to see them being made.
— Otto von Bismarck (German-Prussian politician, 1st Chancellor of Germany, 1815–1898)

Last Day of Q2 Bearish for Dow, Down 15 of Last 21
But Bullish for NASDAQ, Up 13 of 20, Although Down 6 of Last 7

FRIDAY
D 28.6
S 33.3
N 61.9
28

New indicator: CFO Magazine gave Excellence awards to WorldCom's Scott Sullivan (1998), Enron's Andrew Fastow (1999), and to Tyco's Mark Swartz (2000). All were subsequently indicted.
— Roger Lowenstein (Financial journalist and author, *Origins Of The Crash*, b. 1954)

SATURDAY
29

July Almanac Investor Seasonalities: See Pages 92, 94 and 96

SUNDAY
30

JULY ALMANAC

JULY						
S	M	T	W	T	F	S
	1	2	3	4	5	6
7	8	9	10	11	12	13
14	15	16	17	18	19	20
21	22	23	24	25	26	27
28	29	30	31			

AUGUST						
S	M	T	W	T	F	S
				1	2	3
4	5	6	7	8	9	10
11	12	13	14	15	16	17
18	19	20	21	22	23	24
25	26	27	28	29	30	31

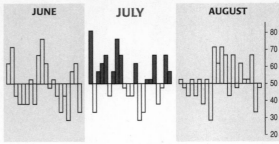

Market Probability Chart above is a graphic representation of the S&P 500 Recent Market Probability Calendar on page 124.

◆ July is the best month of the third quarter except for NASDAQ (page 62) ◆ Start of 2nd half brings an inflow of retirement funds ◆ First trading day Dow up 19 of last 23 ◆ Graph above shows strength in the beginning and end of July ◆ Huge gain in July usually provides better buying opportunity over next 4 months ◆ Start of NASDAQ's worst four months of the year (page 58) ◆ Post-presidential election Julys are ranked #1 Dow (up 12, down 3), #1 S&P (up 9, down 6), and #2 NASDAQ (up 8, down 2).

July Vital Statistics

	DJIA		S&P 500		NASDAQ		Russell 1K		Russell 2K	
Rank	4		6		11		8		10	
Up	38		33		20		14		16	
Down	24		29		21		19		17	
Average % Change	1.2%		0.9%		0.02%		0.5%		−0.5%	
Post-Election Year	2.0%		2.0%		3.1%		3.1%		2.6%	
Best & Worst July										
	% Change		% Change		% Change		% Change		% Change	
Best	1989	9.0	1989	8.8	1997	10.5	1989	8.2	1980	11.0
Worst	1969	−6.6	2002	−7.9	2002	−9.2	2002	−7.5	2002	−15.2
Best & Worst July Weeks										
Best	7/17/09	7.3	7/17/09	7.0	7/17/09	7.4	7/17/09	7.0	7/17/09	8.0
Worst	7/19/02	−7.7	7/19/02	−8.0	7/28/00	−10.5	7/19/02	−7.4	7/2/10	−7.2
Best & Worst July Days										
Best	7/24/02	6.4	7/24/02	5.7	7/29/02	5.8	7/24/02	5.6	7/29/02	4.9
Worst	7/19/02	−4.6	7/19/02	−3.8	7/28/00	−4.7	7/19/02	−3.6	7/23/02	−4.1
First Trading Day of Expiration Week: 1980–2011										
Record (#Up–#Down)	19–13		20–12		21–11		19–13		17–15	
Current streak	D1		D1		D1		D2		D2	
Avg % Change	0.08		0.01		0.01		−0.02		−0.11	
Options Expiration Day: 1980–2011										
Record (#Up–#Down)	15–15		16–16		14–18		16–16		12–20	
Current streak	U1		U1		U1		U1		U1	
Avg % Change	−0.27		−0.32		−0.48		−0.34		−0.51	
Options Expiration Week: 1980–2011										
Record (#Up–#Down)	19–13		16–16		16–16		16–16		17–15	
Current streak	D2		D2		D2		D2		D2	
Avg % Change	0.40		0.05		−0.05		−0.01		−0.16	
Week After Options Expiration: 1980–2011										
Record (#Up–#Down)	16–16		15–17		13–19		15–17		12–20	
Current streak	U3		U3		U4		U3		U4	
Avg % Change	−0.02		−0.20		−0.52		−0.22		−0.34	
First Trading Day Performance										
% of Time Up	64.5		69.4		58.5		69.7		60.6	
Avg % Change	0.25		0.24		0.06		0.29		−0.01	
Last Trading Day Performance										
% of Time Up	53.2		64.5		51.2		60.6		66.7	
Avg % Change	0.07		0.11		0.01		0.04		0.04	

Dow & S&P 1950–April 2012, NASDAQ 1971–April 2012, Russell 1K & 2K 1979–April 2012.

When Dow and S&P in July are inferior,
NASDAQ days tend to be even drearier.

A PROFITABLE LITTLE SERIES

The Little Book, Big Profits® series presents the biggest and brightest icons in the financial world writing on topics that range from tomorrow's hottest trends to the tried-and-true investment strategies we've all come to appreciate.

978-1-118-27011-0

978-0-470-92004-6

978-0-470-56799-9

978-1-118-15005-4

978-0-470-38378-0

978-1-118-15913-2

978-0-470-56805-7

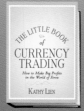

978-0-470-77035-1

978-0-470-62166-0

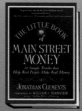

978-0-470-47323-8

978-0-470-39852-4

978-0-470-93293-3

978-0-470-90341-4

978-1-118-06350-7

978-1-118-00477-7

978-0-470-05589-2

978-0-470-22651-3

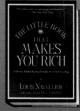

978-0-470-13772-7

978-0-470-25004-4

978-0-470-62415-9

978-0-470-68602-7

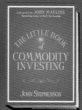

978-0-470-67837-4

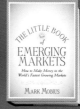

978-1-118-15381-9

978-1-118-24525-5

www.littlebook-series.com

WILEY

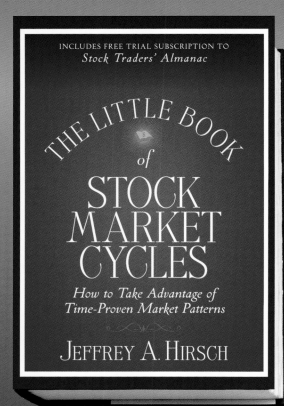

First Trading Day in July, Dow Up 19 of Last 23

MONDAY
D 81.0
S 81.0
N 71.4

1

The common denominator: Something that matters! Something that counts! Something that defines!
Something that is imbued with soul. And with life!
— Tom Peters (referring to projects, *Reinventing Work*, 1999, b. 1942)

TUESDAY
D 38.1
S 33.3
N 38.1

2

The critical ingredient is getting off your butt and doing something. It's as simple as that. A lot of people
have ideas, but there are few who decide to do something about them now. Not tomorrow. Not next week. But
today. The true entrepreneur is a doer, not a dreamer.
— Nolan Bushnell (Founder Atari & Chuck E. Cheese's, b. 1943)

(Shortened Trading Day)

WEDNESDAY
D 52.4
S 57.1
N 42.9

3

I've never been poor, only broke. Being poor is a frame of mind. Being broke is only a temporary situation.
— Mike Todd (Movie Producer, 1903–1958)

Independence Day
(Market Closed)

THURSDAY

4

Press on. Nothing in the world can take the place of persistence. Talent will not: nothing is more common than
unrewarded talent. Education alone will not: the world is full of educated failures. Persistence alone is omnipotent.
— Calvin Coolidge (30th U.S. President, 1872–1933)

FRIDAY
D 57.1
S 61.9
N 57.1

5

It wasn't raining when Noah built the ark.
— Warren Buffett (CEO Berkshire Hathaway, investor & philanthropist, b. 1930)

SATURDAY

6

SUNDAY

7

2011 DAILY DOW POINT CHANGES
(DOW JONES INDUSTRIAL AVERAGE)

Week #		Monday**	Tuesday	Wednsday	Thursday	Friday**	Weekly Dow Close	Net Point Change
1						2010 Close	11577.51	
2		93.24	20.43	31.71	−25.58	−22.55	11674.76	97.25
3	J	−37.31	34.43	83.56	−23.54	55.48	11787.38	112.62
4	A	Holiday	50.55	−12.64	−2.49	49.04	11871.84	84.46
5	N	108.68	−3.33	8.25	4.39	−166.13	11823.70	−48.14
6		68.23	148.23	1.81	20.29	29.89	12092.15	268.45
7		69.48	71.52	6.74	−10.60	43.97	12273.26	181.11
8	F	−5.07	−41.55	61.53	29.97	73.11	12391.25	117.99
9	E B	Holiday	−178.46	−107.01	−37.28	61.95	12130.45	−260.80
10		95.89	−168.32	8.78	191.40	−88.32	12169.88	39.43
11		−79.85	124.35	−1.29	−228.48	59.79	12044.40	−125.48
12	M A	−51.24	−137.74	−242.12	161.29	83.93	11858.52	−185.88
13	R	178.01	−17.90	67.39	84.54	50.03	12220.59	362.07
14		−22.71	81.13	71.60	−30.88	56.99	12376.72	156.13
15		23.31	−6.13	32.85	−17.26	−29.44	12380.05	3.33
16	A	1.06	−117.53	7.41	14.16	56.68	12341.83	−38.22
17	P R	−140.24	65.16	186.79	52.45	Holiday	12505.99	164.16
18		−26.11	115.49	95.59	72.35	47.23	12810.54	304.55
19		−3.18	0.15	−83.93	−139.41	54.57	12638.74	−171.80
20	M	45.94	75.68	−130.33	65.89	−100.17	12595.75	−42.99
21	A Y	−47.38	−68.79	80.60	45.14	−93.28	12512.04	−83.71
22		−130.78	−25.05	38.45	8.10	38.82	12441.58	−70.46
23		Holiday	128.21	−279.65	−41.59	−97.29	12151.26	−290.32
24	J	−61.30	−19.15	−21.87	75.42	−172.45	11951.91	−199.35
25	U N	1.06	123.14	−178.84	64.25	42.84	12004.36	52.45
26		76.02	109.63	−80.34	−59.67	−115.42	11934.58	−69.78
27		108.98	145.13	72.73	152.92	168.43	12582.77	648.19
28	J	Holiday	−12.90	56.15	93.47	−62.29	12657.20	74.43
29	U L	−151.44	−58.88	44.73	−54.49	42.61	12479.73	−177.47
30		−94.57	202.26	−15.51	152.50	−43.25	12681.16	201.43
31		−88.36	−91.50	−198.75	−62.44	−96.87	12143.24	−537.92
32		−10.75	−265.87	29.82	−512.76	60.93	11444.61	−698.63
33	A	−634.76	429.92	−519.83	423.37	125.71	11269.02	−175.59
34	U G	213.88	−76.97	4.28	−419.63	−172.93	10817.65	−451.37
35		37.00	322.11	143.95	−170.89	134.72	11284.54	466.89
36		254.71	20.70	53.58	−119.96	−253.31	11240.26	−44.28
37	S	Holiday	−100.96	275.56	−119.05	−303.68	10992.13	−248.13
38	E P	68.99	44.73	140.88	186.45	75.91	11509.09	516.96
39		−108.08	7.65	−283.82	−391.01	37.65	10771.48	−737.61
40		272.38	146.83	−179.79	143.08	−240.60	10913.38	141.90
41		−258.08	153.41	131.24	183.38	−20.21	11103.12	189.74
42	O	330.06	−16.88	102.55	−40.72	166.36	11644.49	541.37
43	C T	−247.49	180.05	−72.43	37.16	267.01	11808.79	164.30
44		104.83	−207.00	162.42	339.51	22.56	12231.11	422.32
45		−276.10	−297.05	178.08	208.43	−61.23	11983.24	−247.87
46		85.15	101.79	−389.24	112.85	259.89	12153.68	170.44
47	N	−74.70	17.18	−190.57	−134.86	25.43	11796.16	−357.52
48	O V	−248.85	−53.59	−236.17	Holiday	−25.77	11231.78	−564.38
49		291.23	32.62	490.05	−25.65	−0.61	12019.42	787.64
50		78.41	52.30	46.24	−198.67	186.56	12184.26	164.84
51	D	−162.87	−66.45	−131.46	45.33	−2.42	11866.39	−317.87
52	E C	−100.13	337.32	4.16	61.91	124.35	12294.00	427.61
53		Holiday	−2.65	−139.94	135.63	-69.48	12217.56	−76.44
TOTALS		−571.02	1423.66	−776.05	246.27	317.19		640.05

Bold Color: Down Friday, Down Monday   ** Shortened trading day: Nov 25*

** Monday denotes first trading day of week, Friday denotes last trading day of week

Market Subject to Elevated Volatility After July 4th

Beware of inside information ... all inside information.
— Jesse Livermore (Early 20th century stock trader and speculator, *How to Trade in Stocks*, 1877–1940)

Even being right 3 or 4 times out of 10 should yield a person a fortune, if he has the sense to cut his losses quickly on the ventures where he has been wrong.
— Bernard Baruch (Financier, speculator, statesman, presidential adviser, 1870–1965)

July Begins NASDAQ's "Worst Four Months" (Pages 56, 58 and 148)

What's going on ... is the end of Silicon Valley as we know it. The next big thing ain't computers ... it's biotechnology.
— Larry Ellison (Oracle CEO, quoted in *The Wall Street Journal*, April 8, 2003)

In a study of 3000 companies, researchers at the University of Pennsylvania found that spending 10% of revenue on capital improvements boosts productivity by 3.9%, but a similar investment in developing human capital increases productivity by 8.5%.
— John A. Byrne (Editor-in-Chief, Fast *Company Magazine*)

July is the Best Performing Dow and S&P Month of the Third Quarter

Have not great merchants, great manufacturers, great inventors done more for the world than preachers and philanthropists. Can there be any doubt that cheapening the cost of necessities and conveniences of life is the most powerful agent of civilization and progress?
— Charles Elliott Perkins (Railroad magnate, 1888, 1840–1907)

DON'T SELL STOCKS ON MONDAY OR FRIDAY

Since 1989, Monday*, Tuesday, and Wednesday have been the most consistently bullish days of the week for the Dow; Thursday and Friday* the most bearish, as traders have become reluctant to stay long going into the weekend. Since 1989, Mondays, Tuesdays, and Wednesdays gained 12,825.92 Dow points, while Thursday and Friday combined for a total loss of 2,758.52 points. Also broken out are the last eleven and a third years to illustrate Monday's and Friday's poor performance in bear market years 2001–2002 and 2008–2009. During uncertain market times, traders often sell before the weekend and are reluctant to jump in on Monday. See pages 66, 78, and 141–144 for more.

ANNUAL DOW POINT CHANGES FOR DAYS OF THE WEEK SINCE 1953

Year	Monday*	Tuesday	Wednesday	Thursday	Friday*	Year's DJIA Closing	Year's Point Change
1953	−36.16	−7.93	19.63	5.76	7.70	280.90	−11.00
1954	15.68	3.27	24.31	33.96	46.27	404.39	123.49
1955	−48.36	26.38	46.03	−0.66	60.62	488.40	84.01
1956	−27.15	−9.36	−15.41	8.43	64.56	499.47	11.07
1957	−109.50	−7.71	64.12	3.32	−14.01	435.69	−63.78
1958	17.50	23.59	29.10	22.67	55.10	583.65	147.96
1959	−44.48	29.04	4.11	13.60	93.44	679.36	95.71
1960	−111.04	−3.75	−5.62	6.74	50.20	615.89	−63.47
1961	−23.65	10.18	87.51	−5.96	47.17	731.14	115.25
1962	−101.60	26.19	9.97	−7.70	−5.90	652.10	−79.04
1963	−8.88	47.12	16.23	22.39	33.99	762.95	110.85
1964	−0.29	−17.94	39.84	5.52	84.05	874.13	111.18
1965	−73.23	39.65	57.03	3.20	68.48	969.26	95.13
1966	−153.24	−27.73	56.13	−46.19	−12.54	785.69	−183.57
1967	−68.65	31.50	25.42	92.25	38.90	905.11	119.42
1968†	6.41	34.94	25.16	−72.06	44.19	943.75	38.64
1969	−164.17	−36.70	18.33	23.79	15.36	800.36	−143.39
1970	−100.05	−46.09	116.07	−3.48	72.11	838.92	38.56
1971	−2.99	9.56	13.66	8.04	23.01	890.20	51.28
1972	−87.40	−1.23	65.24	8.46	144.75	1020.02	129.82
1973	−174.11	10.52	−5.94	36.67	−36.30	850.86	−169.16
1974	−149.37	47.51	−20.31	−13.70	−98.75	616.24	−234.62
1975	39.46	−109.62	56.93	124.00	125.40	852.41	236.17
1976	70.72	71.76	50.88	−33.70	−7.42	1004.65	152.24
1977	−65.15	−44.89	−79.61	−5.62	21.79	831.17	−173.48
1978	−31.29	−70.84	71.33	−64.67	69.31	805.01	−26.16
1979	−32.52	9.52	−18.84	75.18	0.39	838.74	33.73
1980	−86.51	135.13	137.67	−122.00	60.96	963.99	125.25
1981	−45.68	−49.51	−13.95	−14.67	34.82	875.00	−88.99
1982	5.71	86.20	28.37	−1.47	52.73	1046.54	171.54
1983	30.51	−30.92	149.68	61.16	1.67	1258.64	212.10
1984	−73.80	78.02	−139.24	92.79	−4.84	1211.57	−47.07
1985	80.36	52.70	51.26	46.32	104.46	1546.67	335.10
1986	−39.94	97.63	178.65	29.31	83.63	1895.95	349.28
1987	−559.15	235.83	392.03	139.73	−165.56	1938.83	42.88
1988	268.12	166.44	−60.48	−230.84	86.50	2168.57	229.74
1989	−53.31	143.33	233.25	90.25	171.11	2753.20	584.63
SubTotal	*−1937.20*	*941.79*	*1708.54*	*330.82*	*1417.35*		*2461.30*
1990	219.90	−25.22	47.96	−352.55	−9.63	2633.66	−119.54
1991	191.13	47.97	174.53	254.79	−133.25	3168.83	535.17
1992	237.80	−49.67	3.12	108.74	−167.71	3301.11	132.28
1993	322.82	−37.03	243.87	4.97	−81.65	3754.09	452.98
1994	206.41	−95.33	29.98	−168.87	108.16	3834.44	80.35
1995	262.97	210.06	357.02	140.07	312.56	5117.12	1282.68
1996	626.41	155.55	−34.24	268.52	314.91	6448.27	1331.15
1997	1136.04	1989.17	−590.17	−949.80	−125.26	7908.25	1459.98
1998	649.10	679.95	591.63	−1579.43	931.93	9181.43	1273.18
1999	980.49	−1587.23	826.68	735.94	1359.81	11497.12	2315.69
2000	2265.45	306.47	−1978.34	238.21	−1542.06	10786.85	−710.27
SubTotal	*7098.52*	*1594.69*	*−327.96*	*−1299.41*	*967.81*		*8033.65*
2001	−389.33	336.86	−396.53	976.41	−1292.76	10021.50	−765.35
2002	−1404.94	−823.76	1443.69	−428.12	−466.74	8341.63	−1679.87
2003	978.87	482.11	−425.46	566.22	510.55	10453.92	2112.29
2004	201.12	523.28	358.76	−409.72	−344.35	10783.01	329.09
2005	316.23	−305.62	27.67	−128.75	24.96	10717.50	−65.51
2006	95.74	573.98	1283.87	193.34	−401.28	12463.15	1745.65
2007	278.23	−157.93	1316.74	−766.63	131.26	13264.82	801.67
2008	−1387.20	1704.51	−3073.72	−940.88	−791.14	8776.39	−4488.43
2009	−45.22	161.76	617.56	932.68	−15.12	10428.05	1651.66
2010	1236.88	−421.80	1019.66	−76.73	−608.55	11577.51	1149.46
2011	−571.02	1423.66	−776.05	246.27	317.19	12217.56	640.05
2012‡	361.84	−42.54	−61.23	489.23	−144.26		
Subtotal	*−328.80*	*3454.51*	*1334.96*	*653.32*	*−3080.24*		*1430.71*
Totals	**4832.52**	**5990.99**	**2715.54**	**−315.27**	**−695.08**		**11925.66**

* Monday denotes first trading day of week, Friday denotes last trading day of week
†Most Wednesdays closed last 7 months of 1968   ‡Partial year through May 11, 2012

JULY

Monday Before July Expiration, Dow Up 7 of Last 9

MONDAY
D 52.4
S 47.6
N 61.9
15

Get to the Point! Blurt it out! Tell me plainly what's in it for me!
— Roy H. Williams (*The Wizard of Ads*, A reader's mental response to a poorly constructed advertisement. Quoted in *Your Company*, 12/98)

TUESDAY
D 52.4
S 42.9
N 47.6
16

The first stocks to double in a bull market will usually double again.
— Michael L. Burke (*Investors Intelligence*)

WEDNESDAY
D 47.6
S 42.9
N 47.6
17

If the market does not rally, as it should during bullish seasonal periods, it is a sign that other forces are stronger and that when the seasonal period ends those forces will really have their say.
— Edson Gould (Stock market analyst, *Findings & Forecasts*, 1902–1987)

THURSDAY
D 61.9
S 61.9
N 61.9
18

Charts not only tell what was, they tell what is; and a trend from was to is (projected linearly into the will be) contains better percentages than clumsy guessing.
— Robert A. Levy (Chairman, Cato Institute, founder, CDA Investment Technologies, *The Relative Strength Concept of Common Stock Forecasting*, 1968, b. 1941)

July Expiration Day, Dow Down 7 of Last 12, –4.6% in 2002 and –2.5% in 2010

FRIDAY
D 33.3
S 28.6
N 33.3
19

Your organization will never get better unless you are willing to admit that there is something wrong with it.
— General Norman Schwartzkof (Ret. Commander of Allied Forces in 1990–1991 Gulf War)

SATURDAY
20

SUNDAY
21

A RALLY FOR ALL SEASONS

Most years, especially when the market sells off during the first half, prospects for the perennial summer rally become the buzz on the street. Parameters for this "rally" were defined by the late Ralph Rotnem as the lowest close in the Dow Jones Industrials in May or June to the highest close in July, August, or September. Such a big deal is made of the summer rally that one might get the impression the market puts on its best performance in the summertime. Nothing could be further from the truth! Not only does the market "rally" in every season of the year, but it does so with more gusto in the winter, spring, and fall than in the summer.

Winters in 49 years averaged a 13.1% gain, as measured from the low in November or December to the first quarter closing high. Spring rose 11.5% followed by fall with 11.0%. Last and least was the average 9.2% summer rally. Even 2009's impressive 19.7% summer rally was outmatched by spring. Nevertheless, no matter how thick the gloom or grim the outlook, don't despair! There's always a rally for all seasons, statistically.

SEASONAL GAINS IN DOW JONES INDUSTRIALS

	WINTER RALLY Nov/Dec Low to Q1 High	SPRING RALLY Feb/Mar Low to Q2 High	SUMMER RALLY May/Jun Low to Q3 High	FALL RALLY Aug/Sep Low to Q4 High
1964	15.3%	6.2%	9.4%	8.3%
1965	5.7	6.6	11.6	10.3
1966	5.9	4.8	3.5	7.0
1967	11.6	8.7	11.2	4.4
1968	7.0	11.5	5.2	13.3
1969	0.9	7.7	1.9	6.7
1970	5.4	6.2	22.5	19.0
1971	21.6	9.4	5.5	7.4
1972	19.1	7.7	5.2	11.4
1973	8.6	4.8	9.7	15.9
1974	13.1	8.2	1.4	11.0
1975	36.2	24.2	8.2	8.7
1976	23.3	6.4	5.9	4.6
1977	8.2	3.1	2.8	2.1
1978	2.1	16.8	11.8	5.2
1979	11.0	8.9	8.9	6.1
1980	13.5	16.8	21.0	8.5
1981	11.8	9.9	0.4	8.3
1982	4.6	9.3	18.5	37.8
1983	15.7	17.8	6.3	10.7
1984	5.9	4.6	14.1	9.7
1985	11.7	7.1	9.5	19.7
1986	31.1	18.8	9.2	11.4
1987	30.6	13.6	22.9	5.9
1988	18.1	13.5	11.2	9.8
1989	15.1	12.9	16.1	5.7
1990	8.8	14.5	12.4	8.6
1991	21.8	11.2	6.6	9.3
1992	14.9	6.4	3.7	3.3
1993	8.9	7.7	6.3	7.3
1994	9.7	5.2	9.1	5.0
1995	13.6	19.3	11.3	13.9
1996	19.2	7.5	8.7	17.3
1997	17.7	18.4	18.4	7.3
1998	20.3	13.6	8.2	24.3
1999	15.1	21.6	8.2	12.6
2000	10.8	15.2	9.8	3.5
2001	6.4	20.8	1.7	23.1
2002	14.8	7.9	2.8	17.6
2003	6.5	23.9	14.3	15.7
2004	11.6	5.2	4.4	10.6
2005	9.0	2.1	5.6	5.3
2006	8.8	8.3	9.5	13.0
2007	6.7	13.5	6.6	10.3
2008	2.5	11.2	3.8	4.5
2009	19.6	34.4	19.7	15.5
2010	11.6	13.1	11.1	16.0
2011	12.6	10.3	7.0	14.7
2012	18.0	4.5*		
Totals	**642.0%**	**561.3%**	**443.1%**	**527.6%**
Average	**13.1%**	**11.5%**	**9.2%**	**11.0%**

As of 5/18/2012

70

MONDAY
D 38.1
S 33.3
N 38.1
22

Technology will gradually strengthen democracies in every country and at every level.
— William H. Gates (Microsoft founder)

Week After July Expiration Prone to Wild Swings, Dow Mixed Last 15 years
1998 −4.3%, 2002 +3.1%, 2006 +3.2%, 2007 −4.2%, 2009 +4.0%, 2010 +3.2

TUESDAY
D 47.6
S 52.4
N 52.4
23

The Clairvoyant Society of London will not meet Tuesday because of unforeseen circumstances.
— Advertisement in the London Financial Times

WEDNESDAY
D 52.4
S 52.4
N 52.4
24

Nothing is more uncertain than the favor of the crowd.
— Marcus Tullius Cicero (Great Roman Orator, Politician, 106–43 B.C.)

Beware the "Summer Rally" Hype
Historically the Weakest Rally of All Seasons (Page 70)

THURSDAY
D 66.7
S 66.7
N 71.4
25

A bank is a place where they lend you an umbrella in fair weather and ask for it back again when it begins to rain.
— Robert Frost (American poet, 1874–1963)

FRIDAY
D 38.1
S 38.1
N 52.4
26

When investment decisions need to consider the speed of light, something is seriously wrong.
— Frank M. Bifulco (Senior Portfolio Manager Alcott Capital Management, *Barron's Letters to the Editor*, 5/24/2010)

SATURDAY
27

August Almanac Investor Seasonalities: See Pages 92, 94 and 96

SUNDAY
28

AUGUST ALMANAC

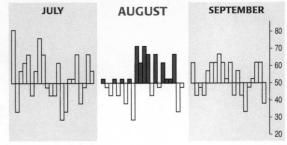

AUGUST							SEPTEMBER						
S	M	T	W	T	F	S	S	M	T	W	T	F	S
				1	2	3							1
4	5	6	7	8	9	10	2	3	4	5	6	7	8
11	12	13	14	15	16	17	9	10	11	12	13	14	15
18	19	20	21	22	23	24	16	17	18	19	20	21	22
25	26	27	28	29	30	31	23	24	25	26	27	28	29
							30						

Market Probability Chart above is a graphic representation of the S&P 500 Recent Market Probability Calendar on page 124.

◆ Harvesting made August the best stock market month 1901–1951 ◆ Now that about 2% farm, August is the worst Dow, S&P, and NASDAQ (2000 up 11.7%, 2001 down 10.9) month since 1987 ◆ Shortest bear in history (45 days) caused by turmoil in Russia, currency crisis and hedge fund debacle ended here in 1998, 1344.22-point drop in the Dow, second worst behind October 2008, off 15.1% ◆ Saddam Hussein triggered a 10.0% slide in 1990 ◆ Best Dow gains: 1982 (11.5%) and 1984 (9.8%) as bear markets ended ◆ Next to last day S&P up only three times last 16 years ◆ Post-presidential election year Augusts' rankings #11 S&P and NASDAQ, #12 Dow.

August Vital Statistics

	DJIA	S&P 500	NASDAQ	Russell 1K	Russell 2K
Rank	10	9	10	9	9
Up	35	34	22	21	19
Down	27	28	19	12	14
Average % Change	–0.1%	–0.04%	0.1%	0.3%	0.3%
Post-Election Year	–1.6%	–1.4%	–1.5%	–1.4%	–0.4%
Best & Worst August					
	% Change	% Change	% Change	% Change	% Change
Best	1982 11.5	1982 11.6	2000 11.7	1982 11.3	1984 11.5
Worst	1998 –15.1	1998 –14.6	1998 –19.9	1998 –15.1	1998 –19.5
Best & Worst August Weeks					
Best	8/20/82 10.3	8/20/82 8.8	8/3/84 7.4	8/20/82 8.5	8/3/84 7.0
Worst	8/23/74 –6.1	8/5/11 –7.2	8/28/98 –8.8	8/5/11 –7.7	8/5/11 –10.3
Best & Worst August Days					
Best	8/17/82 4.9	8/17/82 4.8	8/9/11 5.3	8/9/11 5.0	8/9/11 6.9
Worst	8/31/98 –6.4	8/31/98 –6.8	8/31/98 –8.6	8/8/11 –6.9	8/8/11 –8.9
First Trading Day of Expiration Week: 1980–2011					
Record (#Up–#Down)	21–11	24–8	23–9	24–8	20–12
Current streak	U1	U2	U2	U1	U2
Avg % Change	0.30	0.30	0.31	0.27	0.25
Options Expiration Day: 1980–2011					
Record (#Up–#Down)	17–15	18–14	18–14	18–14	20–12
Current streak	D1	D2	D1	D2	D2
Avg % Change	–0.06	0.01	–0.09	0.004	0.11
Options Expiration Week: 1980–2011					
Record (#Up–#Down)	16–16	19–13	18–14	19–13	20–12
Current streak	D2	D2	D1	D2	D1
Avg % Change	0.25	0.43	0.56	0.44	0.64
Week After Options Expiration: 1980–2011					
Record (#Up–#Down)	20–12	21–11	20–12	21–11	20–12
Current streak	U1	U1	U1	U1	U2
Avg % Change	0.30	0.31	0.45	0.30	0.05
First Trading Day Performance					
% of Time Up	48.4	51.6	53.7	48.5	51.5
Avg % Change	0.03	0.05	–0.08	0.11	0.04
Last Trading Day Performance					
% of Time Up	61.3	64.5	68.3	60.6	72.7
Avg % Change	0.13	0.13	0.06	–0.04	0.08

Dow & S&P 1950–April 2012, NASDAQ 1971–April 2012, Russell 1K & 2K 1979–April 2012.

August's a good month to go on vacation;
Trading stocks will likely lead to frustration.

MONDAY

D 42.9
S 47.6
N 47.6

29

Change is the law of life. And those who look only to the past or present are certain to miss the future.
— John F. Kennedy (35th U.S. President, 1917–1963)

TUESDAY

D 61.9
S 66.7
N 71.4

30

The bigger a man's head gets, the easier it is to fill his shoes.
— Anonymous

Last Trading Day in July, NASDAQ Down 6 of Last 7
FOMC Meeting (2 Days)

WEDNESDAY

D 47.6
S 57.1
N 47.6

31

Six words that spell business success: create concept, communicate concept, sustain momentum.
— Yale Hirsch (Creator of *Stock Trader's Almanac*, b. 1923)

First Trading Day in August, Dow Down 10 of Last 15, But Up 3 of Last 5
Russell 2000 Up 6 of Last 8

THURSDAY

D 42.9
S 52.4
N 57.1

1

What's money? A man is a success if he gets up in the morning and goes to bed at night and in between does what he wants to do.
— Bob Dylan (American singer-songwriter, musician and artist, b. 1941)

First Nine Trading Days of August Are Historically Weak (Pages 72 and 124)

FRIDAY

D 52.4
S 47.6
N 42.9

2

I would rather be positioned as a petrified bull rather than a penniless bear.
— John L. Person (Professional trader, author, speaker, *Commodity Trader's Almanac*, nationalfutures.com, 11/3/2010, b. 1961)

SATURDAY

3

SUNDAY

4

REPUBLICAN CONGRESS & DEMOCRATIC PRESIDENT BEST FOR THE MARKET

Six possible political alignments exist in Washington: Republican president with a Republican Congress, Democratic Congress, or split Congress; and a Democratic president with a Democratic Congress, Republican Congress, or split Congress. Data presented in the chart below begins in 1949 with the first full presidential term following WWII. Lopsided market moves during the first half of the 20th century prior to latter-day improvements to financial systems, including the Depression, have been omitted to focus on the modern era.

First looking at just the historical performance of the Dow under Democratic and Republican presidents we see a pattern that is contrary to popular belief. Under a Democrat, the Dow has performed better than under a Republican. The Dow has historically returned 10.0% under Democrats compared to 6.8% under a Republican executive. Congressional results are the opposite and much more dramatic. Republican Congresses since 1949 have yielded an average 16.8% gain in the Dow compared to a 6.1% return when Democrats have controlled the Hill.

With total Republican control of Washington, the Dow has been up on average 14.1%. Democrats in power of the two branches have produced an average Dow gain of 7.4%. When power is split, with a Republican president and a Democratic Congress or a split Congress, the Dow has not done very well, averaging only a 5.4% gain. The best scenario for all investors has been a Democrat in the White House and Republican control of Congress, with average gains of 19.5%. A Democratic president and a split Congress has occurred just once, 2011–2012.

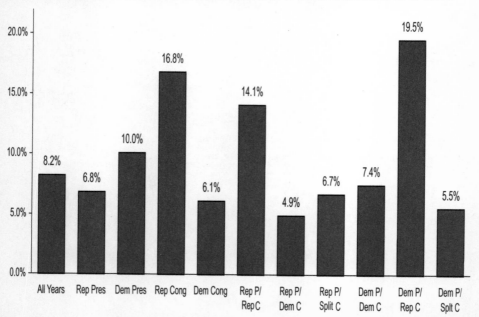

DOW JONES INDUSTRIALS AVERAGE ANNUAL % CHANGE SINCE 1949–2011

All Years	8.2%
Rep Pres	6.8%
Dem Pres	10.0%
Rep Cong	16.8%
Dem Cong	6.1%
Rep P/ Rep C	14.1%
Rep P/ Dem C	4.9%
Rep P/ Split C	6.7%
Dem P/ Dem C	7.4%
Dem P/ Rep C	19.5%
Dem P/ Splt C	5.5%

MONDAY

D 42.9
S 42.9
N 38.1

5

If banking institutions are protected by the taxpayer and they are given free rein to speculate, I may not live long enough to see the crisis, but my soul is going to come back and haunt you.
— Paul A. Volcker (Fed Chairman 1979–1987, Chair Economic Recovery Advisory Board, 2/2/2010, b. 1927)

August Worst Dow and S&P Month 1988–2011
Harvesting Made August Best Dow Month 1901–1951

TUESDAY

D 47.6
S 52.4
N 52.4

6

Nothing has a stronger influence psychologically on their environment and especially on their children than the unlived life of the parent.
— C.G. Jung (Swiss psychiatrist)

WEDNESDAY

D 52.4
S 42.9
N 42.9

7

Bankruptcy was designed to forgive stupidity, not reward criminality.
— William P. Barr (Verizon General Counsel, calling for government liquidation of MCI-WorldCom in Chap. 7, 4/14/2003)

THURSDAY

D 42.9
S 52.4
N 38.1

8

An economist is someone who sees something happen, and then wonders if it would work in theory.
— Ronald Reagan (40th U.S. President, 1911–2004)

FRIDAY

D 42.9
S 38.1
N 38.1

9

I'm not nearly so concerned about the return on my capital as I am the return of my capital.
— Will Rogers (American humorist and showman, 1879–1935)

SATURDAY

10

SUNDAY

11

AURA OF THE TRIPLE WITCH—4TH QUARTER MOST BULLISH: DOWN WEEKS TRIGGER MORE WEAKNESS WEEK AFTER

Options expire the third Friday of every month, but in March, June, September, and December, a powerful coven gathers. Since the S&P index futures began trading on April 21, 1982, stock options, index options, as well as index futures all expire at the same time four times each year—known as Triple Witching. Traders have long sought to understand and master the magic of this quarterly phenomenon.

The market for single-stock and ETF futures continues to grow. However, their impact on the market has thus far been subdued. As their availability continues to expand, trading volumes and market influence are also likely to broaden. Until such time, we do not believe the term "quadruple witching" is applicable just yet.

We have analyzed what the market does prior, during, and following Triple Witching expirations in search of consistent trading patterns. Here are some of our findings of how the Dow Jones Industrials perform around Triple-Witching Week (TWW).

- TWWs became more bullish since 1990, except in the second quarter.
- Following weeks became more bearish. Since Q1 2000, only 17 of 48 were up, and 8 occurred in December, 6 in March, 3 in September, none in June.
- TWWs have tended to be down in flat periods and dramatically so during bear markets.
- DOWN WEEKS TEND TO FOLLOW DOWN TWWs is a most interesting pattern. Since 1991, of 29 down TWWs, 21 following weeks were also down. This is surprising, inasmuch as the previous decade had an exactly opposite pattern: There were 13 down TWWs then, but 12 up weeks followed them.
- TWWs in the second and third quarter (Worst Six Months May through October) are much weaker, and the weeks following, horrendous. But in the first and fourth quarter (Best Six Months period November through April), only the week after Q1 expiration is negative.

Throughout the *Almanac* you will also see notations on the performance of Mondays and Fridays of TWW, as we place considerable significance on the beginnings and ends of weeks (pages 66, 68, 78, and 141–144).

TRIPLE WITCHING WEEK AND WEEK AFTER DOW POINT CHANGES

	Expiration Week Q1	Week After	Expiration Week Q2	Week After	Expiration Week Q3	Week After	Expiration Week Q4	Week After
1991	−6.93	−89.36	−34.98	−58.81	33.54	−13.19	20.12	167.04
1992	40.48	−44.95	−69.01	−2.94	21.35	−76.73	9.19	12.97
1993	43.76	−31.60	−10.24	−3.88	−8.38	−70.14	10.90	6.15
1994	32.95	−120.92	3.33	−139.84	58.54	−101.60	116.08	26.24
1995	38.04	65.02	86.80	75.05	96.85	−33.42	19.87	−78.76
1996	114.52	51.67	55.78	−50.60	49.94	−15.54	179.53	76.51
1997	−130.67	−64.20	14.47	−108.79	174.30	4.91	−82.01	−76.98
1998	303.91	−110.35	−122.07	231.67	100.16	133.11	81.87	314.36
1999	27.20	−81.31	365.05	−303.00	−224.80	−524.30	32.73	148.33
2000	666.41	517.49	−164.76	−44.55	−293.65	−79.63	−277.95	200.60
2001	−821.21	−318.63	−353.36	−19.05	−1369.70	611.75	224.19	101.65
2002	34.74	−179.56	−220.42	−10.53	−326.67	−284.57	77.61	−207.54
2003	662.26	−376.20	83.63	−211.70	173.27	−331.74	236.06	46.45
2004	−53.48	26.37	6.31	−44.57	−28.61	−237.22	106.70	177.20
2005	−144.69	−186.80	110.44	−325.23	−36.62	−222.35	97.01	7.68
2006	203.31	0.32	122.63	−25.46	168.66	−52.67	138.03	−102.30
2007	−165.91	370.60	215.09	−279.22	377.67	75.44	110.80	−84.78
2008	410.23	−144.92	−464.66	−496.18	−33.55	−245.31	−50.57	−63.56
2009	54.40	497.80	−259.53	−101.34	214.79	−155.01	−142.61	191.21
2010	117.29	108.38	239.57	−306.83	145.08	252.41	81.59	81.58
2011	−185.88	362.07	52.45	−69.78	516.96	−737.61	−317.87	427.61
2012	310.60	−151.89						
Up	15	9	12	2	13	5	16	15
Down	7	13	9	19	8	16	5	6

Monday Before August Expiration, Dow Up 12 of Last 17, Average Gain 0.4%

MONDAY

D 52.4
S 52.4
N 47.6

12

Don't be the last bear or last bull standing, let history guide you, be contrary to the crowd, and let the tape tell you when to act.
— Jeffrey A. Hirsch (Editor, *Stock Trader's Almanac*, b. 1966)

TUESDAY

D 28.6
S 28.6
N 42.9

13

To know values is to know the meaning of the market.
— Charles Dow (Co-founder Dow Jones & Co, 1851–1902)

Mid-August Stronger Than Beginning and End

WEDNESDAY

D 66.7
S 71.4
N 71.4

14

Analysts are supposed to be critics of corporations. They often end up being public relations spokesmen for them.
— Ralph Wanger (Chief Investment Officer, Acorn Fund)

THURSDAY

D 47.6
S 61.9
N 61.9

15

A market is the combined behavior of thousands of people responding to information, misinformation and whim.
— Kenneth Chang (*NY Times* journalist)

August Expiration Day Bullish Lately, Dow Up 7 in a Row 2003–2009
Up 156 Points (1.7%) in 2009

FRIDAY

D 61.9
S 71.4
N 66.7

16

Cooperation is essential to address 21st-century challenges; you can't fire cruise missiles at the global financial crisis.
— Nicholas D. Kristof (*NY Times* columnist, 10/23/2008)

SATURDAY

17

SUNDAY

18

TAKE ADVANTAGE OF DOWN FRIDAY/ DOWN MONDAY WARNING

Fridays and Mondays are the most important days of the week. Friday is the day for squaring positions—trimming longs or covering shorts before taking off for the weekend. Traders want to limit their exposure (particularly to stocks that are not acting well) since there could be unfavorable developments before trading resumes two or more days later.

Monday is important because the market then has the chance to reflect any weekend news, plus what traders think after digesting the previous week's action and the many Monday morning research and strategy comments.

For over 30 years, a down Friday followed by down Monday has frequently corresponded to important market inflection points that exhibit a clearly negative bias, often coinciding with market tops and, on a few climactic occasions, such as in October 2002 and March 2009, near major market bottoms.

One simple way to get a quick reading on which way the market may be heading is to keep track of the performance of the Dow Jones Industrial Average on Fridays and the following Mondays. Since 1995, there have been 179 occurrences of Down Friday/Down Monday (DF/DM), with 57 falling in the bear market years of 2001, 2002, 2008, and 2011, producing an average decline of 12.8%.

To illustrate how Down Friday/ Down Monday can telegraph market inflection points we created the chart below of the Dow Jones Industrials

DOWN FRIDAY/DOWN MONDAYS

Year	Total Number Down Friday/ Down Monday	Subsequent Average % Dow Loss*	Average Number of Days it took
1995	8	−1.2%	18
1996	9	−3.0%	28
1997	6	−5.1%	45
1998	9	−6.4%	47
1999	9	−6.4%	39
2000	11	−6.6%	32
2001	13	−13.5%	53
2002	18	−11.9%	54
2003	9	−3.0%	17
2004	9	−3.7%	51
2005	10	−3.0%	37
2006	11	−2.0%	14
2007	8	−6.0%	33
2008	15	−17.0%	53
2009	10	−8.7%	15
2010	7	−3.1%	10
2011	11	−9.0%	53
2012**	6	−3.8%	45
Average	**10**	**−6.3%**	**36**

*Over next 3 months, ** Ending May 18, 2012*

from November 2010 to May 18, 2012 with arrows pointing to occurrences of DF/DM. Use DF/DM as a warning to examine market conditions carefully. Unprecedented central bank liquidity has tempered subsequent pullbacks, but has not eliminated them.

DOW JONES INDUSTRIALS (NOVEMBER 2010–MAY 18, 2012)

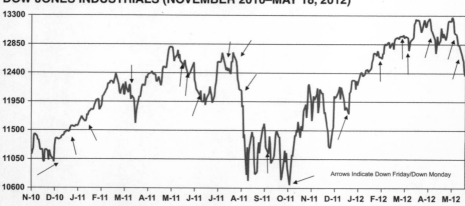

Arrows Indicate Down Friday/Down Monday

AUGUST

MONDAY
19
D 61.9
S 66.7
N 61.9

The market can stay irrational longer than you can stay solvent.
— John Maynard Keynes (British economist, 1883–1946)

TUESDAY
20
D 47.6
S 42.9
N 42.9

There's no trick to being a humorist when you have the whole government working for you.
— Will Rogers (American humorist and showman, 1879–1935)

End of August Stronger Last 9 Years

WEDNESDAY
21
D 66.7
S 66.7
N 85.7

Stock option plans reward the executive for doing the wrong thing. Instead of asking, "Are we making the right decision?" he asks, "How did we close today?" It is encouragement to loot the corporation.
— Peter Drucker (Austrian-born pioneer management theorist, 1909–2005)

THURSDAY
22
D 47.6
S 47.6
N 52.4

If you spend more than 14 minutes a year worrying about the market, you've wasted 12 minutes.
— Peter Lynch (Fidelity Investments, *One Up On Wall Street*, b. 1944)

FRIDAY
23
D 57.1
S 61.9
N 47.6

If you are ready to give up everything else – to study the whole history and background of the market and all the principal companies . . . as carefully as a medical student studies anatomy – . . . and, in addition, you have the cool nerves of a great gambler, the sixth sense of a clairvoyant, and the courage of a lion, you have a ghost of a chance.
— Bernard Baruch (Financier, speculator, statesman, presidential adviser, 1870–1965)

SATURDAY
24

SUNDAY
25

SEPTEMBER ALMANAC

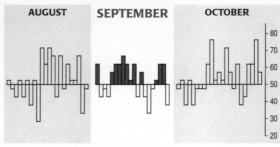

SEPTEMBER								OCTOBER						
S	M	T	W	T	F	S		S	M	T	W	T	F	S
1	2	3	4	5	6	7				1	2	3	4	5
8	9	10	11	12	13	14		6	7	8	9	10	11	12
15	16	17	18	19	20	21		13	14	15	16	17	18	19
22	23	24	25	26	27	28		20	21	22	23	24	25	26
29	30							27	28	29	30	31		

Market Probability Chart above is a graphic representation of the S&P 500 Recent Market Probability Calendar on page 124.

◆ Start of business year, end of vacations, and back to school made September a leading barometer month in first 60 years of 20th century; now portfolio managers back after Labor Day tend to clean house ◆ Biggest % loser on the S&P, Dow, and NASDAQ since (pages 44 & 56) ◆ Streak of four great Dow Septembers averaging 4.2% gains ended in 1999 with six losers in a row averaging –5.9% (see page 152), up three straight 2005–2007, down 6% in 2008 and 2011 ◆ Day after Labor Day Dow up 13 of last 18 ◆ S&P opened strong 12 of last 17 years but tends to close weak due to end-of-quarter mutual fund portfolio restructuring, last trading day: S&P down 13 of past 19 ◆ September Triple-Witching Week can be dangerous; week after is pitiful (see page 76).

September Vital Statistics

	DJIA		S&P 500		NASDAQ		Russell 1K		Russell 2K	
Rank	12		12		12		12		12	
Up	24		27		22		16		18	
Down	38		34		19		17		15	
Average % Change	–0.9%		–0.6%		–0.7%		–0.8%		–0.6%	
Post-Election Year	–0.9%		–0.9%		–0.9%		–1.2%		–1.6%	
Best & Worst September										
	% Change		% Change		% Change		% Change		% Change	
Best	2010	7.7	2010	8.8	1998	13.0	2010	9.0	2010	12.3
Worst	2002	–12.4	1974	–11.9	2001	–17.0	2002	–10.9	2001	–13.6
Best & Worst September Weeks										
Best	9/28/01	7.4	9/28/01	7.8	9/16/11	6.3	9/28/01	7.6	9/28/01	6.9
Worst	9/21/01	–14.3	9/21/01	–11.6	9/21/01	–16.1	9/21/01	–11.7	9/21/01	–14.0
Best & Worst September Days										
Best	9/8/98	5.0	9/30/08	5.4	9/8/98	6.0	9/30/08	5.3	9/18/08	7.0
Worst	9/17/01	–7.1	9/29/08	–8.8	9/29/08	–9.1	9/29/08	–8.7	9/29/08	–6.7
First Trading Day of Expiration Week: 1980–2011										
Record (#Up–#Down)	21–11		18–14		13–19		18–14		13–19	
Current streak	U3		U3		U3		U3		U3	
Avg % Change	–0.11		–0.14		–0.33		–0.16		–0.22	
Options Expiration Day: 1980–2011										
Record (#Up–#Down)	17–15		19–13		22–10		19–13		22–10	
Current streak	U8		U8		U8		U8		U7	
Avg % Change	0.05		0.18		0.19		0.16		0.21	
Options Expiration Week: 1980–2011										
Record (#Up–#Down)	17–15		19–13		18–14		19–13		17–15	
Current streak	U3		U6		U6		U6		U6	
Avg % Change	–0.30		–0.03		0.002		–0.03		0.13	
Week After Options Expiration: 1980–2011										
Record (#Up–#Down)	12–20		10–22		14–18		10–21		11–21	
Current streak	D1		D1		D1		D1		D1	
Avg % Change	–0.72		–0.75		–0.85		–0.76		–1.35	
First Trading Day Performance										
% of Time Up	61.3		62.9		53.7		51.5		48.5	
Avg % Change	0.05		0.02		–0.02		–0.02		0.01	
Last Trading Day Performance										
% of Time Up	38.7		41.9		48.8		48.5		63.6	
Avg % Change	–0.13		–0.08		–0.04		0.01		0.29	

Dow & S&P 1950–April 2012, NASDAQ 1971–April 2012, Russell 1K & 2K 1979–April 2012.

September is when leaves and stocks tend to fall;
On Wall Street it's the worst month of all.

MONDAY

D 52.4
S 52.4
N 52.4

26

If you bet on a horse, that's gambling. If you bet you can make three spades, that's entertainment. If you bet cotton will go up three points, that's business. See the difference?
— Blackie Sherrod (Sportswriter, b. 1919)

TUESDAY

D 42.9
S 52.4
N 42.9

27

So at last I was going to America! Really, really going, at last! The boundaries burst. The arch of heaven soared! A million suns shone out for every star. The winds rushed in from outer space, roaring in my ears, "America! America!"
— Mary Antin (1881–1949, Immigrant writer, *The Promised Land*, 1912)

WEDNESDAY

D 66.7
S 66.7
N 76.2

28

Everyone blames the foreigners when the economy goes south. Always. It is human nature to blame others, and it is the same all over the world.
— Jim Rogers (Financier, *Adventure Capitalist*, b. 1942)

August's Next-to-Last Trading Day, S&P Down 13 of Last 16 Years

THURSDAY

D 33.3
S 33.3
N 61.9

29

I have seen it repeatedly throughout the world: politicians get a country in trouble but swear everything is okay in the face of overwhelming evidence to the contrary.
— Jim Rogers (Financier, *Adventure Capitalist*, b. 1942)

FRIDAY

D 47.6
S 47.6
N 52.4

30

I have noticed over the years the difficulty some people have in cutting losses, admitting an error, and moving on. I am rather frequently—and on occasion, quite spectacularly—wrong. However, if we expect to be wrong, then there should be no ego tied up in admitting the error, honoring the stop loss, selling the loser—and preserving your capital.
— Barry L. Ritholtz (CEO Fusion IQ, *Bailout Nation*, The Big Picture blog, 8/12/2010, b. 1961)

SATURDAY

31

September Almanac Investor Seasonalities: See Pages 92, 94 and 96

SUNDAY

1

A CORRECTION FOR ALL SEASONS

While there's a rally for every season (page 70), almost always there's a decline or correction, too. Fortunately, corrections tend to be smaller than rallies, and that's what gives the stock market its long-term upward bias. In each season the average bounce outdoes the average setback. On average, the net gain between the rally and the correction is smallest in summer and fall.

The summer setback tends to be slightly outdone by the average correction in the fall. Tax selling and portfolio cleaning are the usual explanations—individuals sell to register a tax loss and institutions like to get rid of their losers before preparing year-end statements. The October jinx also plays a major part. Since 1964, there have been 17 fall declines of over 10%, and in 10 of them (1966, 1974, 1978, 1979, 1987, 1990, 1997, 2000, 2002, and 2008) much damage was done in October, where so many bear markets end. Recent October lows were also seen in 1998, 1999, 2004, and 2005. Most often, it has paid to buy after fourth quarter or late third quarter "waterfall declines" for a rally that may continue into January or even beyond. Anticipation of war in Iraq put the market down in 2003 Q1. Quick success rallied stocks through Q3. Financial crisis affected the pattern in 2008–2009, producing the worst winter decline since 1932. Easy monetary policy and strong corporate earnings spared Q1 2011 and 2012 from a seasonal slump.

SEASONAL CORRECTIONS IN DOW JONES INDUSTRIALS

	WINTER SLUMP Nov/Dec High to Q1 Low	SPRING SLUMP Feb/Mar High to Q2 Low	SUMMER SLUMP May/Jun High to Q3 Low	FALL SLUMP Aug/Sep High to Q4 Low
1964	−0.1%	−2.4%	−1.0%	−2.1%
1965	−2.5	−7.3	−8.3	−0.9
1966	−6.0	−13.2	−17.7	−12.7
1967	−4.2	−3.9	−5.5	−9.9
1968	−8.8	−0.3	−5.5	+0.4
1969	−8.7	−8.7	−17.2	−8.1
1970	−13.8	−20.2	−8.8	−2.5
1971	−1.4	−4.8	−10.7	−13.4
1972	−0.5	−2.6	−6.3	−5.3
1973	−11.0	−12.8	−10.9	−17.3
1974	−15.3	−10.8	−29.8	−27.6
1975	−6.3	−5.5	−9.9	−6.7
1976	−0.2	−5.1	−4.7	−8.9
1977	−8.5	−7.2	−11.5	−10.2
1978	−12.3	−4.0	−7.0	−13.5
1979	−2.5	−5.8	−3.7	−10.9
1980	−10.0	−16.0	−1.7	−6.8
1981	−6.9	−5.1	−18.6	−12.9
1982	−10.9	−7.5	−10.6	−3.3
1983	−4.1	−2.8	−6.8	−3.6
1984	−11.9	−10.5	−8.4	−6.2
1985	−4.8	−4.4	−2.8	−2.3
1986	−3.3	−4.7	−7.3	−7.6
1987	−1.4	−6.6	−1.7	−36.1
1988	−6.7	−7.0	−7.6	−4.5
1989	−1.7	−2.4	−3.1	−6.6
1990	−7.9	−4.0	−17.3	−18.4
1991	−6.3	−3.6	−4.5	−6.3
1992	+0.1	−3.3	−5.4	−7.6
1993	−2.7	−3.1	−3.0	−2.0
1994	−4.4	−9.6	−4.4	−7.1
1995	−0.8	−0.1	−0.2	−2.0
1996	−3.5	−4.6	−7.5	+0.2
1997	−1.8	−9.8	−2.2	−13.3
1998	−7.0	−3.1	−18.2	−13.1
1999	−2.7	−1.7	−8.0	−11.5
2000	−14.8	−7.4	−4.1	−11.8
2001	−14.5	−13.6	−27.4	−16.2
2002	−5.1	−14.2	−26.7	−19.5
2003	−15.8	−5.3	−3.1	−2.1
2004	−3.9	−7.7	−6.3	−5.7
2005	−4.5	−8.5	−3.3	−4.5
2006	−2.4	−5.4	−7.8	−0.4
2007	−3.7	−3.2	−6.1	−8.4
2008	−14.5	−11.0	−20.6	−35.9
2009	−32.0	−6.3	−7.4	−3.5
2010	−6.1	−10.4	−13.1	−1.0
2011	+0.2	−4.0	−16.3	−12.2
2012	+0.5	−6.7*		
Totals	**−317.4%**	**−328.2%**	**−440.0%**	**−441.7%**
Average	**−6.5%**	**−6.7%**	**−9.2%**	**−9.2%**

* As of 5/18/2012

Labor Day (Market Closed)

MONDAY

2

The way a young man spends his evenings is a part of that thin area between success and failure.
— Robert R. Young (U.S. financier and railroad tycoon, 1897–1958)

First Trading Day in September, S&P Up 12 of Last 17
Day After Labor Day, Dow Up 13 of Last 18, 1997 Up 3.4%, 1998 Up 5.0%

TUESDAY
D 57.1
S 61.9
N 57.1

3

The difference between life and the movies is that a script has to make sense, and life doesn't.
— Joseph L. Mankiewicz (Film director, writer, producer, 1909–1993)

WEDNESDAY
D 57.1
S 42.9
N 57.1

4

Why is it right-wing [conservatives] always stand shoulder to shoulder in solidarity, while liberals always fall out among themselves?
— Yevgeny Yevtushenko (Russian poet, *Babi Yar*, quoted in London *Observer* December 15, 1991, b. 1933)

Rosh Hashanah

THURSDAY
D 52.4
S 47.6
N 52.4

5

In my experience, selling a put is much safer than buying a stock.
— Kyle Rosen (Boston Capital Mgmt., *Barron's* 8/23/04)

FRIDAY
D 38.1
S 42.9
N 52.4

6

When teachers held high expectations of their students that alone was enough to cause an increase of 25 points in the students' IQ scores.
— Warren Bennis (Author, *The Unconscious Conspiracy: Why Leaders Can't Lead*, 1976)

SATURDAY

7

SUNDAY

8

FIRST-TRADING-DAY-OF-THE-MONTH PHENOMENON: DOW GAINS MORE ONE DAY THAN ALL OTHER DAYS

Over the last 15 years the Dow Jones Industrial Average has gained more points on the first trading days of all months than all other days combined. While the Dow has gained 4,746.96 points between September 2, 1997 (7,622.42) and May 18, 2012 (12,369.38), it is incredible that 5,545.13 points were gained on the first trading days of these 177 months. The remaining 3,527 trading days combined lost 798.17 points during the period. This averages out to gains of 31.33 points on first days, in contrast to a loss of 0.23 points on all others.

Note September 1997 through October 2000 racked up a total gain of 2,632.39 Dow points on the first trading days of these 38 months (winners except for seven occasions). But between November 2000 and September 2002, when the 2000–2002 bear markets did the bulk of their damage, frightened investors switched from pouring money into the market on that day to pulling it out, fourteen months out of twenty-three, netting a 404.80 Dow point loss. The 2007–2009 bear market lopped off 964.14 Dow points on first days in 17 months, November 2007–March 2009. First days had their worst year in 2011, declining seven times for a total loss of 644.45 Dow points.

First days of November have performed worst. Triple digit declines in 2007 and 2011 have resulted in the only net loss. In rising market trends, first days perform much better, as institutions are likely anticipating strong performance at each month's outset. S&P 500 first days track the Dow's pattern closely, but NASDAQ first days are not as strong, with weakness in April, August, and October.

DOW POINTS GAINED FIRST DAY OF MONTH
SEPTEMBER 1997 TO MAY 18, 2012

	Jan	Feb	Mar	Apr	May	Jun	Jul	Aug	Sep	Oct	Nov	Dec	Totals
1997									257.36	70.24	232.31	189.98	749.89
1998	56.79	201.28	4.73	68.51	83.70	22.42	96.65	−96.55	288.36	−210.09	114.05	16.99	646.84
1999	2.84	−13.13	18.20	46.35	225.65	36.52	95.62	−9.19	108.60	−63.95	−81.35	120.58	486.74
2000	−139.61	100.52	9.62	300.01	77.87	129.87	112.78	84.97	23.68	49.21	−71.67	−40.95	636.30
2001	−140.70	96.27	−45.14	−100.85	163.37	78.47	91.32	−12.80	47.74	−10.73	188.76	−87.60	268.11
2002	51.90	−12.74	262.73	−41.24	113.41	−215.46	−133.47	−229.97	−355.45	346.86	120.61	−33.52	−126.34
2003	265.89	56.01	−53.22	77.73	−25.84	47.55	55.51	−79.83	107.45	194.14	57.34	116.59	819.32
2004	−44.07	11.11	94.22	15.63	88.43	14.20	−101.32	39.45	−5.46	112.38	26.92	162.20	413.69
2005	−53.58	62.00	63.77	−99.46	59.19	82.39	28.47	−17.76	−21.97	−33.22	−33.30	106.70	143.23
2006	129.91	89.09	60.12	35.62	−23.85	91.97	77.80	−59.95	83.00	−8.72	−49.71	−27.80	397.48
2007	11.37	51.99	−34.29	27.95	73.23	40.47	126.81	150.38	91.12	191.92	−362.14	−57.15	311.66
2008	−220.86	92.83	−7.49	391.47	189.87	−134.50	32.25	−51.70	−26.63	−19.59	−5.18	−679.95	−439.48
2009	258.30	−64.03	−299.64	152.68	44.29	221.11	57.06	114.95	−185.68	−203.00	76.71	126.74	299.49
2010	155.91	118.20	78.53	70.44	143.22	−112.61	−41.49	208.44	254.75	41.63	6.13	249.76	1172.91
2011	93.24	148.23	−168.32	56.99	−3.18	−279.65	168.43	−10.75	−119.96	−258.08	−297.05	25.65	−644.45
2012	179.82	83.55	28.23	52.45	65.69								409.74
Totals	607.15	1021.18	12.05	1054.28	1275.05	22.75	666.42	29.69	546.91	199.00	−77.57	188.22	5545.13

SUMMARY FIRST DAYS VS. OTHER DAYS OF MONTH

	# of Days	Total Points Gained	Average Daily Point Gain
First days	177	5551.13	31.36
Other days	3527	−804.17	−0.23

SEPTEMBER

MONDAY
D 61.9
S 57.1
N 61.9
9

If you can buy more of your best idea, why put [the money] into your 10th-best idea or your 20th-best idea?
The more positions you have, the more average you are.
— Bruce Berkowitz (Fairholme Fund, *Barron's* 3/17/08)

TUESDAY
D 52.4
S 61.9
N 61.9
10

Don't be scared to take big steps—you can't cross a chasm in two small jumps.
— David Lloyd George (British Prime Minister, 1916–1922)

2001 4-Day Market Closing, Longest Since
9-Day Banking Moratorium in March 1933

WEDNESDAY
D 61.9
S 61.9
N 57.1
11

Fortune favors the brave.
— Virgil (Roman Poet, *Aeneid*, 70–19 B.C.)

"In Memory"

THURSDAY
D 71.4
S 66.7
N 71.4
12

The four most expensive words in the English language, "This time it's different."
— Sir John Templeton (Founder Templeton Funds, philanthropist, b. 1912)

FRIDAY
D 52.4
S 61.9
N 76.2
13

In an uptrend, if a higher high is made but fails to carry through, and prices dip below the previous high, the
trend is apt to reverse. The converse is true for downtrends.
— Victor Sperandeo (*Trader Vic—Methods of a Wall Street Master*)

Yom Kippur

SATURDAY
14

SUNDAY
15

MARKET BEHAVIOR THREE DAYS BEFORE AND THREE DAYS AFTER HOLIDAYS

The *Stock Trader's Almanac* has tracked holiday seasonality annually since the first edition in 1968. Stocks used to rise on the day before holidays and sell off the day after, but nowadays, each holiday moves to its own rhythm. Eight holidays are separated into seven groups. Average percentage changes for the Dow, S&P 500, NASDAQ, and Russell 2000 are shown.

The Dow and S&P consist of blue chips and the largest cap stocks, whereas NASDAQ and the Russell 2000 would be more representative of smaller-cap stocks. This is evident on the last day of the year with NASDAQ and the Russell 2000 having a field day, while their larger brethren in the Dow and S&P are showing losses on average.

Thanks to the Santa Claus Rally, the three days before and after New Year's Day and Christmas are best. NASDAQ and the Russell 2000 average gains of 1.1% to 1.8% over the six-day spans. However, trading around the first day of the year has been mixed. Traders have been selling more the first trading day of the year recently, pushing gains and losses into the New Year.

Bullishness before Labor Day and after Memorial Day is affected by strength the first day of September and June. The second worst day after a holiday is the day after Easter. Surprisingly, the following day is one of the best second days after a holiday, right up there with the second day after New Year's Day.

Presidents' Day is the least bullish of all the holidays, bearish the day before and three days after. NASDAQ has dropped 18 of the last 23 days before Presidents' Day (Dow, 16 of 23; S&P, 17 of 23; Russell 2000, 13 of 23).

HOLIDAYS: 3 DAYS BEFORE, 3 DAYS AFTER (Average % change 1980 to April 2012)

	−3	−2	−1	Mixed	+1	+2	+3
S&P 500	0.02	0.30	−0.14	**New Year's**	0.20	0.37	0.05
DJIA	−0.01	0.23	−0.21	**Day**	0.33	0.37	0.18
NASDAQ	0.10	0.34	0.17	*1/1/13*	0.19	0.69	0.22
Russell 2K	0.08	0.46	0.45		0.04	0.24	0.15
S&P 500	0.37	0.01	−0.25	**Negative Before & After**	−0.26	−0.03	−0.13
DJIA	0.37	0.02	−0.17	**Presidents'**	−0.16	−0.09	−0.16
NASDAQ	0.56	0.27	−0.40	**Day**	−0.63	−0.02	−0.06
Russell 2K	0.43	0.15	−0.12	*2/18/13*	−0.49	−0.13	−0.04
S&P 500	0.19	−0.06	0.40	**Positive Before &**	−0.23	0.31	0.14
DJIA	0.16	−0.09	0.31	**Negative After**	−0.16	0.30	0.13
NASDAQ	0.44	0.23	0.52	**Good Friday**	−0.35	0.32	0.25
Russell 2K	0.22	0.09	0.54	*3/29/13*	−0.33	0.21	0.19
S&P 500	0.04	0.06	−0.004	**Positive After**	0.32	0.17	0.26
DJIA	0.01	0.01	−0.06	**Memorial**	0.39	0.18	0.16
NASDAQ	0.10	0.26	0.02	**Day**	0.23	0.004	0.51
Russell 2K	−0.05	0.32	0.08	*5/27/13*	0.22	0.11	0.43
S&P 500	0.04	0.08	0.04	**Negative After**	−0.15	0.07	0.06
DJIA	0.01	0.08	0.04	**Independence**	−0.09	0.11	0.05
NASDAQ	0.15	0.10	0.02	**Day**	−0.18	−0.05	0.22
Russell 2K	0.15	−0.02	−0.08	*7/4/13*	−0.24	0.02	0.03
S&P 500	0.17	−0.22	0.18	**Positive Day Before**	0.04	0.09	−0.15
DJIA	0.14	−0.27	0.18	**Labor**	0.09	0.15	−0.25
NASDAQ	0.39	0.02	0.19	**Day**	−0.07	−0.05	0.01
Russell 2K	0.54	0.06	0.14	*9/2/13*	−0.001	0.15	−0.02
S&P 500	0.09	0.01	0.27	**Positive Before & After**	0.18	−0.44	0.32
DJIA	0.10	0.02	0.28	**Thanksgiving**	0.13	−0.37	0.36
NASDAQ	−0.001	−0.25	0.41	*11/28/13*	0.44	−0.44	0.12
Russell 2K	0.07	−0.14	0.36		0.33	−0.48	0.28
S&P 500	0.16	0.21	0.24	**Christmas**	0.15	−0.01	0.37
DJIA	0.24	0.25	0.30	*12/25/13*	0.19	−0.001	0.32
NASDAQ	−0.12	0.47	0.45		0.13	0.05	0.12
Russell 2K	0.18	0.38	0.38		0.22	0.06	0.55

SEPTEMBER

Monday Before September Triple Witching, Russell 2000 Down 8 of Last 13

MONDAY
D 52.4
S 52.4
N 38.1
16

To find one man in a thousand who is your true friend from unselfish motives is to find one of the great wonders of the world.
— Leopold Mozart (Father of Wolfgang Amadeus, 1719–1787, Quoted by Maynard Solomon, *Mozart*)

Expiration Week 2001, Dow Lost 1370 Points (14.3%)
2nd Worst Weekly Point Loss Ever, 5th Worst Week Overall

TUESDAY
D 52.4
S 61.9
N 66.7
17

Short-term volatility is greatest at turning points and diminishes as a trend becomes established.
— George Soros (Financier, philanthropist, political activist, author and philosopher, b. 1930)

FOMC Meeting (2 Days)

WEDNESDAY
D 33.3
S 42.9
N 52.4
18

The game is lost only when we stop trying.
— Mario Cuomo (Former NY Governor, *C-Span*)

THURSDAY
D 57.1
S 57.1
N 66.7
19

Bill Gates' One-Minus Staffing: For every project, figure out the bare minimum of people needed to staff it. Cut to the absolute muscle and bones, then take out one more. When you understaff, people jump on the loose ball. You find out who the real performers are. Not so when you're overstaffed. People sit around waiting for somebody else to do it.
— Quoted by Rich Karlgaard (Publisher, *Forbes* Dec. 25, 2000)

September Triple Witching, Dow Up 8 Straight and 9 of Last 10

FRIDAY
D 42.9
S 42.9
N 42.9
20

We go to the movies to be entertained, not see rape, ransacking, pillage and looting. We can get all that in the stock market.
— Kennedy Gammage (*The Richland Report*)

SATURDAY
21

SUNDAY
22

MARKET GAINS MORE ON SUPER-8 DAYS EACH MONTH THAN ON ALL 13 REMAINING DAYS COMBINED

For many years, the last day plus the first four days were the best days of the month. The market currently exhibits greater bullish bias from the last three trading days of the previous month through the first two days of the current month, and now shows significant bullishness during the middle three trading days, 9 to 11, due to 401(k) cash inflows (see pages 145 and 146). This pattern was not as pronounced during the boom years of the 1990s, with market strength all month long. It returned in 2000 with monthly bullishness at the ends, beginnings and middles of months versus weakness during the rest of the month. "Super Eight" performance in 2011, was on track as were most seasonal patterns and indicators.

SUPER-8 DAYS* DOW % CHANGES VS. REST OF MONTH

	Super-8 Days	Rest of Month		Super-8 Days	Rest of Month		Super-8 Days	Rest of Month
	2004			**2005**			**2006**	
Jan	3.79%	−1.02%		−1.96%	−1.35%		−0.03%	0.34%
Feb	−1.20	0.83		1.76	−0.07		1.67	0.71
Mar	−1.64	−1.69		0.31	−2.05		0.81	−0.03
Apr	3.20	−0.60		−4.62	1.46		1.69	−0.53
May	−2.92	−0.51		0.57	2.43		−0.66	0.08
Jun	1.15	1.36		1.43	−3.00		2.39	−4.87
Jul	−1.91	−0.88		0.96	1.83		1.65	0.07
Aug	0.51	0.40		1.36	−3.07		1.83	0.41
Sep	0.47	−2.26		0.90	−0.31		1.13	1.64
Oct	0.85	−1.82		1.14	−2.18		1.58	2.59
Nov	3.08	3.20		1.67	3.89		−0.01	−0.31
Dec	2.03	1.13		0.57	−1.96		2.40	−0.05
Totals	**7.41%**	**−1.86%**		**4.09%**	**−4.37%**		**14.45%**	**0.04%**
Average	**0.62%**	**−0.16%**		**0.34%**	**−0.36%**		**1.20%**	**0.003%**
	2007			**2008**			**2009**	
Jan	0.68%	−0.04%		−4.76%	−4.11%		3.16%	−6.92%
Feb	3.02	−1.72		1.83	0.65		−6.05	−4.39
Mar	−5.51	3.64		−4.85	2.92		−4.37	12.84
Apr	2.66	2.82		−0.27	4.09		1.52	−0.24
May	2.21	0.95		2.19	−4.81		2.64	2.98
Jun	3.84	−5.00		0.37	−6.30		1.71	−1.64
Jul	2.59	−1.47		−3.80	−1.99		2.30	5.03
Aug	−2.94	−0.26		1.53	1.06		0.04	4.91
Sep	4.36	1.18		−2.23	−1.19		−0.81	2.21
Oct	1.28	−1.05		−3.39	−13.70		−0.05	2.40
Nov	−0.59	−5.63		6.07	−11.90		0.00	5.57
Dec	−0.04	4.62		−2.54	3.49		0.62	0.46
Totals	**11.56%**	**−1.96%**		**−9.85%**	**−31.79%**		**0.71%**	**23.21%**
Average	**0.96%**	**−0.16%**		**−0.82%**	**−2.65%**		**0.06%**	**1.93%**
	2010			**2011**			**2012**	
Jan	0.66%	−3.92%		1.70%	1.80%		1.90%	1.66%
Feb	3.31	−2.38		0.45	0.57		−0.39	2.33
Mar	1.91	3.51		−1.40	2.21		2.22	−0.55
Apr	1.13	0.18		2.30	0.95		1.00	−1.80
May	−3.08	−5.75		1.03	−2.61			
Jun	4.33	−3.26		−1.64	−1.19			
Jul	−7.07	11.34		3.52	0.31			
Aug	0.20	−5.49		2.04	−11.39			
Sep	3.83	4.22		3.24	−3.96			
Oct	−0.18	3.47		−4.47	10.71			
Nov	−1.20	1.37		1.42	−6.66			
Dec	1.98	1.45		5.74	3.58			
Totals	**5.82%**	**4.74%**		**13.93%**	**−5.68%**		**4.73%**	**1.64%**
Average	**0.49%**	**0.40%**		**1.16%**	**−0.47%**		**1.18%**	**0.41%**

		Super-8 Days*		Rest of Month (13 Days)	
100	Net % Changes	52.85%	Net % Changes	−16.02%
Month	Average Period	0.53%	Average Period	−0.16%
Totals	Average Day	0.07%	Average Day	−0.01%

* Super-8 Days = Last 3 + First 2 + Middle 3

SEPTEMBER

Week After Sepetmber Triple Witching Dow Down 17 of Last 22,
Average Loss Since 1990, –1.2%

MONDAY
D 28.6
S 33.3
N 38.1
23

Q. What kind of grad students do you take? A. I never take a straight-A student. A real scientist tends to be critical, and somewhere along the line, they had to rebel against their teachers.
— Lynn Margulis (U. Mass science professor, *The Scientist*, 6/30/03)

TUESDAY
D 52.4
S 47.6
N 47.6
24

To achieve satisfactory investment results is easier than most people realize. The typical individual investor has a great advantage over the large institutions.
— Benjamin Graham (Economist, investor, *Securities Analysis* 1934, *The Intelligent Investor* 1949, 1894–1976)

WEDNESDAY
D 57.1
S 52.4
N 52.4
25

It was never my thinking that made the big money for me. It was always my sitting. Got that? My sitting tight!
— Jesse Livermore (Early 20th century stock trader & speculator, *How to Trade in Stocks*, 1877–1940)

THURSDAY
D 57.1
S 61.9
N 42.9
26

The single best predictor of overall excellence is a company's ability to attract, motivate, and retain talented people.
— Bruce Pfau (Vice chair human resources KPMG, *Fortune* 1998)

End of September Prone to Weakness
From End-of-Q3 Institutional Portfolio Restructuring

FRIDAY
D 57.1
S 61.9
N 47.6
27

A loss never bothers me after I take it. I forget it overnight. But being wrong—not taking the loss—that is what does damage to the pocketbook and to the soul.
— Jesse Livermore (Early 20th century stock trader and speculator, *How to Trade in Stocks*, 1877–1940)

SATURDAY
28

October Almanac Investor Seasonalities: See Pages 92, 94 and 96

SUNDAY
29

OCTOBER ALMANAC

OCTOBER						
S	M	T	W	T	F	S
		1	2	3	4	5
6	7	8	9	10	11	12
13	14	15	16	17	18	19
20	21	22	23	24	25	26
27	28	29	30	31		

NOVEMBER						
S	M	T	W	T	F	S
					1	2
3	4	5	6	7	8	9
10	11	12	13	14	15	16
17	18	19	20	21	22	23
24	25	26	27	28	29	30

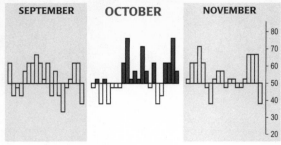

Market Probability Chart above is a graphic representation of the S&P 500 Recent Market Probability Calendar on page 124.

◆ Known as the jinx month because of crashes in 1929, 1987, the 554-point drop on October 27, 1997, back-to-back massacres in 1978 and 1979, Friday the 13th in 1989, and the meltdown in 2008 ◆ Yet October is a "bear killer" and turned the tide in 12 post-WWII bear markets: 1946, 1957, 1960, 1962, 1966, 1974, 1987, 1990, 1998, 2001, 2002, and 2011 ◆ First October Dow top in 2007, 20-year 1987 Crash anniversary −2.6% ◆ Worst six months of the year ends with October (page 48) ◆ No longer worst month (pages 44 & 56) ◆ Best Dow, S&P, and NASDAQ month from 1993 to 2007 ◆ Post-presidential election year Octobers since 1953, Dow, S&P, and NASDAQ rank mid-pack ◆ October is a great time to buy ◆ Big October gains five years 1999–2003 after atrocious Septembers ◆ Can get into Best Six Months earlier using MACD (page 50) ◆ October 2011, second month to gain 1000 Dow points.

October Vital Statistics

	DJIA		S&P 500		NASDAQ		Russell 1K		Russell 2K	
Rank	7		7		8		7		11	
Up	37		37		22		21		18	
Down	25		25		19		12		15	
Average % Change	0.5%		0.8%		0.6%		0.8%		−0.6%	
Post-Election Year	0.5%		0.7%		0.9%		0.3%		−0.1%	
Best & Worst October										
	% Change		% Change		% Change		% Change		% Change	
Best	1982	10.7	1974	16.3	1974	17.2	1982	11.3	2011	15.0
Worst	1987	−23.2	1987	−21.8	1987	−27.2	1987	−21.9	1987	−30.8
Best & Worst October Weeks										
Best	10/11/74	12.6	10/11/74	14.1	10/31/08	10.9	10/31/08	10.8	10/31/08	14.1
Worst	10/10/08	−18.2	10/10/08	−18.2	10/23/87	−19.2	10/10/08	−18.2	10/23/87	−20.4
Best & Worst October Days										
Best	10/13/08	11.1	10/13/08	11.6	10/13/08	11.8	10/13/08	11.7	10/13/08	9.3
Worst	10/19/87	−22.6	10/19/87	−20.5	10/19/87	−11.4	10/19/87	−19.0	10/19/87	−12.5
First Trading Day of Expiration Week: 1980–2011										
Record (#Up–#Down)	26–6		24–8		22–10		25–7		24–8	
Current streak	D1		D1		D1		D1		D3	
Avg % Change	0.83		0.80		0.63		0.77		0.43	
Options Expiration Day: 1980–2011										
Record (#Up–#Down)	14–18		16–16		17–15		16–16		14–18	
Current streak	U1		U2		U2		U2		U1	
Avg % Change	−0.19		−0.27		−0.14		−0.25		−0.17	
Options Expiration Week: 1980–2011										
Record (#Up–#Down)	22–10		22–10		18–14		22–10		19–13	
Current streak	U4		U4		D1		U4		D1	
Avg % Change	0.65		0.66		0.71		0.65		0.30	
Week After Options Expiration: 1980–2011										
Record (#Up–#Down)	14–18		13–19		16–16		13–19		14–18	
Current streak	U2		U2		U2		U2		U2	
Avg % Change	−0.49		−0.52		−0.60		−0.54		−0.72	
First Trading Day Performance										
% of Time Up	48.4		48.4		48.8		51.5		48.5	
Avg % Change	0.07		0.05		−0.16		0.25		−0.28	
Last Trading Day Performance										
% of Time Up	54.8		54.8		68.3		63.6		72.7	
Avg % Change	0.07		0.15		0.53		0.36		0.63	

Dow & S&P 1950–April 2012, NASDAQ 1971–April 2012, Russell 1K & 2K 1979–April 2012.

October has killed many a bear;
Buy techs and small caps and soon wear a grin ear to ear.

SEPTEMBER/OCTOBER

Last Day of Q3, Dow Down 11 of Last 15, Massive 4.7% Rally in 2008

MONDAY

D 38.1
S 38.1
N 38.1

30

First Trading Day in October, Dow Down 5 of Last 7
Off 2.1% in 2009

TUESDAY

D 52.4
S 47.6
N 42.9

1

Start Looking for MACD BUY Signals (Pages 50 and 58)
Almanac Investor Subscribers Emailed When It Triggers (See Insert)

WEDNESDAY

D 47.6
S 52.4
N 52.4

2

THURSDAY

D 42.9
S 38.1
N 47.6

3

FRIDAY

D 61.9
S 52.4
N 61.9

4

SATURDAY

5

SUNDAY

6

SECTOR SEASONALITY: SELECTED PERCENTAGE PLAYS

Sector seasonality was featured in the first 1968 *Almanac*. A Merrill Lynch study showed that buying seven sectors around September or October and selling in the first few months of 1954–1964 tripled the gains of holding them for 10 years. Over the years we have honed this strategy significantly and now devote a large portion of our time and resources to investing and trading during positive and negative seasonal periods for different sectors with Exchange Traded Funds (ETFs).

Updated seasonalities appear in the table below. We specify whether the seasonality starts or finishes in the beginning third (B), middle third (M), or last third (E) of the month. These selected percentage plays are geared to take advantage of the bulk of seasonal sector strength or weakness.

By design, entry points are in advance of the major seasonal moves, providing traders ample opportunity to accumulate positions at favorable prices. Conversely, exit points have been selected to capture the majority of the move.

From the major seasonalities in the table below, we created the Sector Index Seasonality Strategy Calendar on pages 94 and 96. Note the concentration of bullish sector seasonalities during the Best Six Months, November to April, and bearish sector seasonalities during the Worst Six Months, May to October.

Almanac Investor newsletter subscribers receive specific entry and exit points for highly correlated ETFs and detailed analysis in our monthly ETF Lab. Visit *www.stocktradersalmanac.com,* or see the insert for additional details and a special offer for new subscribers. Top 300 ETFs appear on pages 188–190.

SECTOR INDEX SEASONALITY TABLE

Ticker	Sector Index	Type	Start		Finish		15-Year	10-Year	5-Year
					Seasonality		**Average % Return[†]**		
XCI	Computer Tech	Short	January	B	March	B	−7.2	−7.8	−6.6
IIX	Internet	Short	January	B	February	E	−8.6	−6.2	−3.7
XNG	Natural Gas	Long	February	E	June	B	18.5	14.3	18.2
RXP	Healthcare Prod	Long	March	M	June	M	7.0	6.0	6.8
RXH	Healthcare Prov	Long	March	M	June	M	15.2	14.7	19.5
MSH	High-Tech	Long	March	M	July	B	11.8	8.7	12.4
XCI	Computer Tech	Long	April	M	July	M	12.5	5.5	8.0
IIX	Internet	Long	April	M	July	B	11.5	6.0	4.5
CYC	Cyclical	Short	May	M	October	E	−8.6	−5.8	−9.4
XAU	Gold & Silver	Short	May	M	June	E	−8.2	−5.6	−6.4
S5MATR*	Materials	Short	May	M	October	M	−9.5	−6.0	−7.3
BKX	Banking	Short	June	B	July	B	−5.6	−7.3	−10.8
XNG	Natural Gas	Short	June	M	July	E	−8.2	−7.8	−7.7
XAU	Gold & Silver	Long	July	E	December	E	13.5	19.5	9.1
DJT	Transports	Short	July	M	October	M	−8.5	−4.3	−6.4
UTY	Utilities	Long	July	E	January	B	9.2	8.4	3.3
BTK	Biotech	Long	August	B	March	B	28.6	13.0	9.8
RXP	Healthcare Prod	Long	August	B	February	B	11.1	9.7	6.7
MSH	High-Tech	Long	August	M	January	M	17.5	14.3	5.6
IIX	Internet	Long	August	B	January	B	27.5	21.0	6.9
SOX	Semiconductor	Short	August	M	October	E	−12.3	−7.2	−9.6
CMR	Consumer	Long	September	E	June	B	11.6	7.8	4.5
RXH	Healthcare Prov	Short	September	M	November	B	−7.0	−7.1	−9.2
XOI	Oil	Short	September	B	November	E	−4.6	−4.3	−6.0
BKX	Banking	Long	October	B	May	B	14.9	11.9	10.6
XBD	Broker/Dealer	Long	October	B	April	M	32.9	14.5	7.4
XCI	Computer Tech	Long	October	B	January	B	17.8	13.6	9.3
CYC	Cyclical	Long	October	B	May	M	21.5	18.3	15.4
RXH	Healthcare Prov	Long	October	E	January	M	11.7	10.0	10.0
S5MATR*	Materials	Long	October	M	May	M	16.8	14.0	9.6
DRG	Pharmaceutical	Long	October	M	January	B	7.4	6.9	7.1
RMZ	Real Estate	Long	October	E	May	B	13.1	13.0	13.9
SOX	Semiconductor	Long	October	E	December	B	16.6	12.2	5.7
XTC	Telecom	Long	October	M	December	E	11.3	10.5	4.1
DJT	Transports	Long	October	B	May	B	20.3	18.4	18.0
XOI	Oil	Long	December	M	July	B	13.4	13.0	6.4

[†]*Average % Return based on full seasonality completion through May 18, 2012*
* *S5MATR Available @ bloomberg.com*

🐻 **MONDAY**
D 33.3
S 38.1
N 47.6
7

Executives owe it to the organization and to their fellow workers not to tolerate nonperforming individuals in important jobs.
— Peter Drucker (Austria-born pioneer management theorist, 1909–2005)

October Ends Dow and S&P "Worst Six Months" (Pages 44, 48, 50 and 147)
And NASDAQ "Worst Four Months" (Pages 56, 58 and 148)

TUESDAY
D 47.6
S 47.6
N 61.9
8

Prosperity is a great teacher; adversity a greater.
— William Hazlitt (English essayist, 1778–1830)

WEDNESDAY
D 47.6
S 47.6
N 57.1
9

Every successful enterprise requires three people—a dreamer, a businessman, and a son-of-a-bitch.
— Peter McArthur (1904)

Dow Lost 1874 Points (18.2%) on the Week Ending 10/10/08
Worst Dow Week in the History of Wall Street

THURSDAY
D 42.9
S 47.6
N 61.9
10

Based on my own personal experience—both as an investor in recent years and an expert witness in years past—rarely do more than three or four variables really count. Everything else is noise.
— Martin J. Whitman (Founder Third Avenue Funds, b. 1924)

🐂 **FRIDAY**
D 61.9
S 61.9
N 76.2
11

Those who cast the votes decide nothing. Those who count the votes decide everything.
— Joseph Stalin (Ruler USSR 1929–1953, 1879–1953)

SATURDAY
12

SUNDAY
13

Sector Index Seasonality Strategy Calendar*

* Graphic representation of the Sector Index Seasonality Percentage Plays on page 92.
L = Long Trade, S = Short Trade, ——▶ = Start of Trade

(continued on page 96)

Columbus Day (Bond Market Closed)
Monday Before October Expiration, Dow Up 26 of 32

MONDAY
D 76.2
S 76.2
N 71.4
14

Doubt is the father of invention.
— Galileo Galilei (Italian physicist and astronomer, 1564–1642)

TUESDAY
D 52.4
S 52.4
N 52.4
15

Most people have no idea of the giant capacity we can immediately command when we focus all of our resources on mastering a single area of our lives.
— Anthony Robbins (Motivator, advisor, consultant, author, entrepreneur, philanthropist, b. 1960)

October 2011, Second Dow Month to Gain 1000 Points

WEDNESDAY
D 52.4
S 57.1
N 47.6
16

In this age of instant information, investors can experience both fear and greed at the exact same moment.
— Sam Stovall (Chief Investment Strategist Standard & Poor's, October 2003)

THURSDAY
D 42.9
S 52.4
N 38.1
17

The average man desires to be told specifically which particular stock to buy or sell. He wants to get something for nothing. He does not wish to work.
— William LeFevre (Senior analyst Ehrenkrantz King Nussbaum, 1928–1997)

October Expiration Day, Dow Down 6 Straight 2005–2010 and 7 of Last 9
Crash of October 19, 1987, Dow down 22.6% in One Day

FRIDAY
D 66.7
S 71.4
N 71.4
18

I was in search of a one-armed economist so that the guy could never make a statement and then say: "on the other hand."
— Harry S. Truman (33rd U.S. President, 1884–1972)

SATURDAY
19

SUNDAY
20

(continued from page 94)

Sector Index Seasonality Strategy Calendar*

* Graphic representation of the Sector Index Seasonality Percentage Plays on page 92.
L = Long Trade, S = Short Trade, ⟶ = Start of Trade

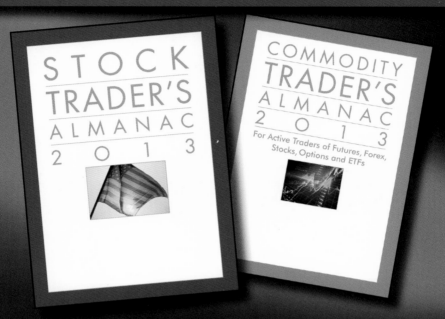

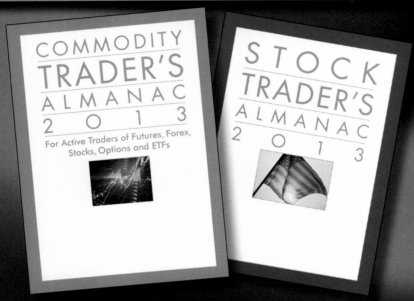

OCTOBER

Late October is Time to Buy Depressed Stocks
Especially Techs and Small Caps

MONDAY
D 47.6
S 57.1
N 47.6
21

Capitalism is the legitimate racket of the ruling class.
— Al Capone (American gangster, 1899–1947)

TUESDAY
D 42.9
S 47.6
N 47.6
22

I will never knowingly buy any company that has a real time quote of their stock price in the building lobby.
— Robert Mahan (A trader commenting on Enron)

WEDNESDAY
D 57.1
S 61.9
N 57.1
23

The greatest lie ever told: Build a better mousetrap and the world will beat a path to your door.
— Yale Hirsch (Creator of *Stock Trader's Almanac*, b. 1923)

THURSDAY
D 42.9
S 38.1
N 38.1
24

Love your enemies, for they tell you your faults.
— Benjamin Franklin (U.S. Founding Father, diplomat, inventor, 1706–1790)

FRIDAY
D 38.1
S 42.9
N 33.3
25

When new money is created on a grand scale, it must go somewhere and have some major consequences. One of these will be greatly increased volatility and instability in the economy and financial system.
— J. Anthony Boeckh, Ph.D (Chairman Bank Credit Analyst 1968–2002, *The Great Reflation, Boeckh Investment Letter*)

SATURDAY
26

SUNDAY
27

NOVEMBER ALMANAC

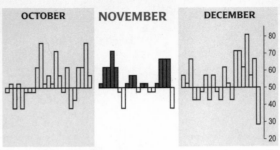

NOVEMBER							DECEMBER						
S	M	T	W	T	F	S	S	M	T	W	T	F	S
					1	2							1
3	4	5	6	7	8	9	2	3	4	5	6	7	8
10	11	12	13	14	15	16	9	10	11	12	13	14	15
17	18	19	20	21	22	23	16	17	18	19	20	21	22
24	25	26	27	28	29	30	23	24	25	26	27	28	29
							30	31					

Market Probability Chart above is a graphic representation of the S&P 500 Recent Market Probability Calendar on page 124.

◆ #3 S&P and Dow month since 1950, #4 on NASDAQ since 1971 (pages 44 & 56) ◆ Start of the "Best Six Months" of the year (page 48), NASDAQ's Best Eight Months and Best Three (pages 147 & 148) ◆ Simple timing indicator almost triples "Best Six Months" strategy (page 50), doubles NASDAQ's Best Eight (page 58) ◆ Day before and after Thanksgiving Day combined, only 13 losses in 60 years (page 102) ◆ Week before Thanksgiving Dow up 15 of last 19 ◆ Post-presidential election year Novembers rank #3 Dow and S&P, #4 NASDAQ.

November Vital Statistics

	DJIA		S&P 500		NASDAQ		Russell 1K		Russell 2K	
Rank	3		3		4		2		4	
Up	41		40		26		23		21	
Down	21		22		15		10		12	
Average % Change	1.5%		1.5%		1.5%		1.7%		1.8%	
Post-Election Year	1.7%		1.7%		2.3%		3.9%		2.6%	
Best & Worst November										
	% Change		% Change		% Change		% Change		% Change	
Best	1962	10.1	1980	10.2	2001	14.2	1980	10.1	2002	8.8
Worst	1973	−14.0	1973	−11.4	2000	−22.9	2000	−9.3	2008	−12.0
Best & Worst November Weeks										
Best	11/28/08	9.7	11/28/08	12.0	11/28/08	10.9	11/28/08	12.5	11/28/08	16.4
Worst	11/21/08	−5.3	11/21/08	−8.4	11/10/00	−12.2	11/21/08	−8.8	11/21/08	−11.0
Best & Worst November Days										
Best	11/13/08	6.7	11/13/08	6.9	11/13/08	6.5	11/13/08	7.0	11/13/08	8.5
Worst	11/20/08	−5.6	11/20/08	−6.7	11/19/08	−6.5	11/20/08	−6.9	11/19/08	−7.9
First Trading Day of Expiration Week: 1980–2011										
Record (#Up–#Down)	16–16		13–19		12–20		14–18		14–18	
Current streak	D1		D2		D2		D2		D1	
Avg % Change	−0.06		−0.09		−0.16		−0.11		−0.11	
Options Expiration Day: 1980–2011										
Record (#Up–#Down)	20–12		18–14		16–16		18–14		15–16	
Current streak	U2		D1		D1		D1		U2	
Avg % Change	0.22		0.15		−0.003		0.14		0.09	
Options Expiration Week: 1980–2011										
Record (#Up–#Down)	21–11		19–13		16–16		18–14		16–16	
Current streak	D1		D1		D4		D1		D1	
Avg % Change	0.28		−0.01		−0.06		−0.04		−0.31	
Week After Options Expiration: 1980–2011										
Record (#Up–#Down)	18–14		19–13		20–12		19–13		18–14	
Current streak	D3		D2		D1		D3		D1	
Avg % Change	0.63		0.61		0.68		0.61		0.68	
First Trading Day Performance										
% of Time Up	62.9		62.9		63.4		69.7		63.6	
Avg % Change	0.26		0.28		0.26		0.37		0.18	
Last Trading Day Performance										
% of Time Up	54.8		54.8		65.9		48.5		72.7	
Avg % Change	0.11		0.15		−0.08		0.03		0.23	

Dow & S&P 1950–April 2012, NASDAQ 1971–April 2012, Russell 1K & 2K 1979–April 2012.

Astute investors always smile and remember,
When stocks seasonally start soaring, and salute November.

OCTOBER/NOVEMBER

84th Anniversary of 1929 Crash, Dow Down 23.0% in Two Days,
October 28 and 29

MONDAY
28

D 57.1
S 61.9
N 52.4

Selling a soybean contract short is worth two years at the Harvard Business School.
— Robert Stovall (Managing director, Wood Asset Management, b. 1926)

TUESDAY
29

D 66.7
S 61.9
N 61.9

Inflation is the modern way that governments default on their debt.
— Mike Epstein (MTA, MIT/Sloan Lab for Financial Engineering)

FOMC Meeting (2 Days)

WEDNESDAY
30

D 66.7
S 76.2
N 71.4

We are all born originals; why is it so many die copies?
— Edward Young (English poet, 1683–1765)

Halloween

THURSDAY
31

D 52.4
S 57.1
N 71.4

When Amercia sneezes, the rest of the word catches cold.
— Anonymous (circa 1929)

First Trading Day in November, Dow Down 5 of Last 7

FRIDAY
1

D 52.4
S 52.4
N 61.9

My best shorts come from research reports where there are recommendations to buy stocks on weakness;
also, where a brokerage firm changes its recommendation from a buy to a hold.
— Marc Howard (Hedge fund manager, *New York Magazine* 1976, b. 1941)

November Almanac Investor Seasonalities: See Pages 92, 94 and 96

SATURDAY
2

Daylight Saving Time Ends

SUNDAY
3

FOURTH QUARTER MARKET MAGIC

Examining market performance on a quarterly basis reveals several intriguing and helpful patterns. Fourth-quarter market gains have been magical, providing the greatest and most consistent gains over the years. First-quarter performance runs a respectable second. This should not be surprising, as cash inflows, trading volume, and buying bias are generally elevated during these two quarters.

Positive market psychology hits a fever pitch, as the holiday season approaches, and does not begin to wane until spring. Professionals drive the market higher, as they make portfolio adjustments to maximize year-end numbers. Bonuses are paid and invested around the turn of the year.

The market's sweet spot of the four-year cycle begins in the fourth quarter of the midterm year. The best two-quarter span runs from the fourth quarter of the midterm year through the first quarter of the pre-election year, averaging 15.3% for the Dow, 16.0% for the S&P 500, and an amazing 23.3% for NASDAQ.

Quarterly strength fades in the latter half of the pre-election year, but stays impressively positive through the election year. Losses dominate the first and third quarters of post-election years and the first and second quarters of midterm years.

QUARTERLY % CHANGES

	Q1	Q2	Q3	Q4	Year	Q2–Q3	Q4–Q1
Dow Jones Industrials (1949 to March 2012)							
Average	2.1%	1.6%	0.4%	3.9%	8.2%	2.0%	6.3%
Post Election	−1.1%	1.6%	0.2%	3.4%	4.4%	1.8%	5.2%
Midterm	1.5%	−1.8%	−0.5%	7.3%	6.7%	−2.2%	15.3%
Pre-Election	7.5%	5.3%	1.6%	2.3%	17.7%	6.8%	3.2%
Election	0.8%	1.2%	0.4%	2.3%	4.6%	1.6%	1.2%
S&P 500 (1949 to March 2012)							
Average	2.0%	1.7%	0.5%	4.1%	8.6%	2.3%	6.6%
Post Election	−1.2%	2.2%	0.4%	3.1%	4.8%	2.7%	4.3%
Midterm	1.0%	−2.8%	0.1%	8.0%	6.4%	−2.7%	16.0%
Pre-Election	7.5%	5.2%	1.1%	3.0%	17.1%	6.3%	4.6%
Election	1.4%	2.1%	0.6%	2.1%	6.1%	2.6%	1.0%
NASDAQ Composite (1971 to March 2012)							
Average	4.4%	3.3%	−0.4%	4.4%	11.9%	3.2%	9.1%
Post Election	−3.3%	6.8%	1.3%	4.2%	8.4%	8.1%	6.3%
Midterm	2.1%	−3.4%	−5.2%	8.9%	1.7%	−8.1%	23.3%
Pre-Election	13.8%	8.0%	1.7%	5.1%	30.9%	12.1%	7.8%
Election	3.9%	1.3%	0.6%	−0.6%	4.8%	2.4%	−3.1%

NOVEMBER

November Begins Dow and S&P "Best Six Months" (Pages 44, 48, 50, 147)
And NASDAQ "Best Eight Months" (Pages 56, 58 and 148)

MONDAY
4
D 52.4
S 61.9
N 61.9

History must repeat itself because we pay such little attention to it the first time.
— Blackie Sherrod (Sportswriter, b. 1919)

Election Day

TUESDAY
5
D 61.9
S 61.9
N 76.2

A president is elected and tries to get rid of the dirty stuff in the economy as quickly as possible, so that by the time the next election comes around, he looks like a hero. The stock market is reacting to what the politicians are doing.
— Yale Hirsch (Creator of *Stock Trader's Almanac*, NY Times 10/10/2010, b. 1923)

WEDNESDAY
6
D 71.4
S 71.4
N 66.7

Thomas Alva Edison said, "Genius is 5% inspiration and 95% perspiration!" Unfortunately, many startup "genius" entrepreneurs mistakenly switch the two percentages around, and then wonder why they can't get their projects off the ground.
— Yale Hirsch (Creator of Stock *Trader's Almanac*, b. 1923)

THURSDAY
7
D 61.9
S 61.9
N 66.7

Establish a no-excuse environment - you will find your own quality will increase as well.
— Jordan Kimmel (Portfolio manager Magnet AE Fund, b. 1958)

FRIDAY
8
D 52.4
S 47.6
N 61.9

As for it being different this time, it is different every time. The question is in what way, and to what extent.
— Tom McClellan (*The McClellan Market Report*)

SATURDAY
9

SUNDAY
10

TRADING THE THANKSGIVING MARKET

For 35 years, the "holiday spirit" gave the Wednesday before Thanksgiving and the Friday after a great track record, except for two occasions. Publishing it in the 1987 *Almanac* was the "kiss of death." Wednesday, Friday, and Monday were all crushed, down 6.6% over the three days in 1987. Since 1988, Wednesday–Friday gained 14 of 24 times, with a total Dow point-gain of 451.20 versus Monday's total Dow point-loss of 619.07, down nine of 14 since 1998. The best strategy appears to be coming into the week long and exiting into strength Friday. Greece's debt crisis cancelled Thanksgiving on Wall Street in 2011.

DOW JONES INDUSTRIALS BEFORE AND AFTER THANKSGIVING

	Tuesday Before	Wednesday Before		Friday After	Total Gain Dow Points	Dow Close	Next Monday
1952	−0.18	1.54		1.22	2.76	283.66	0.04
1953	1.71	0.65		2.45	3.10	280.23	1.14
1954	3.27	1.89		3.16	5.05	387.79	0.72
1955	4.61	0.71		0.26	0.97	482.88	−1.92
1956	−4.49	−2.16		4.65	2.49	472.56	−2.27
1957	−9.04	10.69		3.84	14.53	449.87	−2.96
1958	−4.37	8.63		8.31	16.94	557.46	2.61
1959	2.94	1.41		1.42	2.83	652.52	6.66
1960	−3.44	1.37		4.00	5.37	606.47	−1.04
1961	−0.77	1.10		2.18	3.28	732.60	−0.61
1962	6.73	4.31		7.62	11.93	644.87	−2.81
1963	32.03	−2.52	T	9.52	7.00	750.52	1.39
1964	−1.68	−5.21	H	−0.28	−5.49	882.12	−6.69
1965	2.56	N/C	A	−0.78	−0.78	948.16	−1.23
1966	−3.18	1.84	N	6.52	8.36	803.34	−2.18
1967	13.17	3.07	K	3.58	6.65	877.60	4.51
1968	8.14	−3.17	S	8.76	5.59	985.08	−1.74
1969	−5.61	3.23	G	1.78	5.01	812.30	−7.26
1970	5.21	1.98	I	6.64	8.62	781.35	12.74
1971	−5.18	0.66	V	17.96	18.62	816.59	13.14
1972	8.21	7.29	I	4.67	11.96	1025.21	−7.45
1973	−17.76	10.08	N	−0.98	9.10	854.00	−29.05
1974	5.32	2.03	G	−0.63	1.40	618.66	−15.64
1975	9.76	3.15		2.12	5.27	860.67	−4.33
1976	−6.57	1.66		5.66	7.32	956.62	−6.57
1977	6.41	0.78		1.12	1.90	844.42	−4.85
1978	−1.56	2.95		3.12	6.07	810.12	3.72
1979	−6.05	−1.80		4.35	2.55	811.77	16.98
1980	3.93	7.00		3.66	10.66	993.34	−23.89
1981	18.45	7.90		7.80	15.70	885.94	3.04
1982	−9.01	9.01		7.36	16.37	1007.36	−4.51
1983	7.01	−0.20		1.83	1.63	1277.44	−7.62
1984	9.83	6.40		18.78	25.18	1220.30	−7.95
1985	0.12	18.92		−3.56	15.36	1472.13	−14.22
1986	6.05	4.64		−2.53	2.11	1914.23	−1.55
1987	40.45	−16.58	D	−36.47	−53.05	1910.48	−76.93
1988	11.73	14.58	A	−17.60	−3.02	2074.68	6.76
1989	7.25	17.49	Y	18.77	36.26	2675.55	19.42
1990	−35.15	9.16		−12.13	−2.97	2527.23	5.94
1991	14.08	−16.10		−5.36	−21.46	2894.68	40.70
1992	25.66	17.56		15.94	33.50	3282.20	22.96
1993	3.92	13.41		−3.63	9.78	3683.95	−6.15
1994	−91.52	−3.36		33.64	30.28	3708.27	31.29
1995	40.46	18.06		7.23*	25.29	5048.84	22.04
1996	−19.38	−29.07		22.36*	−6.71	6521.70	N/C
1997	41.03	−14.17		28.35*	14.18	7823.13	189.98
1998	−73.12	13.13		18.80*	31.93	9333.08	−216.53
1999	−93.89	12.54		−19.26*	−6.72	10988.91	−40.99
2000	31.85	−95.18		70.91*	−24.27	10470.23	75.84
2001	−75.08	−66.70		125.03*	58.33	9959.71	23.04
2002	−172.98	255.26		−35.59*	219.67	8896.09	−33.52
2003	16.15	15.63		2.89*	18.52	9782.46	116.59
2004	3.18	27.71		1.92*	29.63	10522.23	−46.33
2005	51.15	44.66		15.53*	60.19	10931.62	−40.90
2006	5.05	5.36		−46.78*	−41.42	12280.17	−158.46
2007	51.70	−211.10		181.84*	−29.26	12980.88	−237.44
2008	36.08	247.14		102.43*	349.57	8829.04	−679.95
2009	−17.24	30.69		−154.48*	−123.79	10309.92	34.92
2010	−142.21	150.91		−95.28*	55.63	11092.00	−39.51
2011	−53.59	−236.17		−25.77*	−261.94	11231.78	291.23

*Shortened trading day

102

Veterans' Day
Monday Before November Expiration, Dow Down 8 of Last 13

MONDAY
D 33.3
S 38.1
N 42.9
11

At a time of war, we need you to work for peace. At a time of inequality, we need you to work for opportunity. At a time of so much cynicism and so much doubt, we need you to make us believe again.
— Barack H. Obama (44th U.S. President, Commencement Wesleyan University 5/28/2008, b. 1961)

TUESDAY
D 57.1
S 52.4
N 57.1
12

Individualism, private property, the law of accumulation of wealth and the law of competition . . . are the highest result of human experience, the soil in which, so far, has produced the best fruit.
— Andrew Carnegie (Scottish-born U.S. industrialist, philanthropist, The Gospel Of Wealth, 1835–1919)

WEDNESDAY
D 61.9
S 57.1
N 61.9
13

Self-discipline is a form of freedom. Freedom from laziness and lethargy, freedom from expectations and demands of others, freedom from weakness and fear—and doubt.
— Harvey A. Dorfman (Sports psychologist, The *Mental ABC's of Pitching*, b. 1935)

THURSDAY
D 61.9
S 57.1
N 57.1
14

All great truths begin as blasphemies.
— George Bernard Shaw (Irish dramatist, 1856–1950)

November Expiration Day, Dow Up 8 of Last 10
Dow Surged in 2008, Up 494 Points (6.5%)

FRIDAY
D 57.1
S 47.6
N 42.9
15

I'm very big on having clarified principles. I don't believe in being reactive. You can't do that in the markets effectively. I can't. I need perspective. I need a game plan.
— Ray Dalio (Money manager, founder Bridgewater Associates, *Fortune* 3/16/2009, b. 1949)

SATURDAY
16

SUNDAY
17

MOST OF THE SO-CALLED "JANUARY EFFECT" TAKES PLACE IN THE LAST HALF OF DECEMBER

Over the years we reported annually on the fascinating January Effect, showing that small-cap stocks handily outperformed large-cap stocks during January 40 out of 43 years between 1953 and 1995. Readers saw that "Cats and Dogs" on average quadrupled the returns of blue chips in this period. Then, the January Effect disappeared over the next four years.

Looking at the graph on page 108, comparing the Russell 1000 index of large-capitalization stocks to the Russell 2000 smaller-capitalization stocks, shows small-cap stocks beginning to outperform the blue chips in mid-December. Narrowing the comparison down to half-month segments was an inspiration and proved to be quite revealing, as you can see in the table below.

25-YEAR AVERAGE RATES OF RETURN (DEC 1987 TO FEB 2012)

From	Russell 1000		Russell 2000	
mid-Dec*	Change	Annualized	Change	Annualized
12/15–12/31	1.9%	53.9%	3.5%	119.9%
12/15–01/15	2.4	31.2	4.2	60.2
12/15–01/31	2.7	24.2	4.4	41.9
12/15–02/15	3.7	24.4	6.2	43.5
12/15–02/28	3.0	16.1	6.0	34.1
end-Dec*				
12/31–01/15	0.4	8.7	0.5	11.0
12/31–01/31	0.5	6.2	0.7	8.7
12/31–02/15	1.4	11.6	2.2	18.7
12/31–02/28	0.7	4.5	1.9	12.6

33-YEAR AVERAGE RATES OF RETURN (DEC 1979 TO FEB 2012)

From	Russell 1000		Russell 2000	
mid-Dec*	Change	Annualized	Change	Annualized
12/15–12/31	1.7%	47.1%	3.0%	96.8%
12/15–01/15	2.4	31.2	4.4	63.8
12/15–01/31	2.7	24.2	4.7	45.3
12/15–02/15	3.4	22.2	6.1	42.7
12/15–02/28	2.9	15.2	6.0	33.4
end-Dec*				
12/31–01/15	0.7	15.8	1.3	31.2
12/31–01/31	1.1	14.0	1.6	21.0
12/31–02/15	1.8	15.1	3.0	26.2
12/31–02/28	1.3	8.3	2.9	19.2

Mid-month dates are the 11th trading day of the month, month end dates are monthly closes

Small-cap strength in the last half of December became even more magnified after the 1987 market crash. Note the dramatic shift in gains in the last half of December during the 25-year period starting in 1987, versus the 33 years from 1979 to 2012. With all the beaten-down small stocks being dumped for tax loss purposes, it generally pays to get a head start on the January Effect in mid-December. You don't have to wait until December either; the small-cap sector often begins to turn around toward the end of October and November.

MONDAY

D 42.9
S 52.4
N 47.6

18

Make sure you have a jester because people in high places are seldom told the truth.
— Radio caller to President Ronald Reagan

TUESDAY

D 47.6
S 52.4
N 47.6

19

Only those who will risk going too far can possibly find out how far one can go.
— T.S. Eliot (English poet, essayist and critic, *The Wasteland*, 1888–1965)

Week Before Thanksgiving, Dow Up 15 of Last 19, 2003 –1.4%, 2004 –0.8%, 2008 –5.3%, 2011 –2.9%

WEDNESDAY

D 52.4
S 47.6
N 57.1

20

Oil has fostered massive corruption in almost every country that has been "blessed" with it, and the expectation that oil wealth will transform economies has lead to disastrous policy choices.
— Ted Tyson (Chief Investment Officer, Mastholm Asset Management)

THURSDAY

D 57.1
S 47.6
N 57.1

21

What investors really get paid for is holding dogs. Small stocks tend to have higher average returns than big stocks, and value stocks tend to have higher average returns than growth stocks.
— Kenneth R. French (Economist, Dartmouth, NBER, b. 1954)

FRIDAY

D 57.1
S 52.4
N 52.4

22

Unless you love EVERYBODY, you can't sell ANYBODY.
— (From Jerry Maguire, 1996)

SATURDAY

23

SUNDAY

24

DECEMBER ALMANAC

DECEMBER								JANUARY						
S	M	T	W	T	F	S		S	M	T	W	T	F	S
1	2	3	4	5	6	7					1	2	3	4
8	9	10	11	12	13	14		5	6	7	8	9	10	11
15	16	17	18	19	20	21		12	13	14	15	16	17	18
22	23	24	25	26	27	28		19	20	21	22	23	24	25
29	30	31						26	27	28	29	30	31	

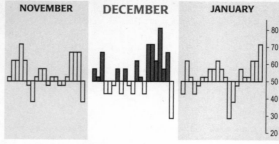

Market Probability Chart above is a graphic representation of the S&P 500 Recent Market Probability Calendar on page 124.

◆ #1 S&P (+1.7%) and #2 Dow (+1.7%) month since 1950 (page 44), #2 NASDAQ (2.0%) since 1971 ◆ 2002 worst December since 1931, down over 6% Dow and S&P, –9.7% on NASDAQ (pages 152, 155, & 157) ◆ "Free lunch" served on Wall Street before Christmas (page 110) ◆ Small caps start to outperform larger caps near middle of month (pages 104 and 108) ◆ "Santa Claus Rally" visible in graph above and on page 112 ◆ In 1998 was part of best fourth quarter since 1928 (page 167) ◆ Fourth quarter expiration week most bullish triple witching week, Dow up 16 of last 21 (page 76) ◆ In post-presidential election years Decembers' rankings slip: #7 S&P and NASDAQ, #5 Dow month.

December Vital Statistics

	DJIA		S&P 500		NASDAQ		Russell 1K		Russell 2K	
Rank	2		1		2		1		1	
Up	44		47		24		26		26	
Down	18		15		17		7		7	
Average % Change	1.7%		1.7%		2.0%		1.7%		2.8%	
Post-Election Year	0.8%		0.4%		0.8%		1.2%		2.6%	
Best & Worst December										
	% Change		% Change		% Change		% Change		% Change	
Best	1991	9.5	1991	11.2	1999	22.0	1991	11.2	1999	11.2
Worst	2002	–6.2	2002	–6.0	2002	–9.7	2002	–5.8	2002	–5.7
Best & Worst December Weeks										
Best	12/2/11	7.0	12/2/11	7.4	12/8/00	10.3	12/2/11	7.4	12/2/11	10.3
Worst	12/4/87	–7.5	12/6/74	–7.1	12/15/00	–9.1	12/4/87	–7.0	12/12/80	–6.5
Best & Worst December Days										
Best	12/16/08	4.2	12/16/08	5.1	12/5/00	10.5	12/16/08	5.2	12/16/08	6.7
Worst	12/1/08	–7.7	12/1/08	–8.9	12/1/08	–9.0	12/1/08	–9.1	12/1/08	–11.9
First Trading Day of Expiration Week: 1980–2011										
Record (#Up–#Down)	18–14		19–13		13–19		19–13		14–18	
Current streak	D1		D1		D2		D2		D2	
Avg % Change	0.15		0.10		–0.10		0.07		–0.21	
Options Expiration Day: 1980–2011										
Record (#Up–#Down)	21–11		24–8		23–9		24–8		21–11	
Current streak	D2		U6		U6		U6		U5	
Avg % Change	0.37		0.43		0.39		0.41		0.45	
Options Expiration Week: 1980–2011										
Record (#Up–#Down)	24–8		23–9		18–14		22–10		16–16	
Current streak	D1		D1		D1		D1		D1	
Avg % Change	0.66		0.66		0.12		0.60		0.45	
Week After Options Expiration: 1980–2011										
Record (#Up–#Down)	22–9		19–13		20–12		1–13		22–10	
Current streak	U3		U3		U3		U3		U3	
Avg % Change	0.79		0.52		0.71		0.55		0.87	
First Trading Day Performance										
% of Time Up	48.4		51.6		63.4		54.5		54.5	
Avg % Change	–0.05		–0.03		0.17		–0.03		–0.08	
Last Trading Day Performance										
% of Time Up	53.2		61.3		73.2		51.5		69.7	
Avg % Change	0.06		0.10		0.34		–0.09		0.45	

Dow & S&P 1950–April 2012, NASDAQ 1971–April 2012, Russell 1K & 2K 1979–April 2012.

If Santa Claus should fail to call,
Bears may come to Broad and Wall.

NOVEMBER/DECEMBER

Trading Thanksgiving Market: Long into Weakness Prior,
Exit into Strength After (Page 102)

MONDAY
D 66.7
S 66.7
N 57.1
25

Benjamin Graham was correct in suggesting that while the stock market in the short run may be a voting
mechanism, in the long run it is a weighing mechanism. True value will win out in the end.
— Burton G. Malkiel (Economist, April 2003 Princeton Paper, *A Random Walk Down Wall Street*, b. 1932)

TUESDAY
D 61.9
S 66.7
N 57.1
26

Every man with a new idea is a crank until the idea succeeds.
— Mark Twain (American novelist and satirist, pen name of Samuel Longhorne Clemens, 1835–1910)

WEDNESDAY
D 52.4
S 66.7
N 66.7
27

The task of leadership is not to put greatness into humanity, but to elicit it, for the greatness is already there.
— Sir John Buchan (Scottish author, Governor General of Canada 1935–1940, 1875–1940)

Thanksgiving and Chanukah (Market Closed)

THURSDAY
28

I'd be a bum on the street with a tin cup, if the markets were always efficient.
— Warren Buffett (CEO Berkshire Hathaway, investor & philanthropist, b. 1930)

(Shortened Trading Day)
Last Trading Day of November, S&P Up 5 of Last 6

FRIDAY
D 52.4
S 38.1
N 52.4
29

If there is something you really want to do, make your plan and do it. Otherwise, you'll just regret it forever.
— Richard Rocco (PostNet franchisee, Entrepreneur Magazine 12/2006, b. 1946)

SATURDAY
30

December Almanac Investor Seasonalities: See Pages 92, 94 and 96

SUNDAY
1

JANUARY EFFECT NOW STARTS IN MID-DECEMBER

Small-cap stocks tend to outperform big caps in January. Known as the "January Effect," the tendency is clearly revealed by the graph below. Thirty-four years of daily data for the Russell 2000 index of smaller companies are divided by the Russell 1000 index of largest companies, and then compressed into a single year to show an idealized yearly pattern. When the graph is descending, big blue chips are outperforming smaller companies; when the graph is rising, smaller companies are moving up faster than their larger brethren.

In a typical year, the smaller fry stay on the sidelines while the big boys are on the field. Then, around late October, small stocks begin to wake up, and in mid-December, they take off. Anticipated year-end dividends, payouts, and bonuses could be a factor. Other major moves are quite evident just before Labor Day—possibly because individual investors are back from vacations—and off the low points in late October and November. Small caps hold the lead through the beginning of May.

RUSSELL 2000/RUSSELL 1000 ONE-YEAR SEASONAL PATTERN

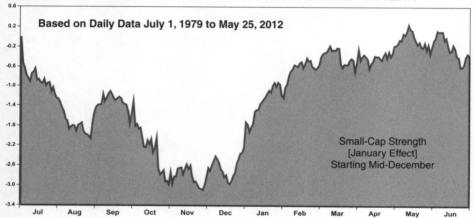

Based on Daily Data July 1, 1979 to May 25, 2012

Small-Cap Strength
[January Effect]
Starting Mid-December

The bottom graph shows the actual ratio of the Russell 2000 divided by the Russell 1000 from 1979. Smaller companies had the upper hand for five years into 1983, as the last major bear trend wound to a close and the nascent bull market logged its first year. After falling behind for about eight years, they came back after the Persian Gulf War bottom in 1990, moving up until 1994, when big caps ruled the latter stages of the millennial bull. For six years, the picture was bleak for small fry, as the blue chips and tech stocks moved to stratospheric PE ratios. Small caps spiked in late 1999 and early 2000 and reached a peak in early 2006, as the four-year-old bull entered its final year. Note how the small-cap advantage has waned during major bull moves and intensified during weak market times. Look for a clear move lower to confirm a major bull move is in place.

RUSSELL 2000/RUSSELL 1000 (1979 TO APRIL 2012)

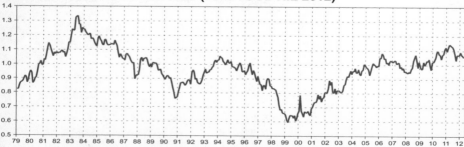

DECEMBER

MONDAY

D 52.4
S 57.1
N 71.4

2

To succeed in the markets, it is essential to make your own decisions. Numerous traders cited listening to others as their worst blunder.
— Jack D. Schwager (Investment manager, author, *Stock Market Wizards: Interviews with America's Top Stock Traders*, b. 1948)

TUESDAY

D 47.6
S 52.4
N 66.7

3

There are ways for the individual investor to make money in the securities markets. Buying value and holding long term while collecting dividends has been proven over and over again.
— Robert M. Sharp (Author, *The Lore and Legends of Wall Street*)

WEDNESDAY

D 61.9
S 66.7
N 66.7

4

People who can take a risk, who believe in themselves enough to walk away [from a company] are generally people who bring about change.
— Cynthia Danaher (Exiting GM of Hewlett-Packard's Medical Products Group, *Newsweek*)

THURSDAY

D 57.1
S 42.9
N 52.4

5

Never overpay for a stock. More money is lost than in any other way by projecting above-average growth and paying an extra multiple for it.
— Charles Neuhauser (Bear Stearns)

FRIDAY

D 42.9
S 42.9
N 38.1

6

You have to find something that you love enough to be able to take risks, jump over the hurdles and break through the brick walls that are always going to be placed in front of you. If you don't have that kind of feeling for what it is you're doing, you'll stop at the first giant hurdle.
— George Lucas (Star Wars director)

SATURDAY

7

SUNDAY

8

WALL STREET'S ONLY "FREE LUNCH" SERVED BEFORE CHRISTMAS

Investors tend to get rid of their losers near year-end for tax purposes, often hammering these stocks down to bargain levels. Over the years, the *Almanac* has shown that NYSE stocks selling at their lows on December 15 will usually outperform the market by February 15 in the following year. Preferred stocks, closed-end funds, splits, and new issues are eliminated. When there are a huge number of new lows, stocks down the most are selected, even though there are usually good reasons why some stocks have been battered.

BARGAIN STOCKS VS. THE MARKET*

Short Span* Late Dec–Jan/Feb	New Lows Late Dec	% Change Jan/Feb	% Change NYSE Composite	Bargain Stocks Advantage
1974–75	112	48.9%	22.1%	26.8%
1975–76	21	34.9	14.9	20.0
1976–77	2	1.3	−3.3	4.6
1977–78	15	2.8	−4.5	7.3
1978–79	43	11.8	3.9	7.9
1979–80	5	9.3	6.1	3.2
1980–81	14	7.1	−2.0	9.1
1981–82	21	−2.6	−7.4	4.8
1982–83	4	33.0	9.7	23.3
1983–84	13	−3.2	−3.8	0.6
1984–85	32	19.0	12.1	6.9
1985–86	4	−22.5	3.9	−26.4
1986–87	22	9.3	12.5	−3.2
1987–88	23	13.2	6.8	6.4
1988–89	14	30.0	6.4	23.6
1989–90	25	−3.1	−4.8	1.7
1990–91	18	18.8	12.6	6.2
1991–92	23	51.1	7.7	43.4
1992–93	9	8.7	0.6	8.1
1993–94	10	−1.4	2.0	−3.4
1994–95	25	14.6	5.7	8.9
1995–96	5	−11.3	4.5	−15.8
1996–97	16	13.9	11.2	2.7
1997–98	29	9.9	5.7	4.2
1998–99	40	−2.8	4.3	−7.1
1999–00	26	8.9	−5.4	14.3
2000–01	51	44.4	0.1	44.3
2001–02	12	31.4	−2.3	33.7
2002–03	33	28.7	3.9	24.8
2003–04	15	16.7	2.3	14.4
2004–05	36	6.8	−2.8	9.6
2005–06	71	12.0	2.6	9.4
2006–07	43	5.1	−0.5	5.6
2007–08	71	−3.2	−9.4	6.2
2008–09	88	11.4	−2.4	13.8
2009–10	25	1.8	−3.0	4.8
2010–11	20	8.3%	3.4%	4.9%
2011–12	65	18.1%	6.1%	12.0%
38-Year Totals		**481.1%**	**119.5%**	**361.6%**
Average		**12.7%**	**3.1%**	**9.5%**

* Dec 15 – Feb 15 (1974–1999), Dec 1999–2012 based on actual newsletter advice

In response to changing market conditions, we tweaked the strategy the last 13 years, adding selections from NASDAQ, AMEX, and the OTC Bulletin Board and selling in mid-January some years. We e-mail the list of stocks to our *Almanac Investor* newsletter subscribers. Visit *www.stocktradersalmanac.com,* or see the insert for additional details and a special offer for new subscribers.

We have come to the conclusion that the most prudent course of action is to compile our list from the stocks making new lows on Triple-Witching Friday before Christmas, capitalizing on the Santa Claus Rally (page 112). This also gives us the weekend to evaluate the issues in greater depth and weed out any glaringly problematic stocks. Subscribers will receive the list of stocks selected from the new lows made on December 21, 2012 and December 20, 2013 via e-mail.

This "Free Lunch" strategy is only an extremely short-term strategy reserved for the nimblest traders. It has performed better after market corrections and when there are more new lows to choose from. The object is to buy bargain stocks near their 52-week lows and sell any quick, generous gains, as these issues can often be real dogs.

MONDAY

D 47.6
S 47.6
N 52.4

9

History is a collection of agreed upon lies.
— Voltaire (French philosopher, 1694–1778)

TUESDAY

D 57.1
S 57.1
N 52.4

10

What lies behind us and what lies before us are tiny matters, compared to what lies within us.
— Ralph Waldo Emerson (American author, poet and philosopher, *Self-Reliance*, 1803–1882)

WEDNESDAY

D 52.4
S 42.9
N 42.9

11

The secret to business is to know something that nobody else knows.
— Aristotle Onassis (Greek shipping billionaire)

Small Cap Strength Starts in Mid-December (Page 104)

THURSDAY

D 52.4
S 57.1
N 47.6

12

The first panacea for a mismanaged nation is inflation of the currency; the second is war. Both bring a temporary prosperity; both bring a permanent ruin. But both are the refuge of political and economic opportunists.
— Ernest Hemingway (American writer, 1954 Nobel Prize, 1899–1961)

FRIDAY

D 52.4
S 47.6
N 42.9

13

Experience is helpful, but it is judgment that matters.
— General Colin Powell (Chairman Joint Chiefs 1989–93, Secretary of State 2001–05, *NY Times* 10/22/2008, b. 1937)

SATURDAY

14

SUNDAY

15

IF SANTA CLAUS SHOULD FAIL TO CALL, BEARS MAY COME TO BROAD AND WALL

Santa Claus tends to come to Wall Street nearly every year, bringing a short, sweet, respectable rally within the last five days of the year and the first two in January. This has been good for an average 1.6% gain since 1969 (1.5% since 1950). Santa's failure to show tends to precede bear markets, or times stocks could be purchased later in the year at much lower prices. We discovered this phenomenon in 1972.

DAILY % CHANGE IN S&P 500 AT YEAR END

	Trading Days Before Year End						First Days in January			Rally %
	6	5	4	3	2	1	1	2	3	Change
1969	−0.4	1.1	0.8	−0.7	0.4	0.5	1.0	0.5	−0.7	3.6
1970	0.1	0.6	0.5	1.1	0.2	−0.1	−1.1	0.7	0.6	1.9
1971	−0.4	0.2	1.0	0.3	−0.4	0.3	−0.4	0.4	1.0	1.3
1972	−0.3	−0.7	0.6	0.4	0.5	1.0	0.9	0.4	−0.1	3.1
1973	−1.1	−0.7	3.1	2.1	−0.2	0.01	0.1	2.2	−0.9	6.7
1974	−1.4	1.4	0.8	−0.4	0.03	2.1	2.4	0.7	0.5	7.2
1975	0.7	0.8	0.9	−0.1	−0.4	0.5	0.8	1.8	1.0	4.3
1976	0.1	1.2	0.7	−0.4	0.5	0.5	−0.4	−1.2	−0.9	0.8
1977	0.8	0.9	0.0	0.1	0.2	0.2	−1.3	−0.3	−0.8	−0.3
1978	0.03	1.7	1.3	−0.9	−0.4	−0.2	0.6	1.1	0.8	3.3
1979	−0.6	0.1	0.1	0.2	−0.1	0.1	−2.0	−0.5	1.2	−2.2
1980	−0.4	0.4	0.5	−1.1	0.2	0.3	0.4	1.2	0.1	2.0
1981	−0.5	0.2	−0.2	−0.5	0.5	0.2	0.2	−2.2	−0.7	−1.8
1982	0.6	1.8	−1.0	0.3	−0.7	0.2	−1.6	2.2	0.4	1.2
1983	−0.2	−0.03	0.9	0.3	−0.2	0.05	−0.5	1.7	1.2	2.1
1984	−0.5	0.8	−0.2	−0.4	0.3	0.6	−1.1	−0.5	−0.5	−0.6
1985	−1.1	−0.7	0.2	0.9	0.5	0.3	−0.8	0.6	−0.1	1.1
1986	−1.0	0.2	0.1	−0.9	−0.5	−0.5	1.8	2.3	0.2	2.4
1987	1.3	−0.5	−2.6	−0.4	1.3	−0.3	3.6	1.1	0.1	2.2
1988	−0.2	0.3	−0.4	0.1	0.8	−0.6	−0.9	1.5	0.2	0.9
1989	0.6	0.8	−0.2	0.6	0.5	0.8	1.8	−0.3	−0.9	4.1
1990	0.5	−0.6	0.3	−0.8	0.1	0.5	−1.1	−1.4	−0.3	−3.0
1991	2.5	0.6	1.4	0.4	2.1	0.5	0.04	0.5	−0.3	5.7
1992	−0.3	0.2	−0.1	−0.3	0.2	−0.7	−0.1	−0.2	0.04	−1.1
1993	0.01	0.7	0.1	−0.1	−0.4	−0.5	−0.2	0.3	0.1	−0.1
1994	0.01	0.2	0.4	−0.3	0.1	−0.4	−0.03	0.3	−0.1	0.2
1995	0.8	0.2	0.4	0.04	−0.1	0.3	0.8	0.1	−0.6	1.8
1996	−0.3	0.5	0.6	0.1	−0.4	−1.7	−0.5	1.5	−0.1	0.1
1997	−1.5	−0.7	0.4	1.8	1.8	−0.04	0.5	0.2	−1.1	4.0
1998	2.1	−0.2	−0.1	1.3	−0.8	−0.2	−0.1	1.4	2.2	1.3
1999	1.6	−0.1	0.04	0.4	0.1	0.3	−1.0	−3.8	0.2	−4.0
2000	0.8	2.4	0.7	1.0	0.4	−1.0	−2.8	5.0	−1.1	5.7
2001	0.4	−0.02	0.4	0.7	0.3	−1.1	0.6	0.9	0.6	1.8
2002	0.2	−0.5	−0.3	−1.6	0.5	0.05	3.3	−0.05	2.2	1.2
2003	0.3	−0.2	0.2	1.2	0.01	0.2	−0.3	1.2	0.1	2.4
2004	0.1	−0.4	0.7	−0.01	0.01	−0.1	−0.8	−1.2	−0.4	−1.8
2005	0.4	0.04	−1.0	0.1	−0.3	−0.5	1.6	0.4	0.002	0.4
2006	−0.4	−0.5	0.4	0.7	−0.1	−0.5	−0.1	0.1	−0.6	0.003
2007	1.7	0.8	0.1	−1.4	0.1	−0.7	−1.4	0.0	−2.5	−2.5
2008	−1.0	0.6	0.5	−0.4	2.4	1.4	3.2	−0.5	0.8	7.4
2009	0.2	0.5	0.1	−0.1	0.02	−1.0	1.6	0.3	0.05	1.4
2010	−0.2	0.1	0.1	0.1	−0.2	−0.02	1.1	−0.1	0.5	1.1
2011	0.8	0.9	0.01	−1.3	1.1	−0.4	1.6	0.02	0.3	1.9
Avg	0.11	0.33	0.28	0.05	0.23	0.01	0.22	0.43	0.04	1.6

The couplet above was certainly on the mark in 1999, as the period suffered a horrendous 4.0% loss. On January 14, 2000, the Dow started its 33-month 37.8% slide to the October 2002 midterm election year bottom. NASDAQ cracked eight weeks later, falling 37.3% in 10 weeks, eventually dropping 77.9% by October 2002. Saddam Hussein cancelled Christmas by invading Kuwait in 1990. Energy prices and Middle East terror woes may have grounded Santa in 2004. In 2007, the third worst reading since 1950 was recorded, as subprime mortgages and their derivatives led to a full-blown financial crisis and the second worst bear market in history.

DECEMBER

Monday Before December Triple Witching S&P Up 8 of Last 12

MONDAY

D 47.6
S 42.9
N 47.6

16

The more feted by the media, the worse a pundit's accuracy.
— Sharon Begley (Senior editor *Newsweek*, 2/23/2009, referencing Philip E. Tetlock's 2005 *Expert Political Judgment*)

December Triple Witching Week, S&P Up 22 of Last 28
2009 Broke 8-Year Bull Run

TUESDAY

D 57.1
S 61.9
N 52.4

17

Sight and Sound function differently in the mind, with sound being the surer investment. WIN THE EARS OF THE PEOPLE, THEIR EYES WILL FOLLOW.
— Roy H. Williams (*The Wizard of Ads*)

FOMC Meeting (2 Days)

WEDNESDAY

D 47.6
S 52.4
N 42.9

18

The inherent vice of capitalism is the unequal sharing of blessings; the inherent virtue of socialism is the equal sharing of miseries.
— Winston Churchill (British statesman, 1874–1965)

THURSDAY

D 47.6
S 42.9
N 52.4

19

That's the American way. If little kids don't aspire to make money like I did, what the hell good is this country?
— Lee Iacocca (American industrialist, Former Chrysler CEO, b. 1924)

December Triple Witching, S&P Up 22 of 30,
Average Gain 0.4%

FRIDAY

D 76.2
S 71.4
N 57.1

20

If there's anything duller than being on a board in Corporate America, I haven't found it.
— H. Ross Perot (American businessman, *NY Times*, 10/28/92, 2-time presidential candidate 1992 & 1996, b. 1930)

SATURDAY

21

The Only FREE LUNCH on Wall Street is Served (Page 110)
Almanac Investors Emailed Alert Before the Open, Monday (See Insert)

SUNDAY

22

BEST INVESTMENT BOOK OF THE YEAR

What's Behind the Numbers: A Guide to Exposing Financial Chicanery and Avoiding Huge Losses in Your Portfolio

By John Del Vecchio and Tom Jacobs

As we prepared for our annual Best Six Months Sell Signal back in March 2012 we began informing readers that we would be recommending the **AdvisorShares Active Bear ETF** (HDGE) exchange traded fund for our defensive play this year in addition to the bond ETFs. HDGE produced better results in down markets than the mutual funds we had recommended in previous years, and now that it had been trading for more than a year with healthy volume we were comfortable using it as our Worst Six Months timing vehicle. Being an ETF, fees are much lower than the mutual funds and you can trade in and out of it intraday like any stock. It was a no brainer.

We began revealing our bearish outlook in April 2012 and our downside protection picks for the Worst Six Months. We spoke frequently about HDGE and added it to the *Almanac Investor* ETF Portfolio on April 3 at 20.63 on our Sell Signal. At the end of May HDGE was up 18.5% and climbing as the major U.S. equity indices were down 6 to 9% and falling. *(Full Disclosure: At press time the Editor in Chief held a position in HDGE.)*

Our coverage of HDGE initiated a dialogue with the portfolio managers. They of course were pleased we were recommending their ETF and wanted us to be fully aware of the fund's inner workings and holdings. After several discussions and exchanges we had a candid conversation with HDGE's portfolio managers, John Del Vecchio and Brad Lamensdorf, that was published May 10, 2012, in the Investor Alert "Inside the Bear's Lair" at *www.stocktradersalmanac.com*.

Then Mr. Del Vecchio sent us a review copy of his upcoming book. Once we began to pour through it we knew this had to be our 2013 Best Investment Book of the Year. In a witty, pithy, and easy-to-read style Del Vecchio and co-author Tom Jacobs show you how to uncover *What's Behind the Numbers*. Under their tutelage forensic accounting is reduced to Math 101. You will learn how to employ the metrics they use to expose financial chicanery in companies and unearth the best short sales and to protect yourself from owning those stocks most likely to blow up and wreak havoc on your portfolio.

We have long believed that the price-to-sales ratio was the best metric for stock valuation as revenue is much harder to manipulate than earnings. This concept was made famous by renowned money manager Ken Fisher in the 1980s and affirmed by James P. O'Shaughnessy in his landmark book, *What Works on Wall Street*. But as companies and their managers have come increasingly under pressure to meet and exceed expectations they have developed ever-better ways to manipulate revenue as well as earnings. Del Vecchio and Jacobs teach us how to better value stocks by understanding and recognizing aggressive revenue recognition, excessive accounts receivable, and the power of earnings quality. Read *What's Behind the Numbers* so you can keep your portfolio clear of ticking stock bombs.

McGraw-Hill, $30.00, *http://www.deljacobs.com*. **2013 Best Investment Book of the Year**.

YEAR'S TOP INVESTMENT BOOKS

The Little Book of Stock Market Cycles, Jeffrey A. Hirsch, Wiley, $22.95. Forty-six years of research and analysis into why these cycles occur with the historical evidence to prove it. Don't subscribe to the buy-and-hold mantra. Simple, actionable ideas that have stood the test of time and consistently outperformed the market.

(continued on page 116)

DECEMBER

Watch for the Santa Claus Rally (Page 112)

MONDAY
D 71.4
S 71.4
N 76.2
23

Over the last 25 years, computer processing capacity has risen more than a millionfold, while communication capacity has risen over a thousandfold.
— Richard Worzel (Futurist, *Facing the Future*, b. 1950)

(Shortened Trading Day)
Last Trading Day Before Christmas, Dow Up Last 5 Years

TUESDAY
D 57.1
S 61.9
N 66.7
24

[The Fed] is very smart, but [it] doesn't run the markets. In the end, the markets will run [the Fed]. The markets are bigger than any man or any group of men. The markets can even break a president...
— Richard Russell (*Dow Theory Letters*, 8/4/04)

Christmas Day (Market Closed)

WEDNESDAY
25

We do not believe any group of men adequate enough or wise enough to operate without scrutiny or without criticism... the only way to avoid error is to detect it, that the only way to detect it is to be free to inquire... in secrecy error undetected will flourish and subvert.
— J. Robert Oppenheimer (American physicist, father of A-bomb, 1904–1967)

THURSDAY
D 85.7
S 81.0
N 76.2
26

We can guarantee cash benefits as far out and at whatever size you like, but we cannot guarantee their purchasing power.
— Alan Greenspan (Fed Chairman 1987–2006, on funding Social Security to Senate Banking Committee 2/15/05)

FRIDAY
D 57.1
S 57.1
N 57.1
27

I'm not better than the next trader, just quicker at admitting my mistakes and moving on to the next opportunity.
— George Soros (Financier, philanthropist, political activist, author and philosopher, b. 1930)

SATURDAY
28

January Almanac Investor Seasonalities: See Pages 92, 94 and 96

SUNDAY
29

YEAR'S TOP INVESTMENT BOOKS

(continued from page 114)

The Indomitable Investor: Why a Few Succeed in the Stock Market When Everyone Else Fails, Steven M. Sears, Wiley, $29.95. *Barron's* columnist and options expert candidly enlightens us with what makes the market tick.

Backstage Wall Street: An Insider's Guide to Knowing Who to Trust, Who to Run From, and How to Maximize Your Investments, Joshua M. Brown, McGraw-Hill, $28.00. Sometimes barbed, always salient and entertaining, Brown's stock broker experiences will help you avoid many portfolio pitfalls.

Mastering Elliott Wave Principle: Elementary Concepts, Wave Patterns, and Practice Exercises, Constance Brown, Bloomberg Press, $75.00. Serious technical analysis, not for the faint of heart. Ms. Brown's *Technical Analysis for the Trading Professional*, 2nd Edition, is required reading for the Market Technicians Association's final CMT (Chartered Market Technician) certification exam.

The Behavior Gap: Simple Ways to Stop Doing Dumb Things with Money, Carl Richards, Portfolio/Penguin, $24.95. We keep a signed framed copy of Carl's iconic drawing on our wall: "Greed/Buy, Fear/Sell ... Repeat Until Broke!" Cocktail-napkin charting on steroids.

Survival of the Fittest for Investors: Using Darwin's Laws of Evolution to Build a Winning Portfolio, Dick Stoken, McGraw-Hill, $29.95. Shows how, with heightened insight and a powerful algorithm, you can survive and thrive in volatile markets by following the simple principles of evolution.

The Trader's Book of Volume: The Definitive Guide to Volume Trading, Mark Leibovit, McGraw-Hill, $50.00. Shows how to use volume to identify and assess the strength of trade-worthy trends. Also provides in-depth techniques and strategies for trading volume indicators for profit.

Markets Never Forget (But People Do): How Your Memory Is Costing You Money—and Why This Time Isn't Different, Ken Fisher and Lara Hoffmans, Wiley, $29.95. Billion-dollar money manager and market sage insists that we remember the past and profit from history.

Investing Without Wall Street: The Five Essentials of Financial Freedom, Sheldon Jacobs, Wiley, $24.00. A skeptical, clearheaded approach to investing. Complete portfolio diversification with only two funds. Use the media to get the best advice and recommendations.

The Era of Uncertainty: Global Investment Strategies for Inflation, Deflation, and the Middle Ground, Francois Trahan, Katherine Krantz, Wiley, $29.95. Proof that macro matters. Macro trends will be important for investment success during the next several years of tumultuous market conditions and crucial for spotting the next boom.

Gents with No Cents, Ron DeLegge II, Half Full Publishing, $24.99. Take a walk on the light side of Wall Street.

The Reinventors: How Extraordinary Companies Pursue Radical Continuous Change, Jason Jennings, Portfolio/Penguin, $26.95. Bestselling author Jennings explores the most urgent question facing companies today: How do you continually adapt, grow, and stay vital when the game rules always change?

End This Depression NOW!, Paul Krugman, Norton, $24.95. Nobelist Krugman tells us that what we need now for a rapid, powerful recovery is a burst of government spending to jumpstart the economy.

That Used To Be Us: How America Fell Behind in the World It Invented and How We Can Come Back, Thomas L. Friedman and Michael Mandelbaum, Farrar, Straus and Giroux, $28.00. Authors show how America's history offers a 5-part formula for prosperity that will enable us to cope with future challenges.

Economic Warfare: Secrets of Wealth Creation in the Age of Welfare Politics, Ziad K. Abdelnour, Wiley, $34.95. Ziad stirs up the fire in the belly of America and revives our "animal spirits" in a call to rein in wasteful government so our economy can thrive.

Private Empire: ExxonMobil and American Power, Steve Coll, Penguin, $36.00. This is the first hard-hitting book-length examination of the word's most powerful and notoriously secretive company.

Breakout Nations: In Pursuit of the Next Economic Miracles, Ruchir Sharma, Norton, $26.95. Morgan Stanley Emerging Markets head reassesses former superstars of emerging markets and highlights lesser-known economies that, even in these tough times, are poised to become the new breakout nations.

Why Nations Fail: The Origins of Power, Prosperity, and Poverty, Daron Acemoglu and James A. Robinson, Crown Business, $30.00. From the Roman Empire through modern times the authors illustrate the common causes behind success and failure and what can be done to build widespread prosperity.

The Third Industrial Revolution: How Lateral Power Is Transforming Energy, the Economy, and the World, Jeremy Rifkin, Palgrave Macmillan, $27.00. Just imagine hundreds of millions of people producing their own green energy in their homes, offices, and factories, and sharing it on an "energy Internet."

DECEMBER/JANUARY 2014

MONDAY
D 47.6
S 66.7
N 57.1
30

We may face more inflation pressure than currently shows up in formal data.
— William Poole (Economist, president Federal Reserve Bank St. Louis 1998–2008, June 2006 speech, b. 1937)

Last Trading Day of the Year, NASDAQ Down 11 of last 12
NASDAQ Was Up 29 Years in a Row 1971–1999

TUESDAY
D 38.1
S 28.6
N 47.6
31

Our philosophy here is identifying change, anticipating change. Change is what drives earnings growth, and if you identify the underlying change, you recognize the growth before the market, and the deceleration of that growth.
— Peter Vermilye (Baring America Asset Management, 1987)

New Year's Day

WEDNESDAY
1

There is a habitual nature to society and human activity. People's behavior and what they do with their money and time bears upon economics and the stock market.
— Jeffrey A. Hirsch (Editor, *Stock Trader's Almanac*, b. 1966)

Small Caps Punished First Trading Day of Year
Russell 2000 Down 14 of Last 23, But Up Last 4

THURSDAY
D 66.7
S 42.9
N 61.9
2

When you're one step ahead of the crowd, you're a genius. When you're two steps ahead, you're a crackpot.
— Shlomo Riskin (Rabbi, author, b. 1940)

Second Trading Day of the Year, Dow Up 14 of Last 19
Santa Claus Rally Ends (Page 112)

FRIDAY
D 66.7
S 61.9
N 66.7
3

Our firm conviction is that, sooner or later, capitalism will give way to socialism . . . We will bury you.
— Nikita Khrushchev (Soviet leader 1953–1964, 1894–1971)

SATURDAY
4

SUNDAY
5

2014 STRATEGY CALENDAR

(Option expiration dates circled)

	MONDAY	TUESDAY	WEDNESDAY	THURSDAY	FRIDAY	SATURDAY	SUNDAY
JANUARY	30	31	1 JANUARY New Year's Day	2	3	4	5
	6	7	8	9	10	11	12
	13	14	15	16	(17)	18	19
	20 Martin Luther King Day	21	22	23	24	25	26
	27	28	29	30	31	1 FEBRUARY	2
FEBRUARY	3	4	5	6	7	8	9
	10	11	12	13	14 ♥	15	16
	17 Presidents' Day	18	19	20	(21)	22	23
	24	25	26	27	28	1 MARCH	2
MARCH	3	4	5 Ash Wednesday	6	7	8	9 Daylight Saving Time Begins
	10	11	12	13	14	15	16
	17 ♣ St. Patrick's Day	18	19	20	(21)	22	23
	24	25	26	27	28	29	30
APRIL	31	1 APRIL	2	3	4	5	6
	7	8	9	10	11	12	13
	14	15 Tax Deadline Passover	16	(17)	18 Good Friday	19	20 Easter
	21	22	23	24	25	26	27
	28	29	30	1 MAY	2	3	4
MAY	5	6	7	8	9	10	11 Mother's Day
	12	13	14	15	(16)	17	18
	19	20	21	22	23	24	25
	26 Memorial Day	27	28	29	30	31	1 JUNE
JUNE	2	3	4	5	6	7	8
	9	10	11	12	13	14	15 Father's Day
	16	17	18	19	(20)	21	22
	23	24	25	26	27	28	29

Market closed on shaded weekdays; closes early when half-shaded.

2014 STRATEGY CALENDAR
(Option expiration dates circled)

MONDAY	TUESDAY	WEDNESDAY	THURSDAY	FRIDAY	SATURDAY	SUNDAY	
30	1	2	3	4 Independence Day	5	6	JULY
7	8	9	10	11	12	13	
14	15	16	17	(18)	19	20	
21	22	23	24	25	26	27	
28	29	30	31	1 AUGUST	2	3	
4	5	6	7	8	9	10	AUGUST
11	12	13	14	(15)	16	17	
18	19	20	21	22	23	24	
25	26	27	28	29	30	31	
1 SEPTEMBER Labor Day	2	3	4	5	6	7	SEPTEMBER
8	9	10	11	12	13	14	
15	16	17	18	(19)	20	21	
22	23	24	25 Rosh Hashanah	26	27	28	
29	30	1 OCTOBER	2	3	4 Yom Kippur	5	OCTOBER
6	7	8	9	10	11	12	
13 Columbus Day	14	15	16	(17)	18	19	
20	21	22	23	24	25	26	
27	28	29	30	31	1 NOVEMBER	2 Daylight Saving Time Ends	
3	4 Election Day	5	6	7	8	9	NOVEMBER
10	11 Veterans' Day	12	13	14	15	16	
17	18	19	20	(21)	22	23	
24	25	26	27 Thanksgiving	28	29	30	
1 DECEMBER	2	3	4	5	6	7	DECEMBER
8	9	10	11	12	13	14	
15	16	17	18	(19)	20 Chanukah	21	
22	23	24	25 Christmas	26	27	28	
29	30	31	1 JANUARY New Year's Day	2	3	4	

DIRECTORY OF TRADING PATTERNS AND DATABANK

CONTENTS

DOW JONES INDUSTRIALS MARKET PROBABILITY CALENDAR 2013

THE % CHANCE OF THE MARKET RISING ON ANY TRADING DAY OF THE YEAR*
(Based on the number of times the DJIA rose on a particular trading day during January 1953 to December 2011)

Date	Jan	Feb	Mar	Apr	May	Jun	Jul	Aug	Sep	Oct	Nov	Dec
1	H	59.3	64.4	61.0	57.6	S	64.4	45.8	S	47.5	61.0	S
2	57.6	S	S	59.3	66.1	S	59.3	45.8	H	59.3	S	45.8
3	72.9	S	S	54.2	49.2	55.9	61.0	S	59.3	50.8	S	54.2
4	49.2	55.9	64.4	59.3	S	54.2	H	S	57.6	61.0	52.5	64.4
5	S	37.3	59.3	54.2	S	50.8	57.6	49.2	57.6	S	67.8	57.6
6	S	54.2	49.2	S	49.2	55.9	S	50.8	45.8	S	57.6	45.8
7	55.9	47.5	45.8	S	44.1	50.8	S	54.2	S	45.8	47.5	S
8	45.8	40.7	54.2	57.6	52.5	S	64.4	44.1	S	52.5	59.3	S
9	47.5	S	S	61.0	50.8	S	55.9	47.5	49.2	44.1	S	44.1
10	47.5	S	S	62.7	50.8	44.1	50.8	S	44.1	39.0	S	54.2
11	49.2	45.8	59.3	55.9	S	37.3	40.7	S	55.9	54.2	50.8	57.6
12	S	61.0	54.2	71.2	S	55.9	62.7	49.2	59.3	S	61.0	45.8
13	S	45.8	54.2	S	45.8	61.0	S	45.8	45.8	S	47.5	52.5
14	57.6	47.5	52.5	S	54.2	59.3	S	62.7	S	59.3	49.2	S
15	55.9	54.2	59.3	64.4	54.2	S	49.2	57.6	S	52.5	57.6	S
16	59.3	S	S	55.9	44.1	S	45.8	50.8	54.2	50.8	S	45.8
17	37.3	S	S	57.6	52.5	49.2	50.8	S	54.2	42.4	S	57.6
18	35.6	H	62.7	54.2	S	47.5	50.8	S	39.0	61.0	49.2	47.5
19	S	39.0	57.6	55.9	S	50.8	42.4	47.5	49.2	S	49.2	54.2
20	S	49.2	52.5	S	45.8	45.8	S	55.9	45.8	S	50.8	57.6
21	H	50.8	39.0	S	49.2	40.7	S	61.0	S	50.8	64.4	S
22	40.7	35.6	47.5	49.2	42.4	S	47.5	49.2	S	47.5	57.6	S
23	59.3	S	S	52.5	33.9	S	49.2	52.5	40.7	44.1	S	50.8
24	47.5	S	S	52.5	49.2	37.3	47.5	S	52.5	47.5	S	61.0
25	55.9	45.8	45.8	57.6	S	47.5	59.3	S	55.9	27.1	64.4	H
26	S	59.3	55.9	54.2	S	45.8	50.8	49.2	52.5	S	59.3	71.2
27	S	45.8	42.4	S	H	54.2	S	45.8	49.2	S	52.5	49.2
28	59.3	52.5	40.7	S	44.1	52.5	S	57.6	S	54.2	H	S
29	52.5		H	49.2	45.8	S	45.8	42.4	S	54.2	52.5	S
30	59.3		S	50.8	55.9	S	62.7	61.0	39.0	61.0	S	57.6
31	61.0		S		61.0		52.5	S		54.2		54.2

* See new trends developing on pages 68, 88, 141–146.

121

RECENT DOW JONES INDUSTRIALS MARKET PROBABILITY CALENDAR 2013

THE % CHANCE OF THE MARKET RISING ON ANY TRADING DAY OF THE YEAR*
(Based on the number of times the DJIA rose on a particular trading day during January 1991 to December 2011**)

Date	Jan	Feb	Mar	Apr	May	Jun	Jul	Aug	Sep	Oct	Nov	Dec
1	H	71.4	57.1	76.2	71.4	S	81.0	42.9	S	52.4	52.4	S
2	66.7	S	S	66.7	71.4	S	38.1	52.4	H	47.6	S	52.4
3	66.7	S	S	52.4	33.3	71.4	52.4	S	57.1	42.9	S	47.6
4	47.6	52.4	52.4	66.7	S	52.4	H	S	57.1	61.9	52.4	61.9
5	S	42.9	61.9	42.9	S	47.6	57.1	42.9	52.4	S	61.9	57.1
6	S	52.4	42.9	S	42.9	47.6	S	47.6	38.1	S	71.4	42.9
7	52.4	52.4	57.1	S	33.3	47.6	S	52.4	S	33.3	61.9	S
8	33.3	42.9	42.9	47.6	71.4	S	66.7	42.9	S	47.6	52.4	S
9	52.4	S	S	47.6	66.7	S	47.6	42.9	61.9	47.6	S	47.6
10	52.4	S	S	66.7	61.9	47.6	61.9	S	52.4	42.9	S	57.1
11	52.4	57.1	61.9	61.9	S	42.9	66.7	S	61.9	61.9	33.3	52.4
12	S	57.1	57.1	71.4	S	42.9	61.9	52.4	71.4	S	57.1	52.4
13	S	61.9	47.6	S	52.4	66.7	S	28.6	52.4	S	61.9	52.4
14	52.4	38.1	61.9	S	52.4	76.2	S	66.7	S	76.2	61.9	S
15	61.9	66.7	61.9	71.4	57.1	S	52.4	47.6	S	52.4	57.1	S
16	57.1	S	S	61.9	52.4	S	52.4	61.9	52.4	52.4	S	47.6
17	33.3	S	S	57.1	57.1	52.4	47.6	S	52.4	42.9	S	57.1
18	28.6	H	57.1	66.7	S	52.4	61.9	S	33.3	66.7	42.9	47.6
19	S	47.6	57.1	61.9	S	52.4	33.3	61.9	57.1	S	47.6	47.6
20	S	33.3	66.7	S	52.4	42.9	S	47.6	42.9	S	52.4	76.2
21	H	47.6	38.1	S	57.1	33.3	S	66.7	S	47.6	57.1	S
22	33.3	52.4	57.1	52.4	38.1	S	38.1	47.6	S	42.9	57.1	S
23	47.6	S	S	61.9	33.3	S	47.6	57.1	28.6	57.1	S	71.4
24	42.9	S	S	42.9	52.4	42.9	52.4	S	52.4	42.9	S	57.1
25	61.9	33.3	33.3	52.4	S	38.1	66.7	S	57.1	38.1	66.7	H
26	S	42.9	52.4	52.4	S	52.4	38.1	52.4	57.1	S	61.9	85.7
27	S	42.9	57.1	S	H	52.4	S	42.9	57.1	S	52.4	57.1
28	66.7	42.9	33.3	S	52.4	28.6	S	66.7	S	57.1	H	S
29	61.9		H	66.7	52.4	S	42.9	33.3	S	66.7	52.4	S
30	57.1		S	47.6	71.4	S	61.9	47.6	38.1	66.7	S	47.6
31	66.7		S		52.4		47.6	S		52.4		38.1

* See new trends developing on pages 68, 88, 141–146. ** Based on most recent 21-year period.

S&P 500 MARKET PROBABILITY CALENDAR 2013

THE % CHANCE OF THE MARKET RISING ON ANY TRADING DAY OF THE YEAR*

(Based on the number of times the S&P 500 rose on a particular trading day during January 1953 to December 2011)

Date	Jan	Feb	Mar	Apr	May	Jun	Jul	Aug	Sep	Oct	Nov	Dec
1	H	61.0	61.0	64.4	57.6	S	69.5	49.2	S	47.5	61.0	S
2	47.5	S	S	59.3	69.5	S	55.9	44.1	H	66.1	S	49.2
3	71.2	S	S	55.9	55.9	54.2	55.9	S	62.7	52.5	S	54.2
4	52.5	57.6	59.3	55.9	S	62.7	H	S	54.2	61.0	57.6	62.7
5	S	45.8	62.7	55.9	S	50.8	61.0	49.2	57.6	S	69.5	57.6
6	S	49.2	47.5	S	44.1	54.2	S	50.8	45.8	S	54.2	40.7
7	50.8	50.8	47.5	S	40.7	45.8	S	54.2	S	49.2	49.2	S
8	44.1	42.4	55.9	59.3	52.5	S	62.7	44.1	S	50.8	57.6	S
9	49.2	S	S	61.0	49.2	S	54.2	52.5	50.8	42.4	S	49.2
10	50.8	S	S	54.2	50.8	42.4	50.8	S	52.5	44.1	S	55.9
11	55.9	39.0	59.3	50.8	S	42.4	49.2	S	55.9	52.5	57.6	49.2
12	S	64.4	50.8	62.7	S	55.9	67.8	47.5	62.7	S	59.3	49.2
13	S	52.5	62.7	S	44.1	64.4	S	45.8	50.8	S	47.5	45.8
14	61.0	44.1	47.5	S	50.8	59.3	S	64.4	S	54.2	49.2	S
15	62.7	54.2	61.0	62.7	54.2	S	54.2	62.7	S	52.5	49.2	S
16	54.2	S	S	59.3	49.2	S	42.4	54.2	54.2	54.2	S	45.8
17	49.2	S	S	54.2	54.2	55.9	45.8	S	55.9	40.7	S	59.3
18	44.1	H	62.7	54.2	S	44.1	50.8	S	45.8	67.8	50.8	44.1
19	S	35.6	57.6	52.5	S	55.9	40.7	54.2	52.5	S	54.2	47.5
20	S	52.5	49.2	S	42.4	40.7	S	50.8	49.2	S	52.5	54.2
21	H	44.1	54.2	S	47.5	42.4	S	61.0	S	50.8	62.7	S
22	44.1	40.7	42.4	52.5	49.2	S	40.7	47.5	S	50.8	57.6	S
23	59.3	S	S	45.8	42.4	S	49.2	50.8	39.0	44.1	S	47.5
24	61.0	S	S	45.8	50.8	37.3	45.8	S	50.8	42.4	S	62.7
25	52.5	39.0	47.5	57.6	S	40.7	57.6	S	52.5	32.2	67.8	H
26	S	55.9	55.9	49.2	S	50.8	50.8	47.5	59.3	S	61.0	72.9
27	S	50.8	37.3	S	H	57.6	S	45.8	50.8	S	57.6	52.5
28	54.2	59.3	39.0	S	49.2	49.2	S	57.6	S	59.3	H	S
29	49.2		H	45.8	47.5	S	49.2	44.1	S	57.6	52.5	S
30	62.7		S	57.6	55.9	S	64.4	64.4	42.4	62.7	S	66.1
31	66.1		S		62.7		64.4	S		54.2		62.7

* See new trends developing on pages 68, 88, 141–146.

RECENT S&P 500 MARKET PROBABILITY CALENDAR 2013

THE % CHANCE OF THE MARKET RISING ON ANY TRADING DAY OF THE YEAR*

(Based on the number of times the S&P 500 rose on a particular trading day during January 1991 to December 2011**)

Date	Jan	Feb	Mar	Apr	May	Jun	Jul	Aug	Sep	Oct	Nov	Dec
1	H	71.4	52.4	71.4	71.4	S	81.0	52.4	S	47.6	52.4	S
2	42.9	S	S	66.7	66.7	S	33.3	47.6	H	52.4	S	57.1
3	61.9	S	S	61.9	38.1	61.9	57.1	S	61.9	38.1	S	52.4
4	52.4	57.1	42.9	66.7	S	71.4	H	S	42.9	52.4	61.9	66.7
5	S	42.9	71.4	47.6	S	42.9	61.9	42.9	47.6	S	61.9	42.9
6	S	52.4	42.9	S	33.3	38.1	S	52.4	42.9	S	71.4	42.9
7	42.9	47.6	52.4	S	23.8	38.1	S	42.9	S	38.1	61.9	S
8	47.6	57.1	52.4	52.4	61.9	S	66.7	52.4	S	47.6	47.6	S
9	52.4	S	S	42.9	57.1	S	42.9	38.1	57.1	47.6	S	47.6
10	52.4	S	S	52.4	52.4	38.1	57.1	S	61.9	47.6	S	57.1
11	57.1	42.9	52.4	52.4	S	52.4	76.2	S	61.9	61.9	38.1	42.9
12	S	71.4	47.6	57.1	S	38.1	66.7	52.4	66.7	S	52.4	57.1
13	S	66.7	61.9	S	52.4	66.7	S	28.6	61.9	S	57.1	47.6
14	57.1	38.1	52.4	S	47.6	76.2	S	71.4	S	76.2	57.1	S
15	61.9	71.4	66.7	66.7	57.1	S	47.6	61.9	S	52.4	47.6	S
16	57.1	S	S	66.7	57.1	S	42.9	71.4	52.4	57.1	S	42.9
17	52.4	S	S	57.1	61.9	61.9	42.9	S	61.9	52.4	S	61.9
18	28.6	H	57.1	61.9	S	47.6	61.9	S	42.9	71.4	52.4	52.4
19	S	42.9	66.7	57.1	S	52.4	28.6	66.7	57.1	S	52.4	42.9
20	S	38.1	52.4	S	47.6	42.9	S	42.9	42.9	S	47.6	71.4
21	H	42.9	61.9	S	57.1	33.3	S	66.7	S	57.1	47.6	S
22	38.1	61.9	57.1	57.1	38.1	S	33.3	47.6	S	47.6	52.4	S
23	47.6	S	S	57.1	33.3	S	52.4	61.9	33.3	61.9	S	71.4
24	57.1	S	S	28.6	61.9	42.9	52.4	S	47.6	38.1	S	61.9
25	52.4	38.1	38.1	47.6	S	28.6	66.7	S	52.4	42.9	66.7	H
26	S	42.9	47.6	52.4	S	57.1	38.1	52.4	61.9	S	66.7	81.0
27	S	52.4	38.1	S	H	61.9	S	52.4	61.9	S	66.7	57.1
28	52.4	47.6	38.1	S	57.1	33.3	S	66.7	S	61.9	H	S
29	61.9		H	61.9	57.1	S	47.6	33.3	S	61.9	38.1	S
30	61.9		S	57.1	61.9	S	66.7	47.6	38.1	76.2	S	66.7
31	71.4		S		57.1		57.1	S		57.1		28.6

*See new trends developing on pages 68, 88, 141–146. ** Based on most recent 21-year period.*

NASDAQ COMPOSITE MARKET PROBABILITY CALENDAR 2013

THE % CHANCE OF THE MARKET RISING ON ANY TRADING DAY OF THE YEAR*

(Based on the number of times the NASDAQ rose on a particular trading day during January 1971 to December 2011)

Date	Jan	Feb	Mar	Apr	May	Jun	Jul	Aug	Sep	Oct	Nov	Dec
1	H	70.7	61.0	46.3	61.0	S	58.5	53.7	S	48.8	63.4	S
2	56.1	S	S	63.4	70.7	S	48.8	41.5	H	61.0	S	63.4
3	70.7	S	S	68.3	58.5	58.5	43.9	S	53.7	56.1	S	65.9
4	58.5	68.3	56.1	53.7	S	75.6	H	S	61.0	63.4	56.1	65.9
5	S	56.1	68.3	48.8	S	56.1	53.7	48.8	58.5	S	70.7	58.5
6	S	65.9	53.7	S	53.7	58.5	S	56.1	56.1	S	58.5	41.5
7	63.4	56.1	51.2	S	51.2	48.8	S	56.1	S	61.0	51.2	S
8	53.7	51.2	56.1	61.0	63.4	S	63.4	39.0	S	61.0	53.7	S
9	61.0	S	S	61.0	56.1	S	63.4	51.2	56.1	51.2	S	53.7
10	56.1	S	S	61.0	41.5	41.5	61.0	S	48.8	51.2	S	48.8
11	61.0	46.3	56.1	53.7	S	43.9	70.7	S	51.2	75.6	56.1	46.3
12	S	63.4	51.2	61.0	S	53.7	70.7	48.8	61.0	S	63.4	43.9
13	S	58.5	70.7	S	56.1	63.4	S	53.7	61.0	S	53.7	41.5
14	63.4	61.0	51.2	S	56.1	65.9	S	61.0	S	63.4	53.7	S
15	65.9	61.0	51.2	53.7	56.1	S	65.9	58.5	S	51.2	41.5	S
16	68.3	S	S	61.0	56.1	S	46.3	51.2	39.0	48.8	S	43.9
17	58.5	S	S	56.1	51.2	56.1	53.7	S	51.2	36.6	S	58.5
18	41.5	H	63.4	56.1	S	43.9	56.1	S	51.2	70.7	46.3	48.8
19	S	46.3	58.5	56.1	S	51.2	41.5	58.5	63.4	S	51.2	53.7
20	S	56.1	63.4	S	43.9	46.3	S	51.2	51.2	S	53.7	58.5
21	H	39.0	56.1	S	48.8	46.3	S	70.7	S	43.9	65.9	S
22	46.3	46.3	46.3	58.5	48.8	S	41.5	53.7	S	58.5	56.1	S
23	51.2	S	S	56.1	48.8	S	51.2	51.2	46.3	48.8	S	65.9
24	58.5	S	S	51.2	53.7	46.3	53.7	S	53.7	41.5	S	68.3
25	46.3	53.7	46.3	46.3	S	46.3	58.5	S	46.3	31.7	58.5	H
26	S	61.0	53.7	70.7	S	58.5	46.3	53.7	48.8	S	65.9	73.2
27	S	53.7	53.7	S	H	68.3	S	53.7	48.8	S	63.4	51.2
28	68.3	56.1	65.9	S	53.7	65.9	S	63.4	S	46.3	H	S
29	63.4		H	63.4	61.0	S	43.9	61.0	S	56.1	65.9	S
30	53.7		S	68.3	58.5	S	56.1	68.3	48.8	61.0	S	68.3
31	65.9		S		73.2		51.2	S		68.3		73.2

See new trends developing on pages 68, 88, 141–146.
Based on NASDAQ composite, prior to February 5, 1971 based on National Quotation Bureau indices.

RECENT NASDAQ COMPOSITE MARKET PROBABILITY CALENDAR 2013

THE % CHANCE OF THE MARKET RISING ON ANY TRADING DAY OF THE YEAR*

(Based on the number of times the NASDAQ rose on a particular trading day during January 1991 to December 2011**)

Date	Jan	Feb	Mar	Apr	May	Jun	Jul	Aug	Sep	Oct	Nov	Dec
1	H	81.0	52.4	57.1	71.4	S	71.4	57.1	S	42.9	61.9	S
2	61.9	S	S	57.1	61.9	S	38.1	42.9	H	52.4	S	71.4
3	66.7	S	S	76.2	57.1	61.9	42.9	S	57.1	47.6	S	66.7
4	52.4	61.9	38.1	57.1	S	81.0	H	S	57.1	61.9	61.9	66.7
5	S	47.6	71.4	38.1	S	52.4	57.1	38.1	52.4	S	76.2	52.4
6	S	61.9	42.9	S	47.6	42.9	S	52.4	52.4	S	66.7	38.1
7	52.4	52.4	47.6	S	33.3	33.3	S	42.9	S	47.6	66.7	S
8	52.4	57.1	42.9	52.4	76.2	S	71.4	38.1	S	61.9	61.9	S
9	66.7	S	S	42.9	57.1	S	61.9	38.1	61.9	57.1	S	52.4
10	52.4	S	S	57.1	38.1	28.6	66.7	S	61.9	61.9	S	52.4
11	57.1	42.9	47.6	52.4	S	47.6	76.2	S	57.1	76.2	42.9	42.9
12	S	57.1	47.6	57.1	S	38.1	71.4	47.6	71.4	S	57.1	47.6
13	S	57.1	66.7	S	52.4	52.4	S	42.9	76.2	S	61.9	42.9
14	57.1	52.4	47.6	S	42.9	66.7	S	71.4	S	71.4	57.1	S
15	52.4	57.1	42.9	42.9	52.4	S	61.9	61.9	S	52.4	42.9	S
16	66.7	S	S	52.4	61.9	S	47.6	66.7	38.1	47.6	S	47.6
17	61.9	S	S	52.4	66.7	61.9	47.6	S	66.7	38.1	S	52.4
18	33.3	H	61.9	61.9	S	38.1	61.9	S	52.4	71.4	47.6	42.9
19	S	38.1	61.9	57.1	S	52.4	33.3	61.9	66.7	S	47.6	52.4
20	S	47.6	66.7	S	42.9	42.9	S	42.9	42.9	S	57.1	57.1
21	H	42.9	57.1	S	71.4	28.6	S	85.7	S	47.6	57.1	S
22	38.1	57.1	61.9	61.9	47.6	S	38.1	52.4	S	47.6	52.4	S
23	52.4	S	S	57.1	42.9	S	52.4	47.6	38.1	57.1	S	76.2
24	61.9	S	S	52.4	52.4	42.9	52.4	S	47.6	38.1	S	66.7
25	42.9	52.4	42.9	42.9	S	38.1	71.4	S	52.4	33.3	57.1	H
26	S	47.6	42.9	61.9	S	61.9	52.4	52.4	42.9	S	57.1	76.2
27	S	52.4	47.6	S	H	71.4	S	42.9	47.6	S	66.7	57.1
28	81.0	42.9	57.1	S	52.4	61.9	S	76.2	S	52.4	H	S
29	71.4		H	71.4	61.9	S	47.6	61.9	S	61.9	52.4	S
30	52.4		S	66.7	76.2	S	71.4	52.4	38.1	71.4	S	57.1
31	61.9		S		66.7		47.6	S		71.4		47.6

* See new trends developing on pages 68, 88, 141–146. ** Based on most recent 21-year period.

RUSSELL 1000 INDEX MARKET PROBABILITY CALENDAR 2013

THE % CHANCE OF THE MARKET RISING ON ANY TRADING DAY OF THE YEAR*

(Based on the number of times the RUSSELL 1000 rose on a particular trading day during January 1979 to December 2011)

Date	Jan	Feb	Mar	Apr	May	Jun	Jul	Aug	Sep	Oct	Nov	Dec
1	H	66.7	57.6	60.6	54.5	S	69.7	48.5	S	51.5	69.7	S
2	42.4	S	S	63.6	66.7	S	42.4	42.4	H	57.6	S	54.5
3	63.6	S	S	57.6	54.5	57.6	45.5	S	51.5	51.5	S	57.6
4	60.6	57.6	48.5	57.6	S	63.6	H	S	48.5	60.6	57.6	63.6
5	S	54.5	63.6	48.5	S	48.5	60.6	48.5	51.5	S	60.6	42.4
6	S	51.5	39.4	S	39.4	54.5	S	48.5	39.4	S	57.6	39.4
7	54.5	60.6	42.4	S	36.4	33.3	S	54.5	S	45.5	48.5	S
8	48.5	48.5	57.6	63.6	57.6	S	60.6	54.5	S	54.5	54.5	S
9	60.6	S	S	54.5	60.6	S	48.5	45.5	51.5	39.4	S	48.5
10	51.5	S	S	51.5	48.5	39.4	57.6	S	54.5	39.4	S	54.5
11	57.6	39.4	54.5	45.5	S	45.5	66.7	S	60.6	63.6	45.5	45.5
12	S	69.7	48.5	57.6	S	51.5	75.8	48.5	66.7	S	60.6	48.5
13	S	63.6	60.6	S	57.6	57.6	S	42.4	60.6	S	57.6	45.5
14	60.6	42.4	45.5	S	51.5	60.6	S	63.6	S	66.7	54.5	S
15	69.7	63.6	57.6	66.7	57.6	S	51.5	63.6	S	57.6	48.5	S
16	66.7	S	S	60.6	57.6	S	48.5	60.6	51.5	48.5	S	51.5
17	39.4	S	S	48.5	57.6	60.6	45.5	S	48.5	39.4	S	60.6
18	30.3	H	60.6	54.5	S	45.5	57.6	S	42.4	75.8	45.5	48.5
19	S	33.3	60.6	48.5	S	63.6	39.4	66.7	51.5	S	63.6	45.5
20	S	45.5	48.5	S	51.5	39.4	S	63.6	39.4	S	48.5	69.7
21	H	39.4	48.5	S	51.5	39.4	S	72.7	S	51.5	60.6	S
22	42.4	42.4	51.5	51.5	48.5	S	36.4	48.5	S	54.5	60.6	S
23	54.5	S	S	57.6	39.4	S	48.5	57.6	36.4	48.5	S	57.6
24	51.5	S	S	42.4	60.6	36.4	42.4	S	42.4	36.4	S	63.6
25	51.5	42.4	39.4	54.5	S	36.4	75.8	S	51.5	33.3	66.7	H
26	S	54.5	48.5	54.5	S	51.5	51.5	45.5	66.7	S	72.7	72.7
27	S	54.5	42.4	S	H	60.6	S	54.5	57.6	S	63.6	60.6
28	66.7	60.6	45.5	S	63.6	48.5	S	54.5	S	57.6	H	S
29	60.6		H	51.5	57.6	S	45.5	48.5	S	54.5	48.5	S
30	57.6		S	57.6	54.5	S	66.7	60.6	48.5	69.7	S	69.7
31	63.6		S		60.6		60.6	S		63.6		51.5

* See new trends developing on pages 68, 88, 141–146.

RUSSELL 2000 INDEX MARKET PROBABILITY CALENDAR 2013

THE % CHANCE OF THE MARKET RISING ON ANY TRADING DAY OF THE YEAR*

(Based on the number of times the RUSSELL 2000 rose on a particular trading day during **January 1979 to December 2011**)

Date	Jan	Feb	Mar	Apr	May	Jun	Jul	Aug	Sep	Oct	Nov	Dec
1	H	66.7	63.6	48.5	63.6	S	60.6	51.5	S	48.5	63.6	S
2	45.5	S	S	63.6	63.6	S	51.5	48.5	H	48.5	S	54.5
3	66.7	S	S	51.5	63.6	63.6	42.4	S	48.5	51.5	S	63.6
4	60.6	63.6	60.6	54.5	S	72.7	H	S	60.6	69.7	72.7	69.7
5	S	51.5	66.7	45.5	S	51.5	54.5	48.5	54.5	S	66.7	60.6
6	S	66.7	54.5	S	57.6	54.5	S	48.5	63.6	S	57.6	42.4
7	63.6	66.7	60.6	S	48.5	54.5	S	48.5	S	45.5	54.5	S
8	57.6	60.6	51.5	57.6	54.5	S	54.5	45.5	S	48.5	54.5	S
9	63.6	S	S	60.6	63.6	S	57.6	57.6	54.5	48.5	S	57.6
10	51.5	S	S	60.6	45.5	33.3	51.5	S	57.6	54.5	S	48.5
11	69.7	45.5	54.5	51.5	S	51.5	63.6	S	60.6	69.7	48.5	51.5
12	S	72.7	42.4	54.5	S	54.5	60.6	51.5	66.7	S	72.7	39.4
13	S	60.6	60.6	S	60.6	60.6	S	48.5	57.6	S	51.5	45.5
14	66.7	63.6	54.5	S	48.5	66.7	S	75.8	S	63.6	54.5	S
15	66.7	57.6	48.5	60.6	48.5	S	57.6	63.6	S	57.6	48.5	S
16	69.7	S	S	57.6	57.6	S	48.5	60.6	33.3	39.4	S	36.4
17	69.7	S	S	48.5	54.5	57.6	48.5	S	48.5	45.5	S	57.6
18	30.3	H	60.6	60.6	S	45.5	51.5	S	42.4	72.7	18.2	57.6
19	S	51.5	69.7	48.5	S	42.4	39.4	60.6	45.5	S	60.6	60.6
20	S	45.5	54.5	S	54.5	42.4	S	51.5	48.5	S	45.5	63.6
21	H	36.4	51.5	S	54.5	45.5	S	72.7	S	54.5	60.6	S
22	48.5	48.5	51.5	63.6	48.5	S	42.4	48.5	S	54.5	57.6	S
23	54.5	S	S	54.5	51.5	S	42.4	57.6	42.4	48.5	S	66.7
24	54.5	S	S	51.5	57.6	42.4	51.5	S	45.5	42.4	S	78.8
25	45.5	57.6	45.5	60.6	S	45.5	63.6	S	33.3	36.4	63.6	H
26	S	57.6	51.5	63.6	S	57.6	63.6	54.5	54.5	S	63.6	69.7
27	S	63.6	51.5	S	H	72.7	S	57.6	60.6	S	66.7	57.6
28	69.7	60.6	84.8	S	54.5	66.7	S	63.6	S	42.4	H	S
29	60.6		H	57.6	69.7	S	45.5	63.6	S	54.5	72.7	S
30	54.5		S	69.7	66.7	S	57.6	72.7	63.6	60.6	S	66.7
31	75.8		S		72.7		66.7	S		72.7		69.7

See new trends developing on pages 68, 88, 141–146.

DECENNIAL CYCLE: A MARKET PHENOMENON

By arranging each year's market gain or loss so the first and succeeding years of each decade fall into the same column, certain interesting patterns emerge— strong fifth and eighth years; weak first, seventh, and zero years.

This fascinating phenomenon was first presented by Edgar Lawrence Smith in *Common Stocks and Business Cycles* (William-Frederick Press, 1959). Anthony Gaubis co-pioneered the decennial pattern with Smith.

When Smith first cut graphs of market prices into 10-year segments and placed them above one another, he observed that each decade tended to have three bull market cycles and that the longest and strongest bull markets seem to favor the middle years of a decade.

Don't place too much emphasis on the decennial cycle nowadays, other than the extraordinary fifth and zero years, as the stock market is more influenced by the quadrennial presidential election cycle, shown on page 130. Also, the last half-century, which has been the most prosperous in U.S. history, has distributed the returns among most years of the decade. Interestingly, NASDAQ suffered its worst bear market ever in a zero year.

Third years have the fifth worst record within the Decennial Cycle and 2013 is a post-presidential election year, which has the worst record of the 4-year presidential election cycle. Of the last three post-presidential election years since the Depression that were also third years, just 1993 was positive. As historical patterns continue to assert themselves, the likelihood of a banner 2013 is falling (see pages 24, 26, 30, 32, 34, 52, 74, and 130).

THE 10-YEAR STOCK MARKET CYCLE
Annual % Change in Dow Jones Industrial Average
Year of Decade

DECADES	1st	2nd	3rd	4th	5th	6th	7th	8th	9th	10th
1881–1890	3.0%	−2.9%	−8.5%	−18.8%	20.1%	12.4%	−8.4%	4.8%	5.5%	−14.1%
1891–1900	17.6	−6.6	−24.6	−0.6	2.3	−1.7	21.3	22.5	9.2	7.0
1901–1910	−8.7	−0.4	−23.6	41.7	38.2	−1.9	−37.7	46.6	15.0	−17.9
1911–1920	0.4	7.6	−10.3	−5.4	81.7	−4.2	−21.7	10.5	30.5	−32.9
1921–1930	12.7	21.7	−3.3	26.2	30.0	0.3	28.8	48.2	−17.2	−33.8
1931–1940	−52.7	−23.1	66.7	4.1	38.5	24.8	−32.8	28.1	−2.9	−12.7
1941–1950	−15.4	7.6	13.8	12.1	26.6	−8.1	2.2	−2.1	12.9	17.6
1951–1960	14.4	8.4	−3.8	44.0	20.8	2.3	−12.8	34.0	16.4	−9.3
1961–1970	18.7	−10.8	17.0	14.6	10.9	−18.9	15.2	4.3	−15.2	4.8
1971–1980	6.1	14.6	−16.6	−27.6	38.3	17.9	−17.3	−3.1	4.2	14.9
1981–1990	−9.2	19.6	20.3	−3.7	27.7	22.6	2.3	11.8	27.0	−4.3
1991–2000	20.3	4.2	13.7	2.1	33.5	26.0	22.6	16.1	25.2	−6.2
2001–2010	−7.1	−16.8	25.3	3.1	−0.6	16.3	6.4	−33.8	18.8	11.0
2011–2020	5.5									
Total % Change	5.6%	23.1%	66.1%	91.8%	368.0%	87.3%	−31.9%	187.9%	129.4%	−75.9%
Avg % Change	0.4%	1.8%	5.1%	7.1%	28.3%	6.8%	−2.5%	14.5%	10.0%	−5.8%
Up Years	9	7	6	8	12	8	7	10	10	5
Down Years	5	6	7	5	1	5	6	3	3	8

Based on annual close; Cowles indices 1881–1885; 12 Mixed Stocks, 10 Rails, 2 Inds 1886–1889;

20 Mixed Stocks, 18 Rails, 2 Inds 1890–1896; Railroad average 1897 (First industrial average published May 26, 1896).

PRESIDENTIAL ELECTION/STOCK MARKET CYCLE: THE 179-YEAR SAGA CONTINUES

It is no mere coincidence that the last two years (pre-election year and election year) of the 45 administrations since 1833 produced a total net market gain of 724.0%, dwarfing the 273.1% gain of the first two years of these administrations.

Presidential elections every four years have a profound impact on the economy and the stock market. Wars, recessions, and bear markets tend to start or occur in the first half of the term; prosperous times and bull markets, in the latter half. After nine straight annual Dow gains during the millennial bull, the four-year election cycle reasserted its overarching domination of market behavior the last 12 years. Despite European debt concerns, the Dow maintained its streak of no losses in pre-election years since 1939.

STOCK MARKET ACTION SINCE 1833
Annual % Change In Dow Jones Industrial Average[1]

4-Year Cycle Beginning	Elected President	Post-Election Year	Mid-Term Year	Pre-Election Year	Election Year
1833	Jackson (D)	−0.9	13.0	3.1	−11.7
1837	Van Buren (D)	−11.5	1.6	−12.3	5.5
1841*	W.H. Harrison (W)**	−13.3	−18.1	45.0	15.5
1845*	Polk (D)	8.1	−14.5	1.2	−3.6
1849*	Taylor (W)	N/C	18.7	−3.2	19.6
1853*	Pierce (D)	−12.7	−30.2	1.5	4.4
1857	Buchanan (D)	−31.0	14.3	−10.7	14.0
1861*	Lincoln (R)	−1.8	55.4	38.0	6.4
1865	Lincoln (R)**	−8.5	3.6	1.6	10.8
1869	Grant (R)	1.7	5.6	7.3	6.8
1873	Grant (R)	−12.7	2.8	−4.1	−17.9
1877	Hayes (R)	−9.4	6.1	43.0	18.7
1881	Garfield (R)**	3.0	−2.9	−8.5	−18.8
1885*	Cleveland (D)	20.1	12.4	−8.4	4.8
1889*	B. Harrison (R)	5.5	−14.1	17.6	−6.6
1893*	Cleveland (D)	−24.6	−0.6	2.3	−1.7
1897*	McKinley (R)	21.3	22.5	9.2	7.0
1901	McKinley (R)**	−8.7	−0.4	−23.6	41.7
1905	T. Roosevelt (R)	38.2	−1.9	−37.7	46.6
1909	Taft (R)	15.0	−17.9	0.4	7.6
1913*	Wilson (D)	−10.3	−5.4	81.7	−4.2
1917	Wilson (D)	−21.7	10.5	30.5	−32.9
1921*	Harding (R)**	12.7	21.7	−3.3	26.2
1925	Coolidge (R)	30.0	0.3	28.8	48.2
1929	Hoover (R)	−17.2	−33.8	−52.7	−23.1
1933*	F. Roosevelt (D)	66.7	4.1	38.5	24.8
1937	F. Roosevelt (D)	−32.8	28.1	−2.9	−12.7
1941	F. Roosevelt (D)	−15.4	7.6	13.8	12.1
1945	F. Roosevelt (D)**	26.6	−8.1	2.2	−2.1
1949	Truman (D)	12.9	17.6	14.4	8.4
1953*	Eisenhower (R)	−3.8	44.0	20.8	2.3
1957	Eisenhower (R)	−12.8	34.0	16.4	−9.3
1961*	Kennedy (D)**	18.7	−10.8	17.0	14.6
1965	Johnson (D)	10.9	−18.9	15.2	4.3
1969*	Nixon (R)	−15.2	4.8	6.1	14.6
1973	Nixon (R)***	−16.6	−27.6	38.3	17.9
1977*	Carter (D)	−17.3	−3.1	4.2	14.9
1981*	Reagan (R)	−9.2	19.6	20.3	−3.7
1985	Reagan (R)	27.7	22.6	2.3	11.8
1989	G. H. W. Bush (R)	27.0	−4.3	20.3	4.2
1993*	Clinton (D)	13.7	2.1	33.5	26.0
1997	Clinton (D)	22.6	16.1	25.2	−6.2
2001*	G. W. Bush (R)	−7.1	−16.8	25.3	3.1
2005	G. W. Bush (R)	−0.6	16.3	6.4	−33.8
2009*	Obama (D)	18.8	11.0	5.5	
Total % Gain		**86.1%**	**187.0%**	**469.5%**	**254.5%**
Average % Gain		**2.0%**	**4.2%**	**10.4%**	**5.8%**
# Up		20	27	34	29
# Down		24	18	11	15

*Party in power ousted   **Death in office   ***Resigned   **D**–Democrat, **W**–Whig, **R**–Republican
[1] Based on annual close; Prior to 1886 based on Cowles and other indices; 12 Mixed Stocks, 10 Rails, 2 Inds 1886–1889; 20 Mixed Stocks, 18 Rails, 2 Inds 1890–1896; Railroad average 1897 (First industrial average published May 26, 1896).

DOW JONES INDUSTRIALS BULL AND BEAR MARKETS SINCE 1900

Bear markets begin at the end of one bull market and end at the start of the next bull market (7/17/90 to 10/11/90 as an example). The high at Dow 3978.36 on 1/31/94, was followed by a 9.7 percent correction. A 10.3 percent correction occurred between the 5/22/96 closing high of 5778 and the intraday low on 7/16/96. The longest bull market on record ended on 7/17/98, and the shortest bear market on record ended on 8/31/98, when the new bull market began. The greatest bull super cycle in history that began 8/12/82 ended in 2000 after the Dow gained 1409% and NASDAQ climbed 3072%. The Dow gained only 497% in the eight-year super bull from 1921 to the top in 1929. NASDAQ suffered its worst loss ever from the 2000 top to the 2002 bottom, down 77.9%, nearly as much as the 89.2% drop in the Dow from the 1929 top to the 1932 bottom. The third longest Dow bull since 1900 that began 10/9/02 ended on its fifth anniversary. The ensuing bear market was the second worst bear market since 1900, slashing the Dow 53.8%. European debt concerns in 2011 triggered a 16.8% Dow slide, ending the recovery bull shortly after its second anniversary. At press time, the current bull market was under pressure, as the European debt contagion was flaring up. (See page 132 for S&P 500 and NASDAQ bulls and bears.)

DOW JONES INDUSTRIALS BULL AND BEAR MARKETS SINCE 1900

— Beginning —		— Ending —		Bull		Bear	
Date	DJIA	Date	DJIA	% Gain	Days	% Change	Days
9/24/00	38.80	6/17/01	57.33	47.8%	266	−46.1%	875
11/9/03	30.88	1/19/06	75.45	144.3	802	−48.5	665
11/15/07	38.83	11/19/09	73.64	89.6	735	−27.4	675
9/25/11	53.43	9/30/12	68.97	29.1	371	−24.1	668
7/30/14	52.32	11/21/16	110.15	110.5	845	−40.1	393
12/19/17	65.95	11/3/19	119.62	81.4	684	−46.6	660
8/24/21	63.90	3/20/23	105.38	64.9	573	−18.6	221
10/27/23	85.76	9/3/29	381.17	344.5	2138	−47.9	71
11/13/29	198.69	4/17/30	294.07	48.0	155	−86.0	813
7/8/32	41.22	9/7/32	79.93	93.9	61	−37.2	173
2/27/33	50.16	2/5/34	110.74	120.8	343	−22.8	171
7/26/34	85.51	3/10/37	194.40	127.3	958	−49.1	386
3/31/38	98.95	11/12/38	158.41	60.1	226	−23.3	147
4/8/39	121.44	9/12/39	155.92	28.4	157	−40.4	959
4/28/42	92.92	5/29/46	212.50	128.7	1492	−23.2	353
5/17/47	163.21	6/15/48	193.16	18.4	395	−16.3	363
6/13/49	161.60	1/5/53	293.79	81.8	1302	−13.0	252
9/14/53	255.49	4/6/56	521.05	103.9	935	−19.4	564
10/22/57	419.79	1/5/60	685.47	63.3	805	−17.4	294
10/25/60	566.05	12/13/61	734.91	29.8	414	−27.1	195
6/26/62	535.76	2/9/66	995.15	85.7	1324	−25.2	240
10/7/66	744.32	12/3/68	985.21	32.4	788	−35.9	539
5/26/70	631.16	4/28/71	950.82	50.6	337	−16.1	209
11/23/71	797.97	1/11/73	1051.70	31.8	415	−45.1	694
12/6/74	577.60	9/21/76	1014.79	75.7	655	−26.9	525
2/28/78	742.12	9/8/78	907.74	22.3	192	−16.4	591
4/21/80	759.13	4/27/81	1024.05	34.9	371	−24.1	472
8/12/82	776.92	11/29/83	1287.20	65.7	474	−15.6	238
7/24/84	1086.57	8/25/87	2722.42	150.6	1127	−36.1	55
10/19/87	1738.74	7/17/90	2999.75	72.5	1002	−21.2	86
10/11/90	2365.10	7/17/98	9337.97	294.8	2836	−19.3	45
8/31/98	7539.07	1/14/00	11722.98	55.5	501	−29.7	616
9/21/01	8235.81	3/19/02	10635.25	29.1	179	−31.5	204
10/9/02	7286.27	10/9/07	14164.53	94.4	1826	−53.8	517
3/9/09	6547.05	4/29/11	12810.54	95.7	781	−16.8	157
10/3/11	10655.30	4/2/12	13264.49	24.5*	183*	*At Press Time – not in averages	
		Average		**86.0%**	**756**	**− 31.1%**	**402**

Based on Dow Jones industrial average.   1900–2000 Data: Ned Davis Research
The NYSE was closed from 7/31/1914 to 12/11/1914 due to World War I.
DJIA figures were then adjusted back to reflect the composition change from 12 to 20 stocks in September 1916.

STANDARD & POOR'S 500 BULL & BEAR MARKETS SINCE 1929 NASDAQ COMPOSITE SINCE 1971

A constant debate of the definition and timing of bull and bear markets permeates Wall Street like the bell that signals the open and close of every trading day. We have relied on the Ned Davis Research parameters for years to track bulls and bears on the Dow (see page 131). Standard & Poor's 500 index has been a stalwart indicator for decades and at times marched to a different beat than the Dow. The moves of the S&P 500 and NASDAQ have been correlated to the bull and bear dates on page 131. Many dates line up for the three indices, but you will notice quite a lag or lead on several occasions, including NASDAQ's independent cadence from 1975 to 1980.

STANDARD & POOR'S 500 BULL AND BEAR MARKETS

— Beginning —		— Ending —		Bull		Bear	
Date	S&P 500	Date	S&P 500	% Gain	Days	% Change	Days
11/13/29	17.66	4/10/30	25.92	46.8%	148	−83.0%	783
6/1/32	4.40	9/7/32	9.31	111.6	98	−40.6	173
2/27/33	5.53	2/6/34	11.82	113.7	344	−31.8	401
3/14/35	8.06	3/6/37	18.68	131.8	723	−49.0	390
3/31/38	8.50	11/9/38	13.79	62.2	223	−26.2	150
4/8/39	10.18	10/25/39	13.21	29.8	200	−43.5	916
4/28/42	7.47	5/29/46	19.25	157.7	1492	−28.8	353
5/17/47	13.71	6/15/48	17.06	24.4	395	−20.6	363
6/13/49	13.55	1/5/53	26.66	96.8	1302	−14.8	252
9/14/53	22.71	8/2/56	49.74	119.0	1053	−21.6	446
10/22/57	38.98	8/3/59	60.71	55.7	650	−13.9	449
10/25/60	52.30	12/12/61	72.64	38.9	413	−28.0	196
6/26/62	52.32	2/9/66	94.06	79.8	1324	−22.2	240
10/7/66	73.20	11/29/68	108.37	48.0	784	−36.1	543
5/26/70	69.29	4/28/71	104.77	51.2	337	−13.9	209
11/23/71	90.16	1/11/73	120.24	33.4	415	−48.2	630
10/3/74	62.28	9/21/76	107.83	73.1	719	−19.4	531
3/6/78	86.90	9/12/78	106.99	23.1	190	−8.2	562
3/27/80	98.22	11/28/80	140.52	43.1	246	−27.1	622
8/12/82	102.42	10/10/83	172.65	68.6	424	−14.4	288
7/24/84	147.82	8/25/87	336.77	127.8	1127	−33.5	101
12/4/87	223.92	7/16/90	368.95	64.8	955	−19.9	87
10/11/90	295.46	7/17/98	1186.75	301.7	2836	−19.3	45
8/31/98	957.28	3/24/00	1527.46	59.6	571	−36.8	546
9/21/01	965.80	1/4/02	1172.51	21.4	105	−33.8	278
10/9/02	776.76	10/9/07	1565.15	101.5	1826	−56.8	517
3/9/09	676.53	4/29/11	1363.61	101.6	781	−19.4	157
10/3/11	1099.23	4/2/12	1419.04	29.1*	182*	*At Press Time–not in averages	
		Average		**81.0%**	**729**	**−30.2%**	**379**

NASDAQ COMPOSITE BULL AND BEAR MARKETS

— Beginning —		— Ending —		Bull		Bear	
Date	NASDAQ	Date	NASDAQ	% Gain	Days	% Change	Days
11/23/71	100.31	1/11/73	136.84	36.4%	415	−59.9%	630
10/3/74	54.87	7/15/75	88.00	60.4	285	−16.2	63
9/16/75	73.78	9/13/78	139.25	88.7	1093	−20.4	62
11/14/78	110.88	2/8/80	165.25	49.0	451	−24.9	48
3/27/80	124.09	5/29/81	223.47	80.1	428	−28.8	441
8/13/82	159.14	6/24/83	328.91	106.7	315	−31.5	397
7/25/84	225.30	8/26/87	455.26	102.1	1127	−35.9	63
10/28/87	291.88	10/9/89	485.73	66.4	712	−33.0	372
10/16/90	325.44	7/20/98	2014.25	518.9	2834	−29.5	80
10/8/98	1419.12	3/10/00	5048.62	255.8	519	−71.8	560
9/21/01	1423.19	1/4/02	2059.38	44.7	105	−45.9	278
10/9/02	1114.11	10/31/07	2859.12	156.6	1848	−55.6	495
3/9/09	1268.64	4/29/11	2873.54	126.5	781	−18.7	157
10/3/11	2335.83	3/26/12	3122.57	33.7*	175*	*At Press Time– not in averages	
		Average		**130.2%**	**839**	**−36.3%**	**280**

JANUARY DAILY POINT CHANGES DOW JONES INDUSTRIALS

Previous Month Close	2003	2004	2005	2006	2007	2008	2009	2010	2011	2012
	8341.63	10453.92	10783.01	10717.50	12463.15	13264.82	8776.39	10428.05	11577.51	12217.56
1	H	H	S	S	H	H	H	H	S	S
2	265.89	-44.07	S	H	H*	-220.86	258.30	S	S	H
3	-5.83	S	-53.58	129.91	11.37	12.76	S	S	93.24	179.82
4	S	S	-98.65	32.74	6.17	-256.54	S	155.91	20.43	21.04
5	S	134.22	-32.95	2.00	-82.68	S	-81.80	-11.94	31.71	-2.72
6	171.88	-5.41	25.05	77.16	S	S	62.21	1.66	-25.58	-55.78
7	-32.98	-9.63	-18.92	S	S	27.31	-245.40	33.18	-22.55	S
8	-145.28	63.41	S	S	25.48	-238.42	-27.24	11.33	S	S
9	180.87	-133.55	S	52.59	-6.89	146.24	-143.28	S	S	32.77
10	8.71	S	17.07	-0.32	25.56	117.78	S	S	-37.31	69.78
11	S	S	-64.81	31.86	72.82	-246.79	S	45.80	34.43	-13.02
12	S	26.29	61.56	-81.08	41.10	S	-125.21	-36.73	83.56	21.57
13	1.09	-58.00	-111.95	-2.49	S	S	-25.41	53.51	-23.54	-48.96
14	56.64	111.19	52.17	S	S	171.85	-248.42	29.78	55.48	S
15	-119.44	15.48	S	S	H	-277.04	12.35	-100.90	S	S
16	-25.31	46.66	S	H	26.51	-34.95	68.73	S	S	H
17	-111.13	S	H	-63.55	-5.44	-306.95	S	S	H	60.01
18	S	S	70.79	-41.46	-9.22	-59.91	S	H	50.55	96.88
19	S	H	-88.82	25.85	-2.40	S	H	115.78	-12.64	45.03
20	H	-71.85	-68.50	-213.32	S	S	-332.13	-122.28	-2.49	96.50
21	-143.84	94.96	-78.48	S	S	H	279.01	-213.27	49.04	S
22	-124.17	-0.44	S	S	-88.37	-128.11	-105.30	-216.90	S	S
23	50.74	-54.89	S	21.38	56.64	298.98	-45.24	S	S	-11.66
24	-238.46	S	-24.38	23.45	87.97	108.44	S	S	108.68	-33.07
25	S	S	92.95	-2.48	-119.21	-171.44	S	23.88	-3.33	81.21
26	S	134.22	37.03	99.73	-15.54	S	38.47	-2.57	8.25	-22.33
27	-141.45	-92.59	-31.19	97.74	S	S	58.70	41.87	4.39	-74.17
28	99.28	-141.55	-40.20	S	S	176.72	200.72	-115.70	-166.13	S
29	21.87	41.92	S	S	3.76	96.41	-226.44	-53.13	S	S
30	-165.58	-22.22	S	-7.29	32.53	-37.47	-148.15	S	S	-6.74
31	108.68	S	62.74	-35.06	98.38	207.53	S	S	68.23	-20.81
Close	8053.81	10488.07	10489.94	10864.86	12621.69	12650.36	8000.86	10067.33	11891.93	12632.91
Change	-287.82	34.15	-293.07	147.36	158.54	-614.46	-775.53	-360.72	314.42	415.35

* Ford funeral

FEBRUARY DAILY POINT CHANGES DOW JONES INDUSTRIALS

Previous Month Close	2003	2004	2005	2006	2007	2008	2009	2010	2011	2012
	8053.81	10488.07	10489.94	10864.86	12621.69	12650.36	8000.86	10067.33	11891.93	12632.91
1	S	S	62.00	89.09	51.99	92.83	S	118.20	148.23	83.55
2	S	11.11	44.85	-101.97	-20.19	S	-64.03	111.32	1.81	-11.05
3	56.01	6.00	-3.69	-58.36	S	-108.03	141.53	-26.30	20.29	156.82
4	-96.53	-34.44	123.03	S	S	S	-121.70	-268.37	29.89	S
5	-28.11	24.81	S	S	8.25	-370.03	106.41	10.05	S	S
6	-55.88	97.48	S	4.65	4.57	-65.03	217.52	S	S	-17.10
7	-65.07	S	-0.37	-48.51	0.56	46.90	S	S	69.48	33.07
8	S	S	8.87	108.86	-29.24	-64.87	S	-103.84	71.52	5.75
9	S	-14.00	-60.52	24.73	-56.80	S	-9.72	150.25	6.74	6.51
10	55.88	34.82	85.50	35.70	S	S	-381.99	-20.26	-10.60	-89.23
11	-77.00	123.85	46.40	S	S	57.88	50.65	105.81	43.97	S
12	-84.94	-43.63	S	S	-28.28	133.40	-6.77	-45.05	S	S
13	-8.30	-66.22	S	-26.73	102.30	178.83	-82.35	S	S	72.81
14	158.93	S	-4.88	136.07	87.01	-175.26	S	S	-5.07	4.24
15	S	S	46.19	30.58	23.15	-28.77	S	H	-41.55	-97.33
16	S	H	-2.44	61.71	2.56	S	H	169.67	61.53	123.13
17	H	87.03	-80.62	-5.36	S	S	-297.81	40.43	29.97	45.79
18	132.35	-42.89	30.96	S	S	H	3.03	83.66	73.11	S
19	-40.55	-7.26	S	S	H	-10.99	-89.68	9.45	S	S
20	-85.64	-45.70	S	H	19.07	90.04	-100.28	S	S	H
21	103.15	S	H	-46.26	-48.23	-142.96	S	S	H	15.82
22	S	S	-174.02	68.11	-52.39	96.72	S	-18.97	-178.46	-27.02
23	S	-9.41	62.59	-67.95	-38.54	S	-250.89	-100.97	-107.01	46.02
24	-159.87	-43.25	75.00	-7.37	S	S	236.16	91.75	-37.28	-1.74
25	51.26	35.25	92.81	S	S	189.20	-80.05	-53.13	61.95	S
26	-102.52	-21.48	S	S	-15.22	114.70	-88.81	4.23	S	S
27	78.01	3.78	S	35.70	-416.02	9.36	-119.15	S	S	-1.44
28	6.09	S	-75.37	-104.14	52.39	-112.10	S	S	95.89	23.61
29	—	S	—	—	—	-315.79	—	—	—	-53.05
Close	7891.08	10583.92	10766.23	10993.41	12268.63	12266.39	7062.93	10325.26	12226.34	12952.07
Change	-162.73	95.85	276.29	128.55	-353.06	-383.97	-937.93	257.93	334.41	319.16

MARCH DAILY POINT CHANGES DOW JONES INDUSTRIALS

Previous Month	2003	2004	2005	2006	2007	2008	2009	2010	2011	2012
Close	7891.08	10583.92	10766.23	10993.41	12268.63	12266.39	7062.93	10325.26	12226.34	12952.07
1	S	94.22	63.77	60.12	-34.29	S	S	78.53	-168.32	28.23
2	S	-86.66	-18.03	-28.02	-120.24	S	-299.64	2.19	8.78	-2.73
3	-53.22	1.63	21.06	-3.92	S	-7.49	-37.27	-9.22	191.40	S
4	-132.99	-5.11	107.52	S	S	-45.10	149.82	47.38	-88.32	S
5	70.73	7.55	S	S	-63.69	41.19	-281.40	122.06	S	-14.76
6	-101.61	S	S	-63.00	157.18	-214.60	32.50	S	S	-203.66
7	66.04	S	-3.69	22.10	-15.14	-146.70	S	S	-79.85	78.18
8	S	-66.07	-24.24	25.05	68.25	S	S	-13.68	124.35	70.61
9	S	-72.52	-107.00	-33.46	15.62	S	-79.89	11.86	-1.29	14.08
10	-171.85	-160.07	45.89	104.06	S	-153.54	379.44	2.95	-228.48	S
11	-44.12	-168.51	-77.15	S	S	416.66	3.91	44.51	59.79	S
12	28.01	111.70	S	S	42.30	-46.57	239.66	12.85	S	37.69
13	269.68	S	S	-0.32	-242.66	35.50	53.92	S	S	217.97
14	37.96	S	30.15	75.32	57.44	-194.65	S	S	-51.24	16.42
15	S	-137.19	-59.41	58.43	26.28	S	S	17.46	-137.74	58.66
16	S	81.78	-112.03	43.47	-49.27	S	-7.01	43.83	-242.12	-20.14
17	282.21	115.63	-6.72	26.41	S	21.16	178.73	47.69	161.29	S
18	52.31	-4.52	3.32	S	S	420.41	90.88	45.50	83.93	S
19	71.22	-109.18	S	S	115.76	-293.00	-85.78	-37.19	S	6.51
20	21.15	S	S	-5.12	61.93	261.66	-122.42	S	S	-68.94
21	235.37	S	-64.28	-39.06	159.42	H	S	S	178.01	-45.57
22	S	-121.85	-94.88	81.96	13.62	S	S	43.91	-17.90	-78.48
23	S	-1.11	-14.49	-47.14	19.87	S	497.48	102.94	67.39	34.59
24	-307.29	-15.41	-13.15	9.68	S	187.32	-115.89	-52.68	84.54	S
25	65.55	170.59	H	S	S	-16.04	89.84	5.06	50.03	S
26	-50.35	-5.85	S	S	-11.94	-109.74	174.75	9.15	S	160.90
27	-28.43	S	S	-29.86	-71.78	-120.40	-148.38	S	S	-43.90
28	-55.68	S	42.78	-95.57	-96.93	-86.06	S	S	-22.71	-71.52
29	S	116.66	-79.95	61.16	48.39	S	S	45.50	81.13	19.61
30	S	52.07	135.23	-65.00	5.60	S	-254.16	11.56	71.60	66.22
31	-153.64	-24.00	-37.17	-41.38	S	46.49	86.90	-50.79	-30.88	S
Close	7992.13	10357.70	10503.76	11109.32	12354.35	12262.89	7608.92	10856.63	12319.73	13212.04
Change	101.05	-226.22	-262.47	115.91	85.72	-3.50	545.99	531.37	93.39	259.97

APRIL DAILY POINT CHANGES DOW JONES INDUSTRIALS

Previous Month	2003	2004	2005	2006	2007	2008	2009	2010	2011	2012
Close	7992.13	10357.70	10503.76	11109.32	12354.35	12262.89	7608.92	10856.63	12319.73	13212.04
1	77.73	15.63	-99.46	S	S	391.47	152.68	70.44	56.99	S
2	215.20	97.26	S	S	27.95	-48.53	216.48	H	S	52.45
3	-44.68	S	S	35.62	128.00	20.20	39.51	S	S	-64.94
4	36.77	S	16.84	58.91	19.75	-16.61	S	S	23.31	-124.80
5	S	87.78	37.32	35.70	30.15	S	S	46.48	-6.13	-14.61
6	S	12.44	27.56	-23.05	H	S	-41.74	-3.56	32.85	H
7	23.26	-90.66	60.30	-96.46	S	3.01	-186.29	-72.47	-17.26	S
8	-1.49	-38.12	-84.98	S	S	-35.99	47.55	29.55	-29.44	S
9	-100.98	H	S	S	8.94	-49.18	246.27	70.28	S	-130.55
10	23.39	S	S	21.29	4.71	54.72	H	S	S	-213.66
11	-17.92	S	-12.78	-51.70	-89.23	-256.56	S	S	1.06	89.46
12	S	73.53	59.41	40.34	68.34	S	S	8.62	-117.53	181.19
13	S	-134.28	-104.04	7.68	59.17	S	-25.57	13.45	7.41	-136.99
14	147.69	-3.33	-125.18	H	S	-23.36	-137.63	103.69	14.16	S
15	51.26	19.51	-191.24	S	S	60.41	109.44	21.46	56.68	S
16	-144.75	54.51	S	S	108.33	256.80	95.81	-125.91	S	71.82
17	80.04	S	S	-63.87	52.58	1.22	5.90	S	S	194.13
18	H	S	-16.26	194.99	30.80	228.87	S	S	-140.24	-82.79
19	S	-14.12	56.16	10.00	4.79	S	S	73.39	65.16	-68.65
20	S	-123.35	-115.05	64.12	153.35	S	-289.60	25.01	186.79	65.16
21	-8.75	2.77	206.24	4.56	S	-24.34	127.83	7.86	52.45	S
22	156.09	143.93	-60.89	S	S	-104.79	-82.99	9.37	H	S
23	30.67	11.64	S	S	-42.58	42.99	70.49	69.99	S	-102.09
24	-75.62	S	S	-11.13	34.54	85.73	119.23	S	S	74.39
25	-133.69	S	84.76	-53.07	135.95	42.91	S	S	-26.11	89.16
26	S	-28.11	-91.34	71.24	15.61	S	S	0.75	115.49	113.90
27	S	33.43	47.67	28.02	15.44	S	-51.29	-213.04	95.59	23.69
28	165.26	-135.56	-18.43	-15.37	S	-20.11	-8.05	53.28	72.35	S
29	31.38	-70.33	122.14	S	S	-39.81	168.78	122.05	47.23	S
30	-22.90	-46.70	S	S	-58.03	-11.81	-17.61	-158.71	S	-14.68
Close	8480.09	10225.57	10192.51	11367.14	13062.91	12820.13	8168.12	11008.61	12810.54	13213.63
Change	487.96	-132.13	-311.25	257.82	708.56	557.24	559.20	151.98	490.81	1.59

MAY DAILY POINT CHANGES DOW JONES INDUSTRIALS

Previous Month	2002	2003	2004	2005	2006	2007	2008	2009	2010	2011
Close	9946.22	8480.09	10225.57	10192.51	11367.14	13062.91	12820.13	8168.12	11008.61	12810.54
1	113.41	−25.84	S	S	−23.85	73.23	189.87	44.29	S	S
2	32.24	128.43	S	59.19	73.16	75.74	48.20	S	S	−3.18
3	−85.24	S	88.43	5.25	−16.17	29.50	S	S	143.22	0.15
4	S	S	3.20	127.69	38.58	23.24	S	214.33	−225.06	−83.93
5	S	−51.11	−6.25	−44.26	138.88	S	−88.66	−16.09	−58.65	−139.41
6	−198.59	56.79	−69.69	5.02	S	S	51.29	101.63	−347.80	54.57
7	28.51	−27.73	−123.92	S	S	48.35	−206.48	−102.43	−139.89	S
8	305.28	−69.41	S	S	6.80	−3.90	52.43	164.80	S	S
9	−104.41	113.38	S	38.94	55.23	53.80	−120.90	S	S	45.94
10	−97.50	S	−127.32	−103.23	2.88	−147.74	S	S	404.71	75.68
11	S	S	29.45	19.14	−141.92	111.09	S	−155.88	−36.88	−130.33
12	169.74	122.13	25.69	−110.77	−119.74	S	130.43	50.34	148.65	65.89
13	188.48	−47.48	−34.42	−49.36	S	S	−44.13	−184.22	−113.96	−100.17
14	−54.46	−31.43	2.13	S	S	20.56	66.20	46.43	−162.79	S
15	45.53	65.32	S	S	47.78	37.06	94.28	−62.68	S	S
16	63.87	−34.17	S	112.17	−8.88	103.69	−5.86	S	S	−47.38
17	S	S	−105.96	79.59	−214.28	−10.81	S	S	5.67	−68.79
18	S	S	61.60	132.57	−77.32	79.81	S	235.44	−114.88	80.60
19	S	−185.58	−30.80	28.74	15.77	S	41.36	−29.23	−66.58	45.14
20	−123.58	−2.03	−0.07	−21.28	S	S	−199.48	−52.81	−376.36	−93.28
21	−123.79	25.07	29.10	S	S	−13.65	−227.49	−129.91	125.38	S
22	52.17	77.59	S	S	−18.73	−2.93	24.43	−14.81	S	S
23	58.20	7.36	S	51.65	−26.98	−14.30	−145.99	S	S	−130.78
24	−111.82	S	−8.31	−19.88	18.97	−84.52	S	S	−126.82	−25.05
25	S	S	159.19	−45.88	93.73	66.15	S	H	−22.82	38.45
26	S	H	−7.73	79.80	67.56	S	H	196.17	−69.30	8.10
27	H	179.97	95.31	4.95	S	S	68.72	−173.47	284.54	38.82
28	−122.68	11.77	−16.75	S	S	H	45.68	103.78	−122.36	S
29	−58.54	−81.94	S	S	H	14.06	52.19	96.53	S	S
30	−11.35	139.08	S	S	−184.18	111.74	−7.90	S	S	H
31	13.56	S	H	−75.07	73.88	−5.44	S	S	H	128.21
Close	9925.25	8850.26	10188.45	10467.48	11168.31	13627.64	12638.32	8500.33	10136.63	12569.79
Change	−20.97	370.17	−37.12	274.97	−198.83	564.73	−181.81	332.21	−871.98	−240.75

JUNE DAILY POINT CHANGES DOW JONES INDUSTRIALS

Previous Month	2002	2003	2004	2005	2006	2007	2008	2009	2010	2011
Close	9925.25	8850.26	10188.45	10467.48	11168.31	13627.64	12638.32	8500.33	10136.63	12569.79
1	S	S	14.20	82.39	91.97	40.47	S	221.11	−112.61	−279.65
2	S	47.55	60.32	3.62	−12.41	S	−134.50	19.43	225.52	−41.59
3	−215.46	25.14	−67.06	−92.52	S	S	−100.97	−65.59	5.74	−97.29
4	−21.95	116.03	46.91	S	S	8.21	−12.37	74.96	−323.31	S
5	108.96	2.32	S	S	−199.15	−80.86	213.97	12.89	S	S
6	−172.16	21.49	S	6.06	−46.58	−129.79	−394.64	S	S	−61.30
7	−34.97	S	148.26	16.04	−71.24	−198.94	S	S	−115.48	−19.15
8	S	S	41.44	−6.21	7.92	157.66	S	1.36	123.49	−21.87
9	S	−82.79	−64.08	26.16	−46.90	S	70.51	−1.43	−40.73	75.42
10	55.73	74.89	41.66	9.61	S	S	9.44	−24.04	273.28	−172.45
11	−128.14	128.33	H*	S	S	0.57	−205.99	31.90	38.54	S
12	100.45	13.33	S	S	−99.34	−129.95	57.81	28.34	S	S
13	−114.91	−79.43	S	9.93	−86.44	187.34	165.77	S	S	1.06
14	−28.59	S	−75.37	25.01	110.78	71.37	S	S	−20.18	123.14
15	S	S	45.70	18.80	198.27	85.76	S	−187.13	213.88	−178.84
16	S	201.84	−0.85	12.28	−0.64	S	−38.27	−107.46	4.69	64.25
17	213.21	4.06	−2.06	44.42	S	S	−108.78	−7.49	24.71	42.84
18	18.70	−29.22	38.89	S	S	−26.50	−131.24	58.42	16.47	S
19	−144.55	−114.27	S	S	−72.44	22.44	34.03	−15.87	S	S
20	−129.80	21.22	S	−13.96	32.73	−146.00	−220.40	S	−8.23	76.02
21	−177.98	S	−44.94	−9.44	104.62	56.42	S	S		109.63
22	S	S	23.60	−11.74	−60.35	−185.58	S	−200.72	−148.89	−80.34
23	S	−127.80	84.50	−166.49	−30.02	S	−0.33	−16.10	4.92	−59.67
24	28.03	36.90	−35.76	−123.60	S	S	−34.93	−23.05	−145.64	−115.42
25	−155.00	−98.32	−71.97	S	S	−8.21	4.40	172.54	−8.99	S
26	−6.71	67.51	S	S	56.19	−14.39	−358.41	−34.01	S	S
27	149.81	−89.99	S	−7.06	−120.54	90.07	−106.91	S	S	108.98
28	−26.66	S	S	114.85	48.82	−5.45	S	S	−5.29	145.13
29	S	S	56.34	−31.15	217.24	−13.66	S	90.99	−268.22	72.73
30	S	−3.61	22.05	−99.51	−40.58	S	3.50	−82.38	−96.28	152.92
Close	9243.26	8985.44	10435.48	10274.97	11150.22	13408.62	11350.01	8447.00	9774.02	12414.34
Change	−681.99	135.18	247.03	−192.51	−18.09	−219.02	−1288.31	−53.33	−362.61	−155.45

* Reagan funeral

JULY DAILY POINT CHANGES DOW JONES INDUSTRIALS

Previous Month	2002	2003	2004	2005	2006	2007	2008	2009	2010	2011
Close	9243.26	8985.44	10435.48	10274.97	11150.22	13408.62	11350.01	8447.00	9774.02	12414.34
1	−133.47	55.51	−101.32	28.47	S	S	32.25	57.06	−41.49	168.43
2	−102.04	101.89	−51.33	S	S	126.81	−166.75	−223.32	−46.05	S
3	47.22	−72.63*	S	S	77.80*	41.87*	73.03*	H	S	S
4	H	H	S	H	H	H	H	S	S	H
5	324.53*	S	H	68.36	−76.20	−11.46	S	S	H	−12.90
6	S	S	−63.49	−101.12	73.48	45.84	S	44.13	57.14	56.15
7	S	146.58	20.95	31.61	−134.63	S	−56.58	−161.27	274.66	93.47
8	−104.60	6.30	−68.73	146.85	S	S	152.25	14.81	120.71	−62.29
9	−178.81	−66.88	41.66	S	S	38.29	−236.77	4.76	59.04	S
10	−282.59	−120.17	S	S	12.88	−148.27	81.58	−36.65	S	S
11	−11.97	83.55	S	70.58	31.22	76.17	−128.48	S	S	−151.44
12	−117.00	S	25.00	−5.83	−121.59	283.86	S	S	18.24	−58.88
13	S	S	9.37	43.50	−166.89	45.52	S	185.16	146.75	44.73
14	S	57.56	−38.79	71.50	−106.94	S	−45.35	27.81	3.70	−54.49
15	−45.34	−48.18	−45.64	11.94	S	S	−92.65	256.72	−7.41	42.61
16	−166.08	−34.38	−23.38	S	S	43.73	276.74	95.61	−261.41	S
17	69.37	−43.77	S	S	8.01	20.57	207.38	32.12	S	S
18	−132.99	137.33	S	−65.84	51.87	−53.33	49.91	S	S	−94.57
19	−390.23	S	−45.72	71.57	212.19	82.19	S	S	56.53	202.26
20	S	S	55.01	42.59	−83.32	−149.33	S	104.21	75.53	−15.51
21	S	−91.46	−102.94	−61.38	−59.72	S	−29.23	67.79	−109.43	152.50
22	−234.68	61.76	4.20	23.41	S	S	135.16	−34.68	201.77	−43.25
23	−82.24	35.79	−88.11	S	S	92.34	29.88	188.03	102.32	S
24	488.95	−81.73	S	S	182.67	−226.47	−283.10	23.95	S	S
25	−4.98	172.06	S	−54.70	52.66	68.12	21.41	S	S	−88.36
26	78.08	S	−0.30	−16.71	−1.20	−311.50	S	S	100.81	−91.50
27	S	S	123.22	57.32	−2.08	−208.10	S	15.27	12.26	−198.75
28	S	−18.06	31.93	68.46	119.27	S	−239.61	−11.79	−39.81	−62.44
29	447.49	−62.05	12.17	−64.64	S	S	266.48	−26.00	−30.72	−96.87
30	−31.85	−4.41	10.47	S	S	92.84	186.13	83.74	−1.22	S
31	56.56	33.75	S	S	−34.02	−146.32	−205.67	17.15	S	S
Close	8736.59	9233.80	10139.71	10640.91	11185.68	13211.99	11378.02	9171.61	10465.94	12143.24
Change	−506.67	248.36	−295.77	365.94	35.46	−196.63	28.01	724.61	691.92	−271.10

* Shortened trading day

AUGUST DAILY POINT CHANGES DOW JONES INDUSTRIALS

Previous Month	2002	2003	2004	2005	2006	2007	2008	2009	2010	2011
Close	8736.59	9233.80	10139.71	10640.91	11185.68	13211.99	11378.02	9171.61	10465.94	12143.24
1	−229.97	−79.83	S	−17.76	−59.95	150.38	−51.70	S	S	−10.75
2	−193.49	S	39.45	60.59	74.20	100.96	S	S	208.44	−265.87
3	S	S	−58.92	13.85	42.66	−281.42	S	114.95	−38.00	29.82
4	S	32.07	6.27	−87.49	−2.24	S	−42.17	33.63	44.05	−512.76
5	−269.50	−149.72	−163.48	−52.07	S	S	331.62	−39.22	−5.45	60.93
6	230.46	25.42	−147.70	S	S	286.87	40.30	−24.71	−21.42	S
7	182.06	64.71	S	S	−20.97	35.52	−224.64	113.81	S	S
8	255.87	64.64	S	−21.10	−45.79	153.56	302.89	S	S	−634.76
9	33.43	S	−0.67	78.74	−97.41	−387.18	S	S	45.19	429.92
10	S	S	130.01	−21.26	48.19	−31.14	S	−32.12	−54.50	−519.83
11	S	26.26	−6.35	91.48	−36.34	S	48.03	−96.50	−265.42	423.37
12	−56.56	92.71	−123.73	−85.58	S	S	−139.88	120.16	−58.88	125.71
13	−206.50	−38.30	10.76	S	S	−3.01	−109.51	36.58	−16.80	S
14	260.92	38.80	S	S	9.84	−207.61	82.97	−76.79	S	S
15	74.83	11.13	S	34.07	132.39	−167.45	43.97	S	S	213.88
16	−40.08	S	129.20	−120.93	96.86	−15.69	S	S	−1.14	−76.97
17	S	S	18.28	37.26	7.84	233.30	S	−186.06	103.84	4.28
18	S	90.76	110.32	4.22	46.51	S	−180.51	82.60	9.69	−419.63
19	212.73	16.45	−42.33	4.30	S	S	−130.84	61.22	−144.33	−172.93
20	−118.72	−31.39	69.32	S	S	42.27	68.88	70.89	−57.59	S
21	85.16	26.17	S	S	−36.42	−30.49	12.78	155.91	S	S
22	96.41	−74.81	S	10.66	−5.21	145.27	197.85	S	S	37.00
23	−180.68	S	−37.09	−50.31	−41.94	−0.25	S	S	−39.21	322.11
24	S	S	25.58	−84.71	6.56	142.99	S	3.32	−133.96	143.95
25	S	−31.23	83.11	15.76	−20.41	S	−241.81	30.01	19.61	−170.89
26	46.05	22.81	−8.33	−53.34	S	S	26.62	4.23	−74.25	134.72
27	−94.60	−6.66	21.60	S	S	−56.74	89.64	37.11	164.84	S
28	−130.32	40.42	S	S	67.96	−280.28	212.67	−36.43	S	S
29	−23.10	41.61	S	65.76	17.93	247.44	−171.63	S	S	254.71
30	−7.49	S	−72.49	−50.23	12.97	−50.56	S	S	−140.92	20.70
31	S	S	51.40	68.78	−1.76	119.01	S	−47.92	4.99	53.58
Close	8663.50	9415.82	10173.92	10481.60	11381.15	13357.74	11543.55	9496.28	10014.72	11613.53
Change	−73.09	182.02	34.21	−159.31	195.47	145.75	165.53	324.67	−451.22	−529.71

SEPTEMBER DAILY POINT CHANGES DOW JONES INDUSTRIALS

Previous Month Close	2002	2003	2004	2005	2006	2007	2008	2009	2010	2011
	8663.50	9415.82	10173.92	10481.60	11381.15	13357.74	11543.55	9496.28	10014.72	11613.53
1	S	H	-5.46	-21.97	83.00	S	H	-185.68	254.75	-119.96
2	H	107.45	121.82	-12.26	S	S	-26.63	-29.93	50.63	-253.31
3	-355.45	45.19	-30.08	S	S	H	15.96	63.94	157.83	S
4	117.07	19.44	S	S	H	91.12	-344.65	96.66	S	S
5	-141.42	-84.56	S	H	5.13	-143.39	32.73	S	S	H
6	143.50	S	H	141.87	-63.08	57.88	S	S	H	-100.96
7	S	S	82.59	44.26	-74.76	-249.97	S	H	-137.24	275.56
8	S	82.95	-29.43	-37.57	60.67	S	289.78	56.07	46.32	-119.05
9	92.18	-79.09	-24.26	82.63	S	S	-280.01	49.88	28.23	-303.68
10	83.23	-86.74	23.97	S	S	14.47	38.19	80.26	47.53	S
11	-21.44	39.30	S	S	4.73	180.54	164.79	-22.07	S	S
12	-201.76	11.79	S	4.38	101.25	-16.74	-11.72	S	S	68.99
13	-66.72	S	1.69	-85.50	45.23	133.23	S	S	81.36	44.73
14	S	S	3.40	-52.54	-15.93	17.64	S	21.39	-17.64	140.88
15	S	-22.74	-86.80	13.85	33.38	S	-504.48	56.61	46.24	186.45
16	67.49	118.53	13.13	83.19	S	S	141.51	108.30	22.10	75.91
17	-172.63	-21.69	39.97	S	S	-39.10	-449.36	-7.79	13.02	S
18	-35.10	113.48	S	S	-5.77	335.97	410.03	36.28	S	S
19	-230.06	-14.31	S	-84.31	-14.09	76.17	368.75	S	S	-108.08
20	43.63	S	-79.57	-76.11	72.28	-48.86	S	S	145.77	7.65
21	S	S	40.04	-103.49	-79.96	53.49	S	-41.34	7.41	-283.82
22	S	-109.41	-135.75	44.02	-25.13	S	-372.75	51.01	-21.72	-391.01
23	-113.87	40.63	-70.28	-2.46	S	S	-161.52	-81.32	-76.89	37.65
24	-189.02	-150.53	8.34	S	S	-61.13	-29.00	-41.11	197.84	S
25	158.69	-81.55	S	S	67.71	19.59	196.89	-42.25	S	S
26	155.30	-30.88	S	24.04	93.58	99.50	121.07	S	S	272.38
27	-295.67	S	-58.70	12.58	19.85	34.79	S	S	-48.22	146.83
28	S	S	88.86	16.88	29.21	-17.31	S	124.17	46.10	-179.79
29	S	67.16	58.84	79.69	-39.38	S	-777.68	-47.16	-22.86	143.08
30	-109.52	-105.18	-55.97	15.92	S	S	485.21	-29.92	-47.23	-240.60
Close	7591.93	9275.06	10080.27	10568.70	11679.07	13895.63	10850.66	9712.28	10788.05	10913.38
Change	-1071.57	-140.76	-93.65	87.10	297.92	537.89	-692.89	216.00	773.33	-700.15

OCTOBER DAILY POINT CHANGES DOW JONES INDUSTRIALS

Previous Month Close	2002	2003	2004	2005	2006	2007	2008	2009	2010	2011
	7591.93	9275.06	10080.27	10568.70	11679.07	13895.63	10850.66	9712.28	10788.05	10913.38
1	346.86	194.14	112.38	S	S	191.92	-19.59	-203.00	41.63	S
2	-183.18	18.60	S	S	-8.72	-40.24	-348.22	-21.61	S	S
3	-38.42	84.51	S	-33.22	56.99	-79.26	-157.47	S	S	-258.08
4	-188.79	S	23.89	-94.37	123.27	6.26	S	S	-78.41	153.41
5	S	S	-38.86	-123.75	16.08	91.70	S	112.08	193.45	131.24
6	S	22.67	62.24	-30.26	-16.48	S	-369.88	131.50	22.93	183.38
7	-105.56	59.63	-114.52	5.21	S	S	-508.39	-5.67	-19.07	-20.21
8	78.65	-23.71	-70.20	S	S	-22.28	-189.01	61.29	57.90	S
9	-215.22	49.11	S	S	7.60	120.80	-678.91	78.07	S	S
10	247.68	-5.33	S	-53.55	9.36	-85.84	-128.00	S	S	330.06
11	316.34	S	26.77	14.41	-15.04	-63.57	S	S	3.86	-16.88
12	S	S	-4.79	-36.26	95.57	77.96	S	20.86	10.06	102.55
13	S	89.70	-74.85	-0.32	12.81	S	936.42	-14.74	75.68	-40.72
14	27.11	48.60	-107.88	70.75	S	S	-76.62	144.80	-1.51	166.36
15	378.28	-9.93	38.93	S	S	-108.28	-733.08	47.08	-31.79	S
16	-219.65	-11.33	S	S	20.09	-71.86	401.35	-67.03	S	S
17	239.01	-69.93	S	60.76	-30.58	-20.40	-127.04	S	S	-247.49
18	47.36	S	22.94	-62.84	42.66	-3.58	S	S	80.91	180.05
19	S	S	-58.70	128.87	19.05	-366.94	S	96.28	-165.07	-72.43
20	S	56.15	-10.69	-133.03	-9.36	S	413.21	-50.71	129.35	37.16
21	215.84	-30.30	-21.17	-65.88	S	S	-231.77	-92.12	38.60	267.01
22	-88.08	-149.87	-107.95	S	S	44.95	-514.45	131.95	-14.01	S
23	44.11	14.89	S	S	114.54	109.26	172.04	-109.13	S	S
24	-176.93	-30.67	S	169.78	10.97	-0.98	-312.30	S	S	104.83
25	126.65	S	-7.82	-7.13	6.80	-3.33	S	S	31.49	-207.00
26	S	S	138.49	-32.89	28.98	134.78	S	-104.22	5.41	162.42
27	S	25.70	113.55	-115.03	-73.40	S	-203.18	14.21	-43.18	339.51
28	-75.95	140.15	2.51	172.82	S	S	889.35	-119.48	-12.33	22.56
29	0.90	26.22	22.93	S	S	63.56	-74.16	199.89	4.54	S
30	58.47	12.08	S	S	-3.76	-77.79	189.73	-249.85	S	S
31	-30.38	14.51	S	37.30	-5.77	137.54	144.32	S	S	-276.10
Close	8397.03	9801.12	10027.47	10440.07	12080.73	13930.01	9325.01	9712.73	11118.49	11955.01
Change	805.10	526.06	-52.80	-128.63	401.66	34.38	-1525.65	0.45	330.44	1041.63

NOVEMBER DAILY POINT CHANGES DOW JONES INDUSTRIALS

Previous Month	2002	2003	2004	2005	2006	2007	2008	2009	2010	2011
Close	8397.03	9801.12	10027.47	10440.07	12080.73	13930.01	9325.01	9712.73	11118.49	11955.01
1	120.61	S	26.92	-33.30	-49.71	-362.14	S	S	6.13	-297.05
2	S	S	-18.66	65.96	-12.48	27.23	S	76.71	64.10	178.08
3	S	57.34	101.32	49.86	-32.50	S	-5.18	-17.53	26.41	208.43
4	53.96	-19.63	177.71	8.17	S	S	305.45	30.23	219.71	-61.23
5	106.67	-18.00	72.78	S	S	-51.70	-486.01	203.82	9.24	S
6	92.74	36.14	S	S	119.51	117.54	-443.48	17.46	S	S
7	-184.77	-47.18	S	55.47	51.22	-360.92	248.02	S	S	85.15
8	-49.11	S	3.77	-46.51	19.77	-33.73	S	S	-37.24	101.79
9	S	S	-4.94	6.49	-73.24	-223.55	S	203.52	-60.09	-389.24
10	S	-53.26	-0.89	93.89	5.13	S	-73.27	20.03	10.29	112.85
11	-178.18	-18.74	84.36	45.94	S	S	-176.58	44.29	-73.94	259.89
12	27.05	111.04	69.17	S	S	-55.19	-411.30	-93.79	-90.52	S
13	12.49	-10.89	S	S	23.45	319.54	552.59	73.00	S	S
14	143.64	-69.26	S	11.13	86.13	-76.08	-337.94	S	S	-74.70
15	36.96	S	11.23	-10.73	33.70	-120.96	S	S	9.39	17.18
16	S	S	-62.59	-11.68	54.11	66.74	S	136.49	-178.47	-190.57
17	S	-57.85	61.92	45.46	36.74	S	-223.73	30.46	-15.62	-134.86
18	-92.52	-86.67	22.98	46.11	S	S	151.17	-11.11	173.35	25.43
19	-11.79	66.30	-115.64	S	S	-218.35	-427.47	-93.87	22.32	S
20	148.23	-71.04	S	53.95	-26.02	51.70	-444.99	-14.28	S	S
21	222.14	9.11	S	51.15	5.05	-211.10	494.13	S	S	-248.85
22	-40.31	S	32.51	51.15	5.36	H	S	S	-24.97	-53.59
23	S	S	3.18	44.66	H	181.84*	S	132.79	-142.21	-236.17
24	S	119.26	27.71	H	-46.78*	S	396.97	-17.24	150.91	H
25	44.56	16.15	H	15.53*	S	S	36.08	30.69	H	-25.77*
26	-172.98	15.63	1.92*	S	S	-237.44	247.14	H	-95.28*	S
27	255.26	H	S	S	-158.46	215.00	H	-154.48*	S	S
28	H	2.89*	S	-40.90	14.74	331.01	102.43*	S	S	291.23
29	-35.59*	S	-46.33	-2.56	90.28	22.28	S	S	-39.51	32.62
30	S	S	-47.88	-82.29	-4.80	59.99	S	34.92	-46.47	490.05
Close	8896.09	9782.46	10428.02	10805.87	12221.93	13371.72	8829.04	10344.84	11006.02	12045.68
Change	499.06	-18.66	400.55	365.80	141.20	-558.29	-495.97	632.11	-112.47	90.67

* Shortened trading day

DECEMBER DAILY POINT CHANGES DOW JONES INDUSTRIALS

Previous Month	2002	2003	2004	2005	2006	2007	2008	2009	2010	2011
Close	8896.09	9782.46	10428.02	10805.87	12221.93	13371.72	8829.04	10344.84	11006.02	12045.68
1	S	116.59	162.20	106.70	-27.80	S	-679.95	126.74	249.76	-25.65
2	-33.52	-45.41	-5.10	-35.06	S	S	270.00	-18.90	106.63	-0.61
3	-119.64	19.78	7.09	S	S	-57.15	172.60	-86.53	19.68	S
4	-5.08	57.40	S	S	89.72	-65.84	-215.45	22.75	S	S
5	-114.57	-68.14	S	-42.50	47.75	196.23	259.18	S	S	78.41
6	22.49	S	-45.15	21.85	-22.35	174.93	S	S	-19.90	52.30
7	S	S	-106.48	-45.95	-30.84	5.69	S	1.21	-3.03	46.24
8	S	102.59	53.65	-55.79	29.08	S	298.76	-104.14	13.32	-198.67
9	-172.36	-41.85	58.59	23.46	S	S	-242.85	51.08	-2.42	186.56
10	100.85	-1.56	-9.60	S	S	101.45	70.09	68.78	40.26	S
11	14.88	86.30	S	S	20.99	-294.26	-196.33	65.67	S	S
12	-50.74	34.00	S	-10.81	-12.90	41.13	64.59	S	S	-162.87
13	-104.69	S	95.10	55.95	1.92	44.06	S	S	18.24	-66.45
14	S	S	38.13	59.79	99.26	-178.11	S	29.55	47.98	-131.46
15	S	-19.34	15.00	-1.84	28.76	S	-65.15	-49.05	-19.07	45.33
16	193.69	106.74	14.19	-6.08	S	S	359.61	-10.88	41.78	-2.42
17	-92.01	15.70	-55.72	S	S	-172.65	-99.80	-132.86	-7.34	S
18	-88.04	102.82	S	S	-4.25	65.27	-219.35	20.63	S	S
19	-82.55	30.14	S	-39.06	30.05	-25.20	-25.88	S	S	-100.13
20	146.52	S	11.68	-30.98	-7.45	38.37	S	S	-13.78	337.32
21	S	S	97.83	28.18	-42.62	205.01	S	85.25	55.03	4.16
22	S	59.78	56.46	55.71	-78.03	S	-59.34	50.79	26.33	61.91
23	-18.03	3.26	11.23	-6.17	S	S	-100.28	1.51	14.00	124.35
24	-45.18*	-36.07*	H	S	S	98.68*	48.99*	53.66*	H	S
25	H	H	S	S	H	H	H	H	S	S
26	-15.50	19.48*	S	H	64.41	2.36	47.07	S	S	H
27	-128.83	S	-50.99	-105.50	102.94	-192.08	S	S	-18.46	-2.65
28	S	S	78.41	18.49	-9.05	6.26	S	26.98	20.51	-139.94
29	S	125.33	-25.35	-11.44	-38.37	S	-31.62	-1.67	9.84	135.63
30	29.07	-24.96	-28.89	-67.32	S	S	184.46	3.10	-15.67	-69.48
31	8.78	28.88	-17.29	S	S	-101.05	108.00	-120.46	7.80	S
Close	8341.63	10453.92	10783.01	10717.50	12463.15	13264.82	8776.39	10428.05	11577.51	12217.56
Change	-554.46	671.46	354.99	-88.37	241.22	-106.90	-52.65	83.21	571.49	171.88

* Shortened trading day

A TYPICAL DAY IN THE MARKET

Half-hourly data became available for the Dow Jones Industrial Average starting in January 1987. The NYSE switched 10:00 a.m. openings to 9:30 a.m. in October 1985. Below is the comparison between half-hourly performance from January 1987 to April 27, 2012 and hourly performance from November 1963 to June 1985. Stronger openings and closings in a more bullish climate are evident. Morning and afternoon weaknesses appear an hour earlier.

MARKET % PERFORMANCE EACH HALF-HOUR OF THE DAY
(January 1987 to April 27, 2012)

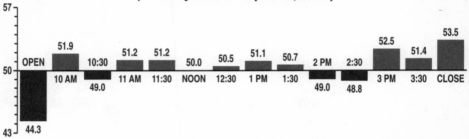

Based on the number of times the Dow Jones Industrial Average increased over previous half-hour.

MARKET % PERFORMANCE EACH HOUR OF THE DAY
(November 1963 to June 1985)

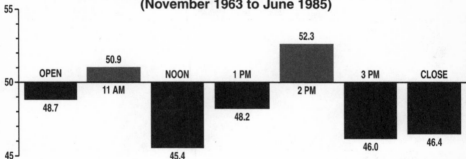

Based on the number of times the Dow Jones Industrial Average increased over previous hour.

On the next page, half-hourly movements since January 1987 are separated by day of the week. From 1953 to 1989, Monday was the worst day of the week, especially during long bear markets, but times changed. Monday reversed positions and became the best day of the week and on the plus side eleven years in a row from 1990 to 2000.

During the last twelve years (2001–May 11, 2012) Monday and Friday are net losers. Tuesday and Wednesday are solid gainers, Tuesday the best (page 68). On all days stocks do tend to firm up near the close with weakness early morning and from 2 to 2:30 frequently.

THROUGH THE WEEK ON A HALF-HOURLY BASIS

From the chart showing the percentage of times the Dow Jones Industrial Average rose over the preceding half-hour (January 1987 to April 27, 2012*), the typical week unfolds.

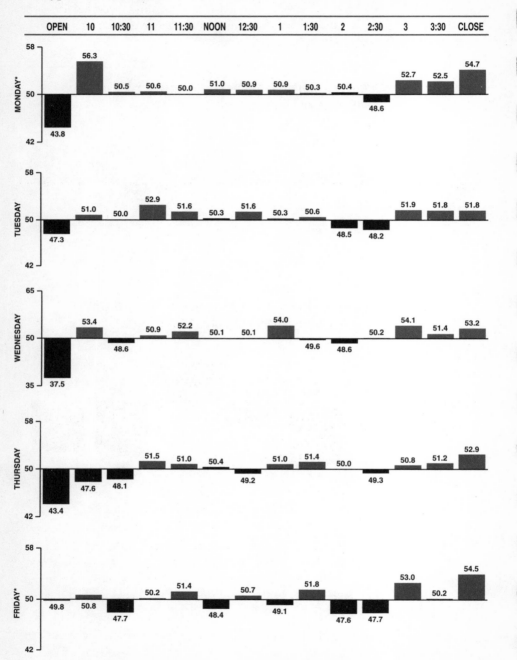

*Monday denotes first trading day of the week, Friday denotes last trading day of the week.

TUESDAY MOST PROFITABLE DAY OF WEEK

Between 1952 and 1989, Monday was the worst trading day of the week. The first trading day of the week (including Tuesday, when Monday is a holiday) rose only 44.3% of the time, while the other trading days closed higher 54.8% of the time. (NYSE Saturday trading was discontinued June 1952.)

MARKET % PERFORMANCE EACH DAY OF THE WEEK
(June 1952 to December 1989)

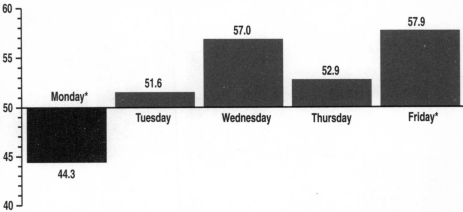

A dramatic reversal occurred in 1990—Monday became the most powerful day of the week. However, during the last eleven and a third years, Tuesday has produced the most gains. Since the top in 2000, traders have not been inclined to stay long over the weekend nor buy up equities at the outset of the week. This is not uncommon during uncertain market times. Monday was the worst day during the 2007–2009 bear, and only Tuesday was a net gainer. Since the March 2009 bottom, Monday is best. See pages 68 and 143.

MARKET % PERFORMANCE EACH DAY OF THE WEEK
(January 1990 to May 4, 2012)

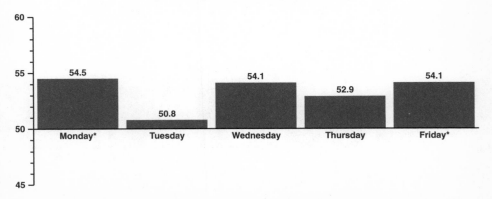

Charts based on the number of times S&P 500 index closed higher than previous day.
*Monday denotes first trading day of the week, Friday denotes last trading day of the week.

NASDAQ STRONGEST LAST 3 DAYS OF WEEK

Despite 20 years less data, daily trading patterns on NASDAQ through 1989 appear to be fairly similar to the S&P on page 141, except for more bullishness on Thursdays. During the mostly flat markets of the 1970s and early 1980s, it would appear that apprehensive investors decided to throw in the towel over weekends and sell on Mondays and Tuesdays.

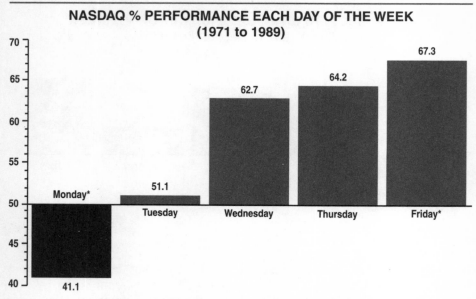

NASDAQ % PERFORMANCE EACH DAY OF THE WEEK (1971 to 1989)

Notice the vast difference in the daily trading pattern between NASDAQ and S&P from January 1, 1990, to recent times. The reason for so much more bullishness is that NASDAQ moved up 1010%, over three times as much during the 1990 to 2000 period. The gain for the S&P was 332% and for the Dow Jones industrials, 326%. NASDAQ's weekly patterns are beginning to move in step with the rest of the market. Notice the similarities to the S&P since 2001 on pages 143 and 144—Monday and Friday weakness, midweek strength.

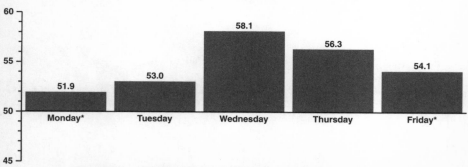

NASDAQ % PERFORMANCE EACH DAY OF THE WEEK (1990 to May 4, 2012)

Based on NASDAQ composite, prior to February 5, 1971, based on National Quotation Bureau indices.
*Monday denotes first trading day of the week, Friday denotes last trading day of the week.

S&P DAILY PERFORMANCE EACH YEAR SINCE 1952

To determine if market trend alters performance of different days of the week, we separated 22 bear years—1953, '56, '57, '60, '62, '66, '69, '70, '73, '74, '77, '78, '81, '84, '87, '90, '94, 2000, 2001, 2002, 2008, and 2011—from 38 bull market years. While Tuesday and Thursday did not vary much between bull and bear years, Mondays and Fridays were sharply affected. There was a swing of 10.6 percentage points in Monday's and 9.5 in Friday's performance. Wednesday is developing a reputation as the best day of the week based upon total points gained. See page 68.

PERCENTAGE OF TIMES MARKET CLOSED HIGHER THAN PREVIOUS DAY
(June 1952 to May 4, 2012)

	Monday*	Tuesday	Wednesday	Thursday	Friday*
1952	48.4%	55.6%	58.1%	51.9%	66.7%
1953	32.7	50.0	54.9	57.5	56.6
1954	50.0	57.5	63.5	59.2	73.1
1955	50.0	45.7	63.5	60.0	78.9
1956	36.5	39.6	46.9	50.0	59.6
1957	25.0	54.0	66.7	48.9	44.2
1958	59.6	52.0	59.6	68.1	72.6
1959	42.3	53.1	55.8	48.9	69.8
1960	34.6	50.0	44.2	54.0	59.6
1961	52.9	54.4	64.7	56.0	67.3
1962	28.3	52.1	54.0	51.0	50.0
1963	46.2	63.3	51.0	57.5	69.2
1964	40.4	48.0	61.5	58.7	77.4
1965	44.2	57.5	55.8	51.0	71.2
1966	36.5	47.8	53.9	42.0	57.7
1967	38.5	50.0	60.8	64.0	69.2
1968†	49.1	57.5	64.3	42.6	54.9
1969	30.8	45.8	50.0	67.4	50.0
1970	38.5	46.0	63.5	48.9	52.8
1971	44.2	64.6	57.7	55.1	51.9
1972	38.5	60.9	57.7	51.0	67.3
1973	32.1	51.1	52.9	44.9	44.2
1974	32.7	57.1	51.0	36.7	30.8
1975	53.9	38.8	61.5	56.3	55.8
1976	55.8	55.3	55.8	40.8	58.5
1977	40.4	40.4	46.2	53.1	53.9
1978	51.9	43.5	59.6	54.0	48.1
1979	54.7	53.2	58.8	66.0	44.2
1980	55.8	54.2	71.7	35.4	59.6
1981	44.2	38.8	55.8	53.2	47.2
1982	46.2	39.6	44.2	44.9	50.0
1983	55.8	46.8	61.5	52.0	55.8
1984	39.6	63.8	31.4	46.0	44.2
1985	44.2	61.2	54.9	56.3	53.9
1986	51.9	44.9	67.3	58.3	55.8
1987	51.9	57.1	63.5	61.7	49.1
1988	51.9	61.7	51.9	48.0	59.6
1989	51.9	47.8	69.2	58.0	69.2
1990	67.9	53.2	52.9	40.0	51.9
1991	44.2	46.9	52.9	49.0	51.9
1992	51.9	49.0	53.9	56.3	45.3
1993	65.4	41.7	55.8	44.9	48.1
1994	55.8	46.8	52.9	48.0	59.6
1995	63.5	56.5	63.5	62.0	63.5
1996	54.7	44.9	51.0	57.1	63.5
1997	67.3	67.4	42.3	41.7	57.7
1998	57.7	62.5	57.7	38.3	60.4
1999	46.2	29.8	67.3	53.1	57.7
2000	51.9	43.5	40.4	56.0	46.2
2001	45.3	51.1	44.0	59.2	43.1
2002	40.4	37.5	56.9	38.8	48.1
2003	59.6	62.5	42.3	58.3	50.0
2004	51.9	61.7	59.6	52.1	52.8
2005	59.6	47.8	59.6	56.0	55.8
2006	55.8	55.6	67.3	52.0	48.1
2007	47.2	50.0	64.0	50.0	61.5
2008	42.3	50.0	41.5	60.4	55.8
2009	53.9	50.0	57.7	63.8	52.8
2010	61.5	57.5	55.8	53.1	57.7
2011	48.1	56.5	55.8	56.0	57.7
2012‡	61.1	46.7	50.0	70.6	55.6
Average	**48.1%**	**51.3%**	**55.9%**	**52.9%**	**56.5%**
38 Bull Years	**51.8%**	**52.8%**	**58.5%**	**53.4%**	**60.0%**
22 Bear Years	**41.2%**	**48.9%**	**51.8%**	**51.3%**	**50.5%**

Based on S&P 500

† Most Wednesdays closed last 7 months of 1968 ‡ Through 5/4/2012 only, not included in averages.
*Monday denotes first trading day of the week, Friday denotes last trading day of the week.

NASDAQ DAILY PERFORMANCE EACH YEAR SINCE 1971

After dropping a hefty 77.9% from its 2000 high (versus −37.8% on the Dow and −49.1% on the S&P 500), NASDAQ tech stocks still outpace the blue chips and big caps—but not by nearly as much as they did. From January 1, 1971 through May 4, 2012 NASDAQ, moved up an impressive 3199%. The Dow (up 1454%) and the S&P (up 1386%) gained less than half as much.

Monday's performance on NASDAQ was lackluster during the three-year bear market of 2000–2002. As NASDAQ rebounded (up 50% in 2003), strength returned to Monday during 2003–2006. During the bear market from late 2007 to early 2009, weakness was most consistent on Monday and Friday.

PERCENTAGE OF TIMES NASDAQ CLOSED HIGHER THAN PREVIOUS DAY (1971 to May 4, 2012)

	Monday*	Tuesday	Wednesday	Thursday	Friday*
1971	51.9%	52.1%	59.6%	65.3%	71.2%
1972	30.8	60.9	63.5	57.1	78.9
1973	34.0	48.9	52.9	53.1	48.1
1974	30.8	44.9	52.9	51.0	42.3
1975	44.2	42.9	63.5	64.6	63.5
1976	50.0	63.8	67.3	59.2	58.5
1977	51.9	40.4	53.9	63.3	73.1
1978	48.1	47.8	73.1	72.0	84.6
1979	45.3	53.2	64.7	86.0	82.7
1980	46.2	64.6	84.9	52.1	73.1
1981	42.3	32.7	67.3	76.6	69.8
1982	34.6	47.9	59.6	51.0	63.5
1983	42.3	44.7	67.3	68.0	73.1
1984	22.6	53.2	35.3	52.0	51.9
1985	36.5	59.2	62.8	68.8	66.0
1986	38.5	55.1	65.4	72.9	75.0
1987	42.3	49.0	65.4	68.1	66.0
1988	50.0	55.3	61.5	66.0	63.5
1989	38.5	54.4	71.2	72.0	75.0
1990	54.7	42.6	60.8	46.0	55.8
1991	51.9	59.2	66.7	65.3	51.9
1992	44.2	53.1	59.6	60.4	45.3
1993	55.8	56.3	69.2	57.1	67.3
1994	51.9	46.8	54.9	52.0	55.8
1995	50.0	52.2	63.5	64.0	63.5
1996	50.9	57.1	64.7	61.2	63.5
1997	65.4	59.2	53.9	52.1	55.8
1998	59.6	58.3	65.4	44.7	58.5
1999	61.5	40.4	63.5	57.1	65.4
2000	40.4	41.3	42.3	60.0	57.7
2001	41.5	57.8	52.0	55.1	47.1
2002	44.2	37.5	56.9	46.9	46.2
2003	57.7	60.4	40.4	60.4	46.2
2004	57.7	59.6	53.9	50.0	50.9
2005	61.5	47.8	51.9	48.0	59.6
2006	55.8	51.1	65.4	50.0	44.2
2007	47.2	63.0	66.0	56.0	57.7
2008	34.6	52.1	49.1	54.2	42.3
2009	51.9	54.2	63.5	63.8	50.9
2010	61.5	53.2	61.5	55.1	61.5
2011	50.0	56.5	50.0	64.0	53.9
2012†	44.4	60.0	61.1	70.6	44.4
Average	**47.0%**	**52.2%**	**60.2%**	**59.8%**	**60.1%**
29 Bull Years	**49.7%**	**54.0%**	**63.0%**	**60.8%**	**63.6%**
12 Bear Years	**40.8%**	**46.9%**	**53.3%**	**56.6%**	**53.1%**

Based on NASDAQ composite; prior to February 5, 1971, based on National Quotation Bureau indices.
† Through 5/4/2012 only, not included in averages.
*Monday denotes first trading day of the week, Friday denotes last trading day of the week.

MONTHLY CASH INFLOWS INTO S&P STOCKS

For many years, the last trading day of the month, plus the first four of the following month, were the best market days of the month. This pattern is quite clear in the first chart, showing these five consecutive trading days towering above the other 16 trading days of the average month in the 1953–1981 period. The rationale was that individuals and institutions tended to operate similarly, causing a massive flow of cash into stocks near beginnings of months.

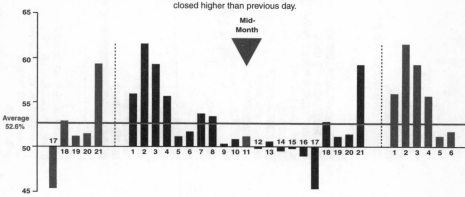

MARKET % PERFORMANCE EACH DAY OF THE MONTH
(January 1953 to December 1981)
Based on the number of times the S&P 500
closed higher than previous day.

Clearly "front-running" traders took advantage of this phenomenon, drastically altering the previous pattern. The second chart from 1982 onward shows the trading shift caused by these "anticipators" to the last three trading days of the month, plus the first two. Another astonishing development shows the ninth, tenth, and eleventh trading days rising strongly as well. Perhaps the enormous growth of 401(k) retirement plans (participants' salaries are usually paid twice monthly) is responsible for this mid-month bulge. First trading days of the month have produced the greatest gains in recent years (see page 84).

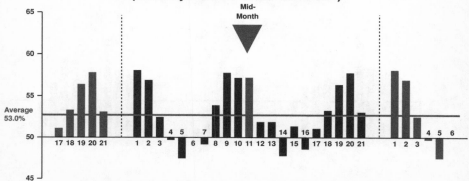

MARKET % PERFORMANCE EACH DAY OF THE MONTH
(January 1982 to December 2011)

Trading Days (excluding Saturdays, Sundays, and holidays).

MONTHLY CASH INFLOWS INTO NASDAQ STOCKS

NASDAQ stocks moved up 58.1% of the time through 1981 compared to 52.6% for the S&P on page 145. Ends and beginnings of the month are fairly similar, specifically the last plus the first four trading days. But notice how investors piled into NASDAQ stocks until mid-month. NASDAQ rose 118.6% from January 1, 1971, to December 31, 1981, compared to 33.0% for the S&P.

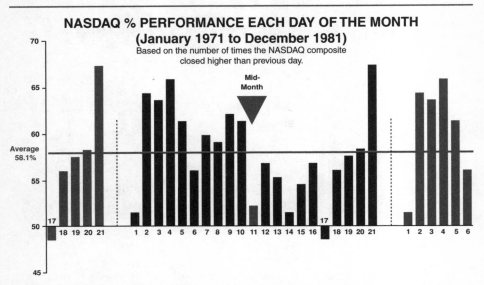

NASDAQ % PERFORMANCE EACH DAY OF THE MONTH
(January 1971 to December 1981)
Based on the number of times the NASDAQ composite closed higher than previous day.

After the air was let out of the tech market 2000–2002, S&P's 926% gain over the last 30 years is more evenly matched with NASDAQ's 1230% gain. Last three, first four, and middle ninth and tenth days rose the most. Where the S&P has five days of the month that go down more often than up, NASDAQ has none. NASDAQ exhibits the most strength on the last trading day of the month; however, over the past 15 years, last days have weakened considerably, down more often then not.

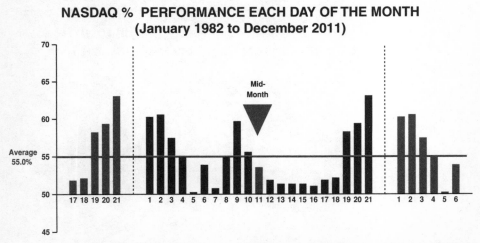

NASDAQ % PERFORMANCE EACH DAY OF THE MONTH
(January 1982 to December 2011)

Trading Days (excluding Saturdays, Sundays, and holidays).
Based on NASDAQ composite, prior to February 5, 1971, based on National Quotation Bureau indices.

NOVEMBER, DECEMBER, AND JANUARY: YEAR'S BEST THREE-MONTH SPAN

The most important observation to be made from a chart showing the average monthly percent change in market prices since 1950 is that institutions (mutual funds, pension funds, banks, etc.) determine the trading patterns in today's market.

The "investment calendar" reflects the annual, semi-annual and quarterly operations of institutions during January, April and July. October, besides being the last campaign month before elections, is also the time when most bear markets seem to end, as in 1946, 1957, 1960, 1966, 1974, 1987, 1990, 1998 and 2002. (August and September tend to combine to make the worst consecutive two-month period.)

S&P 500 MONTHLY % PERFORMANCE
January 1950 to April 2012

Average month-to-month % change in S&P 500
(Based on monthly closing prices.)

Unusual year-end strength comes from corporate and private pension funds, producing a 4.3% gain on average between November 1 and January 31. In 2007–2008, these three months were all down for the fourth time since 1930; previously in 1931–1932, 1940–1941, and 1969–1970, also bear markets. September's dismal performance makes it the worst month of the year. However, in the last 17 years it has been up ten times—down five in a row 1999–2003.

In post-presidential election years since 1950, the best three months are July +2.0% (9–7), May +1.7% (9–7), and November +1.7% (11–4). January, March, April, October, and December are gainers while February, June, August, and September are losers. February is worst, –2.0% (6–9).

See page 44 for monthly performance tables for the S&P 500 and the Dow Jones industrials. See pages 48, 50, and 60 for unique switching strategies.

On page 62, you can see how the first month of the first three quarters far outperforms the second and the third months since 1950, and note the improvement in May's and October's performance since 1991.

NOVEMBER THROUGH JUNE: NASDAQ'S EIGHT-MONTH RUN

The two-and-a-half-year plunge of 77.9% in NASDAQ stocks, between March 10, 2000, and October 9, 2002, brought several horrendous monthly losses (the two greatest were November 2000, −22.9%, and February 2001, −22.4%), which trimmed average monthly performance over the $41^1/_3$-year period. Ample Octobers in ten of the last 14 years, including three huge turnarounds in 2001 (+12.8%), 2002 (+13.5%), and 2011 (+11.1%) have put bear-killing October in the number one spot since 1998. January's 2.9% average gain is still awesome, and twice S&P's 1.1% January average since 1971.

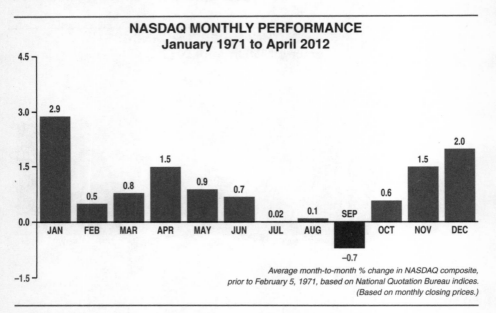

NASDAQ MONTHLY PERFORMANCE
January 1971 to April 2012

Average month-to-month % change in NASDAQ composite, prior to February 5, 1971, based on National Quotation Bureau indices. (Based on monthly closing prices.)

Bear in mind, when comparing NASDAQ to the S&P on page 147, that there are 22 fewer years of data here. During this $41^1/_3$-year (1971–April 2012) period, NASDAQ gained 3300%, while the S&P and the Dow rose only 1417% and 1475%, respectively. On page 56 you can see a statistical monthly comparison between NASDAQ and the Dow.

Year-end strength is even more pronounced in NASDAQ, producing a 6.4% gain on average between November 1 and January 31—1.5 times greater than that of the S&P 500 on page 147. September is the worst month of the year for the over-the-counter index as well, posting an average loss of −0.7%. These extremes underscore NASDAQ's higher volatility—and potential for moves of greater magnitude.

In post-presidential election years since 1971, the best three months are May +3.4% (8–2), July +3.1% (8–2), and April +2.4% (7–3). January, June, October, November, and December are also solid. February, March, August, and September are net losers with February the worst, averaging −4.4% (2–8).

DOW JONES INDUSTRIALS ANNUAL HIGHS, LOWS, & CLOSES SINCE 1901

YEAR	HIGH DATE	HIGH CLOSE	LOW DATE	LOW CLOSE	YEAR CLOSE	YEAR	HIGH DATE	HIGH CLOSE	LOW DATE	LOW CLOSE	YEAR CLOSE
1901	6/17	57.33	12/24	45.07	47.29	1957	7/12	520.77	10/22	419.79	435.69
1902	4/24	50.14	12/15	43.64	47.10	1958	12/31	583.65	2/25	436.89	583.65
1903	2/16	49.59	11/9	30.88	35.98	1959	12/31	679.36	2/9	574.46	679.36
1904	12/5	53.65	3/12	34.00	50.99	1960	1/5	685.47	10/25	566.05	615.89
1905	12/29	70.74	1/25	50.37	70.47	1961	12/13	734.91	1/3	610.25	731.14
1906	1/19	75.45	7/13	62.40	69.12	1962	1/3	726.01	6/26	535.76	652.10
1907	1/7	70.60	11/15	38.83	43.04	1963	12/18	767.21	1/2	646.79	762.95
1908	11/13	64.74	2/13	42.94	63.11	1964	11/18	891.71	1/2	766.08	874.13
1909	11/19	73.64	2/23	58.54	72.56	1965	12/31	969.26	6/28	840.59	969.26
1910	1/3	72.04	7/26	53.93	59.60	1966	2/9	995.15	10/7	744.32	785.69
1911	6/19	63.78	9/25	53.43	59.84	1967	9/25	943.08	1/3	786.41	905.11
1912	9/30	68.97	2/10	58.72	64.37	1968	12/3	985.21	3/21	825.13	943.75
1913	1/9	64.88	6/11	52.83	57.71	1969	5/14	968.85	12/17	769.93	800.36
1914	3/20	61.12	7/30	52.32	54.58	1970	12/29	842.00	5/26	631.16	838.92
1915	12/27	99.21	2/24	54.22	99.15	1971	4/28	950.82	11/23	797.97	890.20
1916	11/21	110.15	4/22	84.96	95.00	1972	12/11	1036.27	1/26	889.15	1020.02
1917	1/3	99.18	12/19	65.95	74.38	1973	1/11	1051.70	12/5	788.31	850.86
1918	10/18	89.07	1/15	73.38	82.20	1974	3/13	891.66	12/6	577.60	616.24
1919	11/3	119.62	2/8	79.15	107.23	1975	7/15	881.81	1/2	632.04	852.41
1920	1/3	109.88	12/21	66.75	71.95	1976	9/21	1014.79	1/2	858.71	1004.65
1921	12/15	81.50	8/24	63.90	81.10	1977	1/3	999.75	11/2	800.85	831.17
1922	10/14	103.43	1/10	78.59	98.73	1978	9/8	907.74	2/28	742.12	805.01
1923	3/20	105.38	10/27	85.76	95.52	1979	10/5	897.61	11/7	796.67	838.74
1924	12/31	120.51	5/20	88.33	120.51	1980	11/20	1000.17	4/21	759.13	963.99
1925	11/6	159.39	3/30	115.00	156.66	1981	4/27	1024.05	9/25	824.01	875.00
1926	8/14	166.64	3/30	135.20	157.20	1982	12/27	1070.55	8/12	776.92	1046.54
1927	12/31	202.40	1/25	152.73	202.40	1983	11/29	1287.20	1/3	1027.04	1258.64
1928	12/31	300.00	2/20	191.33	300.00	1984	1/6	1286.64	7/24	1086.57	1211.57
1929	9/3	381.17	11/13	198.69	248.48	1985	12/16	1553.10	1/4	1184.96	1546.67
1930	4/17	294.07	12/16	157.51	164.58	1986	12/2	1955.57	1/22	1502.29	1895.95
1931	2/24	194.36	12/17	73.79	77.90	1987	8/25	2722.42	10/19	1738.74	1938.83
1932	3/8	88.78	7/8	41.22	59.93	1988	10/21	2183.50	1/20	1879.14	2168.57
1933	7/18	108.67	2/27	50.16	99.90	1989	10/9	2791.41	1/3	2144.64	2753.20
1934	2/5	110.74	7/26	85.51	104.04	1990	7/17	2999.75	10/11	2365.10	2633.66
1935	11/19	148.44	3/14	96.71	144.13	1991	12/31	3168.83	1/9	2470.30	3168.83
1936	11/17	184.90	1/6	143.11	179.90	1992	6/1	3413.21	10/9	3136.58	3301.11
1937	3/10	194.40	11/24	113.64	120.85	1993	12/29	3794.33	1/20	3241.95	3754.09
1938	11/12	158.41	3/31	98.95	154.76	1994	1/31	3978.36	4/4	3593.35	3834.44
1939	9/12	155.92	4/8	121.44	150.24	1995	12/13	5216.47	1/30	3832.08	5117.12
1940	1/3	152.80	6/10	111.84	131.13	1996	12/27	6560.91	1/10	5032.94	6448.27
1941	1/10	133.59	12/23	106.34	110.96	1997	8/6	8259.31	4/11	6391.69	7908.25
1942	12/26	119.71	4/28	92.92	119.40	1998	11/23	9374.27	8/31	7539.07	9181.43
1943	7/14	145.82	1/8	119.26	135.89	1999	12/31	11497.12	1/22	9120.67	11497.12
1944	12/16	152.53	2/7	134.22	152.32	2000	1/14	11722.98	3/7	9796.03	10786.85
1945	12/11	195.82	1/24	151.35	192.91	2001	5/21	11337.92	9/21	8235.81	10021.50
1946	5/29	212.50	10/9	163.12	177.20	2002	3/19	10635.25	10/9	7286.27	8341.63
1947	7/24	186.85	5/17	163.21	181.16	2003	12/31	10453.92	3/11	7524.06	10453.92
1948	6/15	193.16	3/16	165.39	177.30	2004	12/28	10854.54	10/25	9749.99	10783.01
1949	12/30	200.52	6/13	161.60	200.13	2005	3/4	10940.55	4/20	10012.36	10717.50
1950	11/24	235.47	1/13	196.81	235.41	2006	12/27	12510.57	1/20	10667.39	12463.15
1951	9/13	276.37	1/3	238.99	269.23	2007	10/9	14164.53	3/5	12050.41	13264.82
1952	12/30	292.00	5/1	256.35	291.90	2008	5/2	13058.20	11/20	7552.29	8776.39
1953	1/5	293.79	9/14	255.49	280.90	2009	12/30	10548.51	3/9	6547.05	10428.05
1954	12/31	404.39	1/11	279.87	404.39	2010	12/29	11585.38	7/2	9686.48	11577.51
1955	12/30	488.40	1/17	388.20	488.40	2011	4/29	12810.54	10/3	10655.30	12217.56
1956	4/6	521.05	1/23	462.35	499.47	2012*	5/1	13279.32	1/6	12359.92	At Press Time

*Through May 14, 2012

149

S&P 500 ANNUAL HIGHS, LOWS, & CLOSES SINCE 1930

YEAR	HIGH DATE	HIGH CLOSE	LOW DATE	LOW CLOSE	YEAR CLOSE	YEAR	HIGH DATE	HIGH CLOSE	LOW DATE	LOW CLOSE	YEAR CLOSE
1930	4/10	25.92	12/16	14.44	15.34	1972	12/11	119.12	1/3	101.67	118.05
1931	2/24	18.17	12/17	7.72	8.12	1973	1/11	120.24	12/5	92.16	97.55
1932	9/7	9.31	6/1	4.40	6.89	1974	1/3	99.80	10/3	62.28	68.56
1933	7/18	12.20	2/27	5.53	10.10	1975	7/15	95.61	1/8	70.04	90.19
1934	2/6	11.82	7/26	8.36	9.50	1976	9/21	107.83	1/2	90.90	107.46
1935	11/19	13.46	3/14	8.06	13.43	1977	1/3	107.00	11/2	90.71	95.10
1936	11/9	17.69	1/2	13.40	17.18	1978	9/12	106.99	3/6	86.90	96.11
1937	3/6	18.68	11/24	10.17	10.55	1979	10/5	111.27	2/27	96.13	107.94
1938	11/9	13.79	3/31	8.50	13.21	1980	11/28	140.52	3/27	98.22	135.76
1939	1/4	13.23	4/8	10.18	12.49	1981	1/6	138.12	9/25	112.77	122.55
1940	1/3	12.77	6/10	8.99	10.58	1982	11/9	143.02	8/12	102.42	140.64
1941	1/10	10.86	12/29	8.37	8.69	1983	10/10	172.65	1/3	138.34	164.93
1942	12/31	9.77	4/28	7.47	9.77	1984	11/6	170.41	7/24	147.82	167.24
1943	7/14	12.64	1/2	9.84	11.67	1985	12/16	212.02	1/4	163.68	211.28
1944	12/16	13.29	2/7	11.56	13.28	1986	12/2	254.00	1/22	203.49	242.17
1945	12/10	17.68	1/23	13.21	17.36	1987	8/25	336.77	12/4	223.92	247.08
1946	5/29	19.25	10/9	14.12	15.30	1988	10/21	283.66	1/20	242.63	277.72
1947	2/8	16.20	5/17	13.71	15.30	1989	10/9	359.80	1/3	275.31	353.40
1948	6/15	17.06	2/14	13.84	15.20	1990	7/16	368.95	10/11	295.46	330.22
1949	12/30	16.79	6/13	13.55	16.76	1991	12/31	417.09	1/9	311.49	417.09
1950	12/29	20.43	1/14	16.65	20.41	1992	12/18	441.28	4/8	394.50	435.71
1951	10/15	23.85	1/3	20.69	23.77	1993	12/28	470.94	1/8	429.05	466.45
1952	12/30	26.59	2/20	23.09	26.57	1994	2/2	482.00	4/4	438.92	459.27
1953	1/5	26.66	9/14	22.71	24.81	1995	12/13	621.69	1/3	459.11	615.93
1954	12/31	35.98	1/11	24.80	35.98	1996	11/25	757.03	1/10	598.48	740.74
1955	11/14	46.41	1/17	34.58	45.48	1997	12/5	983.79	1/2	737.01	970.43
1956	8/2	49.74	1/23	43.11	46.67	1998	12/29	1241.81	1/9	927.69	1229.23
1957	7/15	49.13	10/22	38.98	39.99	1999	12/31	1469.25	1/14	1212.19	1469.25
1958	12/31	55.21	1/2	40.33	55.21	2000	3/24	1527.46	12/20	1264.74	1320.28
1959	8/3	60.71	2/9	53.58	59.89	2001	2/1	1373.47	9/21	965.80	1148.08
1960	1/5	60.39	10/25	52.30	58.11	2002	1/4	1172.51	10/9	776.76	879.82
1961	12/12	72.64	1/3	57.57	71.55	2003	12/31	1111.92	3/11	800.73	1111.92
1962	1/3	71.13	6/26	52.32	63.10	2004	12/30	1213.55	8/12	1063.23	1211.92
1963	12/31	75.02	1/2	62.69	75.02	2005	12/14	1272.74	4/20	1137.50	1248.29
1964	11/20	86.28	1/2	75.43	84.75	2006	12/15	1427.09	6/13	1223.69	1418.30
1965	11/15	92.63	6/28	81.60	92.43	2007	10/9	1565.15	3/5	1374.12	1468.36
1966	2/9	94.06	10/7	73.20	80.33	2008	1/2	1447.16	11/20	752.44	903.25
1967	9/25	97.59	1/3	80.38	96.47	2009	12/28	1127.78	3/9	676.53	1115.10
1968	11/29	108.37	3/5	87.72	103.86	2010	12/29	1259.78	7/2	1022.58	1257.64
1969	5/14	106.16	12/17	89.20	92.06	2011	4/29	1363.61	10/3	1099.23	1257.60
1970	1/5	93.46	5/26	69.29	92.15	2012*	4/2	1419.04	1/3	1277.06	At Press Time
1971	4/28	104.77	11/23	90.16	102.09						

*Through May 14, 2012

NASDAQ ANNUAL HIGHS, LOWS, & CLOSES SINCE 1971

YEAR	DATE	HIGH CLOSE	DATE	LOW CLOSE	YEAR CLOSE	YEAR	DATE	HIGH CLOSE	DATE	LOW CLOSE	YEAR CLOSE
1971	12/31	114.12	1/5	89.06	114.12	1992	12/31	676.95	6/26	547.84	676.95
1972	12/8	135.15	1/3	113.65	133.73	1993	10/15	787.42	4/26	645.87	776.80
1973	1/11	136.84	12/24	88.67	92.19	1994	3/18	803.93	6/24	693.79	751.96
1974	3/15	96.53	10/3	54.87	59.82	1995	12/4	1069.79	1/3	743.58	1052.13
1975	7/15	88.00	1/2	60.70	77.62	1996	12/9	1316.27	1/15	988.57	1291.03
1976	12/31	97.88	1/2	78.06	97.88	1997	10/9	1745.85	4/2	1201.00	1570.35
1977	12/30	105.05	4/5	93.66	105.05	1998	12/31	2192.69	10/8	1419.12	2192.69
1978	9/13	139.25	1/11	99.09	117.98	1999	12/31	4069.31	1/4	2208.05	4069.31
1979	10/5	152.29	1/2	117.84	151.14	2000	3/10	5048.62	12/20	2332.78	2470.52
1980	11/28	208.15	3/27	124.09	202.34	2001	1/24	2859.15	9/21	1423.19	1950.40
1981	5/29	223.47	9/28	175.03	195.84	2002	1/4	2059.38	10/9	1114.11	1335.51
1982	12/8	240.70	8/13	159.14	232.41	2003	12/30	2009.88	3/11	1271.47	2003.37
1983	6/24	328.91	1/3	230.59	278.60	2004	12/30	2178.34	8/12	1752.49	2175.44
1984	1/6	287.90	7/25	225.30	247.35	2005	12/2	2273.37	4/28	1904.18	2205.32
1985	12/16	325.16	1/2	245.91	324.93	2006	11/22	2465.98	7/21	2020.39	2415.29
1986	7/3	411.16	1/9	323.01	349.33	2007	10/31	2859.12	3/5	2340.68	2652.28
1987	8/26	455.26	10/28	291.88	330.47	2008	1/2	2609.63	11/20	1316.12	1577.03
1988	7/5	396.11	1/12	331.97	381.38	2009	12/30	2291.28	3/9	1268.64	2269.15
1989	10/9	485.73	1/3	378.56	454.82	2010	12/22	2671.48	7/2	2091.79	2652.87
1990	7/16	469.60	10/16	325.44	373.84	2011	4/29	2873.54	10/3	2335.83	2605.15
1991	12/31	586.34	1/14	355.75	586.34	2012*	3/26	3122.57	1/4	2648.36	At Press Time

RUSSELL 1000 ANNUAL HIGHS, LOWS, & CLOSES SINCE 1979

YEAR	DATE	HIGH CLOSE	DATE	LOW CLOSE	YEAR CLOSE	YEAR	DATE	HIGH CLOSE	DATE	LOW CLOSE	YEAR CLOSE
1979	10/5	61.18	2/27	51.83	59.87	1996	12/2	401.21	1/10	318.24	393.75
1980	11/28	78.26	3/27	53.68	75.20	1997	12/5	519.72	4/11	389.03	513.79
1981	1/6	76.34	9/25	62.03	67.93	1998	12/29	645.36	1/9	490.26	642.87
1982	11/9	78.47	8/12	55.98	77.24	1999	12/31	767.97	2/9	632.53	767.97
1983	10/10	95.07	1/3	76.04	90.38	2000	9/1	813.71	12/20	668.75	700.09
1984	1/6	92.80	7/24	79.49	90.31	2001	1/30	727.35	9/21	507.98	604.94
1985	12/16	114.97	1/4	88.61	114.39	2002	3/19	618.74	10/9	410.52	466.18
1986	7/2	137.87	1/22	111.14	130.00	2003	12/31	594.56	3/11	425.31	594.56
1987	8/25	176.22	12/4	117.65	130.02	2004	12/30	651.76	8/13	566.06	650.99
1988	10/21	149.94	1/20	128.35	146.99	2005	12/14	692.09	4/20	613.37	679.42
1989	10/9	189.93	1/3	145.78	185.11	2006	12/15	775.08	6/13	665.81	770.08
1990	7/16	191.56	10/11	152.36	171.22	2007	10/9	852.32	3/5	749.85	799.82
1991	12/31	220.61	1/9	161.94	220.61	2008	1/2	788.62	11/20	402.91	487.77
1992	12/18	235.06	4/8	208.87	233.59	2009	12/28	619.22	3/9	367.55	612.01
1993	10/15	252.77	1/8	229.91	250.71	2010	12/29	698.11	7/2	562.58	696.90
1994	2/1	258.31	4/4	235.38	244.65	2011	4/29	758.45	10/3	604.42	693.36
1995	12/13	331.18	1/3	244.41	328.89	2012*	4/2	784.67	1/4	703.72	At Press Time

RUSSELL 2000 ANNUAL HIGHS, LOWS, & CLOSES SINCE 1979

YEAR	DATE	HIGH CLOSE	DATE	LOW CLOSE	YEAR CLOSE	YEAR	DATE	HIGH CLOSE	DATE	LOW CLOSE	YEAR CLOSE
1979	12/31	55.91	1/2	40.81	55.91	1996	5/22	364.61	1/16	301.75	362.61
1980	11/28	77.70	3/27	45.36	74.80	1997	10/13	465.21	4/25	335.85	437.02
1981	6/15	85.16	9/25	65.37	73.67	1998	4/21	491.41	10/8	310.28	421.96
1982	12/8	91.01	8/12	60.33	88.90	1999	12/31	504.75	3/23	383.37	504.75
1983	6/24	126.99	1/3	88.29	112.27	2000	3/9	606.05	12/20	443.80	483.53
1984	1/12	116.69	7/25	93.95	101.49	2001	5/22	517.23	9/21	378.89	488.50
1985	12/31	129.87	1/2	101.21	129.87	2002	4/16	522.95	10/9	327.04	383.09
1986	7/3	155.30	1/9	128.23	135.00	2003	12/30	565.47	3/12	345.94	556.91
1987	8/25	174.44	10/28	106.08	120.42	2004	12/28	654.57	8/12	517.10	651.57
1988	7/15	151.42	1/12	121.23	147.37	2005	12/2	690.57	4/28	575.02	673.22
1989	10/9	180.78	1/3	146.79	168.30	2006	12/27	797.73	7/21	671.94	787.66
1990	6/15	170.90	10/30	118.82	132.16	2007	7/13	855.77	11/26	735.07	766.03
1991	12/31	189.94	1/15	125.25	189.94	2008	6/5	763.27	11/20	385.31	499.45
1992	12/31	221.01	7/8	185.81	221.01	2009	12/24	634.07	3/9	343.26	625.39
1993	11/2	260.17	2/23	217.55	258.59	2010	12/27	792.35	2/8	586.49	783.65
1994	3/18	271.08	12/9	235.16	250.36	2011	4/29	865.29	10/3	609.49	740.92
1995	9/14	316.12	1/30	246.56	315.97	2012*	3/26	846.13	1/4	747.28	At Press Time

*Through May 14, 2012

151

DOW JONES INDUSTRIALS MONTHLY PERCENT CHANGE SINCE 1950

	Jan	Feb	Mar	Apr	May	Jun	Jul	Aug	Sep	Oct	Nov	Dec	Year's Change
1950	0.8	0.8	1.3	4.0	4.2	– 6.4	0.1	3.6	4.4	– 0.6	1.2	3.4	17.6
1951	5.7	1.3	– 1.6	4.5	– 3.7	– 2.8	6.3	4.8	0.3	– 3.2	– 0.4	3.0	14.4
1952	0.5	– 3.9	3.6	– 4.4	2.1	4.3	1.9	– 1.6	– 1.6	– 0.5	5.4	2.9	8.4
1953	– 0.7	– 1.9	– 1.5	– 1.8	– 0.9	– 1.5	2.7	– 5.1	1.1	4.5	2.0	– 0.2	– 3.8
1954	4.1	0.7	3.0	5.2	2.6	1.8	4.3	– 3.5	7.3	– 2.3	9.8	4.6	44.0
1955	1.1	0.7	– 0.5	3.9	– 0.2	6.2	3.2	0.5	– 0.3	– 2.5	6.2	1.1	20.8
1956	– 3.6	2.7	5.8	0.8	– 7.4	3.1	5.1	– 3.0	– 5.3	1.0	– 1.5	5.6	2.3
1957	– 4.1	– 3.0	2.2	4.1	2.1	– 0.3	1.0	– 4.8	– 5.8	– 3.3	2.0	– 3.2	– 12.8
1958	3.3	– 2.2	1.6	2.0	1.5	3.3	5.2	1.1	4.6	2.1	2.6	4.7	34.0
1959	1.8	1.6	– 0.3	3.7	3.2	– 0.03	4.9	– 1.6	– 4.9	2.4	1.9	3.1	16.4
1960	– 8.4	1.2	– 2.1	– 2.4	4.0	2.4	– 3.7	1.5	– 7.3	0.04	2.9	3.1	– 9.3
1961	5.2	2.1	2.2	0.3	2.7	– 1.8	3.1	2.1	– 2.6	0.4	2.5	1.3	18.7
1962	– 4.3	1.1	– 0.2	– 5.9	– 7.8	– 8.5	6.5	1.9	– 5.0	1.9	10.1	0.4	– 10.8
1963	4.7	– 2.9	3.0	5.2	1.3	– 2.8	– 1.6	4.9	0.5	3.1	– 0.6	1.7	17.0
1964	2.9	1.9	1.6	– 0.3	1.2	1.3	1.2	– 0.3	4.4	– 0.3	0.3	– 0.1	14.6
1965	3.3	0.1	– 1.6	3.7	– 0.5	– 5.4	1.6	1.3	4.2	3.2	– 1.5	2.4	10.9
1966	1.5	– 3.2	– 2.8	1.0	– 5.3	– 1.6	– 2.6	– 7.0	– 1.8	4.2	– 1.9	– 0.7	– 18.9
1967	8.2	– 1.2	3.2	3.6	– 5.0	0.9	5.1	– 0.3	2.8	– 5.1	– 0.4	3.3	15.2
1968	– 5.5	– 1.7	0.02	8.5	– 1.4	– 0.1	– 1.6	1.5	4.4	1.8	3.4	– 4.2	4.3
1969	0.2	– 4.3	3.3	1.6	– 1.3	– 6.9	– 6.6	2.6	– 2.8	5.3	– 5.1	– 1.5	– 15.2
1970	– 7.0	4.5	1.0	– 6.3	– 4.8	– 2.4	7.4	4.1	– 0.5	– 0.7	5.1	5.6	4.8
1971	3.5	1.2	2.9	4.1	– 3.6	– 1.8	– 3.7	4.6	– 1.2	– 5.4	– 0.9	7.1	6.1
1972	1.3	2.9	1.4	1.4	0.7	– 3.3	– 0.5	4.2	– 1.1	0.2	6.6	0.2	14.6
1973	– 2.1	– 4.4	– 0.4	– 3.1	– 2.2	– 1.1	3.9	– 4.2	6.7	1.0	– 14.0	3.5	– 16.6
1974	0.6	0.6	– 1.6	– 1.2	– 4.1	0.03	– 5.6	– 10.4	– 10.4	9.5	– 7.0	– 0.4	– 27.6
1975	14.2	5.0	3.9	6.9	1.3	5.6	– 5.4	0.5	– 5.0	5.3	2.9	– 1.0	38.3
1976	14.4	– 0.3	2.8	– 0.3	– 2.2	2.8	– 1.8	– 1.1	1.7	– 2.6	– 1.8	6.1	17.9
1977	– 5.0	– 1.9	– 1.8	0.8	– 3.0	2.0	– 2.9	– 3.2	– 1.7	– 3.4	1.4	0.2	– 17.3
1978	– 7.4	– 3.6	2.1	10.6	0.4	– 2.6	5.3	1.7	– 1.3	– 8.5	0.8	0.7	– 3.1
1979	4.2	– 3.6	6.6	– 0.8	– 3.8	2.4	0.5	4.9	– 1.0	– 7.2	0.8	2.0	4.2
1980	4.4	– 1.5	– 9.0	4.0	4.1	2.0	7.8	– 0.3	– 0.02	– 0.9	7.4	– 3.0	14.9
1981	– 1.7	2.9	3.0	– 0.6	– 0.6	– 1.5	– 2.5	– 7.4	– 3.6	0.3	4.3	– 1.6	– 9.2
1982	– 0.4	– 5.4	– 0.2	3.1	– 3.4	– 0.9	– 0.4	11.5	– 0.6	10.7	4.8	0.7	19.6
1983	2.8	3.4	1.6	8.5	– 2.1	1.8	– 1.9	1.4	1.4	– 0.6	4.1	– 1.4	20.3
1984	– 3.0	– 5.4	0.9	0.5	– 5.6	2.5	– 1.5	9.8	– 1.4	0.1	– 1.5	1.9	– 3.7
1985	6.2	– 0.2	– 1.3	– 0.7	4.6	1.5	0.9	– 1.0	– 0.4	3.4	7.1	5.1	27.7
1986	1.6	8.8	6.4	– 1.9	5.2	0.9	– 6.2	6.9	– 6.9	6.2	1.9	– 1.0	22.6
1987	13.8	3.1	3.6	– 0.8	0.2	5.5	6.3	3.5	– 2.5	– 23.2	– 8.0	5.7	2.3
1988	1.0	5.8	– 4.0	2.2	– 0.1	5.4	– 0.6	– 4.6	4.0	1.7	– 1.6	2.6	11.8
1989	8.0	– 3.6	1.6	5.5	2.5	– 1.6	9.0	2.9	– 1.6	– 1.8	2.3	1.7	27.0
1990	– 5.9	1.4	3.0	– 1.9	8.3	0.1	0.9	– 10.0	– 6.2	– 0.4	4.8	2.9	– 4.3
1991	3.9	5.3	1.1	– 0.9	4.8	– 4.0	4.1	0.6	– 0.9	1.7	– 5.7	9.5	20.3
1992	1.7	1.4	– 1.0	3.8	1.1	– 2.3	2.3	– 4.0	0.4	– 1.4	2.4	– 0.1	4.2
1993	0.3	1.8	1.9	– 0.2	2.9	– 0.3	0.7	3.2	– 2.6	3.5	0.1	1.9	13.7
1994	6.0	– 3.7	– 5.1	1.3	2.1	– 3.5	3.8	4.0	– 1.8	1.7	– 4.3	2.5	2.1
1995	0.2	4.3	3.7	3.9	3.3	2.0	3.3	– 2.1	3.9	– 0.7	6.7	0.8	33.5
1996	5.4	1.7	1.9	– 0.3	1.3	0.2	– 2.2	1.6	4.7	2.5	8.2	– 1.1	26.0
1997	5.7	0.9	– 4.3	6.5	4.6	4.7	7.2	– 7.3	4.2	– 6.3	5.1	1.1	22.6
1998	– 0.02	8.1	3.0	3.0	– 1.8	0.6	– 0.8	– 15.1	4.0	9.6	6.1	0.7	16.1
1999	1.9	– 0.6	5.2	10.2	– 2.1	3.9	– 2.9	1.6	– 4.5	3.8	1.4	5.7	25.2
2000	– 4.8	– 7.4	7.8	– 1.7	– 2.0	– 0.7	0.7	6.6	– 5.0	3.0	– 5.1	3.6	– 6.2
2001	0.9	– 3.6	– 5.9	8.7	1.6	– 3.8	0.2	– 5.4	– 11.1	2.6	8.6	1.7	– 7.1
2002	– 1.0	1.9	2.9	– 4.4	– 0.2	– 6.9	– 5.5	– 0.8	– 12.4	10.6	5.9	– 6.2	– 16.8
2003	– 3.5	– 2.0	1.3	6.1	4.4	1.5	2.8	2.0	– 1.5	5.7	– 0.2	6.9	25.3
2004	0.3	0.9	– 2.1	– 1.3	– 0.4	2.4	– 2.8	0.3	– 0.9	– 0.5	4.0	3.4	3.1
2005	– 2.7	2.6	– 2.4	– 3.0	2.7	– 1.8	3.6	– 1.5	0.8	– 1.2	3.5	– 0.8	– 0.6
2006	1.4	1.2	1.1	2.3	– 1.7	– 0.2	0.3	1.7	2.6	3.4	1.2	2.0	16.3
2007	1.3	– 2.8	0.7	5.7	4.3	– 1.6	– 1.5	1.1	4.0	0.2	– 4.0	– 0.8	6.4
2008	– 4.6	– 3.0	– 0.03	4.5	– 1.4	– 10.2	0.2	1.5	– 6.0	– 14.1	– 5.3	– 0.6	– 33.8
2009	– 8.8	– 11.7	7.7	7.3	4.1	– 0.6	8.6	3.5	2.3	0.005	6.5	0.8	18.8
2010	– 3.5	2.6	5.1	1.4	– 7.9	– 3.6	7.1	– 4.3	7.7	3.1	– 1.0	5.2	11.0
2011	2.7	2.8	0.8	4.0	– 1.9	– 1.2	– 2.2	– 4.4	– 6.0	9.5	0.8	1.4	5.5
2012	3.4	2.5	2.0	0.01									
TOTALS	66.4	2.8	68.1	124.2	1.0	– 22.9	72.1	– 4.8	– 53.1	32.5	93.3	105.9	
AVG.	1.1	0.04	1.1	2.0	0.02	– 0.4	1.2	– 0.1	– 0.9	0.5	1.5	1.7	
# Up	41	36	41	41	31	28	38	35	24	37	41	44	
# Down	22	27	22	22	31	34	24	27	38	25	21	18	

DOW JONES INDUSTRIALS MONTHLY POINT CHANGES SINCE 1950

	Jan	Feb	Mar	Apr	May	Jun	Jul	Aug	Sep	Oct	Nov	Dec	Year's Close
1950	1.66	1.65	2.61	8.28	9.09	-14.31	0.29	7.47	9.49	-1.35	2.59	7.81	235.41
1951	13.42	3.22	-4.11	11.19	-9.48	-7.01	15.22	12.39	0.91	-8.81	-1.08	7.96	269.23
1952	1.46	-10.61	9.38	-11.83	5.31	11.32	5.30	-4.52	-4.43	-1.38	14.43	8.24	291.90
1953	-2.13	-5.50	-4.40	-5.12	-2.47	-4.02	7.12	-14.16	2.82	11.77	5.56	-0.47	280.90
1954	11.49	2.15	8.97	15.82	8.16	6.04	14.39	-12.12	24.66	-8.32	34.63	17.62	404.39
1955	4.44	3.04	-2.17	15.95	-0.79	26.52	14.47	2.33	-1.56	-11.75	28.39	5.14	488.40
1956	-17.66	12.91	28.14	4.33	-38.07	14.73	25.03	-15.77	-26.79	4.60	-7.07	26.69	499.47
1957	-20.31	-14.54	10.19	19.55	10.57	-1.64	5.23	-24.17	-28.05	-15.26	8.83	-14.18	435.69
1958	14.33	-10.10	6.84	9.10	6.84	15.48	24.81	5.64	23.46	11.13	14.24	26.19	583.65
1959	10.31	9.54	-1.79	22.04	20.04	-0.19	31.28	-10.47	-32.73	14.92	12.58	20.18	679.36
1960	-56.74	7.50	-13.53	-14.89	23.80	15.12	-23.89	9.26	-45.85	0.22	16.86	18.67	615.89
1961	32.31	13.88	14.55	2.08	18.01	-12.76	21.41	14.57	-18.73	2.71	17.68	9.54	731.14
1962	-31.14	8.05	-1.10	-41.62	-51.97	-52.08	36.65	11.25	-30.20	10.79	59.53	2.80	652.10
1963	30.75	-19.91	19.58	35.18	9.26	-20.08	-11.45	33.89	3.47	22.44	-4.71	12.43	762.95
1964	22.39	14.80	13.15	-2.52	9.79	10.94	9.60	-2.62	36.89	-2.29	2.35	-1.30	874.13
1965	28.73	0.62	-14.43	33.26	-4.27	-50.01	13.71	11.36	37.48	30.24	-14.11	22.55	969.26
1966	14.25	-31.62	-27.12	8.91	-49.61	-13.97	-22.72	-58.97	-14.19	32.85	-15.48	-5.90	785.69
1967	64.20	-10.52	26.61	31.07	-44.49	7.70	43.98	-2.95	25.37	-46.92	-3.93	29.30	905.11
1968	-49.64	-14.97	0.17	71.55	-13.22	-1.20	-14.80	13.01	39.78	16.60	32.69	-41.33	943.75
1969	2.30	-40.84	30.27	14.70	-12.62	-64.37	-57.72	21.25	-23.63	42.90	-43.69	-11.94	800.36
1970	-56.30	33.53	7.98	-49.50	-35.63	-16.91	50.59	30.46	-3.90	-5.07	38.48	44.83	838.92
1971	29.58	10.33	25.54	37.38	-33.94	-16.67	-32.71	39.64	-10.88	-48.19	-7.66	58.86	890.20
1972	11.97	25.96	12.57	13.47	6.55	-31.69	-4.29	38.99	-10.46	2.25	62.69	1.81	1020.02
1973	-21.00	-43.95	-4.06	-29.58	-20.02	-9.70	34.69	-38.83	59.53	9.48	-134.33	28.61	850.86
1974	4.69	4.98	-13.85	-9.93	-34.58	0.24	-44.98	-78.85	-70.71	57.65	-46.86	-2.42	616.24
1975	87.45	35.36	29.10	53.19	10.95	46.70	-47.48	3.83	-41.46	42.16	24.63	-8.26	852.41
1976	122.87	-2.67	26.84	-2.60	-21.62	27.55	-18.14	-10.90	16.45	-25.26	-17.71	57.43	1004.65
1977	-50.28	-17.95	-17.29	7.77	-28.24	17.64	-26.23	-28.58	-14.38	-28.76	11.35	1.47	831.17
1978	-61.25	-27.80	15.24	79.96	3.29	-21.66	43.32	14.55	-11.00	-73.37	6.58	5.98	805.01
1979	34.21	-30.40	53.36	-7.28	-32.57	19.65	4.44	41.21	-9.05	-62.88	6.65	16.39	838.74
1980	37.11	-12.71	-77.39	31.31	33.79	17.07	67.40	-2.73	-0.17	-7.93	68.85	-29.35	963.99
1981	-16.72	27.31	29.29	-6.12	-6.00	-14.87	-24.54	-70.87	-31.49	2.57	36.43	-13.98	875.00
1982	-3.90	-46.71	-1.62	25.59	-28.82	-7.61	-3.33	92.71	-5.06	95.47	47.56	7.26	1046.54
1983	29.16	36.92	17.41	96.17	-26.22	21.98	-22.74	16.94	16.97	-7.93	50.82	-17.38	1258.64
1984	-38.06	-65.95	10.26	5.86	-65.90	27.55	-17.12	109.10	-17.67	0.67	-18.44	22.63	1211.57
1985	75.20	-2.76	-17.23	-8.72	57.35	20.05	11.99	-13.44	-5.38	45.68	97.82	74.54	1546.67
1986	24.32	138.07	109.55	-34.63	92.73	16.01	-117.41	123.03	-130.76	110.23	36.42	-18.28	1895.95
1987	262.09	65.95	80.70	-18.33	5.21	126.96	153.54	90.88	-66.67	-602.75	-159.98	105.28	1938.83
1988	19.39	113.40	-83.56	44.27	-1.21	110.59	-12.98	-97.08	81.26	35.74	-34.14	54.06	2168.57
1989	173.75	-83.93	35.23	125.18	61.35	-40.09	220.60	76.61	-44.45	-47.74	61.19	46.93	2753.20
1990	-162.66	36.71	79.96	-50.45	219.90	4.03	24.51	-290.84	-161.88	-10.15	117.32	74.01	2633.66
1991	102.73	145.79	31.68	-25.99	139.63	-120.75	118.07	18.78	-26.83	52.33	-174.42	274.15	3168.83
1992	54.56	44.28	-32.20	123.65	37.76	-78.36	75.26	-136.43	14.31	-45.38	78.88	-4.05	3301.11
1993	8.92	60.78	64.30	-7.56	99.88	-11.35	23.39	111.78	-96.13	125.47	3.36	70.14	3754.09
1994	224.27	-146.34	-196.06	45.73	76.68	-133.41	139.54	148.92	-70.23	64.93	-168.89	95.21	3834.44
1995	9.42	167.19	146.64	163.58	143.87	90.96	152.37	-97.91	178.52	-33.60	319.01	42.63	5117.12
1996	278.18	90.32	101.52	-18.06	74.10	11.45	-125.72	87.30	265.96	147.21	492.32	-73.43	6448.27
1997	364.82	64.65	-294.26	425.51	322.05	341.75	549.82	-600.19	322.84	-503.18	381.05	85.12	7908.25
1998	-1.75	639.22	254.09	263.56	-163.42	52.07	-68.73	-1344.22	303.55	749.48	524.45	64.88	9181.43
1999	177.40	-52.25	479.58	1002.88	-229.30	411.06	-315.65	174.13	-492.33	392.91	147.95	619.31	11497.12
2000	-556.59	-812.22	793.61	-188.01	-211.58	-74.44	74.09	693.12	-564.18	320.22	-556.65	372.36	10786.85
2001	100.51	-392.08	-616.50	856.19	176.97	-409.54	20.41	-573.06	-1102.19	227.58	776.42	169.94	10021.50
2002	-101.50	186.13	297.81	-457.72	-20.97	-681.99	-506.67	-73.09	-1071.57	805.10	499.06	-554.46	8341.63
2003	-287.82	-162.73	101.05	487.96	370.17	135.18	248.36	182.02	-140.76	526.06	-18.66	671.46	10453.92
2004	34.15	95.85	-226.22	-132.13	-37.12	247.03	-295.77	34.21	-93.65	-52.80	400.55	354.99	10783.01
2005	-293.07	276.29	-262.47	-311.25	274.97	-192.51	365.94	-159.31	87.10	-128.63	365.80	-88.37	10717.50
2006	147.36	128.55	115.91	257.82	-198.83	-18.09	35.46	195.47	297.92	401.66	141.20	241.22	12463.15
2007	158.54	-353.06	85.72	708.56	564.73	-219.02	-196.63	145.75	537.89	34.38	-558.29	-106.90	13264.82
2008	-614.46	-383.97	-3.50	557.24	-181.81	-1288.31	28.01	165.53	-692.89	-1525.65	-495.97	-52.65	8776.39
2009	-775.53	-937.93	545.99	559.20	332.21	-53.33	724.61	324.67	216.00	0.45	632.11	83.21	10428.05
2010	-360.72	257.93	531.37	151.98	-871.98	-362.61	691.92	-451.22	773.33	330.44	-112.47	571.49	11577.51
2011	314.42	334.41	93.39	490.81	-240.75	-155.45	-271.10	-529.71	-700.15	1041.63	90.67	171.88	12217.56
2012	415.35	319.16	259.97	1.59									
TOTALS	-24.77	-317.59	2691.26	5485.58	507.51	-2346.63	1844.02	-1640.96	-2536.48	2517.57	3175.44	3658.55	
# Up	41	36	41	41	31	28	38	35	24	37	41	44	
# Down	22	27	22	22	31	34	24	27	38	25	21	18	

153

DOW JONES INDUSTRIALS MONTHLY CLOSING PRICES SINCE 1950

	Jan	Feb	Mar	Apr	May	Jun	Jul	Aug	Sep	Oct	Nov	Dec
1950	201.79	203.44	206.05	214.33	223.42	209.11	209.40	216.87	226.36	225.01	227.60	235.41
1951	248.83	252.05	247.94	259.13	249.65	242.64	257.86	270.25	271.16	262.35	261.27	269.23
1952	270.69	260.08	269.46	257.63	262.94	274.26	279.56	275.04	270.61	269.23	283.66	291.90
1953	289.77	284.27	279.87	274.75	272.28	268.26	275.38	261.22	264.04	275.81	281.37	280.90
1954	292.39	294.54	303.51	319.33	327.49	333.53	347.92	335.80	360.46	352.14	386.77	404.39
1955	408.83	411.87	409.70	425.65	424.86	451.38	465.85	468.18	466.62	454.87	483.26	488.40
1956	470.74	483.65	511.79	516.12	478.05	492.78	517.81	502.04	475.25	479.85	472.78	499.47
1957	479.16	464.62	474.81	494.36	504.93	503.29	508.52	484.35	456.30	441.04	449.87	435.69
1958	450.02	439.92	446.76	455.86	462.70	478.18	502.99	508.63	532.09	543.22	557.46	583.65
1959	593.96	603.50	601.71	623.75	643.79	643.60	674.88	664.41	631.68	646.60	659.18	679.36
1960	622.62	630.12	616.59	601.70	625.50	640.62	616.73	625.99	580.14	580.36	597.22	615.89
1961	648.20	662.08	676.63	678.71	696.72	683.96	705.37	719.94	701.21	703.92	721.60	731.14
1962	700.00	708.05	706.95	665.33	613.36	561.28	597.93	609.18	578.98	589.77	649.30	652.10
1963	682.85	662.94	682.52	717.70	726.96	706.88	695.43	729.32	732.79	755.23	750.52	762.95
1964	785.34	800.14	813.29	810.77	820.56	831.50	841.10	838.48	875.37	873.08	875.43	874.13
1965	902.86	903.48	889.05	922.31	918.04	868.03	881.74	893.10	930.58	960.82	946.71	969.26
1966	983.51	951.89	924.77	933.68	884.07	870.10	847.38	788.41	774.22	807.07	791.59	785.69
1967	849.89	839.37	865.98	897.05	852.56	860.26	904.24	901.29	926.66	879.74	875.81	905.11
1968	855.47	840.50	840.67	912.22	899.00	897.80	883.00	896.01	935.79	952.39	985.08	943.75
1969	946.05	905.21	935.48	950.18	937.56	873.19	815.47	836.72	813.09	855.99	812.30	800.36
1970	744.06	777.59	785.57	736.07	700.44	683.53	734.12	764.58	760.68	755.61	794.09	838.92
1971	868.50	878.83	904.37	941.75	907.81	891.14	858.43	898.07	887.19	839.00	831.34	890.20
1972	902.17	928.13	940.70	954.17	960.72	929.03	924.74	963.73	953.27	955.52	1018.21	1020.02
1973	999.02	955.07	951.01	921.43	901.41	891.71	926.40	887.57	947.10	956.58	822.25	850.86
1974	855.55	860.53	846.68	836.75	802.17	802.41	757.43	678.58	607.87	665.52	618.66	616.24
1975	703.69	739.05	768.15	821.34	832.29	878.99	831.51	835.34	793.88	836.04	860.67	852.41
1976	975.28	972.61	999.45	996.85	975.23	1002.78	984.64	973.74	990.19	964.93	947.22	1004.65
1977	954.37	936.42	919.13	926.90	898.66	916.30	890.07	861.49	847.11	818.35	829.70	831.17
1978	769.92	742.12	757.36	837.32	840.61	818.95	862.27	876.82	865.82	792.45	799.03	805.01
1979	839.22	808.82	862.18	854.90	822.33	841.98	846.42	887.63	878.58	815.70	822.35	838.74
1980	875.85	863.14	785.75	817.06	850.85	867.92	935.32	932.59	932.42	924.49	993.34	963.99
1981	947.27	974.58	1003.87	997.75	991.75	976.88	952.34	881.47	849.98	852.55	888.98	875.00
1982	871.10	824.39	822.77	848.36	819.54	811.93	808.60	901.31	896.25	991.72	1039.28	1046.54
1983	1075.70	1112.62	1130.03	1226.20	1199.98	1221.96	1199.22	1216.16	1233.13	1225.20	1276.02	1258.64
1984	1220.58	1154.63	1164.89	1170.75	1104.85	1132.40	1115.28	1224.38	1206.71	1207.38	1188.94	1211.57
1985	1286.77	1284.01	1266.78	1258.06	1315.41	1335.46	1347.45	1334.01	1328.63	1374.31	1472.13	1546.67
1986	1570.99	1709.06	1818.61	1783.98	1876.71	1892.72	1775.31	1898.34	1767.58	1877.81	1914.23	1895.95
1987	2158.04	2223.99	2304.69	2286.36	2291.57	2418.53	2572.07	2662.95	2596.28	1993.53	1833.55	1938.83
1988	1958.22	2071.62	1988.06	2032.33	2031.12	2141.71	2128.73	2031.65	2112.91	2148.65	2114.51	2168.57
1989	2342.32	2258.39	2293.62	2418.80	2480.15	2440.06	2660.66	2737.27	2692.82	2645.08	2706.27	2753.20
1990	2590.54	2627.25	2707.21	2656.76	2876.66	2880.69	2905.20	2614.36	2452.48	2442.33	2559.65	2633.66
1991	2736.39	2882.18	2913.86	2887.87	3027.50	2906.75	3024.82	3043.60	3016.77	3069.10	2894.68	3168.83
1992	3223.39	3267.67	3235.47	3359.12	3396.88	3318.52	3393.78	3257.35	3271.66	3226.28	3305.16	3301.11
1993	3310.03	3370.81	3435.11	3427.55	3527.43	3516.08	3539.47	3651.25	3555.12	3680.59	3683.95	3754.09
1994	3978.36	3832.02	3635.96	3681.69	3758.37	3624.96	3764.50	3913.42	3843.19	3908.12	3739.23	3834.44
1995	3843.86	4011.05	4157.69	4321.27	4465.14	4556.10	4708.47	4610.56	4789.08	4755.48	5074.49	5117.12
1996	5395.30	5485.62	5587.14	5569.08	5643.18	5654.63	5528.91	5616.21	5882.17	6029.38	6521.70	6448.27
1997	6813.09	6877.74	6583.48	7008.99	7331.04	7672.79	8222.61	7622.42	7945.26	7442.08	7823.13	7908.25
1998	7906.50	8545.72	8799.81	9063.37	8899.95	8952.02	8883.29	7539.07	7842.62	8592.10	9116.55	9181.43
1999	9358.83	9306.58	9786.16	10789.04	10559.74	10970.80	10655.15	10829.28	10336.95	10729.86	10877.81	11497.12
2000	10940.53	10128.31	10921.92	10733.91	10522.33	10447.89	10521.98	11215.10	10650.92	10971.14	10414.49	10786.85
2001	10887.36	10495.28	9878.78	10734.97	10911.94	10502.40	10522.81	9949.75	8847.56	9075.14	9851.56	10021.50
2002	9920.00	10106.13	10403.94	9946.22	9925.25	9243.26	8736.59	8663.50	7591.93	8397.03	8896.09	8341.63
2003	8053.81	7891.08	7992.13	8480.09	8850.26	8985.44	9233.80	9415.82	9275.06	9801.12	9782.46	10453.92
2004	10488.07	10583.92	10357.70	10225.57	10188.45	10435.48	10139.71	10173.92	10080.27	10027.47	10428.02	10783.01
2005	10489.94	10766.23	10503.76	10192.51	10467.48	10274.97	10640.91	10481.60	10568.70	10440.07	10805.87	10717.50
2006	10864.86	10993.41	11109.32	11367.14	11168.31	11150.22	11185.68	11381.15	11679.07	12080.73	12221.93	12463.15
2007	12621.69	12268.63	12354.35	13062.91	13627.64	13408.62	13211.99	13357.74	13895.63	13930.01	13371.72	13264.82
2008	12650.36	12266.39	12262.89	12820.13	12638.32	11350.01	11378.02	11543.55	10850.66	9325.01	8829.04	8776.39
2009	8000.86	7062.93	7608.92	8168.12	8500.33	8447.00	9171.61	9496.28	9712.28	9712.73	10344.84	10428.05
2010	10067.33	10325.26	10856.63	11008.61	10136.63	9774.02	10465.94	10014.72	10788.05	11118.49	11006.02	11577.51
2011	11891.93	12226.34	12319.73	12810.54	12569.79	12414.34	12143.24	11613.53	10913.38	11955.01	12045.68	12217.56
2012	12632.91	12952.07	13212.04	13213.63								

154

STANDARD & POOR'S 500 MONTHLY PERCENT CHANGES SINCE 1950

	Jan	Feb	Mar	Apr	May	Jun	Jul	Aug	Sep	Oct	Nov	Dec	Year's Change
1950	1.7	1.0	0.4	4.5	3.9	– 5.8	0.8	3.3	5.6	0.4	– 0.1	4.6	21.8
1951	6.1	0.6	– 1.8	4.8	– 4.1	– 2.6	6.9	3.9	– 0.1	– 1.4	– 0.3	3.9	16.5
1952	1.6	– 3.6	4.8	– 4.3	2.3	4.6	1.8	– 1.5	– 2.0	– 0.1	4.6	3.5	11.8
1953	– 0.7	– 1.8	– 2.4	– 2.6	– 0.3	– 1.6	2.5	– 5.8	0.1	5.1	0.9	0.2	– 6.6
1954	5.1	0.3	3.0	4.9	3.3	0.1	5.7	– 3.4	8.3	– 1.9	8.1	5.1	45.0
1955	1.8	0.4	– 0.5	3.8	– 0.1	8.2	6.1	– 0.8	1.1	– 3.0	7.5	– 0.1	26.4
1956	– 3.6	3.5	6.9	– 0.2	– 6.6	3.9	5.2	– 3.8	– 4.5	0.5	– 1.1	3.5	2.6
1957	– 4.2	– 3.3	2.0	3.7	3.7	– 0.1	1.1	– 5.6	– 6.2	– 3.2	1.6	– 4.1	– 14.3
1958	4.3	– 2.1	3.1	3.2	1.5	2.6	4.3	1.2	4.8	2.5	2.2	5.2	38.1
1959	0.4	– 0.02	0.1	3.9	1.9	– 0.4	3.5	– 1.5	– 4.6	1.1	1.3	2.8	8.5
1960	– 7.1	0.9	– 1.4	– 1.8	2.7	2.0	– 2.5	2.6	– 6.0	– 0.2	4.0	4.6	– 3.0
1961	6.3	2.7	2.6	0.4	1.9	– 2.9	3.3	2.0	– 2.0	2.8	3.9	0.3	23.1
1962	– 3.8	1.6	– 0.6	– 6.2	– 8.6	– 8.2	6.4	1.5	– 4.8	0.4	10.2	1.3	– 11.8
1963	4.9	– 2.9	3.5	4.9	1.4	– 2.0	– 0.3	4.9	– 1.1	3.2	– 1.1	2.4	18.9
1964	2.7	1.0	1.5	0.6	1.1	1.6	1.8	– 1.6	2.9	0.8	– 0.5	0.4	13.0
1965	3.3	– 0.1	– 1.5	3.4	– 0.8	– 4.9	1.3	2.3	3.2	2.7	– 0.9	0.9	9.1
1966	0.5	– 1.8	– 2.2	2.1	– 5.4	– 1.6	– 1.3	– 7.8	– 0.7	4.8	0.3	– 0.1	– 13.1
1967	7.8	0.2	3.9	4.2	– 5.2	1.8	4.5	– 1.2	3.3	– 2.9	0.1	2.6	20.1
1968	– 4.4	– 3.1	0.9	8.2	1.1	0.9	– 1.8	1.1	3.9	0.7	4.8	– 4.2	7.7
1969	– 0.8	– 4.7	3.4	2.1	– 0.2	– 5.6	– 6.0	4.0	– 2.5	4.4	– 3.5	– 1.9	– 11.4
1970	– 7.6	5.3	0.1	– 9.0	– 6.1	– 5.0	7.3	4.4	3.3	– 1.1	4.7	5.7	0.1
1971	4.0	0.9	3.7	3.6	– 4.2	0.1	– 4.1	3.6	– 0.7	– 4.2	– 0.3	8.6	10.8
1972	1.8	2.5	0.6	0.4	1.7	– 2.2	0.2	3.4	– 0.5	0.9	4.6	1.2	15.6
1973	– 1.7	– 3.7	– 0.1	– 4.1	– 1.9	– 0.7	3.8	– 3.7	4.0	– 0.1	– 11.4	1.7	– 17.4
1974	– 1.0	– 0.4	– 2.3	– 3.9	– 3.4	– 1.5	– 7.8	– 9.0	– 11.9	16.3	– 5.3	– 2.0	– 29.7
1975	12.3	6.0	2.2	4.7	4.4	4.4	– 6.8	– 2.1	– 3.5	6.2	2.5	– 1.2	31.5
1976	11.8	– 1.1	3.1	– 1.1	– 1.4	4.1	– 0.8	– 0.5	2.3	– 2.2	– 0.8	5.2	19.1
1977	– 5.1	– 2.2	– 1.4	0.02	– 2.4	4.5	– 1.6	– 2.1	– 0.2	– 4.3	2.7	0.3	– 11.5
1978	– 6.2	– 2.5	2.5	8.5	0.4	– 1.8	5.4	2.6	– 0.7	– 9.2	1.7	1.5	1.1
1979	4.0	– 3.7	5.5	0.2	– 2.6	3.9	0.9	5.3	N/C	– 6.9	4.3	1.7	12.3
1980	5.8	– 0.4	– 10.2	4.1	4.7	2.7	6.5	0.6	2.5	1.6	10.2	– 3.4	25.8
1981	– 4.6	1.3	3.6	– 2.3	– 0.2	– 1.0	– 0.2	– 6.2	– 5.4	4.9	3.7	– 3.0	– 9.7
1982	– 1.8	– 6.1	– 1.0	4.0	– 3.9	– 2.0	– 2.3	11.6	0.8	11.0	3.6	1.5	14.8
1983	3.3	1.9	3.3	7.5	– 1.2	3.5	– 3.3	1.1	1.0	– 1.5	1.7	– 0.9	17.3
1984	– 0.9	– 3.9	1.3	0.5	– 5.9	1.7	– 1.6	10.6	– 0.3	– 0.01	– 1.5	2.2	1.4
1985	7.4	0.9	– 0.3	– 0.5	5.4	1.2	– 0.5	– 1.2	– 3.5	4.3	6.5	4.5	26.3
1986	0.2	7.1	5.3	– 1.4	5.0	1.4	– 5.9	7.1	– 8.5	5.5	2.1	– 2.8	14.6
1987	13.2	3.7	2.6	– 1.1	0.6	4.8	4.8	3.5	– 2.4	– 21.8	– 8.5	7.3	2.0
1988	4.0	4.2	– 3.3	0.9	0.3	4.3	– 0.5	– 3.9	4.0	2.6	– 1.9	1.5	12.4
1989	7.1	– 2.9	2.1	5.0	3.5	– 0.8	8.8	1.6	– 0.7	– 2.5	1.7	2.1	27.3
1990	– 6.9	0.9	2.4	– 2.7	9.2	– 0.9	– 0.5	– 9.4	– 5.1	– 0.7	6.0	2.5	– 6.6
1991	4.2	6.7	2.2	0.03	3.9	– 4.8	4.5	2.0	– 1.9	1.2	– 4.4	11.2	26.3
1992	– 2.0	1.0	– 2.2	2.8	0.1	– 1.7	3.9	– 2.4	0.9	0.2	3.0	1.0	4.5
1993	0.7	1.0	1.9	– 2.5	2.3	0.1	– 0.5	3.4	– 1.0	1.9	– 1.3	1.0	7.1
1994	3.3	– 3.0	– 4.6	1.2	1.2	– 2.7	3.1	3.8	– 2.7	2.1	– 4.0	1.2	– 1.5
1995	2.4	3.6	2.7	2.8	3.6	2.1	3.2	– 0.03	4.0	– 0.5	4.1	1.7	34.1
1996	3.3	0.7	0.8	1.3	2.3	0.2	– 4.6	1.9	5.4	2.6	7.3	– 2.2	20.3
1997	6.1	0.6	– 4.3	5.8	5.9	4.3	7.8	– 5.7	5.3	– 3.4	4.5	1.6	31.0
1998	1.0	7.0	5.0	0.9	– 1.9	3.9	– 1.2	– 14.6	6.2	8.0	5.9	5.6	26.7
1999	4.1	– 3.2	3.9	3.8	– 2.5	5.4	– 3.2	– 0.6	– 2.9	6.3	1.9	5.8	19.5
2000	– 5.1	– 2.0	9.7	– 3.1	– 2.2	2.4	– 1.6	6.1	– 5.3	– 0.5	– 8.0	0.4	– 10.1
2001	3.5	– 9.2	– 6.4	7.7	0.5	– 2.5	– 1.1	– 6.4	– 8.2	1.8	7.5	0.8	– 13.0
2002	– 1.6	– 2.1	3.7	– 6.1	– 0.9	– 7.2	– 7.9	0.5	– 11.0	8.6	5.7	– 6.0	– 23.4
2003	– 2.7	– 1.7	1.0	8.0	5.1	1.1	1.6	1.8	– 1.2	5.5	0.7	5.1	26.4
2004	1.7	1.2	– 1.6	– 1.7	1.2	1.8	– 3.4	0.2	0.9	1.4	3.9	3.2	9.0
2005	– 2.5	1.9	– 1.9	– 2.0	3.0	– 0.01	3.6	– 1.1	0.7	– 1.8	3.5	– 0.1	3.0
2006	2.5	0.05	1.1	1.2	– 3.1	0.01	0.5	2.1	2.5	3.2	1.6	1.3	13.6
2007	1.4	– 2.2	1.0	4.3	3.3	– 1.8	– 3.2	1.3	3.6	1.5	– 4.4	– 0.9	3.5
2008	– 6.1	– 3.5	– 0.6	4.8	1.1	– 8.6	– 1.0	1.2	– 9.1	– 16.9	– 7.5	0.8	– 38.5
2009	– 8.6	– 11.0	8.5	9.4	5.3	0.02	7.4	3.4	3.6	– 2.0	5.7	1.8	23.5
2010	– 3.7	2.9	5.9	1.5	– 8.2	– 5.4	6.9	– 4.7	8.8	3.7	– 0.2	6.5	12.8
2011	2.3	3.2	– 0.1	2.8	– 1.4	– 1.8	– 2.1	– 5.7	– 7.2	10.8	– 0.5	0.9	– 0.003
2012	4.4	4.1	3.1	– 0.7									
TOTALS	69.6	– 7.4	74.2	95.2	14.1	– 4.5	57.8	– 2.4	– 35.4	49.2	93.3	105.8	
AVG.	1.1	– 0.1	1.2	1.5	0.2	– 0.1	0.9	– 0.04	– 0.6	0.8	1.5	1.7	
# Up	39	34	41	43	35	32	33	34	27	37	40	47	
# Down	24	29	22	20	27	30	29	28	34	25	22	15	

155

STANDARD & POOR'S 500 MONTHLY CLOSING PRICES SINCE 1950

	Jan	Feb	Mar	Apr	May	Jun	Jul	Aug	Sep	Oct	Nov	Dec
1950	17.05	17.22	17.29	18.07	18.78	17.69	17.84	18.42	19.45	19.53	19.51	20.41
1951	21.66	21.80	21.40	22.43	21.52	20.96	22.40	23.28	23.26	22.94	22.88	23.77
1952	24.14	23.26	24.37	23.32	23.86	24.96	25.40	25.03	24.54	24.52	25.66	26.57
1953	26.38	25.90	25.29	24.62	24.54	24.14	24.75	23.32	23.35	24.54	24.76	24.81
1954	26.08	26.15	26.94	28.26	29.19	29.21	30.88	29.83	32.31	31.68	34.24	35.98
1955	36.63	36.76	36.58	37.96	37.91	41.03	43.52	43.18	43.67	42.34	45.51	45.48
1956	43.82	45.34	48.48	48.38	45.20	46.97	49.39	47.51	45.35	45.58	45.08	46.67
1957	44.72	43.26	44.11	45.74	47.43	47.37	47.91	45.22	42.42	41.06	41.72	39.99
1958	41.70	40.84	42.10	43.44	44.09	45.24	47.19	47.75	50.06	51.33	52.48	55.21
1959	55.42	55.41	55.44	57.59	58.68	58.47	60.51	59.60	56.88	57.52	58.28	59.89
1960	55.61	56.12	55.34	54.37	55.83	56.92	55.51	56.96	53.52	53.39	55.54	58.11
1961	61.78	63.44	65.06	65.31	66.56	64.64	66.76	68.07	66.73	68.62	71.32	71.55
1962	68.84	69.96	69.55	65.24	59.63	54.75	58.23	59.12	56.27	56.52	62.26	63.10
1963	66.20	64.29	66.57	69.80	70.80	69.37	69.13	72.50	71.70	74.01	73.23	75.02
1964	77.04	77.80	78.98	79.46	80.37	81.69	83.18	81.83	84.18	84.86	84.42	84.75
1965	87.56	87.43	86.16	89.11	88.42	84.12	85.25	87.17	89.96	92.42	91.61	92.43
1966	92.88	91.22	89.23	91.06	86.13	84.74	83.60	77.10	76.56	80.20	80.45	80.33
1967	86.61	86.78	90.20	94.01	89.08	90.64	94.75	93.64	96.71	93.90	94.00	96.47
1968	92.24	89.36	90.20	97.59	98.68	99.58	97.74	98.86	102.67	103.41	108.37	103.86
1969	103.01	98.13	101.51	103.69	103.46	97.71	91.83	95.51	93.12	97.24	93.81	92.06
1970	85.02	89.50	89.63	81.52	76.55	72.72	78.05	81.52	84.21	83.25	87.20	92.15
1971	95.88	96.75	100.31	103.95	99.63	99.70	95.58	99.03	98.34	94.23	93.99	102.09
1972	103.94	106.57	107.20	107.67	109.53	107.14	107.39	111.09	110.55	111.58	116.67	118.05
1973	116.03	111.68	111.52	106.97	104.95	104.26	108.22	104.25	108.43	108.29	95.96	97.55
1974	96.57	96.22	93.98	90.31	87.28	86.00	79.31	72.15	63.54	73.90	69.97	68.56
1975	76.98	81.59	83.36	87.30	91.15	95.19	88.75	86.88	83.87	89.04	91.24	90.19
1976	100.86	99.71	102.77	101.64	100.18	104.28	103.44	102.91	105.24	102.90	102.10	107.46
1977	102.03	99.82	98.42	98.44	96.12	100.48	98.85	96.77	96.53	92.34	94.83	95.10
1978	89.25	87.04	89.21	96.83	97.24	95.53	100.68	103.29	102.54	93.15	94.70	96.11
1979	99.93	96.28	101.59	101.76	99.08	102.91	103.81	109.32	109.32	101.82	106.16	107.94
1980	114.16	113.66	102.09	106.29	111.24	114.24	121.67	122.38	125.46	127.47	140.52	135.76
1981	129.55	131.27	136.00	132.81	132.59	131.21	130.92	122.79	116.18	121.89	126.35	122.55
1982	120.40	113.11	111.96	116.44	111.88	109.61	107.09	119.51	120.42	133.71	138.54	140.64
1983	145.30	148.06	152.96	164.42	162.39	168.11	162.56	164.40	166.07	163.55	166.40	164.93
1984	163.41	157.06	159.18	160.05	150.55	153.18	150.66	166.68	166.10	166.09	163.58	167.24
1985	179.63	181.18	180.66	179.83	189.55	191.85	190.92	188.63	182.08	189.82	202.17	211.28
1986	211.78	226.92	238.90	235.52	247.35	250.84	236.12	252.93	231.32	243.98	249.22	242.17
1987	274.08	284.20	291.70	288.36	290.10	304.00	318.66	329.80	321.83	251.79	230.30	247.08
1988	257.07	267.82	258.89	261.33	262.16	273.50	272.02	261.52	271.91	278.97	273.70	277.72
1989	297.47	288.86	294.87	309.64	320.52	317.98	346.08	351.45	349.15	340.36	345.99	353.40
1990	329.08	331.89	339.94	330.80	361.23	358.02	356.15	322.56	306.05	304.00	322.22	330.22
1991	343.93	367.07	375.22	375.35	389.83	371.16	387.81	395.43	387.86	392.46	375.22	417.09
1992	408.79	412.70	403.69	414.95	415.35	408.14	424.21	414.03	417.80	418.68	431.35	435.71
1993	438.78	443.38	451.67	440.19	450.19	450.53	448.13	463.56	458.93	467.83	461.79	466.45
1994	481.61	467.14	445.77	450.91	456.50	444.27	458.26	475.49	462.69	472.35	453.69	459.27
1995	470.42	487.39	500.71	514.71	533.40	544.75	562.06	561.88	584.41	581.50	605.37	615.93
1996	636.02	640.43	645.50	654.17	669.12	670.63	639.95	651.99	687.31	705.27	757.02	740.74
1997	786.16	790.82	757.12	801.34	848.28	885.14	954.29	899.47	947.28	914.62	955.40	970.43
1998	980.28	1049.34	1101.75	1111.75	1090.82	1133.84	1120.67	957.28	1017.01	1098.67	1163.63	1229.23
1999	1279.64	1238.33	1286.37	1335.18	1301.84	1372.71	1328.72	1320.41	1282.71	1362.93	1388.91	1469.25
2000	1394.46	1366.42	1498.58	1452.43	1420.60	1454.60	1430.83	1517.68	1436.51	1429.40	1314.95	1320.28
2001	1366.01	1239.94	1160.33	1249.46	1255.82	1224.42	1211.23	1133.58	1040.94	1059.78	1139.45	1148.08
2002	1130.20	1106.73	1147.39	1076.92	1067.14	989.82	911.62	916.07	815.28	885.76	936.31	879.82
2003	855.70	841.15	849.18	916.92	963.59	974.50	990.31	1008.01	995.97	1050.71	1058.20	1111.92
2004	1131.13	1144.94	1126.21	1107.30	1120.68	1140.84	1101.72	1104.24	1114.58	1130.20	1173.82	1211.92
2005	1181.27	1203.60	1180.59	1156.85	1191.50	1191.33	1234.18	1220.33	1228.81	1207.01	1249.48	1248.29
2006	1280.08	1280.66	1294.83	1310.61	1270.09	1270.20	1276.66	1303.82	1335.85	1377.94	1400.63	1418.30
2007	1438.24	1406.82	1420.86	1482.37	1530.62	1503.35	1455.27	1473.99	1526.75	1549.38	1481.14	1468.36
2008	1378.55	1330.63	1322.70	1385.59	1400.38	1280.00	1267.38	1282.83	1166.36	968.75	896.24	903.25
2009	825.88	735.09	797.87	872.81	919.14	919.32	987.48	1020.62	1057.08	1036.19	1095.63	1115.10
2010	1073.87	1104.49	1169.43	1186.69	1089.41	1030.71	1101.60	1049.33	1141.20	1183.26	1180.55	1257.64
2011	1286.12	1327.22	1325.83	1363.61	1345.20	1320.64	1292.28	1218.89	1131.42	1253.30	1246.96	1257.60
2012	1312.41	1365.68	1408.47	1397.91								

156

NASDAQ COMPOSITE MONTHLY PERCENT CHANGES SINCE 1971

	Jan	Feb	Mar	Apr	May	Jun	Jul	Aug	Sep	Oct	Nov	Dec	Year's Change
1971	10.2	2.6	4.6	6.0	-3.6	-0.4	-2.3	3.0	0.6	-3.6	-1.1	9.8	27.4
1972	4.2	5.5	2.2	2.5	0.9	-1.8	-1.8	1.7	-0.3	0.5	2.1	0.6	17.2
1973	-4.0	-6.2	-2.4	-8.2	-4.8	-1.6	7.6	-3.5	6.0	-0.9	-15.1	-1.4	-31.1
1974	3.0	-0.6	-2.2	-5.9	-7.7	-5.3	-7.9	-10.9	-10.7	17.2	-3.5	-5.0	-35.1
1975	16.6	4.6	3.6	3.8	5.8	4.7	-4.4	-5.0	-5.9	3.6	2.4	-1.5	29.8
1976	12.1	3.7	0.4	-0.6	-2.3	2.6	1.1	-1.7	1.7	-1.0	0.9	7.4	26.1
1977	-2.4	-1.0	-0.5	1.4	0.1	4.3	0.9	-0.5	0.7	-3.3	5.8	1.8	7.3
1978	-4.0	0.6	4.7	8.5	4.4	0.05	5.0	6.9	-1.6	-16.4	3.2	2.9	12.3
1979	6.6	-2.6	7.5	1.6	-1.8	5.1	2.3	6.4	-0.3	-9.6	6.4	4.8	28.1
1980	7.0	-2.3	-17.1	6.9	7.5	4.9	8.9	5.7	3.4	2.7	8.0	-2.8	33.9
1981	-2.2	0.1	6.1	3.1	3.1	-3.5	-1.9	-7.5	-8.0	8.4	3.1	-2.7	-3.2
1982	-3.8	-4.8	-2.1	5.2	-3.3	-4.1	-2.3	6.2	5.6	13.3	9.3	0.04	18.7
1983	6.9	5.0	3.9	8.2	5.3	3.2	-4.6	-3.8	1.4	-7.4	4.1	-2.5	19.9
1984	-3.7	-5.9	-0.7	-1.3	-5.9	2.9	-4.2	10.9	-1.8	-1.2	-1.8	2.0	-11.2
1985	12.7	2.0	-1.7	0.5	3.6	1.9	1.7	-1.2	-5.8	4.4	7.3	3.5	31.4
1986	3.3	7.1	4.2	2.3	4.4	1.3	-8.4	3.1	-8.4	2.9	-0.3	-2.8	7.5
1987	12.2	8.4	1.2	-2.8	-0.3	2.0	2.4	4.6	-2.3	-27.2	-5.6	8.3	-5.4
1988	4.3	6.5	2.1	1.2	-2.3	6.6	-1.9	-2.8	3.0	-1.4	-2.9	2.7	15.4
1989	5.2	-0.4	1.8	5.1	4.4	-2.4	4.3	3.4	0.8	-3.7	0.1	-0.3	19.3
1990	-8.6	2.4	2.3	-3.6	9.3	0.7	-5.2	-13.0	-9.6	-4.3	8.9	4.1	-17.8
1991	10.8	9.4	6.5	0.5	4.4	-6.0	5.5	4.7	0.2	3.1	-3.5	11.9	56.8
1992	5.8	2.1	-4.7	-4.2	1.1	-3.7	3.1	-3.0	3.6	3.8	7.9	3.7	15.5
1993	2.9	-3.7	2.9	-4.2	5.9	0.5	0.1	5.4	2.7	2.2	-3.2	3.0	14.7
1994	3.0	-1.0	-6.2	-1.3	0.2	-4.0	2.3	6.0	-0.2	1.7	-3.5	0.2	-3.2
1995	0.4	5.1	3.0	3.3	2.4	8.0	7.3	1.9	2.3	-0.7	2.2	-0.7	39.9
1996	0.7	3.8	0.1	8.1	4.4	-4.7	-8.8	5.6	7.5	-0.4	5.8	-0.1	22.7
1997	6.9	-5.1	-6.7	3.2	11.1	3.0	10.5	-0.4	6.2	-5.5	0.4	-1.9	21.6
1998	3.1	9.3	3.7	1.8	-4.8	6.5	-1.2	-19.9	13.0	4.6	10.1	12.5	39.6
1999	14.3	-8.7	7.6	3.3	-2.8	8.7	-1.8	3.8	0.2	8.0	12.5	22.0	85.6
2000	-3.2	19.2	-2.6	-15.6	-11.9	16.6	-5.0	11.7	-12.7	-8.3	-22.9	-4.9	-39.3
2001	12.2	-22.4	-14.5	15.0	-0.3	2.4	-6.2	-10.9	-17.0	12.8	14.2	1.0	-21.1
2002	-0.8	-10.5	6.6	-8.5	-4.3	-9.4	-9.2	-1.0	-10.9	13.5	11.2	-9.7	-31.5
2003	-1.1	1.3	0.3	9.2	9.0	1.7	6.9	4.3	-1.3	8.1	1.5	2.2	50.0
2004	3.1	-1.8	-1.8	-3.7	3.5	3.1	-7.8	-2.6	3.2	4.1	6.2	3.7	8.6
2005	-5.2	-0.5	-2.6	-3.9	7.6	-0.5	6.2	-1.5	-0.02	-1.5	5.3	-1.2	1.4
2006	4.6	-1.1	2.6	-0.7	-6.2	-0.3	-3.7	4.4	3.4	4.8	2.7	-0.7	9.5
2007	2.0	-1.9	0.2	4.3	3.1	-0.05	-2.2	2.0	4.0	5.8	-6.9	-0.3	9.8
2008	-9.9	-5.0	0.3	5.9	4.6	-9.1	1.4	1.8	-11.6	-17.7	-10.8	2.7	-40.5
2009	-6.4	-6.7	10.9	12.3	3.3	3.4	7.8	1.5	5.6	-3.6	4.9	5.8	43.9
2010	-5.4	4.2	7.1	2.6	-8.3	-6.5	6.9	-6.2	12.0	5.9	-0.4	6.2	16.9
2011	1.8	3.0	-0.04	3.3	-1.3	-2.2	-0.6	-6.4	-6.4	11.1	-2.4	-0.6	-1.8
2012	8.0	5.4	4.2	-1.5									
TOTALS	123.2	19.1	34.8	63.1	37.5	28.6	0.8	3.2	-27.7	24.8	62.6	83.7	
AVG.	2.9	0.5	0.8	1.5	0.9	0.7	0.02	0.1	-0.7	0.6	1.5	2.0	
# Up	28	22	27	27	24	23	20	22	22	22	26	24	
# Down	14	20	15	15	17	18	21	19	19	19	15	17	

Based on NASDAQ composite; prior to February 5, 1971, based on National Quotation Bureau indices.

NASDAQ COMPOSITE MONTHLY CLOSING PRICES SINCE 1971

	Jan	Feb	Mar	Apr	May	Jun	Jul	Aug	Sep	Oct	Nov	Dec
1971	98.77	101.34	105.97	112.30	108.25	107.80	105.27	108.42	109.03	105.10	103.97	114.12
1972	118.87	125.38	128.14	131.33	132.53	130.08	127.75	129.95	129.61	130.24	132.96	133.73
1973	128.40	120.41	117.46	107.85	102.64	100.98	108.64	104.87	111.20	110.17	93.51	92.19
1974	94.93	94.35	92.27	86.86	80.20	75.96	69.99	62.37	55.67	65.23	62.95	59.82
1975	69.78	73.00	75.66	78.54	83.10	87.02	83.19	79.01	74.33	76.99	78.80	77.62
1976	87.05	90.26	90.62	90.08	88.04	90.32	91.29	89.70	91.26	90.35	91.12	97.88
1977	95.54	94.57	94.13	95.48	95.59	99.73	100.65	100.10	100.85	97.52	103.15	105.05
1978	100.84	101.47	106.20	115.18	120.24	120.30	126.32	135.01	132.89	111.12	114.69	117.98
1979	125.82	122.56	131.76	133.82	131.42	138.13	141.33	150.44	149.98	135.53	144.26	151.14
1980	161.75	158.03	131.00	139.99	150.45	157.78	171.81	181.52	187.76	192.78	208.15	202.34
1981	197.81	198.01	210.18	216.74	223.47	215.75	211.63	195.75	180.03	195.24	201.37	195.84
1982	188.39	179.43	175.65	184.70	178.54	171.30	167.35	177.71	187.65	212.63	232.31	232.41
1983	248.35	260.67	270.80	293.06	308.73	318.70	303.96	292.42	296.65	274.55	285.67	278.60
1984	268.43	252.57	250.78	247.44	232.82	239.65	229.70	254.64	249.94	247.03	242.53	247.35
1985	278.70	284.17	279.20	280.56	290.80	296.20	301.29	297.71	280.33	292.54	313.95	324.93
1986	335.77	359.53	374.72	383.24	400.16	405.51	371.37	382.86	350.67	360.77	359.57	349.33
1987	392.06	424.97	430.05	417.81	416.54	424.67	434.93	454.97	444.29	323.30	305.16	330.47
1988	344.66	366.95	374.64	379.23	370.34	394.66	387.33	376.55	387.71	382.46	371.45	381.38
1989	401.30	399.71	406.73	427.55	446.17	435.29	453.84	469.33	472.92	455.63	456.09	454.82
1990	415.81	425.83	435.54	420.07	458.97	462.29	438.24	381.21	344.51	329.84	359.06	373.84
1991	414.20	453.05	482.30	484.72	506.11	475.92	502.04	525.68	526.88	542.98	523.90	586.34
1992	620.21	633.47	603.77	578.68	585.31	563.60	580.83	563.12	583.27	605.17	652.73	676.95
1993	696.34	670.77	690.13	661.42	700.53	703.95	704.70	742.84	762.78	779.26	754.39	776.80
1994	800.47	792.50	743.46	733.84	735.19	705.96	722.16	765.62	764.29	777.49	750.32	751.96
1995	755.20	793.73	817.21	843.98	864.58	933.45	1001.21	1020.11	1043.54	1036.06	1059.20	1052.13
1996	1059.79	1100.05	1101.40	1190.52	1243.43	1185.02	1080.59	1141.50	1226.92	1221.51	1292.61	1291.03
1997	1379.85	1309.00	1221.70	1260.76	1400.32	1442.07	1593.81	1587.32	1685.69	1593.61	1600.55	1570.35
1998	1619.36	1770.51	1835.68	1868.41	1778.87	1894.74	1872.39	1499.25	1693.84	1771.39	1949.54	2192.69
1999	2505.89	2288.03	2461.40	2542.85	2470.52	2686.12	2638.49	2739.35	2746.16	2966.43	3336.16	4069.31
2000	3940.35	4696.69	4572.83	3860.66	3400.91	3966.11	3766.99	4206.35	3672.82	3369.63	2597.93	2470.52
2001	2772.73	2151.83	1840.26	2116.24	2110.49	2160.54	2027.13	1805.43	1498.80	1690.20	1930.58	1950.40
2002	1934.03	1731.49	1845.35	1688.23	1615.73	1463.21	1328.26	1314.85	1172.06	1329.75	1478.78	1335.51
2003	1320.91	1337.52	1341.17	1464.31	1595.91	1622.80	1735.02	1810.45	1786.94	1932.21	1960.26	2003.37
2004	2066.15	2029.82	1994.22	1920.15	1986.74	2047.79	1887.36	1838.10	1896.84	1974.99	2096.81	2175.44
2005	2062.41	2051.72	1999.23	1921.65	2068.22	2056.96	2184.83	2152.09	2151.69	2120.30	2232.82	2205.32
2006	2305.82	2281.39	2339.79	2322.57	2178.88	2172.09	2091.47	2183.75	2258.43	2366.71	2431.77	2415.29
2007	2463.93	2416.15	2421.64	2525.09	2604.52	2603.23	2545.57	2596.36	2701.50	2859.12	2660.96	2652.28
2008	2389.86	2271.48	2279.10	2412.80	2522.66	2292.98	2325.55	2367.52	2091.88	1720.95	1535.57	1577.03
2009	1476.42	1377.84	1528.59	1717.30	1774.33	1835.04	1978.50	2009.06	2122.42	2045.11	2144.60	2269.15
2010	2147.35	2238.26	2397.96	2461.19	2257.04	2109.24	2254.70	2114.03	2368.62	2507.41	2498.23	2652.87
2011	2700.08	2782.27	2781.07	2873.54	2835.30	2773.52	2756.38	2579.46	2415.40	2684.41	2620.34	2605.15
2012	2813.84	2966.89	3091.57	3046.36								

Based on NASDAQ composite; prior to February 5, 1971, based on National Quotation Bureau indices.

RUSSELL 1000 INDEX MONTHLY PERCENT CHANGES SINCE 1979

	Jan	Feb	Mar	Apr	May	Jun	Jul	Aug	Sep	Oct	Nov	Dec	Year's Change
1979	4.2	– 3.5	6.0	0.3	– 2.2	4.3	1.1	5.6	0.02	– 7.1	5.1	2.1	16.1
1980	5.9	– 0.5	– 11.5	4.6	5.0	3.2	6.4	1.1	2.6	1.8	10.1	– 3.9	25.6
1981	– 4.6	1.0	3.8	– 1.9	0.2	– 1.2	– 0.1	– 6.2	– 6.4	5.4	4.0	– 3.3	– 9.7
1982	– 2.7	– 5.9	– 1.3	3.9	– 3.6	– 2.6	– 2.3	11.3	1.2	11.3	4.0	1.3	13.7
1983	3.2	2.1	3.2	7.1	– 0.2	3.7	– 3.2	0.5	1.3	– 2.4	2.0	– 1.2	17.0
1984	– 1.9	– 4.4	1.1	0.3	– 5.9	2.1	– 1.8	10.8	– 0.2	– 0.1	– 1.4	2.2	– 0.1
1985	7.8	1.1	– 0.4	– 0.3	5.4	1.6	– 0.8	– 1.0	– 3.9	4.5	6.5	4.1	26.7
1986	0.9	7.2	5.1	– 1.3	5.0	1.4	– 5.9	6.8	– 8.5	5.1	1.4	– 3.0	13.6
1987	12.7	4.0	1.9	– 1.8	0.4	4.5	4.2	3.8	– 2.4	– 21.9	– 8.0	7.2	0.02
1988	4.3	4.4	– 2.9	0.7	0.2	4.8	– 0.9	– 3.3	3.9	2.0	– 2.0	1.7	13.1
1989	6.8	– 2.5	2.0	4.9	3.8	– 0.8	8.2	1.7	– 0.5	– 2.8	1.5	1.8	25.9
1990	– 7.4	1.2	2.2	– 2.8	8.9	– 0.7	– 1.1	– 9.6	– 5.3	– 0.8	6.4	2.7	– 7.5
1991	4.5	6.9	2.5	– 0.1	3.8	– 4.7	4.6	2.2	– 1.5	1.4	– 4.1	11.2	28.8
1992	– 1.4	0.9	– 2.4	2.3	0.3	– 1.9	4.1	– 2.5	1.0	0.7	3.5	1.4	5.9
1993	0.7	0.6	2.2	– 2.8	2.4	0.4	– 0.4	3.5	– 0.5	1.2	– 1.7	1.6	7.3
1994	2.9	– 2.9	– 4.5	1.1	1.0	– 2.9	3.1	3.9	– 2.6	1.7	– 3.9	1.2	– 2.4
1995	2.4	3.8	2.3	2.5	3.5	2.4	3.7	0.5	3.9	– 0.6	4.2	1.4	34.4
1996	3.1	1.1	0.7	1.4	2.1	– 0.1	– 4.9	2.5	5.5	2.1	7.1	– 1.8	19.7
1997	5.8	0.2	– 4.6	5.3	6.2	4.0	8.0	– 4.9	5.4	– 3.4	4.2	1.9	30.5
1998	0.6	7.0	4.9	0.9	– 2.3	3.6	– 1.3	– 15.1	6.5	7.8	6.1	6.2	25.1
1999	3.5	– 3.3	3.7	4.2	– 2.3	5.1	– 3.2	– 1.0	– 2.8	6.5	2.5	6.0	19.5
2000	– 4.2	– 0.4	8.9	– 3.3	– 2.7	2.5	– 1.8	7.4	– 4.8	– 1.2	– 9.3	1.1	– 8.8
2001	3.2	– 9.5	– 6.7	8.0	0.5	– 2.4	– 1.4	– 6.2	– 8.6	2.0	7.5	0.9	– 13.6
2002	– 1.4	– 2.1	4.0	– 5.8	– 1.0	– 7.5	– 7.5	0.3	– 10.9	8.1	5.7	– 5.8	– 22.9
2003	– 2.5	– 1.7	0.9	7.9	5.5	1.2	1.8	1.9	– 1.2	5.7	1.0	4.6	27.5
2004	1.8	1.2	– 1.5	– 1.9	1.3	1.7	– 3.6	0.3	1.1	1.5	4.1	3.5	9.5
2005	– 2.6	2.0	– 1.7	– 2.0	3.4	0.3	3.8	– 1.1	0.8	– 1.9	3.5	0.01	4.4
2006	2.7	0.01	1.3	1.1	– 3.2	0.003	0.1	2.2	2.3	3.3	1.9	1.1	13.3
2007	1.8	– 1.9	0.9	4.1	3.4	– 2.0	– 3.2	1.2	3.7	1.6	– 4.5	– 0.8	3.9
2008	– 6.1	– 3.3	– 0.8	5.0	1.6	– 8.5	– 1.3	1.2	– 9.7	– 17.6	– 7.9	1.3	– 39.0
2009	– 8.3	– 10.7	8.5	10.0	5.3	0.1	7.5	3.4	3.9	– 2.3	5.6	2.3	25.5
2010	– 3.7	3.1	6.0	1.8	– 8.1	– 5.7	6.8	– 4.7	9.0	3.8	0.1	6.5	13.9
2011	2.3	3.3	0.1	2.9	– 1.3	– 1.9	– 2.3	– 6.0	– 7.6	11.1	– 0.5	0.7	– 0.5
2012	4.8	4.1	3.0	– 0.7									
TOTALS	39.1	2.6	36.9	55.6	36.4	4.0	16.4	10.5	– 25.3	26.5	54.7	56.2	
AVG.	1.2	0.1	1.1	1.6	1.1	0.1	0.5	0.3	– 0.8	0.8	1.7	1.7	
# Up	22	20	23	22	22	19	14	21	16	21	23	26	
# Down	12	14	11	12	11	14	19	12	17	12	10	7	

RUSSELL 1000 INDEX MONTHLY CLOSING PRICES SINCE 1979

	Jan	Feb	Mar	Apr	May	Jun	Jul	Aug	Sep	Oct	Nov	Dec
1979	53.76	51.88	54.97	55.15	53.92	56.25	56.86	60.04	60.05	55.78	58.65	59.87
1980	63.40	63.07	55.79	58.38	61.31	63.27	67.30	68.05	69.84	71.08	78.26	75.20
1981	71.75	72.49	75.21	73.77	73.90	73.01	72.92	68.42	64.06	67.54	70.23	67.93
1982	66.12	62.21	61.43	63.85	61.53	59.92	58.54	65.14	65.89	73.34	76.28	77.24
1983	79.75	81.45	84.06	90.04	89.89	93.18	90.18	90.65	91.85	89.69	91.50	90.38
1984	88.69	84.76	85.73	86.00	80.94	82.61	81.13	89.87	89.67	89.62	88.36	90.31
1985	97.31	98.38	98.03	97.72	103.02	104.65	103.78	102.76	98.75	103.16	109.91	114.39
1986	115.39	123.71	130.07	128.44	134.82	136.75	128.74	137.43	125.70	132.11	133.97	130.00
1987	146.48	152.29	155.20	152.39	152.94	159.84	166.57	172.95	168.83	131.89	121.28	130.02
1988	135.55	141.54	137.45	138.37	138.66	145.31	143.99	139.26	144.68	147.55	144.59	146.99
1989	156.93	152.98	155.99	163.63	169.85	168.49	182.27	185.33	184.40	179.17	181.85	185.11
1990	171.44	173.43	177.28	172.32	187.66	186.29	184.32	166.69	157.83	156.62	166.69	171.22
1991	179.00	191.34	196.15	195.94	203.32	193.78	202.67	207.18	204.02	206.96	198.46	220.61
1992	217.52	219.50	214.29	219.13	219.71	215.60	224.37	218.86	221.15	222.65	230.44	233.59
1993	235.25	236.67	241.80	235.13	240.80	241.78	240.82	249.20	247.91	250.97	246.70	250.71
1994	258.08	250.52	239.19	241.71	244.13	237.11	244.44	254.04	247.49	251.62	241.82	244.65
1995	250.52	260.08	266.01	272.81	282.48	289.29	299.98	301.40	313.28	311.37	324.36	328.89
1996	338.97	342.56	345.01	349.84	357.35	357.10	339.44	347.79	366.77	374.38	401.05	393.75
1997	416.77	417.46	398.19	419.15	445.06	462.95	499.89	475.33	500.78	483.86	504.25	513.79
1998	517.02	553.14	580.31	585.46	572.16	592.57	584.97	496.66	529.11	570.63	605.31	642.87
1999	665.64	643.67	667.49	695.25	679.10	713.61	690.51	683.27	663.83	707.19	724.66	767.97
2000	736.08	733.04	797.99	771.58	750.98	769.68	755.57	811.17	772.60	763.06	692.40	700.09
2001	722.55	654.25	610.36	658.90	662.39	646.64	637.43	597.67	546.46	557.29	599.32	604.94
2002	596.66	583.88	607.35	572.04	566.18	523.72	484.39	486.08	433.22	468.51	495.00	466.18
2003	454.30	446.37	450.35	486.09	512.92	518.94	528.53	538.40	532.15	562.51	568.32	594.56
2004	605.21	612.58	603.42	591.83	599.40	609.31	587.21	589.09	595.66	604.51	629.26	650.99
2005	633.99	646.93	635.78	623.32	644.28	645.92	670.26	663.13	668.53	656.09	679.35	679.42
2006	697.79	697.83	706.74	714.37	691.78	691.80	692.59	707.55	723.48	747.30	761.43	770.08
2007	784.11	768.92	775.97	807.82	835.14	818.17	792.11	801.22	830.59	844.20	806.44	799.82
2008	750.97	726.42	720.32	756.03	768.28	703.22	694.07	702.17	634.08	522.47	481.43	487.77
2009	447.32	399.61	433.67	476.84	501.95	502.27	539.88	558.21	579.97	566.50	598.41	612.01
2010	589.41	607.45	643.79	655.06	601.79	567.37	606.09	577.68	629.78	653.57	654.24	696.90
2011	712.97	736.24	737.07	758.45	748.75	734.48	717.77	674.79	623.45	692.41	688.77	693.36
2012	726.33	756.42	778.92	773.50								

RUSSELL 2000 INDEX MONTHLY PERCENT CHANGES SINCE 1979

	Jan	Feb	Mar	Apr	May	Jun	Jul	Aug	Sep	Oct	Nov	Dec	Year's Change
1979	9.0	-3.2	9.7	2.3	-1.8	5.3	2.9	7.8	-0.7	-11.3	8.1	6.6	38.0
1980	8.2	-2.1	-18.5	6.0	8.0	4.0	11.0	6.5	2.9	3.9	7.0	-3.7	33.8
1981	-0.6	0.3	7.7	2.5	3.0	-2.5	-2.6	-8.0	-8.6	8.2	2.8	-2.0	-1.5
1982	-3.7	-5.3	-1.5	5.1	-3.2	-4.0	-1.7	7.5	3.6	14.1	8.8	1.1	20.7
1983	7.5	6.0	2.5	7.2	7.0	4.4	-3.0	-4.0	1.6	-7.0	5.0	-2.1	26.3
1984	-1.8	-5.9	0.4	-0.7	-5.4	2.6	-5.0	11.5	-1.0	-2.0	-2.9	1.4	-9.6
1985	13.1	2.4	-2.2	-1.4	3.4	1.0	2.7	-1.2	-6.2	3.6	6.8	4.2	28.0
1986	1.5	7.0	4.7	1.4	3.3	-0.2	-9.5	3.0	-6.3	3.9	-0.5	-3.1	4.0
1987	11.5	8.2	2.4	-3.0	-0.5	2.3	2.8	2.9	-2.0	-30.8	-5.5	7.8	-10.8
1988	4.0	8.7	4.4	2.0	-2.5	7.0	-0.9	-2.8	2.3	-1.2	-3.6	3.8	22.4
1989	4.4	0.5	2.2	4.3	4.2	-2.4	4.2	2.1	0.01	-6.0	0.4	0.1	14.2
1990	-8.9	2.9	3.7	-3.4	6.8	0.1	-4.5	-13.6	-9.2	-6.2	7.3	3.7	-21.5
1991	9.1	11.0	6.9	-0.2	4.5	-6.0	3.1	3.7	0.6	2.7	-4.7	7.7	43.7
1992	8.0	2.9	-3.5	-3.7	1.2	-5.0	3.2	-3.1	2.2	3.1	7.5	3.4	16.4
1993	3.2	-2.5	3.1	-2.8	4.3	0.5	1.3	4.1	2.7	2.5	-3.4	3.3	17.0
1994	3.1	-0.4	-5.4	0.6	-1.3	-3.6	1.6	5.4	-0.5	-0.4	-4.2	2.5	-3.2
1995	-1.4	3.9	1.6	2.1	1.5	5.0	5.7	1.9	1.7	-4.6	4.2	2.4	26.2
1996	-0.2	3.0	1.8	5.3	3.9	-4.2	-8.8	5.7	3.7	-1.7	4.0	2.4	14.8
1997	1.9	-2.5	-4.9	-0.2	11.0	4.1	4.6	2.2	7.2	-4.5	-0.8	1.7	20.5
1998	-1.6	7.4	4.1	0.5	-5.4	0.2	-8.2	-19.5	7.6	4.0	5.2	6.1	-3.4
1999	1.2	-8.2	1.4	8.8	1.4	4.3	-2.8	-3.8	-0.1	0.3	5.9	11.2	19.6
2000	-1.7	16.4	-6.7	-6.1	-5.9	8.6	-3.2	7.4	-3.1	-4.5	-10.4	8.4	-4.2
2001	5.1	-6.7	-5.0	7.7	2.3	3.3	-5.4	-3.3	-13.6	5.8	7.6	6.0	1.0
2002	-1.1	-2.8	7.9	0.8	-4.5	-5.1	-15.2	-0.4	-7.3	3.1	8.8	-5.7	-21.6
2003	-2.9	-3.1	1.1	9.4	10.6	1.7	6.2	4.5	-2.0	8.3	3.5	1.9	45.4
2004	4.3	0.8	0.8	-5.2	1.5	4.1	-6.8	-0.6	4.6	1.9	8.6	2.8	17.0
2005	-4.2	1.6	-3.0	-5.8	6.4	3.7	6.3	-1.9	0.2	-3.2	4.7	-0.6	3.3
2006	8.9	-0.3	4.7	-0.1	-5.7	0.5	-3.3	2.9	0.7	5.7	2.5	0.2	17.0
2007	1.6	-0.9	0.9	1.7	4.0	-1.6	-6.9	2.2	1.6	2.8	-7.3	-0.2	-2.7
2008	-6.9	-3.8	0.3	4.1	4.5	-7.8	3.6	3.5	-8.1	-20.9	-12.0	5.6	-34.8
2009	-11.2	-12.3	8.7	15.3	2.9	1.3	9.5	2.8	5.6	-6.9	3.0	7.9	25.2
2010	-3.7	4.4	8.0	5.6	-7.7	-7.9	6.8	-7.5	12.3	4.0	3.4	7.8	25.3
2011	-0.3	5.4	2.4	2.6	-2.0	-2.5	-3.7	-8.8	-11.4	15.0	-0.5	0.5	-5.5
2012	7.0	2.3	2.4	-1.6									
TOTALS	62.4	35.1	43.1	61.4	49.8	11.2	-16.0	9.1	-19.0	-18.3	59.3	93.1	
AVG.	1.8	1.0	1.3	1.8	1.5	0.3	-0.5	0.3	-0.6	-0.6	1.8	2.8	
# Up	19	19	25	22	21	20	16	19	18	18	21	26	
# Down	15	15	9	12	12	13	17	14	15	15	12	7	

RUSSELL 2000 INDEX MONTHLY CLOSING PRICES SINCE 1979

	Jan	Feb	Mar	Apr	May	Jun	Jul	Aug	Sep	Oct	Nov	Dec
1979	44.18	42.78	46.94	48.00	47.13	49.62	51.08	55.05	54.68	48.51	52.43	55.91
1980	60.50	59.22	48.27	51.18	55.26	57.47	63.81	67.97	69.94	72.64	77.70	74.80
1981	74.33	74.52	80.25	82.25	84.72	82.56	80.41	73.94	67.55	73.06	75.14	73.67
1982	70.96	67.21	66.21	69.59	67.39	64.67	63.59	68.38	70.84	80.86	87.96	88.90
1983	95.53	101.23	103.77	111.20	118.94	124.17	120.43	115.60	117.43	109.17	114.66	112.27
1984	110.21	103.72	104.10	103.34	97.75	100.30	95.25	106.21	105.17	103.07	100.11	101.49
1985	114.77	117.54	114.92	113.35	117.26	118.38	121.56	120.10	112.65	116.73	124.62	129.87
1986	131.78	141.00	147.63	149.66	154.61	154.23	139.65	143.83	134.73	139.95	139.26	135.00
1987	150.48	162.84	166.79	161.82	161.02	164.75	169.42	174.25	170.81	118.26	111.70	120.42
1988	125.24	136.10	142.15	145.01	141.37	151.30	149.89	145.74	149.08	147.25	142.01	147.37
1989	153.84	154.56	157.89	164.68	171.53	167.42	174.50	178.20	178.21	167.47	168.17	168.30
1990	153.27	157.72	163.63	158.09	168.91	169.04	161.51	139.52	126.70	118.83	127.50	132.16
1991	144.17	160.00	171.01	170.61	178.34	167.61	172.76	179.11	180.16	185.00	176.37	189.94
1992	205.16	211.15	203.69	196.25	198.52	188.64	194.74	188.79	192.92	198.90	213.81	221.01
1993	228.10	222.41	229.21	222.68	232.19	233.35	236.46	246.19	252.95	259.18	250.41	258.59
1994	266.52	265.53	251.06	252.55	249.28	240.29	244.06	257.32	256.12	255.02	244.25	250.36
1995	246.85	256.57	260.77	266.17	270.25	283.63	299.72	305.31	310.38	296.25	308.58	315.97
1996	315.38	324.93	330.77	348.28	361.85	346.61	316.00	333.88	346.39	340.57	354.11	362.61
1997	369.45	360.05	342.56	343.00	380.76	396.37	414.48	423.43	453.82	433.26	429.92	437.02
1998	430.05	461.83	480.68	482.89	456.62	457.39	419.75	337.95	363.59	378.16	397.75	421.96
1999	427.22	392.26	397.63	432.81	438.68	457.68	444.77	427.83	427.30	428.64	454.08	504.75
2000	496.23	577.71	539.09	506.25	476.18	517.23	500.64	537.89	521.37	497.68	445.94	483.53
2001	508.34	474.37	450.53	485.32	496.50	512.64	484.78	468.56	404.87	428.17	460.78	488.50
2002	483.10	469.36	506.46	510.67	487.47	462.64	392.42	390.96	362.27	373.50	406.35	383.09
2003	372.17	360.52	364.54	398.68	441.00	448.37	476.02	497.42	487.68	528.22	546.51	556.91
2004	580.76	585.56	590.31	559.80	568.28	591.52	551.29	547.93	572.94	583.79	633.77	651.57
2005	624.02	634.06	615.07	579.38	616.71	639.66	679.75	666.51	667.29	646.61	677.29	673.22
2006	733.20	730.64	765.14	764.54	721.01	724.67	700.56	720.53	725.59	766.84	786.12	787.66
2007	800.34	793.30	800.71	814.57	847.19	833.69	776.13	792.86	805.45	828.02	767.77	766.03
2008	713.30	686.18	687.97	716.18	748.28	689.66	714.52	739.50	679.58	537.52	473.14	499.45
2009	443.53	389.02	422.75	487.56	501.58	508.28	556.71	572.07	604.28	562.77	579.73	625.39
2010	602.04	628.56	678.64	716.60	661.61	609.49	650.89	602.06	676.14	703.35	727.01	783.65
2011	781.25	823.45	843.55	865.29	848.30	827.43	797.03	726.81	644.16	741.06	737.42	740.92
2012	792.82	810.94	830.30	816.88								

10 **BEST** DAYS BY PERCENT AND POINT

	BY PERCENT CHANGE				BY POINT CHANGE		
DAY	CLOSE	PNT CHANGE	% CHANGE	DAY	CLOSE	PNT CHANGE	% CHANGE
			DJIA 1901 TO 1949				
3/15/33	62.10	8.26	15.3	10/30/29	258.47	28.40	12.3
10/6/31	99.34	12.86	14.9	11/14/29	217.28	18.59	9.4
10/30/29	258.47	28.40	12.3	10/5/29	341.36	16.19	5.0
9/21/32	75.16	7.67	11.4	10/31/29	273.51	15.04	5.8
8/3/32	58.22	5.06	9.5	10/6/31	99.34	12.86	14.9
2/11/32	78.60	6.80	9.5	11/15/29	228.73	11.45	5.3
11/14/29	217.28	18.59	9.4	6/19/30	228.97	10.13	4.6
12/18/31	80.69	6.90	9.4	9/5/39	148.12	10.03	7.3
2/13/32	85.82	7.22	9.2	11/22/28	290.34	9.81	3.5
5/6/32	59.01	4.91	9.1	10/1/30	214.14	9.24	4.5
			DJIA 1950 TO APRIL 2012				
10/13/08	9387.61	936.42	11.1	10/13/08	9387.61	936.42	11.1
10/28/08	9065.12	889.35	10.9	10/28/08	9065.12	889.35	10.9
10/21/87	2027.85	186.84	10.2	11/13/08	8835.25	552.59	6.7
3/23/09	7775.86	497.48	6.8	3/16/00	10630.60	499.19	4.9
11/13/08	8835.25	552.59	6.7	3/23/09	7775.86	497.48	6.8
11/21/08	8046.42	494.13	6.5	11/21/08	8046.42	494.13	6.5
7/24/02	8191.29	488.95	6.4	11/30/11	12045.68	490.05	4.2
10/20/87	1841.01	102.27	5.9	7/24/02	8191.29	488.95	6.4
3/10/09	6926.49	379.44	5.8	9/30/08	10850.66	485.21	4.7
7/29/02	8711.88	447.49	5.4	7/29/02	8711.88	447.49	5.4
			S&P 500 1930 TO APRIL 2012				
3/15/33	6.81	0.97	16.6	10/13/08	1003.35	104.13	11.6
10/6/31	9.91	1.09	12.4	10/28/08	940.51	91.59	10.8
9/21/32	8.52	0.90	11.8	3/16/00	1458.47	66.32	4.8
10/13/08	1003.35	104.13	11.6	1/3/01	1347.56	64.29	5.0
10/28/08	940.51	91.59	10.8	9/30/08	1166.36	59.97	5.4
2/16/35	10.00	0.94	10.4	11/13/08	911.29	58.99	6.9
8/17/35	11.70	1.08	10.2	3/23/09	822.92	54.38	7.1
3/16/35	9.05	0.82	10.0	3/18/08	1330.74	54.14	4.2
9/12/38	12.06	1.06	9.6	8/9/11	1172.53	53.07	4.7
9/5/39	12.64	1.11	9.6	8/11/11	1172.64	51.88	4.6
			NASDAQ 1971 TO APRIL 2012				
1/3/01	2616.69	324.83	14.2	1/3/01	2616.69	324.83	14.2
10/13/08	1844.25	194.74	11.8	12/5/00	2889.80	274.05	10.5
12/5/00	2889.80	274.05	10.5	4/18/00	3793.57	254.41	7.2
10/28/08	1649.47	143.57	9.5	5/30/00	3459.48	254.37	7.9
4/5/01	1785.00	146.20	8.9	10/19/00	3418.60	247.04	7.8
4/18/01	2079.44	156.22	8.1	10/13/00	3316.77	242.09	7.9
5/30/00	3459.48	254.37	7.9	6/2/00	3813.38	230.88	6.4
10/13/00	3316.77	242.09	7.9	4/25/00	3711.23	228.75	6.6
10/19/00	3418.60	247.04	7.8	4/17/00	3539.16	217.87	6.6
5/8/02	1696.29	122.47	7.8	10/13/08	1844.25	194.74	11.8
			RUSSELL 1000 1979 TO APRIL 2012				
10/13/08	542.98	56.75	11.7	10/13/08	542.98	56.75	11.7
10/28/08	503.74	47.68	10.5	10/28/08	503.74	47.68	10.5
10/21/87	135.85	11.15	8.9	3/16/00	777.86	36.60	4.9
3/23/09	446.90	29.36	7.0	1/3/01	712.63	35.74	5.3
11/13/08	489.83	31.99	7.0	11/13/08	489.83	31.99	7.0
11/24/08	456.14	28.26	6.6	9/30/08	634.08	31.74	5.3
3/10/09	391.01	23.46	6.4	8/9/11	647.85	30.57	5.0
11/21/08	427.88	24.97	6.2	12/5/00	728.44	30.36	4.4
7/24/02	448.05	23.87	5.6	3/23/09	446.90	29.36	7.0
7/29/02	477.61	24.69	5.5	8/11/11	649.44	29.14	4.7
			RUSSELL 2000 1979 TO APRIL 2012				
10/13/08	570.89	48.41	9.3	10/13/08	570.89	48.41	9.3
11/13/08	491.23	38.43	8.5	9/18/08	723.68	47.30	7.0
3/23/09	433.72	33.61	8.4	8/9/11	696.16	45.20	6.9
10/21/87	130.65	9.26	7.6	11/30/11	737.42	41.32	5.9
10/28/08	482.55	34.15	7.6	10/4/11	648.64	39.15	6.4
11/24/08	436.80	30.26	7.4	11/13/08	491.23	38.43	8.5
3/10/09	367.75	24.49	7.1	10/27/11	765.43	38.28	5.3
9/18/08	723.68	47.30	7.0	5/10/10	689.61	36.61	5.6
8/9/11	696.16	45.20	6.9	8/11/11	695.89	35.68	5.4
10/16/08	536.57	34.46	6.9	10/16/08	536.57	34.46	6.9

10 <u>WORST</u> DAYS BY PERCENT AND POINT

	BY PERCENT CHANGE				BY POINT CHANGE		
DAY	CLOSE	PNT CHANGE	% CHANGE	DAY	CLOSE	PNT CHANGE	% CHANGE
DJIA 1901 to 1949							
10/28/29	260.64	–38.33	–12.8	10/28/29	260.64	–38.33	–12.8
10/29/29	230.07	–30.57	–11.7	10/29/29	230.07	–30.57	–11.7
11/6/29	232.13	–25.55	–9.9	11/6/29	232.13	–25.55	–9.9
8/12/32	63.11	–5.79	–8.4	10/23/29	305.85	–20.66	–6.3
3/14/07	55.84	–5.05	–8.3	11/11/29	220.39	–16.14	–6.8
7/21/33	88.71	–7.55	–7.8	11/4/29	257.68	–15.83	–5.8
10/18/37	125.73	–10.57	–7.8	12/12/29	243.14	–15.30	–5.9
2/1/17	88.52	–6.91	–7.2	10/3/29	329.95	–14.55	–4.2
10/5/32	66.07	–5.09	–7.2	6/16/30	230.05	–14.20	–5.8
9/24/31	107.79	–8.20	–7.1	8/9/29	337.99	–14.11	–4.0
DJIA 1950 to APRIL 2012							
10/19/87	1738.74	–508.00	–22.6	9/29/08	10365.45	–777.68	–7.0
10/26/87	1793.93	–156.83	–8.0	10/15/08	8577.91	–733.08	–7.9
10/15/08	8577.91	–733.08	–7.9	9/17/01	8920.70	–684.81	–7.1
12/1/08	8149.09	–679.95	–7.7	12/1/08	8149.09	–679.95	–7.7
10/9/08	8579.19	–678.91	–7.3	10/9/08	8579.19	–678.91	–7.3
10/27/97	7161.15	–554.26	–7.2	8/8/11	10809.85	–634.76	–5.6
9/17/01	8920.70	–684.81	–7.1	4/14/00	10305.77	–617.78	–5.7
9/29/08	10365.45	–777.68	–7.0	10/27/97	7161.15	–554.26	–7.2
10/13/89	2569.26	–190.58	–6.9	8/10/11	10719.94	–519.83	–4.6
1/8/88	1911.31	–140.58	–6.9	10/22/08	8519.21	–514.45	–5.7
S&P 500 1930 to APRIL 2012							
10/19/87	224.84	–57.86	–20.5	9/29/08	1106.39	–106.62	–8.8
3/18/35	8.14	–0.91	–10.1	10/15/08	907.84	–90.17	–9.0
4/16/35	8.22	–0.91	–10.0	4/14/00	1356.56	–83.95	–5.8
9/3/46	15.00	–1.65	–9.9	12/1/08	816.21	–80.03	–8.9
10/18/37	10.76	–1.10	–9.3	8/8/11	1119.46	–79.92	–6.7
10/15/08	907.84	–90.17	–9.0	10/9/08	909.92	–75.02	–7.6
12/1/08	816.21	–80.03	–8.9	8/31/98	957.28	–69.86	–6.8
7/20/33	10.57	–1.03	–8.9	10/27/97	876.99	–64.65	–6.9
9/29/08	1106.39	–106.62	–8.8	10/7/08	996.23	–60.66	–5.7
7/21/33	9.65	–0.92	–8.7	8/4/11	1200.07	–60.27	–4.8
NASDAQ 1971 to APRIL 2012							
10/19/87	360.21	–46.12	–11.4	4/14/00	3321.29	–355.49	–9.7
4/14/00	3321.29	–355.49	–9.7	4/3/00	4223.68	–349.15	–7.6
9/29/08	1983.73	–199.61	–9.1	4/12/00	3769.63	–286.27	–7.1
10/26/87	298.90	–29.55	–9.0	4/10/00	4188.20	–258.25	–5.8
10/20/87	327.79	–32.42	–9.0	1/4/00	3901.69	–229.46	–5.6
12/1/08	1398.07	–137.50	–9.0	3/14/00	4706.63	–200.61	–4.1
8/31/98	1499.25	–140.43	–8.6	5/10/00	3384.73	–200.28	–5.6
10/15/08	1628.33	–150.68	–8.5	5/23/00	3164.55	–199.66	–5.9
4/3/00	4223.68	–349.15	–7.6	9/29/08	1983.73	–199.61	–9.1
1/2/01	2291.86	–178.66	–7.2	10/25/00	3229.57	–190.22	–5.6
RUSSELL 1000 1979 to APRIL 2012							
10/19/87	121.04	–28.40	–19.0	9/29/08	602.34	–57.35	–8.7
10/15/08	489.71	–49.11	–9.1	10/15/08	489.71	–49.11	–9.1
12/1/08	437.75	–43.68	–9.1	4/14/00	715.20	–45.74	–6.0
9/29/08	602.34	–57.35	–8.7	8/8/11	617.28	–45.56	–6.9
10/26/87	119.45	–10.74	–8.3	12/1/08	437.75	–43.68	–9.1
10/9/08	492.13	–40.05	–7.5	10/9/08	492.13	–40.05	–7.5
8/8/11	617.28	–45.56	–6.9	8/31/98	496.66	–35.77	–6.7
11/20/08	402.91	–29.62	–6.9	8/4/11	664.65	–34.92	–5.0
8/31/98	496.66	–35.77	–6.7	10/27/97	465.44	–32.96	–6.6
10/27/97	465.44	–32.96	–6.6	10/7/08	538.15	–32.64	–5.7
RUSSELL 2000 1979 to APRIL 2012							
10/19/87	133.60	–19.14	–12.5	8/8/11	650.96	–63.67	–8.9
12/1/08	417.07	–56.07	–11.9	12/1/08	417.07	–56.07	–11.9
10/15/08	502.11	–52.54	–9.5	10/15/08	502.11	–52.54	–9.5
10/26/87	110.33	–11.26	–9.3	10/9/08	499.20	–47.37	–8.7
10/20/87	121.39	–12.21	–9.1	9/29/08	657.72	–47.07	–6.7
8/8/11	650.96	–63.67	–8.9	8/4/11	726.80	–45.98	–6.0
10/9/08	499.20	–47.37	–8.7	8/18/11	662.51	–41.52	–5.9
11/19/08	412.38	–35.13	–7.9	10/7/08	558.95	–36.96	–6.2
4/14/00	453.72	–35.50	–7.3	11/9/11	718.86	–36.41	–4.8
11/14/08	456.52	–34.71	–7.1	8/10/11	660.21	–35.95	–5.2

10 <u>BEST</u> WEEKS BY PERCENT AND POINT

	BY PERCENT CHANGE				BY POINT CHANGE		
WEEK ENDS	CLOSE	PNT CHANGE	% CHANGE	WEEK ENDS	CLOSE	PNT CHANGE	% CHANGE
DJIA 1901 to 1949							
8/6/32	66.56	12.30	22.7	12/7/29	263.46	24.51	10.3
6/25/38	131.94	18.71	16.5	6/25/38	131.94	18.71	16.5
2/13/32	85.82	11.37	15.3	6/27/31	156.93	17.97	12.9
4/22/33	72.24	9.36	14.9	11/22/29	245.74	17.01	7.4
10/10/31	105.61	12.84	13.8	8/17/29	360.70	15.86	4.6
7/30/32	54.26	6.42	13.4	12/22/28	285.94	15.22	5.6
6/27/31	156.93	17.97	12.9	8/24/29	375.44	14.74	4.1
9/24/32	74.83	8.39	12.6	2/21/29	310.06	14.21	4.8
8/27/32	75.61	8.43	12.6	5/10/30	272.01	13.70	5.3
3/18/33	60.56	6.72	12.5	11/15/30	186.68	13.54	7.8
DJIA 1950 to APRIL 2012							
10/11/74	658.17	73.61	12.6	10/31/08	9325.01	946.06	11.3
10/31/08	9325.01	946.06	11.3	12/2/11	12019.42	787.64	7.0
8/20/82	869.29	81.24	10.3	11/28/08	8829.04	782.62	9.7
11/28/08	8829.04	782.62	9.7	3/17/00	10595.23	666.41	6.7
3/13/09	7223.98	597.04	9.0	3/21/03	8521.97	662.26	8.4
10/8/82	986.85	79.11	8.7	7/1/11	12582.77	648.19	5.4
3/21/03	8521.97	662.26	8.4	9/28/01	8847.56	611.75	7.4
8/3/84	1202.08	87.46	7.9	7/17/09	8743.94	597.42	7.3
9/28/01	8847.56	611.75	7.4	3/13/09	7223.98	597.04	9.0
7/17/09	8743.94	597.42	7.3	7/2/99	11139.24	586.68	5.6
S&P 500 1930 to APRIL 2012							
8/6/32	7.22	1.12	18.4	6/2/00	1477.26	99.24	7.2
6/25/38	11.39	1.72	17.8	11/28/08	896.24	96.21	12.0
7/30/32	6.10	0.89	17.1	10/31/08	968.75	91.98	10.5
4/22/33	7.75	1.09	16.4	12/2/11	1244.28	85.61	7.4
10/11/74	71.14	8.80	14.1	4/20/00	1434.54	77.98	5.8
2/13/32	8.80	1.08	14.0	7/2/99	1391.22	75.91	5.8
9/24/32	8.52	1.02	13.6	3/3/00	1409.17	75.81	5.7
10/10/31	10.64	1.27	13.6	9/28/01	1040.94	75.14	7.8
8/27/32	8.57	1.01	13.4	3/13/09	756.55	73.17	10.7
3/18/33	6.61	0.77	13.2	10/16/98	1056.42	72.10	7.3
NASDAQ 1971 to APRIL 2012							
6/2/00	3813.38	608.27	19.0	6/2/00	3813.38	608.27	19.0
4/12/01	1961.43	241.07	14.0	2/4/00	4244.14	357.07	9.2
11/28/08	1535.57	151.22	10.9	3/3/00	4914.79	324.29	7.1
10/31/08	1720.95	168.92	10.9	4/20/00	3643.88	322.59	9.7
3/13/09	1431.50	137.65	10.6	12/8/00	2917.43	272.14	10.3
4/20/01	2163.41	201.98	10.3	4/12/01	1961.43	241.07	14.0
12/8/00	2917.43	272.14	10.3	7/14/00	4246.18	222.98	5.5
4/20/00	3643.88	322.59	9.7	1/12/01	2626.50	218.85	9.1
10/11/74	60.42	5.26	9.5	4/28/00	3860.66	216.78	6.0
2/4/00	4244.14	357.07	9.0	12/23/99	3969.44	216.38	5.8
RUSSELL 1000 1979 to APRIL 2012							
11/28/08	481.43	53.55	12.5	6/2/00	785.02	57.93	8.0
10/31/08	522.47	50.94	10.8	11/28/08	481.43	53.55	12.5
3/13/09	411.10	39.88	10.7	10/31/08	522.47	50.94	10.8
8/20/82	61.51	4.83	8.5	12/2/11	687.44	47.63	7.4
6/2/00	785.02	57.93	8.0	4/20/00	757.32	42.12	5.9
9/28/01	546.46	38.48	7.6	3/3/00	756.41	41.55	5.8
10/16/98	546.09	38.45	7.6	3/13/09	411.10	39.88	10.7
8/3/84	87.43	6.13	7.5	7/1/11	745.21	39.46	5.6
12/2/11	687.44	47.63	7.4	10/14/11	675.52	38.87	6.1
3/21/03	474.58	32.69	7.4	7/2/99	723.25	38.80	5.7
RUSSELL 2000 1979 to APRIL 2012							
11/28/08	473.14	66.60	16.4	12/2/11	735.02	68.86	10.3
10/31/08	537.52	66.40	14.1	11/28/08	473.14	66.60	16.4
6/2/00	513.03	55.66	12.2	10/31/08	537.52	66.40	14.1
3/13/09	393.09	42.04	12.0	10/14/11	712.46	56.25	8.6
12/2/11	735.02	68.86	10.3	6/2/00	513.03	55.66	12.2
10/14/11	712.46	56.25	8.6	10/28/11	761.00	48.58	6.8
7/17/09	519.22	38.24	8.0	7/1/11	840.04	42.25	5.3
10/16/98	342.87	24.47	7.7	3/13/09	393.09	42.04	12.0
12/18/87	116.94	8.31	7.7	2/1/08	730.50	41.90	6.1
3/3/00	597.88	41.14	7.4	3/3/00	597.88	41.14	7.4

10 <u>WORST</u> WEEKS BY PERCENT AND POINT

	BY PERCENT CHANGE				BY POINT CHANGE		
WEEK ENDS	CLOSE	PNT CHANGE	% CHANGE	WEEK ENDS	CLOSE	PNT CHANGE	% CHANGE
DJIA 1901 to 1949							
7/22/33	88.42	−17.68	−16.7	11/8/29	236.53	−36.98	−13.5
5/18/40	122.43	−22.42	−15.5	12/8/28	257.33	−33.47	−11.5
10/8/32	61.17	−10.92	−15.2	6/21/30	215.30	−28.95	−11.9
10/3/31	92.77	−14.59	−13.6	10/19/29	323.87	−28.82	−8.2
11/8/29	236.53	−36.98	−13.5	5/3/30	258.31	−27.15	−9.5
9/17/32	66.44	−10.10	−13.2	10/31/29	273.51	−25.46	−8.5
10/21/33	83.64	−11.95	−12.5	10/26/29	298.97	−24.90	−7.7
12/12/31	78.93	−11.21	−12.4	5/18/40	122.43	−22.42	−15.5
5/8/15	62.77	−8.74	−12.2	2/8/29	301.53	−18.23	−5.7
6/21/30	215.30	−28.95	−11.9	10/11/30	193.05	−18.05	−8.6
DJIA 1950 to APRIL 2012							
10/10/08	8451.19	−1874.19	−18.2	10/10/08	8451.19	−1874.19	−18.2
9/21/01	8235.81	−1369.70	−14.3	9/21/01	8235.81	−1369.70	−14.3
10/23/87	1950.76	−295.98	−13.2	3/16/01	9823.41	−821.21	−7.7
10/16/87	2246.74	−235.47	−9.5	10/3/08	10325.38	−817.75	−7.3
10/13/89	2569.26	−216.26	−7.8	4/14/00	10305.77	−805.71	−7.3
3/16/01	9823.41	−821.21	−7.7	9/23/11	10771.48	−737.61	−6.4
7/19/02	8019.26	−665.27	−7.7	8/5/11	11444.61	−698.63	−5.8
12/4/87	1766.74	−143.74	−7.5	7/12/02	8684.53	−694.97	−7.4
9/13/74	627.19	−50.69	−7.5	7/19/02	8019.26	−665.27	−7.7
9/12/86	1758.72	−141.03	−7.4	10/15/99	10019.71	−630.05	−5.9
S&P 500 1930 to APRIL 2012							
7/22/33	9.71	−2.20	−18.5	10/10/08	899.22	−200.01	−18.2
10/10/08	899.22	−200.01	−18.2	4/14/00	1356.56	−159.79	−10.5
5/18/40	9.75	−2.05	−17.4	9/21/01	965.80	−126.74	−11.6
10/8/32	6.77	−1.38	−16.9	10/3/08	1099.23	−113.78	−9.4
9/17/32	7.50	−1.28	−14.6	8/5/11	1199.38	−92.90	−7.2
10/21/33	8.57	−1.31	−13.3	10/15/99	1247.41	−88.61	−6.6
10/3/31	9.37	−1.36	−12.7	3/16/01	1150.53	−82.89	−6.7
10/23/87	248.22	−34.48	−12.2	1/28/00	1360.16	−81.20	−5.6
12/12/31	8.20	−1.13	−12.1	9/23/11	1136.43	−79.58	−6.5
3/26/38	9.20	−1.21	−11.6	1/18/08	1325.19	−75.83	−5.4
NASDAQ 1971 to APRIL 2012							
4/14/00	3321.29	−1125.16	−25.3	4/14/00	3321.29	−1125.16	−25.3
10/23/87	328.45	−77.88	−19.2	7/28/00	3663.00	−431.45	−10.5
9/21/01	1423.19	−272.19	−16.1	11/10/00	3028.99	−422.59	−12.2
10/10/08	1649.51	−297.88	−15.3	3/31/00	4572.83	−390.20	−7.9
11/10/00	3028.99	−422.59	−12.2	1/28/00	3887.07	−348.33	−8.2
10/3/08	1947.39	−235.95	−10.8	10/6/00	3361.01	−311.81	−8.5
7/28/00	3663.00	−431.45	−10.5	10/10/08	1649.51	−297.88	−15.3
10/24/08	1552.03	−159.26	−9.3	5/12/00	3529.06	−287.76	−7.5
12/15/00	2653.27	−264.16	−9.1	9/21/01	1423.19	−272.19	−16.1
12/1/00	2645.29	−259.09	−8.9	12/15/00	2653.27	−264.16	−9.1
RUSSELL 1000 1979 to APRIL 2012							
10/10/08	486.23	−108.31	−18.2	10/10/08	486.23	−108.31	−18.2
10/23/87	130.19	−19.25	−12.9	4/14/00	715.20	−90.39	−11.2
9/21/01	507.98	−67.59	−11.7	9/21/01	507.98	−67.59	−11.7
4/14/00	715.20	−90.39	−11.2	10/3/08	594.54	−65.15	−9.9
10/3/08	594.54	−65.15	−9.9	8/5/11	662.84	−54.93	−7.7
10/16/87	149.44	−14.42	−8.8	9/23/11	627.56	−45.42	−6.8
11/21/08	427.88	−41.15	−8.8	10/15/99	646.79	−43.89	−6.4
9/12/86	124.95	−10.87	−8.0	3/16/01	605.71	−43.88	−6.8
8/5/11	662.84	−54.93	−7.7	5/7/10	611.63	−43.43	−6.6
7/19/02	450.64	−36.13	−7.4	7/27/07	793.72	−41.97	−5.0
RUSSELL 2000 1979 to APRIL 2012							
10/23/87	121.59	−31.15	−20.4	10/10/08	522.48	−96.92	−15.7
4/14/00	453.72	−89.27	−16.4	4/14/00	453.72	−89.27	−16.4
10/10/08	522.48	−96.92	−15.7	10/3/08	619.40	−85.39	−12.1
9/21/01	378.89	−61.84	−14.0	8/5/11	714.63	−82.40	−10.3
10/3/08	619.40	−85.39	−12.1	5/7/10	653.00	−63.60	−8.9
11/21/08	406.54	−49.98	−11.0	9/23/11	652.43	−61.88	−8.7
10/24/08	471.12	−55.31	−10.5	9/21/01	378.89	−61.84	−14.0
8/5/11	714.63	−82.40	−10.3	7/27/07	777.83	−58.61	−7.0
3/6/09	351.05	−37.97	−9.8	10/24/08	471.12	−55.31	−10.5
11/14/08	456.52	−49.27	−9.7	11/25/11	666.16	−53.26	−7.4

10 **BEST** MONTHS BY PERCENT AND POINT

	BY PERCENT CHANGE				BY POINT CHANGE		
MONTH	CLOSE	PNT CHANGE	% CHANGE	MONTH	CLOSE	PNT CHANGE	% CHANGE
DJIA 1901 to 1949							
APR-1933	77.66	22.26	40.2	NOV-1928	293.38	41.22	16.3
AUG-1932	73.16	18.90	34.8	JUN-1929	333.79	36.38	12.2
JUL-1932	54.26	11.42	26.7	AUG-1929	380.33	32.63	9.4
JUN-1938	133.88	26.14	24.3	JUN-1938	133.88	26.14	24.3
APR-1915	71.78	10.95	18.0	AUG-1928	240.41	24.41	11.3
JUN-1931	150.18	21.72	16.9	APR-1933	77.66	22.26	40.2
NOV-1928	293.38	41.22	16.3	FEB-1931	189.66	22.11	13.2
NOV-1904	52.76	6.59	14.3	JUN-1931	150.18	21.72	16.9
MAY-1919	105.50	12.62	13.6	AUG-1932	73.16	18.90	34.8
SEP-1939	152.54	18.13	13.5	JAN-1930	267.14	18.66	7.5
DJIA 1950 to APRIL 2012							
JAN-1976	975.28	122.87	14.4	OCT-2011	11955.01	1041.63	9.5
JAN-1975	703.69	87.45	14.2	APR-1999	10789.04	1002.88	10.2
JAN-1987	2158.04	262.09	13.8	APR-2001	10734.97	856.19	8.7
AUG-1982	901.31	92.71	11.5	OCT-2002	8397.03	805.10	10.6
OCT-1982	991.72	95.47	10.7	MAR-2000	10921.92	793.61	7.8
OCT-2002	8397.03	805.10	10.6	NOV-2001	9851.56	776.42	8.6
APR-1978	837.32	79.96	10.6	SEP-2010	10788.05	773.33	7.7
APR-1999	10789.04	1002.88	10.2	OCT-1998	8592.10	749.48	9.6
NOV-1962	649.30	59.53	10.1	JUL-2009	9171.61	724.61	8.6
NOV-1954	386.77	34.63	9.8	APR-2007	13062.91	708.56	5.7
S&P 500 1930 to APRIL 2012							
APR-1933	8.32	2.47	42.2	MAR-2000	1498.58	132.16	9.7
JUL-1932	6.10	1.67	37.7	OCT-2011	1253.30	121.88	10.8
AUG-1932	8.39	2.29	37.5	SEP-2010	1141.20	91.87	8.8
JUN-1938	11.56	2.29	24.7	APR-2001	1249.46	89.13	7.7
SEP-1939	13.02	1.84	16.5	AUG-2000	1517.68	86.85	6.1
OCT-1974	73.90	10.36	16.3	OCT-1998	1098.67	81.66	8.0
MAY-1933	9.64	1.32	15.9	DEC-1999	1469.25	80.34	5.8
APR-1938	9.70	1.20	14.1	OCT-1999	1362.93	80.22	6.3
JUN-1931	14.83	1.81	13.9	NOV-2001	1139.45	79.67	7.5
JAN-1987	274.08	31.91	13.2	DEC-2010	1257.64	77.09	6.5
NASDAQ 1971 to APRIL 2012							
DEC-1999	4069.31	733.15	22.0	FEB-2000	4696.69	756.34	19.2
FEB-2000	4696.69	756.34	19.2	DEC-1999	4069.31	733.15	22.0
OCT-1974	65.23	9.56	17.2	JUN-2000	3966.11	565.20	16.6
JAN-1975	69.78	9.96	16.6	AUG-2000	4206.35	439.36	11.7
JUN-2000	3966.11	565.20	16.6	NOV-1999	3336.16	369.73	12.5
APR-2001	2116.24	275.98	15.0	JAN-1999	2505.89	313.20	14.3
JAN-1999	2505.89	313.20	14.3	JAN-2001	2772.73	302.21	12.2
NOV-2001	1930.58	240.38	14.2	APR-2001	2116.24	275.98	15.0
OCT-2002	1329.75	157.69	13.5	OCT-2011	2684.41	269.01	11.1
OCT-1982	212.63	24.98	13.3	SEP-2010	2368.62	254.59	12.0
RUSSELL 1000 1979 to APRIL 2012							
JAN-1987	146.48	16.48	12.7	OCT-2011	692.41	68.96	11.1
OCT-1982	73.34	7.45	11.3	MAR-2000	797.99	64.95	8.9
AUG-1982	65.14	6.60	11.3	AUG-2000	811.17	55.60	7.4
DEC-1991	220.61	22.15	11.2	SEP-2010	629.78	52.10	9.0
OCT-2011	692.41	68.96	11.1	APR-2001	658.90	48.54	8.0
AUG-1984	89.87	8.74	10.8	OCT-1999	707.19	43.36	6.5
NOV-1980	78.26	7.18	10.1	DEC-1999	767.97	43.31	6.0
APR-2009	476.84	43.17	10.0	APR-2009	476.84	43.17	10.0
SEP-2010	629.78	52.10	9.0	DEC-2010	696.90	42.66	6.5
MAY-1990	187.66	15.34	8.0	NOV-2001	599.32	42.03	7.0
RUSSELL 2000 1979 to APRIL 2012							
FEB-2000	577.71	81.48	16.4	OCT-2011	741.06	96.90	15.0
APR-2009	487.56	64.81	15.3	FEB-2000	577.71	81.48	16.4
OCT-2011	741.06	96.90	15.0	SEP-2010	676.14	74.08	12.3
OCT-1982	80.86	10.02	14.1	APR-2009	487.56	64.81	15.3
JAN-1985	114.77	13.28	13.1	JAN-2006	733.20	59.98	8.9
SEP-2010	676.14	74.08	12.3	DEC-2010	783.65	56.64	7.8
AUG-1984	106.21	10.96	11.5	JAN-2012	792.82	51.90	7.0
JAN-1987	150.48	15.48	11.5	DEC-1999	504.75	50.67	11.2
DEC-1999	504.75	50.67	11.2	MAR-2010	678.64	50.08	8.0
JUL-1980	63.81	6.34	11.0	NOV-2004	633.77	49.98	8.6

10 <u>WORST</u> MONTHS BY PERCENT AND POINT

	BY PERCENT CHANGE				BY POINT CHANGE		
MONTH	CLOSE	PNT CHANGE	% CHANGE	MONTH	CLOSE	PNT CHANGE	% CHANGE
DJIA 1901 to 1949							
SEP-1931	96.61	−42.80	−30.7	OCT-1929	273.51	−69.94	−20.4
MAR-1938	98.95	−30.69	−23.7	JUN-1930	226.34	−48.73	−17.7
APR-1932	56.11	−17.17	−23.4	SEP-1931	96.61	−42.80	−30.7
MAY-1940	116.22	−32.21	−21.7	SEP-1929	343.45	−36.88	−9.7
OCT-1929	273.51	−69.94	−20.4	SEP-1930	204.90	−35.52	−14.8
MAY-1932	44.74	−11.37	−20.3	NOV-1929	238.95	−34.56	−12.6
JUN-1930	226.34	−48.73	−17.7	MAY-1940	116.22	−32.21	−21.7
DEC-1931	77.90	−15.97	−17.0	MAR-1938	98.95	−30.69	−23.7
FEB-1933	51.39	−9.51	−15.6	SEP-1937	154.57	−22.84	−12.9
MAY-1931	128.46	−22.73	−15.0	MAY-1931	128.46	−22.73	−15.0
DJIA 1950 to APRIL 2012							
OCT-1987	1993.53	−602.75	−23.2	OCT-2008	9325.01	−1525.65	−14.1
AUG-1998	7539.07	−1344.22	−15.1	AUG-1998	7539.07	−1344.22	−15.1
OCT-2008	9325.01	−1525.65	−14.1	JUN-2008	11350.01	−1288.31	−10.2
NOV-1973	822.25	−134.33	−14.0	SEP-2001	8847.56	−1102.19	−11.1
SEP-2002	7591.93	−1071.57	−12.4	SEP-2002	7591.93	−1071.57	−12.4
FEB-2009	7062.93	−937.93	−11.7	FEB-2009	7062.93	−937.93	−11.7
SEP-2001	8847.56	−1102.19	−11.1	MAY-2010	10136.63	−871.98	−7.9
SEP-1974	607.87	−70.71	−10.4	FEB-2000	10128.31	−812.22	−7.4
AUG-1974	678.58	−78.85	−10.4	JAN-2009	8000.86	−775.53	−8.8
JUN-2008	11350.01	−1288.31	−10.2	SEP-2011	10913.38	−700.15	−6.0
S&P 500 1930 to APRIL 2012							
SEP-1931	9.71	−4.15	−29.9	OCT-2008	968.75	−197.61	−16.9
MAR-1938	8.50	−2.84	−25.0	AUG-1998	957.28	−163.39	−14.6
MAY-1940	9.27	−2.92	−24.0	FEB-2001	1239.94	−126.07	−9.2
MAY-1932	4.47	−1.36	−23.3	JUN-2008	1280.00	−120.38	−8.6
OCT-1987	251.79	−70.04	−21.8	SEP-2008	1166.36	−116.47	−9.1
APR-1932	5.83	−1.48	−20.2	NOV-2000	1314.95	−114.45	−8.0
FEB-1933	5.66	−1.28	−18.4	SEP-2002	815.28	−100.79	−11.0
OCT-2008	968.75	−197.61	−16.9	MAY-2010	1089.41	−97.28	−8.2
JUN-1930	20.46	−4.03	−16.5	SEP-2001	1040.94	−92.64	−8.2
AUG-1998	957.28	−163.39	−14.6	FEB-2009	735.09	−90.79	−11.0
NASDAQ 1971 to APRIL 2012							
OCT-1987	323.30	−120.99	−27.2	NOV-2000	2597.93	−771.70	−22.9
NOV-2000	2597.93	−771.70	−22.9	APR-2000	3860.66	−712.17	−15.6
FEB-2001	2151.83	−620.90	−22.4	FEB-2001	2151.83	−620.90	−22.4
AUG-1998	1499.25	−373.14	−19.9	SEP-2000	3672.82	−533.53	−12.7
OCT-2008	1720.95	−370.93	−17.7	MAY-2000	3400.91	−459.75	−11.9
MAR-1980	131.00	−27.03	−17.1	AUG-1998	1499.25	−373.14	−19.9
SEP-2001	1498.80	−306.63	−17.0	OCT-2008	1720.95	−370.93	−17.7
OCT-1978	111.12	−21.77	−16.4	MAR-2001	1840.26	−311.57	−14.5
APR-2000	3860.66	−712.17	−15.6	SEP-2001	1498.80	−306.63	−17.0
NOV-1973	93.51	−16.66	−15.1	OCT-2000	3369.63	−303.19	−8.3
RUSSELL 1000 1979 to APRIL 2012							
OCT-1987	131.89	−36.94	−21.9	OCT-2008	522.47	−111.61	−17.6
OCT-2008	522.47	−111.61	−17.6	AUG-1998	496.66	−88.31	−15.1
AUG-1998	496.66	−88.31	−15.1	NOV-2000	692.40	−70.66	−9.3
MAR-1980	55.79	−7.28	−11.5	FEB-2001	654.25	−68.30	−9.5
SEP-2002	433.22	−52.86	−10.9	SEP-2008	634.08	−68.09	−9.7
FEB-2009	399.61	−47.71	−10.7	JUN-2008	703.22	−65.06	−8.5
SEP-2008	634.08	−68.09	−9.7	MAY-2010	601.79	−53.27	−8.1
AUG-1990	166.69	−17.63	−9.6	SEP-2002	433.22	−52.86	−10.9
FEB-2001	654.25	−68.30	−9.5	SEP-2011	623.45	−51.34	−7.6
NOV-2000	692.40	−70.66	−9.3	SEP-2001	546.46	−51.21	−8.6
RUSSELL 2000 1979 to APRIL 2012							
OCT-1987	118.26	−52.55	−30.8	OCT-2008	537.52	−142.06	−20.9
OCT-2008	537.52	−142.06	−20.9	SEP-2011	644.16	−82.65	−11.4
AUG-1998	337.95	−81.80	−19.5	AUG-1998	337.95	−81.80	−19.5
MAR-1980	48.27	−10.95	−18.5	JUL-2002	392.42	−70.22	−15.2
JUL-2002	392.42	−70.22	−15.2	AUG-2011	726.81	−70.22	−8.8
AUG-1990	139.52	−21.99	−13.6	NOV-2008	473.14	−64.38	−12.0
SEP-2001	404.87	−63.69	−13.6	SEP-2001	404.87	−63.69	−13.6
FEB-2009	389.02	−54.51	−12.3	NOV-2007	767.77	−60.25	−7.3
NOV-2008	473.14	−64.38	−12.0	SEP-2008	679.58	−59.92	−8.1
SEP-2011	644.16	−82.65	−11.4	JUN-2008	689.66	−58.62	−7.8

10 <u>BEST</u> QUARTERS BY PERCENT AND POINT

	BY PERCENT CHANGE				BY POINT CHANGE		
QUARTER	CLOSE	PNT CHANGE	% CHANGE	QUARTER	CLOSE	PNT CHANGE	% CHANGE
DJIA 1901 to 1949							
JUN-1933	98.14	42.74	77.1	DEC-1928	300.00	60.57	25.3
SEP-1932	71.56	28.72	67.0	JUN-1933	98.14	42.74	77.1
JUN-1938	133.88	34.93	35.3	MAR-1930	286.10	37.62	15.1
SEP-1915	90.58	20.52	29.3	JUN-1938	133.88	34.93	35.3
DEC-1928	300.00	60.57	25.3	SEP-1927	197.59	31.36	18.9
DEC-1904	50.99	8.80	20.9	SEP-1928	239.43	28.88	13.7
JUN-1919	106.98	18.13	20.4	SEP-1932	71.56	28.72	67.0
SEP-1927	197.59	31.36	18.9	JUN-1929	333.79	24.94	8.1
DEC-1905	70.47	10.47	17.4	SEP-1939	152.54	21.91	16.8
JUN-1935	118.21	17.40	17.3	SEP-1915	90.58	20.52	29.3
DJIA 1950 to APRIL 2012							
MAR-1975	768.15	151.91	24.7	DEC-1998	9181.43	1338.81	17.1
MAR-1987	2304.69	408.74	21.6	DEC-2011	12217.56	1304.18	12.0
MAR-1986	1818.61	271.94	17.6	SEP-2009	9712.28	1265.28	15.0
MAR-1976	999.45	147.04	17.2	JUN-1999	10970.80	1184.64	12.1
DEC-1998	9181.43	1338.81	17.1	DEC-2003	10453.92	1178.86	12.7
DEC-1982	1046.54	150.29	16.8	DEC-2001	10021.50	1173.94	13.3
JUN-1997	7672.79	1089.31	16.5	DEC-1999	11497.12	1160.17	11.2
DEC-1985	1546.67	218.04	16.4	JUN-1997	7672.79	1089.31	16.5
SEP-2009	9712.28	1265.28	15.0	JUN-2007	13408.62	1054.27	8.5
JUN-1975	878.99	110.84	14.4	SEP-2010	10788.05	1014.03	10.4
S&P 500 1930 to APRIL 2012							
JUN-1933	10.91	5.06	86.5	DEC-1998	1229.23	212.22	20.9
SEP-1932	8.08	3.65	82.4	DEC-1999	1469.25	186.54	14.5
JUN-1938	11.56	3.06	36.0	MAR-2012	1408.47	150.87	12.0
MAR-1975	83.36	14.80	21.6	SEP-2009	1057.08	137.76	15.0
DEC-1998	1229.23	212.22	20.9	MAR-1998	1101.75	131.32	13.5
JUN-1935	10.23	1.76	20.8	JUN-1997	885.14	128.02	16.9
MAR-1987	291.70	49.53	20.5	DEC-2011	1257.60	126.18	11.2
SEP-1939	13.02	2.16	19.9	JUN-2003	974.50	125.32	14.8
MAR-1943	11.58	1.81	18.5	JUN-2009	919.32	121.45	15.2
MAR-1930	25.14	3.69	17.2	DEC-2010	1257.64	116.44	10.2
NASDAQ 1971 to APRIL 2012							
DEC-1999	4069.31	1323.15	48.2	DEC-1999	4069.31	1323.15	48.2
DEC-2001	1950.40	451.60	30.1	MAR-2000	4572.83	503.52	12.4
DEC-1998	2192.69	498.85	29.5	DEC-1998	2192.69	498.85	29.5
MAR-1991	482.30	108.46	29.0	MAR-2012	3091.57	486.42	18.7
MAR-1975	75.66	15.84	26.5	DEC-2001	1950.40	451.60	30.1
DEC-1982	232.41	44.76	23.9	JUN-2001	2160.54	320.28	17.4
MAR-1987	430.05	80.72	23.1	JUN-2009	1835.04	306.45	20.0
JUN-2003	1622.80	281.63	21.0	SEP-2009	2122.42	287.38	15.7
JUN-1980	157.78	26.78	20.4	DEC-2010	2652.87	284.25	12.0
JUN-2009	1835.04	306.45	20.0	JUN-2003	1622.80	281.63	21.0
RUSSELL 1000 1979 to APRIL 2012							
DEC-1998	642.87	113.76	21.5	DEC-1998	642.87	113.76	21.5
MAR-1987	155.20	25.20	19.4	DEC-1999	767.97	104.14	15.7
DEC-1982	77.24	11.35	17.2	MAR-2012	778.92	85.56	12.3
JUN-1997	462.95	64.76	16.3	SEP-2009	579.97	77.70	15.5
DEC-1985	114.39	15.64	15.8	DEC-2011	693.36	69.91	11.2
JUN-2009	502.27	68.60	15.8	JUN-2009	502.27	68.60	15.8
DEC-1999	767.97	104.14	15.7	JUN-2003	518.94	68.59	15.2
SEP-2009	579.97	77.70	15.5	DEC-2010	696.90	67.12	10.7
JUN-2003	518.94	68.59	15.2	MAR-1998	580.31	66.52	12.9
MAR-1991	196.15	24.93	14.6	JUN-1997	462.95	64.76	16.3
RUSSELL 2000 1979 to APRIL 2012							
MAR-1991	171.01	38.85	29.4	DEC-2010	783.65	107.51	15.9
DEC-1982	88.90	18.06	25.5	DEC-2011	740.92	96.76	15.0
MAR-1987	166.79	31.79	23.5	SEP-2009	604.28	96.00	18.9
JUN-2003	448.37	83.83	23.0	MAR-2006	765.14	91.92	13.7
SEP-1980	69.94	12.47	21.7	MAR-2012	830.30	89.38	12.1
DEC-2001	488.50	83.63	20.7	JUN-2009	508.28	85.53	20.2
JUN-1983	124.17	20.40	19.7	JUN-2003	448.37	83.83	23.0
JUN-1980	57.47	9.20	19.1	DEC-2001	488.50	83.63	20.7
DEC-1999	504.75	77.45	18.1	DEC-2004	651.57	78.63	13.7
SEP-2009	604.28	96.00	18.9	DEC-1999	504.75	77.45	18.1

10 <u>WORST</u> QUARTERS BY PERCENT AND POINT

	BY PERCENT CHANGE				BY POINT CHANGE		
QUARTER	CLOSE	PNT CHANGE	% CHANGE	QUARTER	CLOSE	PNT CHANGE	% CHANGE
DJIA 1901 to 1949							
JUN-1932	42.84	−30.44	−41.5	DEC-1929	248.48	−94.97	−27.7
SEP-1931	96.61	−53.57	−35.7	JUN-1930	226.34	−59.76	−20.9
DEC-1929	248.48	−94.97	−27.7	SEP-1931	96.61	−53.57	−35.7
SEP-1903	33.55	−9.73	−22.5	DEC-1930	164.58	−40.32	−19.7
DEC-1937	120.85	−33.72	−21.8	DEC-1937	120.85	−33.72	−21.8
JUN-1930	226.34	−59.76	−20.9	SEP-1946	172.42	−33.20	−16.1
DEC-1930	164.58	−40.32	−19.7	JUN-1932	42.84	−30.44	−41.5
DEC-1931	77.90	−18.71	−19.4	JUN-1940	121.87	−26.08	−17.6
MAR-1938	98.95	−21.90	−18.1	MAR-1939	131.84	−22.92	−14.8
JUN-1940	121.87	−26.08	−17.6	JUN-1931	150.18	−22.18	−12.9
DJIA 1950 to APRIL 2012							
DEC-1987	1938.83	−657.45	−25.3	DEC-2008	8776.39	−2074.27	−19.1
SEP-1974	607.87	−194.54	−24.2	SEP-2001	8847.56	−1654.84	−15.8
JUN-1962	561.28	−145.67	−20.6	SEP-2002	7591.93	−1651.33	−17.9
DEC-2008	8776.39	−2074.27	−19.1	SEP-2011	10913.38	−1500.96	−12.1
SEP-2002	7591.93	−1651.33	−17.9	MAR-2009	7608.92	−1167.47	−13.3
SEP-2001	8847.56	−1654.84	−15.8	JUN-2002	9243.26	−1160.68	−11.2
SEP-1990	2452.48	−428.21	−14.9	SEP-1998	7842.62	−1109.40	−12.4
MAR-2009	7608.92	−1167.47	−13.3	JUN-2010	9774.02	−1082.61	−10.0
SEP-1981	849.98	−126.90	−13.0	MAR-2008	12262.89	−1001.93	−7.6
JUN-1970	683.53	−102.04	−13.0	JUN-2008	11350.01	−912.88	−7.4
S&P 500 1930 to APRIL 2012							
JUN-1932	4.43	−2.88	−39.4	DEC-2008	903.25	−263.11	−22.6
SEP-1931	9.71	−5.12	−34.5	SEP-2011	1131.42	−189.22	−14.3
SEP-1974	63.54	−22.46	−26.1	SEP-2001	1040.94	−183.48	−15.0
DEC-1937	10.55	−3.21	−23.3	SEP-2002	815.28	−174.54	−17.6
DEC-1987	247.08	−74.75	−23.2	MAR-2001	1160.33	−159.95	−12.1
DEC-2008	903.25	−263.11	−22.6	JUN-2002	989.82	−157.57	−13.7
JUN-1962	54.75	−14.80	−21.3	MAR-2008	1322.70	−145.66	−9.9
MAR-1938	8.50	−2.05	−19.4	JUN-2010	1030.71	−138.72	−11.9
JUN-1970	72.72	−16.91	−18.9	SEP-1998	1017.01	−116.83	−10.3
SEP-1946	14.96	−3.47	−18.8	DEC-2000	1320.28	−116.23	−8.1
NASDAQ 1971 to APRIL 2012							
DEC-2000	2470.52	−1202.30	−32.7	DEC-2000	2470.52	−1202.30	−32.7
SEP-2001	1498.80	−661.74	−30.6	SEP-2001	1498.80	−661.74	−30.6
SEP-1974	55.67	−20.29	−26.7	MAR-2001	1840.26	−630.26	−25.5
DEC-1987	330.47	−113.82	−25.6	JUN-2000	3966.11	−606.72	−13.3
MAR-2001	1840.26	−630.26	−25.5	DEC-2008	1577.03	−514.85	−24.6
SEP-1990	344.51	−117.78	−25.5	JUN-2002	1463.21	−382.14	−20.7
DEC-2008	1577.03	−514.85	−24.6	MAR-2008	2279.10	−373.18	−14.1
JUN-2002	1463.21	−382.14	−20.7	SEP-2011	2415.40	−358.12	−12.9
SEP-2002	1172.06	−291.15	−19.9	SEP-2000	3672.82	−293.29	−7.4
JUN-1974	75.96	−16.31	−17.7	SEP-2002	1172.06	−291.15	−19.9
RUSSELL 1000 1979 to APRIL 2012							
DEC-2008	487.77	−146.31	−23.1	DEC-2008	487.77	−146.31	−23.1
DEC-1987	130.02	−38.81	−23.0	SEP-2011	623.45	−111.03	−15.1
SEP-2002	433.22	−90.50	−17.3	SEP-2001	546.46	−100.18	−15.5
SEP-2001	546.46	−100.18	−15.5	SEP-2002	433.22	−90.50	−17.3
SEP-1990	157.83	−28.46	−15.3	MAR-2001	610.36	−89.73	−12.8
SEP-2011	623.45	−111.03	−15.1	JUN-2002	523.72	−83.63	−13.8
JUN-2002	523.72	−83.63	−13.8	MAR-2008	720.32	−79.50	−9.9
MAR-2001	610.36	−89.73	−12.8	JUN-2010	567.37	−76.42	−11.9
SEP-1981	64.06	−8.95	−12.3	DEC-2000	700.09	−72.51	−9.4
JUN-2010	567.37	−76.42	−11.9	SEP-2008	634.08	−69.14	−9.8
RUSSELL 2000 1979 to APRIL 2012							
DEC-1987	120.42	−50.39	−29.5	SEP-2011	644.16	−183.27	−22.1
DEC-2008	499.45	−180.13	−26.5	DEC-2008	499.45	−180.13	−26.5
SEP-1990	126.70	−42.34	−25.0	SEP-2001	404.87	−107.77	−21.0
SEP-2011	644.16	−183.27	−22.1	SEP-2002	362.27	−100.37	−21.7
SEP-2002	362.27	−100.37	−21.7	SEP-1998	363.59	−93.80	−20.5
SEP-2001	404.87	−107.77	−21.0	MAR-2001	687.97	−78.06	−10.2
SEP-1998	363.59	−93.80	−20.5	MAR-2009	422.75	−76.70	−15.4
SEP-1981	67.55	−15.01	−18.2	JUN-2010	609.49	−69.15	−10.2
MAR-2009	422.75	−76.70	−15.4	DEC-1987	120.42	−50.39	−29.5
MAR-1980	48.27	−7.64	−13.7	JUN-2002	462.64	−43.82	−8.7

10 <u>BEST</u> YEARS BY PERCENT AND POINT

	BY PERCENT CHANGE				BY POINT CHANGE		
YEAR	CLOSE	PNT CHANGE	% CHANGE	YEAR	CLOSE	PNT CHANGE	% CHANGE
DJIA 1901 to 1949							
1915	99.15	44.57	81.7	1928	300.00	97.60	48.2
1933	99.90	39.97	66.7	1927	202.40	45.20	28.8
1928	300.00	97.60	48.2	1915	99.15	44.57	81.7
1908	63.11	20.07	46.6	1945	192.91	40.59	26.6
1904	50.99	15.01	41.7	1935	144.13	40.09	38.5
1935	144.13	40.09	38.5	1933	99.90	39.97	66.7
1905	70.47	19.48	38.2	1925	156.66	36.15	30.0
1919	107.23	25.03	30.5	1936	179.90	35.77	24.8
1925	156.66	36.15	30.0	1938	154.76	33.91	28.1
1927	202.40	45.20	28.8	1919	107.23	25.03	30.5
DJIA 1950 to APRIL 2012							
1954	404.39	123.49	44.0	1999	11497.12	2315.69	25.2
1975	852.41	236.17	38.3	2003	10453.92	2112.29	25.3
1958	583.65	147.96	34.0	2006	12463.15	1745.65	16.3
1995	5117.12	1282.68	33.5	2009	10428.05	1651.66	18.8
1985	1546.67	335.10	27.7	1997	7908.25	1459.98	22.6
1989	2753.20	584.63	27.0	1996	6448.27	1331.15	26.0
1996	6448.27	1331.15	26.0	1995	5117.12	1282.68	33.5
2003	10453.92	2112.29	25.3	1998	9181.43	1273.18	16.1
1999	11497.12	2315.69	25.2	2010	11577.51	1149.46	11.0
1997	7908.25	1459.98	22.6	2007	13264.82	801.67	6.4
S&P 500 1930 to APRIL 2012							
1933	10.10	3.21	46.6	1998	1229.23	258.80	26.7
1954	35.98	11.17	45.0	1999	1469.25	240.02	19.5
1935	13.43	3.93	41.4	2003	1111.92	232.10	26.4
1958	55.21	15.22	38.1	1997	970.43	229.69	31.0
1995	615.93	156.66	34.1	2009	1115.10	211.85	23.5
1975	90.19	21.63	31.5	2006	1418.30	170.01	13.6
1997	970.43	229.69	31.0	1995	615.93	156.66	34.1
1945	17.36	4.08	30.7	2010	1257.64	142.54	12.8
1936	17.18	3.75	27.9	1996	740.74	124.81	20.3
1989	353.40	75.68	27.3	2004	1211.92	100.00	9.0
NASDAQ 1971 to APRIL 2012							
1999	4069.31	1876.62	85.6	1999	4069.31	1876.62	85.6
1991	586.34	212.50	56.8	2009	2269.15	692.12	43.9
2003	2003.37	667.86	50.0	2003	2003.37	667.86	50.0
2009	2269.15	692.12	43.9	1998	2192.69	622.34	39.6
1995	1052.13	300.17	39.9	2010	2652.87	383.72	16.9
1998	2192.69	622.34	39.6	1995	1052.13	300.17	39.9
1980	202.34	51.20	33.9	1997	1570.35	279.32	21.6
1985	324.93	77.58	31.4	1996	1291.03	238.90	22.7
1975	77.62	17.80	29.8	2007	2652.28	236.99	9.8
1979	151.14	33.16	28.1	1991	586.34	212.50	56.8
RUSSELL 1000 1979 to APRIL 2012							
1995	328.89	84.24	34.4	1998	642.87	129.08	25.1
1997	513.79	120.04	30.5	2003	594.56	128.38	27.5
1991	220.61	49.39	28.8	1999	767.97	125.10	19.5
2003	594.56	128.38	27.5	2009	612.01	124.24	25.5
1985	114.39	24.08	26.7	1997	513.79	120.04	30.5
1989	185.11	38.12	25.9	2006	770.08	90.66	13.3
1980	75.20	15.33	25.6	2010	696.90	84.89	13.9
2009	612.01	124.24	25.5	1995	328.89	84.24	34.4
1998	642.87	129.08	25.1	1996	393.75	64.86	19.7
1996	393.75	64.86	19.7	2004	650.99	56.43	9.5
RUSSELL 2000 1979 to APRIL 2012							
2003	556.91	173.82	45.4	2003	556.91	173.82	45.4
1991	189.94	57.78	43.7	2010	783.65	158.26	25.3
1979	55.91	15.39	38.0	2009	625.39	125.94	25.2
1980	74.80	18.89	33.8	2006	787.66	114.44	17.0
1985	129.87	28.38	28.0	2004	651.57	94.66	17.0
1983	112.27	23.37	26.3	1999	504.75	82.79	19.6
1995	315.97	65.61	26.2	1997	437.02	74.41	20.5
2010	783.65	158.26	25.3	1995	315.97	65.61	26.2
2009	625.39	125.94	25.2	1991	189.94	57.78	43.7
1988	147.37	26.95	22.4	1996	362.61	46.64	14.8

169

10 **WORST** YEARS BY PERCENT AND POINT

	BY PERCENT CHANGE				BY POINT CHANGE		
YEAR	CLOSE	PNT CHANGE	% CHANGE	YEAR	CLOSE	PNT CHANGE	% CHANGE
DJIA 1901 to 1949							
1931	77.90	−86.68	−52.7	1931	77.90	−86.68	−52.7
1907	43.04	−26.08	−37.7	1930	164.58	−83.90	−33.8
1930	164.58	−83.90	−33.8	1937	120.85	−59.05	−32.8
1920	71.95	−35.28	−32.9	1929	248.48	−51.52	−17.2
1937	120.85	−59.05	−32.8	1920	71.95	−35.28	−32.9
1903	35.98	−11.12	−23.6	1907	43.04	−26.08	−37.7
1932	59.93	−17.97	−23.1	1917	74.38	−20.62	−21.7
1917	74.38	−20.62	−21.7	1941	110.96	−20.17	−15.4
1910	59.60	−12.96	−17.9	1940	131.13	−19.11	−12.7
1929	248.48	−51.52	−17.2	1932	59.93	−17.97	−23.1
DJIA 1950 to APRIL 2012							
2008	8776.39	−4488.43	−33.8	2008	8776.39	−4488.43	−33.8
1974	616.24	−234.62	−27.6	2002	8341.63	−1679.87	−16.8
1966	785.69	−183.57	−18.9	2001	10021.50	−765.35	−7.1
1977	831.17	−173.48	−17.3	2000	10786.85	−710.27	−6.2
2002	8341.63	−1679.87	−16.8	1974	616.24	−234.62	−27.6
1973	850.86	−169.16	−16.6	1966	785.69	−183.57	−18.9
1969	800.36	−143.39	−15.2	1977	831.17	−173.48	−17.3
1957	435.69	−63.78	−12.8	1973	850.86	−169.16	−16.6
1962	652.10	−79.04	−10.8	1969	800.36	−143.39	−15.2
1960	615.89	−63.47	−9.3	1990	2633.66	−119.54	−4.3
S&P 500 1930 to APRIL 2012							
1931	8.12	−7.22	−47.1	2008	903.25	−565.11	−38.5
1937	10.55	−6.63	−38.6	2002	879.82	−268.26	−23.4
2008	903.25	−565.11	−38.5	2001	1148.08	−172.20	−13.0
1974	68.56	−28.99	−29.7	2000	1320.28	−148.97	−10.1
1930	15.34	−6.11	−28.5	1974	68.56	−28.99	−29.7
2002	879.82	−268.26	−23.4	1990	330.22	−23.18	−6.6
1941	8.69	−1.89	−17.9	1973	97.55	−20.50	−17.4
1973	97.55	−20.50	−17.4	1981	122.55	−13.21	−9.7
1940	10.58	−1.91	−15.3	1977	95.10	−12.36	−11.5
1932	6.89	−1.23	−15.1	1966	80.33	−12.10	−13.1
NASDAQ 1971 to APRIL 2012							
2008	1577.03	−1075.25	−40.5	2000	2470.52	−1598.79	−39.3
2000	2470.52	−1598.79	−39.3	2008	1577.03	−1075.25	−40.5
1974	59.82	−32.37	−35.1	2002	1335.51	−614.89	−31.5
2002	1335.51	−614.89	−31.5	2001	1950.40	−520.12	−21.1
1973	92.19	−41.54	−31.1	1990	373.84	−80.98	−17.8
2001	1950.40	−520.12	−21.1	2011	2605.15	−47.72	−1.8
1990	373.84	−80.98	−17.8	1973	92.19	−41.54	−31.1
1984	247.35	−31.25	−11.2	1974	59.82	−32.37	−35.1
1987	330.47	−18.86	−5.4	1984	247.35	−31.25	−11.2
1981	195.84	−6.50	−3.2	1994	751.96	−24.84	−3.2
RUSSELL 1000 1979 to APRIL 2012							
2008	487.77	−312.05	−39.0	2008	487.77	−312.05	−39.0
2002	466.18	−138.76	−22.9	2002	466.18	−138.76	−22.9
2001	604.94	−95.15	−13.6	2001	604.94	−95.15	−13.6
1981	67.93	−7.27	−9.7	2000	700.09	−67.88	−8.8
2000	700.09	−67.88	−8.8	1990	171.22	−13.89	−7.5
1990	171.22	−13.89	−7.5	1981	67.93	−7.27	−9.7
1994	244.65	−6.06	−2.4	1994	244.65	−6.06	−2.4
2011	693.36	−3.54	−0.5	2011	693.36	−3.54	−0.5
1984	90.31	−0.07	−0.1	1984	90.31	−0.07	−0.1
1987	130.02	0.02	0.02	1987	130.02	0.02	0.02
RUSSELL 2000 1979 to APRIL 2012							
2008	499.45	−266.58	−34.8	2008	499.45	−266.58	−34.8
2002	383.09	−105.41	−21.6	2002	383.09	−105.41	−21.6
1990	132.16	−36.14	−21.5	2011	740.92	−42.73	−5.5
1987	120.42	−14.58	−10.8	1990	132.16	−36.14	−21.5
1984	101.49	−10.78	−9.6	2007	766.03	−21.63	−2.7
2011	740.92	−42.73	−5.5	2000	483.53	−21.22	−4.2
2000	483.53	−21.22	−4.2	1998	421.96	−15.06	−3.4
1998	421.96	−15.06	−3.4	1987	120.42	−14.58	−10.8
1994	250.36	−8.23	−3.2	1984	101.49	−10.78	−9.6
2007	766.03	−21.63	−2.7	1994	250.36	−8.23	−3.2

STRATEGY PLANNING AND RECORD SECTION

CONTENTS

These forms are available at our website www.stocktradersalmanac.com.

PORTFOLIO AT START OF 2013

DATE ACQUIRED	NO. OF SHARES	SECURITY	PRICE	TOTAL COST	PAPER PROFITS	PAPER LOSSES

ADDITIONAL PURCHASES

DATE ACQUIRED	NO. OF SHARES	SECURITY	PRICE	TOTAL COST	REASON FOR PURCHASE PRIME OBJECTIVE, ETC.

ADDITIONAL PURCHASES

DATE ACQUIRED	NO. OF SHARES	SECURITY	PRICE	TOTAL COST	REASON FOR PURCHASE PRIME OBJECTIVE, ETC.

SHORT-TERM TRANSACTIONS

Pages 175–178 can accompany next year's income tax return (Schedule D). Enter transactions as completed to avoid last-minute pressures.

NO. OF SHARES	SECURITY	DATE ACQUIRED	DATE SOLD	SALE PRICE	COST	LOSS	GAIN

TOTALS: Carry over to next page

175

SHORT-TERM TRANSACTIONS *(continued)*

NO. OF SHARES	SECURITY	DATE ACQUIRED	DATE SOLD	SALE PRICE	COST	LOSS	GAIN

TOTALS:

LONG-TERM TRANSACTIONS

Pages 175–178 can accompany next year's income tax return (Schedule D). Enter transactions as completed to avoid last-minute pressures.

NO. OF SHARES	SECURITY	DATE ACQUIRED	DATE SOLD	SALE PRICE	COST	LOSS	GAIN

TOTALS: Carry over to next page

LONG-TERM TRANSACTIONS *(continued)*

NO. OF SHARES	SECURITY	DATE ACQUIRED	DATE SOLD	SALE PRICE	COST	LOSS	GAIN

TOTALS:

178

INTEREST/DIVIDENDS RECEIVED DURING 2013

SHARES	STOCK/BOND	FIRST QUARTER		SECOND QUARTER		THIRD QUARTER		FOURTH QUARTER	
		$		$		$		$	

BROKERAGE ACCOUNT DATA 2013

	MARGIN INTEREST	TRANSFER TAXES	CAPITAL ADDED	CAPITAL WITHDRAWN
JAN				
FEB				
MAR				
APR				
MAY				
JUN				
JUL				
AUG				
SEP				
OCT				
NOV				
DEC				

PORTFOLIO PRICE RECORD 2013 (FIRST HALF)

Place purchase price above stock name and weekly closes below.

STOCKS										
Week Ending	1	2	3	4	5	6	7	8	9	10
JANUARY 4										
11										
18										
25										
FEBRUARY 1										
8										
15										
22										
MARCH 1										
8										
15										
22										
29										
APRIL 5										
12										
19										
26										
MAY 3										
10										
17										
24										
31										
JUNE 7										
14										
21										
28										

PORTFOLIO PRICE RECORD 2013 (SECOND HALF)

Place purchase price above stock name and weekly closes below.

STOCKS Week Ending	1	2	3	4	5	6	7	8	9	10
JULY 5										
12										
19										
26										
AUGUST 2										
9										
16										
23										
30										
SEPTEMBER 6										
13										
20										
27										
OCTOBER 4										
11										
18										
25										
NOVEMBER 1										
8										
15										
22										
29										
DECEMBER 6										
13										
20										
27										
3										

WEEKLY INDICATOR DATA 2013 (FIRST HALF)

	Dow Jones Industrial Average	Net Change for Week	Net Change on Friday	Net Change Next Monday	S&P or NASDAQ	NYSE Advances	NYSE Declines	New Highs	New Lows	CBOE Put/Call Ratio	90-Day Treas. Rate	Moody's AAA Rate
JANUARY												
4												
11												
18												
25												
FEBRUARY												
1												
8												
15												
22												
MARCH												
1												
8												
15												
22												
29												
APRIL												
5												
12												
19												
26												
MAY												
3												
10												
17												
24												
31												
JUNE												
7												
14												
21												
28												

WEEKLY INDICATOR DATA 2013 (SECOND HALF)

Week Ending		Dow Jones Industrial Average	Net Change for Week	Net Change on Friday	Net Change Next Monday	S&P or NASDAQ	NYSE Ad-vances	NYSE De-clines	New Highs	New Lows	CBOE Put/Call Ratio	90-Day Treas. Rate	Moody's AAA Rate
JULY	5												
	12												
	19												
	26												
AUGUST	2												
	9												
	16												
	23												
	30												
SEPTEMBER	6												
	13												
	20												
	27												
OCTOBER	4												
	11												
	18												
	25												
NOVEMBER	1												
	8												
	15												
	22												
	29												
DECEMBER	6												
	13												
	20												
	27												
	3												

MONTHLY INDICATOR DATA 2013

	DJIA% Last 3 + 1st 2 Days	DJIA% 9th to 11th Trading Days	DJIA% Change Rest of Month	DJIA% Change Whole Month	% Change Your Stocks	Gross Domestic Product	Prime Rate	Trade Deficit $ Billion	CPI % Change	% Unem- ployment Rate
JAN										
FEB										
MAR										
APR										
MAY										
JUN										
JUL										
AUG										
SEP										
OCT										
NOV										
DEC										

INSTRUCTIONS:

Weekly Indicator Data (pages 182–183). Keeping data on several indicators may give you a better feel of the market. In addition to the closing DJIA and its net change for the week, post the net change for Friday's Dow and also the following Monday's. A series of "down Fridays" followed by "down Mondays" often precedes a downswing. Tracking either the S&P or NASDAQ composite, and advances and declines, will help prevent the Dow from misleading you. New highs and lows and put/call ratios (www.cboe.com) are also useful indicators. All these weekly figures appear in weekend papers or *Barron's*. Data for 90-day Treasury Rate and Moody's AAA Bond Rate are quite important for tracking short- and long-term interest rates. These figures are available from:

> Weekly U.S. Financial Data
> Federal Reserve Bank of St. Louis
> P.O. Box 442
> St. Louis MO 63166
> **http://research.stlouisfed.org**

Monthly Indicator Data. The purpose of the first three columns is to enable you to track the market's bullish bias near the end, beginning, and middle of the month, which has been shifting lately (see pages 88, 145, and 146). Market direction, performance of your stocks, gross domestic product, prime rate, trade deficit, Consumer Price Index, and unemployment rate are worthwhile indicators to follow. Or, readers may wish to gauge other data.

PORTFOLIO AT END OF 2013

DATE ACQUIRED	NO. OF SHARES	SECURITY	PRICE	TOTAL COST	PAPER PROFITS	PAPER LOSSES

IF YOU DON'T PROFIT FROM YOUR INVESTMENT MISTAKES, SOMEONE ELSE WILL

No matter how much we may deny it, almost every successful person in Wall Street pays a great deal of attention to trading suggestions—especially when they come from "the right sources."

One of the hardest things to learn is to distinguish between good tips and bad ones. Usually, the best tips have a logical reason in back of them, which accompanies the tip. Poor tips usually have no reason to support them.

The important thing to remember is that the market discounts. It does not review, it does not reflect. The Street's real interest in "tips," inside information, buying and selling suggestions, and everything else of this kind emanates from a desire to find out just what the market has on hand to discount. The process of finding out involves separating the wheat from the chaff—and there is plenty of chaff.

HOW TO MAKE USE OF STOCK "TIPS"

- The source should be **reliable**. (By listing all "tips" and suggestions on a Performance Record of Recommendations, such as the form below, and then periodically evaluating the outcomes, you will soon know the "batting average" of your sources.)

- The story should make sense. Would the merger violate antitrust laws? Are there too many computers on the market already? How many years will it take to become profitable?

- The stock should not have had a recent sharp run-up. Otherwise, the story may already be discounted, and confirmation or denial in the press would most likely be accompanied by a sell-off in the stock.

PERFORMANCE RECORD OF RECOMMENDATIONS

STOCK RECOMMENDED	BY WHOM	DATE	PRICE	REASON FOR RECOMMENDATION	SUBSEQUENT ACTION OF STOCK

INDIVIDUAL RETIREMENT ACCOUNTS: MOST AWESOME INVESTMENT INCENTIVE EVER DEVISED

MAX IRA INVESTMENTS OF $5,000* A YEAR COMPOUNDED AT VARIOUS INTEREST RATES OF RETURN FOR DIFFERENT PERIODS

Annual Rate	5 Yrs	10 Yrs	15 Yrs	20 Yrs	25 Yrs	30 Yrs	35 Yrs	40 Yrs	45 Yrs	50 Yrs
1%	$25,760	$52,834	$81,289	$111,196	$142,628	$175,664	$210,384	$246,876	$285,229	$325,539
2%	26,541	55,844	88,196	123,917	163,355	206,897	254,972	308,050	366,653	431,355
3%	27,342	59,039	95,784	138,382	187,765	245,013	311,380	388,316	477,507	580,904
4%	28,165	62,432	104,123	154,846	216,559	291,642	382,992	494,133	629,353	793,869
5%	29,010	66,034	113,287	173,596	250,567	348,804	474,182	634,199	838,426	1,099,077
6%	29,877	69,858	123,363	194,964	290,782	419,008	590,604	820,238	1,127,541	1,538,780
7%	30,766	73,918	134,440	219,326	338,382	505,365	739,567	1,068,048	1,528,759	2,174,930
8%	31,680	78,227	146,621	247,115	394,772	611,729	930,511	1,398,905	2,087,130	3,098,359
9%	32,617	82,801	160,017	278,823	461,620	742,876	1,175,624	1,841,459	2,865,930	4,442,205
10%	33,578	87,656	174,749	315,012	540,909	904,717	1,490,634	2,434,259	3,953,977	6,401,497
11%	34,564	92,807	190,950	356,326	634,994	1,104,566	1,895,822	3,229,135	5,475,844	9,261,680
12%	35,576	98,273	208,766	403,494	746,670	1,351,463	2,417,316	4,295,712	7,606,088	13,440,102
13%	36,614	104,072	228,359	457,350	879,250	1,656,576	3,088,747	5,727,429	10,589,030	19,546,215
14%	37,678	110,223	249,902	518,842	1,036,664	2,033,685	3,953,364	7,649,543	14,766,219	28,468,772
15%	38,769	116,746	273,587	589,051	1,223,560	2,499,785	5,066,728	10,229,769	20,614,489	41,501,869
16%	39,887	123,665	299,625	669,203	1,445,441	3,075,808	6,500,135	13,692,392	28,798,589	60,526,763
17%	41,034	131,000	328,244	760,693	1,708,813	3,787,519	8,344,972	18,336,953	40,243,850	88,273,585
18%	42,210	138,776	359,695	865,105	2,021,361	4,666,593	10,718,245	24,562,957	56,236,305	128,697,253
19%	43,415	147,018	394,251	984,237	2,392,153	5,751,937	13,769,572	32,902,482	78,560,374	187,516,251
20%	44,650	155,752	432,211	1,120,128	2,831,886	7,091,289	17,690,047	44,063,147	109,687,860	272,983,145

* At Press Time, 2013 Contribution Limit will be indexed to inflation.

TOP 300 EXCHANGE TRADED FUNDS (As of 4/30/2012)

By Average Daily Volume. See pages 92, 94 and 96, Almanac Investor & stocktradersalmanac.com for more.

SPY	SPDR S&P 500	GDXJ	Market Vectors Junior Gold Miners
XLF	Financial Select Sector SPDR	HYG	iShares iBoxx $ High Yield Corporate Bd
IWM	iShares Russell 2000	KRE	SPDR S&P Regional Banking
QQQ	PowerShares QQQ	EWA	iShares MSCI Australia
TZA	Direxion Daily Small Cap Bear 3X Shares	EPI	WisdomTree India Earnings
VWO	Vanguard MSCI Emerging Markets	SH	ProShares Short S&P500
EFA	iShares MSCI EAFE	UPRO	ProShares UltraPro S&P500
SLV	iShares Silver	EWW	iShares MSCI Mexico Investable Mkt
SDS	ProShares UltraShort S&P500	MDY	SPDR S&P MidCap 400
FXI	iShares FTSE China 25 Fund	VEA	Vanguard MSCI EAFE
EWJ	iShares MSCI Japan	TWM	ProShares UltraShort Russell2000
FAZ	Direxion Daily Financial Bear 3X Shares	AGQ	ProShares Ultra Silver
XLI	Industrial Select Sector SPDR	EWY	iShares MSCI South Korea
TNA	Direxion Daily Small Cap Bull 3X Shares	IWF	iShares Russell 1000 Growth
XLE	Energy Select Sector SPDR	UWM	ProShares Ultra Russell2000
EWZ	iShares MSCI Brazil	VNQ	Vanguard REIT
GDX	Market Vectors Gold Miners	VTI	Vanguard Total Stock Market
GLD	SPDR Gold Shares	EUO	ProShares UltraShort Euro
TBT	ProShares UltraShort 20+ Year Treasury	ERY	Direxion Daily Energy Bear 3X Shares
SPXU	ProShares UltraPro Short S&P500	LQD	iShares iBoxx $ Invest Grade Corp Bond
XLK	Technology Select Sector SPDR	DBC	PowerShares DB Commodity Tracking
XLB	Materials Select Sector SPDR	EDZ	Direxion Daily Emrg Mkts Bear 3X Shares
UNG	United States Natural Gas	IWN	iShares Russell 2000 Value
USO	United States Oil	ITB	iShares DJ US Home Construction
TLT	iShares Barclays 20+ Year Treas Bond	ERX	Direxion Daily Energy Bull 3X Shares
FAS	Direxion Daily Financial Bull 3X Shares	EWU	iShares MSCI United Kingdom
XHB	SPDR S&P Homebuilders	IWO	iShares Russell 2000 Growth
SSO	ProShares Ultra S&P500	EWC	iShares MSCI Canada
EWT	iShares MSCI Taiwan	AMLP	ALPS Alerian MLP
DIA	SPDR Dow Jones Industrial Average	SMH	Market Vectors Semiconductor
XLU	Utilities Select Sector SPDR	NUGT	Direxion Daily Gold Miners Bull 3X Shrs
XRT	SPDR S&P Retail	EWM	iShares MSCI Malaysia
IAU	iShares Gold	EWS	iShares MSCI Singapore
ZSL	ProShares UltraShort Silver	DXD	ProShares UltraShort Dow30
XLP	Consumer Staples Select Sector SPDR	IWD	iShares Russell 1000 Value
XLY	Consumer Discret Select Sector SPDR	BGZ	Direxion Daily Large Cap Bear 3X Shares
IYR	iShares Dow Jones US Real Estate	UCO	ProShares Ultra DJ-UBS Crude Oil
XLV	Health Care Select Sector SPDR	IJR	iShares S&P SmallCap 600
EWG	iShares MSCI Germany	PFF	iShares S&P U.S. Preferred Stock
EWH	iShares MSCI Hong Kong	VGK	Vanguard MSCI Europe
JNK	SPDR Barclays Capital High Yield Bond	SCO	ProShares UltraShort DJ-UBS Crude Oil
OIH	Market Vectors Oil Services	SHY	iShares Barclays 1-3 Year Treasury Bond
QID	ProShares UltraShort QQQ	RWM	ProShares Short Russell2000
XOP	SPDR S&P Oil & Gas Exploration & Prod	DVY	iShares Dow Jones Select Dividend
RSX	Market Vectors Russia	UYG	ProShares Ultra Financials
XME	SPDR S&P Metals & Mining	SRTY	ProShares UltraPro Short Russell2000
KBE	SPDR S&P Bank	IWB	iShares Russell 1000
IVV	iShares S&P 500	BND	Vanguard Total Bond Market
QLD	ProShares Ultra QQQ	VIG	Vanguard Dividend Appreciation
UUP	PowerShares DB US Dollar Bullish	PHYS	Sprott Physical Gold ETV

TOP 300 EXCHANGE TRADED FUNDS (As of 4/30/2012)

By Average Daily Volume. See pages 92, 94 and 96, Almanac Investor & stocktradersalmanac.com for more.

FXE	CurrencyShares Euro	DOG	ProShares Short Dow30
SKF	ProShares UltraShort Financials	ICF	iShares Cohen & Steers Realty Majors
TIP	iShares Barclays TIPS Bond	UYM	ProShares Ultra Basic Materials
SDY	SPDR S&P Dividend	EWI	iShares MSCI Italy
ILF	iShares S&P Latin America 40	SHM	SPDR Nuveen Barclays Cap S/T Muni Bd
AGG	iShares Barclays Aggregate Bond	YCS	ProShares UltraShort Yen
IJH	iShares S&P MidCap 400	FCG	First Trust ISE-Revere Natural Gas
SPLV	PowerShares S&P 500 Low Volatility	TMV	Direxion Daily 20+ Yr Trsy Bear 3X Shrs
BGU	Direxion Daily Large Cap Bull 3X Shares	IYZ	iShares Dow Jones US Telecom
DBA	PowerShares DB Agriculture	FXY	CurrencyShares Japanese Yen
GLL	ProShares UltraShort Gold	IVE	iShares S&P 500 Value
VEU	Vanguard FTSE All-World ex-US	FXU	First Trust Utilities AlphaDEX
PSLV	Sprott Physical Silver ETV	MBB	iShares Barclays MBS Bond
PSQ	ProShares Short QQQ	FXP	ProShares UltraShort FTSE China 25
DDM	ProShares Ultra Dow30	IYF	iShares Dow Jones US Financial Sector
VOO	Vanguard S&P 500	VTV	Vanguard Value
IEF	iShares Barclays 7-10 Year Treasury	IDX	Market Vectors Indonesia
PCY	PowerShares Emerging Mkts Svrgn Debt	VIXY	ProShares VIX Short-Term Futures
PHB	PowerShares Fundamental HY Corp Bd	TAN	Guggenheim Solar
ACWI	iShares MSCI ACWI	SOXL	Direxion Daily Semicondct Bull 3X Shares
TYP	Direxion Daily Technology Bear 3X Shares	PGF	PowerShares Financial Preferred
SDOW	ProShares UltraPro Short Dow30	IWR	iShares Russell Midcap
IYT	iShares Dow Jones Transports	PEY	PowerShares Hi-Yield Eq Div Achievers
URTY	ProShares UltraPro Russell2000	VB	Vanguard Small Cap
IWP	iShares Russell Midcap Growth	SCZ	iShares MSCI EAFE Small Cap
PIN	PowerShares India	CWB	SPDR Barclays Capital Convertible Secs
TYH	Direxion Daily Technology Bull 3X Shares	DIG	ProShares Ultra Oil & Gas
BIL	SPDR Barclays Capital 1-3 Month T-Bill	SCPB	SPDR Barclays Capital Short Term Corp Bd
IWS	iShares Russell Midcap Value	EZU	iShares MSCI EMU
EDC	Direxion Daily Emrg Mkts Bull 3X Shares	FXG	First Trust Consumer Staples AlphaDEX
DEM	WisdomTree Emerging Markets Equity Inc	CIU	iShares Barclays Intermediate Credit Bd
MOO	Market Vectors Agribusiness	FEZ	SPDR EURO STOXX 50
AAXJ	iShares MSCI All Country Asia ex Jpn	IYM	iShares Dow Jones US Basic Materials
OEF	iShares S&P 100	TFI	SPDR Nuveen Barclays Capital Muni Bond
TBF	ProShares Short 20+ Year Treasury	MUB	iShares S&P National AMT-Free Muni Bond
RSP	Guggenheim S&P 500 Equal Weight	IJS	iShares S&P SmallCap 600 Value
BSV	Vanguard Short-Term Bond	CVY	Guggenheim Multi-Asset Income
EMB	iShares JPMorgan USD Emerg Markets Bd	TUR	iShares MSCI Turkey Invest Mkt
PGX	PowerShares Preferred	IDV	iShares Dow Jones Intl Select Div
DUG	ProShares UltraShort Oil & Gas	EMLC	Market Vectors EM Local Curr Bond
IBB	iShares Nasdaq Biotechnology	BIV	Vanguard Intermediate-Term Bond
CSJ	iShares Barclays 1-3 Year Credit Bond	UGL	ProShares Ultra Gold
IVW	iShares S&P 500 Growth	EEV	ProShares UltraShort MSCI Emerging Mkts
EWQ	iShares MSCI France	EZA	iShares MSCI South Africa
VUG	Vanguard Growth	SIVR	ETFS Physical Silver Shares
EPP	iShares MSCI Pacific ex-Japan	BRF	Market Vectors Brazil Small-Cap
RWX	SPDR Dow Jones Intl Real Estate	DRN	Direxion Daily Real Estate Bull 3X Shrs
SMN	ProShares UltraShort Basic Materials	MVV	ProShares Ultra MidCap400
VYM	Vanguard High Dividend Yield Indx	RTH	Market Vectors Retail
DBO	PowerShares DB Oil	ELD	WisdomTree Emerging Markets Local Debt

189

TOP 300 EXCHANGE TRADED FUNDS (As of 4/30/2012)

By Average Daily Volume. See pages 92, 94 and 96, Almanac Investor & stocktradersalmanac.com for more.

SOXX	iShares PHLX SOX Semiconductor Sector	VV	Vanguard Large Cap
HYD	Market Vectors High-Yield Muni	XES	SPDR S&P Oil & Gas Equipment & Services
BWX	SPDR Barclays Capital Intl Treasury Bond	WIP	SPDR DB Intl Govt Infl-Protected Bond
FXO	First Trust Financials AlphaDEX	EWL	iShares MSCI Switzerland
DWX	SPDR S&P International Dividend	PID	PowerShares Intl Dividend Achievers
SRS	ProShares UltraShort Real Estate	EPV	ProShares UltraShort MSCI Europe
URE	ProShares Ultra Real Estate	ECH	iShares MSCI Chile Investable Mkt
PHO	PowerShares Water Resources	IEZ	iShares Dow Jones US Oil Equipment
VNM	Market Vectors Vietnam	IGE	iShares S&P North Amer Natural Resources
EWP	iShares MSCI Spain	FXL	First Trust Technology AlphaDEX
SCHB	Schwab U.S. Broad Market	SCHE	Schwab Emerging Markets Equity
THD	iShares MSCI Thailand Invest Mkt	DGS	WisdomTree Emerging Mkts SmallCap Div
REM	iShares FTSE NAREIT Mort Plus Cp	IYE	iShares Dow Jones US Energy
URA	Global X Uranium	IJK	iShares S&P MidCap 400 Growth
FXR	First Trust Indust/Producer Dur AlphaDEX	ACWX	iShares MSCI ACWI ex US
BKF	iShares MSCI BRIC	SCHX	Schwab U.S. Large-Cap
IEV	iShares S&P Europe 350	VBK	Vanguard Small Cap Growth
FDL	First Trust Morningstar Div Leaders	IJJ	iShares S&P MidCap 400 Value
DUST	Direxion Daily Gold Miners Bear 3X Shrs	MCHI	iShares MSCI China
GSG	iShares S&P GSCI Commodity	GCC	GreenHaven Continuous Commodity
KOL	Market Vectors Coal	SOXS	Direxion Daily Semicondct Bear 3X Shares
VGT	Vanguard Information Technology	DBV	PowerShares DB G10 Currency Harvest
EPU	iShares MSCI All Peru Capped	IJT	iShares S&P SmallCap 600 Growth
HDGE	Active Bear	SCHA	Schwab U.S. Small-Cap
FXA	CurrencyShares Australian Dollar	DBB	PowerShares DB Base Metals
EWD	iShares MSCI Sweden	SCHF	Schwab International Equity
XBI	SPDR S&P Biotech	FRI	First Trust S&P REIT
IWV	iShares Russell 3000	TMF	Direxion Daily 20+ Yr Trsy Bull 3X Shrs
IXC	iShares S&P Global Energy	PFM	PowerShares Dividend Achievers
GXC	SPDR S&P China	PDP	PowerShares DWA Technical Leaders
SHV	iShares Barclays Short Treasury Bond	DRV	Direxion Daily Real Estate Bear 3X Shrs
BKLN	PowerShares Senior Loan Port	FXH	First Trust Health Care AlphaDEX
PSP	PowerShares Global Listed Private Eq	EUM	ProShares Short MSCI Emerging Markets
SIL	Global X Silver Miners	IEO	iShares Dow Jones US Oil & Gas Ex
RWR	SPDR Dow Jones REIT	BIK	SPDR S&P BRIC 40
IYW	iShares Dow Jones US Technology	FXZ	First Trust Materials AlphaDEX
PZA	PowerShares Insured National Muni Bond	FVD	First Trust Value Line Dividend
DXJ	WisdomTree Japan Hedged Equity	UDOW	ProShares UltraPro Dow30
VPL	Vanguard MSCI Pacific	VXF	Vanguard Extended Market
FXD	First Trust Consumer Disc AlphaDEX	EFZ	ProShares Short MSCI EAFE
VT	Vanguard Total World Stock	ECON	EGShares Emerging Markets Consumer
PBW	PowerShares WilderHill Clean Energy	EWX	SPDR S&P Emerging Markets Small Cap
HDV	iShares High Dividend Equity	STPZ	PIMCO 1-5 Year US TIPS
DTN	WisdomTree Dividend ex-Financials	EWO	iShares MSCI Austria Investable Mkt
DLN	WisdomTree LargeCap Dividend	VOT	Vanguard Mid-Cap Growth
ITM	Market Vectors Intermediate Muni	PVI	PowerShares VRDO Tax-Free Weekly
IEI	iShares Barclays 3-7 Year Treasury Bond	EFV	iShares MSCI EAFE Value
VO	Vanguard Mid-Cap	HAO	Guggenheim China Small Cap
VFH	Vanguard Financials	IWC	iShares Russell Microcap
PPH	Market Vectors Pharmaceutical	IWL	iShares Russell Top 200

G. M. LOEB'S "BATTLE PLAN" FOR INVESTMENT SURVIVAL

LIFE IS CHANGE: Nothing can ever be the same a minute from now as it was a minute ago. Everything you own is changing in price and value. You can find that last price of an active security on the stock ticker, but you cannot find the next price anywhere. The value of your money is changing. Even the value of your home is changing, though no one walks in front of it with a sandwich board consistently posting the changes.

RECOGNIZE CHANGE: Your basic objective should be to profit from change. The art of investing is being able to recognize change and to adjust investment goals accordingly.

WRITE THINGS DOWN: You will score more investment success and avoid more investment failures if you write things down. Very few investors have the drive and inclination to do this.

KEEP A CHECKLIST: If you aim to improve your investment results, get into the habit of keeping a checklist on every issue you consider buying. Before making a commitment, it will pay you to write down the answers to at least some of the basic questions—How much am I investing in this company? How much do I think I can make? How much do I have to risk? How long do I expect to take to reach my goal?

HAVE A SINGLE RULING REASON: Above all, writing things down is the best way to find "the ruling reason." When all is said and done, there is invariably a single reason that stands out above all others, why a particular security transaction can be expected to show a profit. All too often, many relatively unimportant statistics are allowed to obscure this single important point.

Any one of a dozen factors may be the point of a particular purchase or sale. It could be a technical reason—an increase in earnings or dividend not yet discounted in the market price—a change of management—a promising new product—an expected improvement in the market's valuation of earnings—or many others. But, in any given case, one of these factors will almost certainly be more important than all the rest put together.

CLOSING OUT A COMMITMENT: If you have a loss, the solution is automatic, provided you decide what to do at the time you buy. Otherwise, the question divides itself into two parts. Are we in a bull or bear market? Few of us really know until it is too late. For the sake of the record, if you think it is a bear market, just put that consideration first and sell as much as your conviction suggests and your nature allows.

If you think it is a bull market, or at least a market where some stocks move up, some mark time, and only a few decline, do not sell unless:

✓ You see a bear market ahead.

✓ You see trouble for a particular company in which you own shares.

✓ Time and circumstances have turned up a new and seemingly far better buy than the issue you like least in your list.

✓ Your shares stop going up and start going down.

A subsidiary question is, which stock to sell first? Two further observations may help:

✓ Do not sell solely because you think a stock is "overvalued."

✓ If you want to sell some of your stocks and not all, in most cases it is better to go against your emotional inclinations and sell first the issues with losses, small profits, or none at all, the weakest, the most disappointing, etc.

Mr. Loeb is the author of *The Battle for Investment Survival*, John Wiley & Sons.

G. M. LOEB'S INVESTMENT SURVIVAL CHECKLIST

OBJECTIVES AND RISKS

Security		Price	Shares	Date

"Ruling reason" for commitment	Amount of commitment
	$_____
	% of my investment capital
	_____%

Price objective	Est. time to achieve it	I will risk _____ points	Which would be $_____

TECHNICAL POSITION

Price action of stock:

❑ Hitting new highs   ❑ In a trading range

❑ Pausing in an uptrend   ❑ Moving up from low ground

❑ Acting stronger than market   ❑ _____

Dow Jones Industrial Average

Trend of market

SELECTED YARDSTICKS

	Price Range		Earnings Per Share Actual or Projected	Price/Earnings Ratio Actual or Projected
	High	Low		
Current year Previous year				

Merger possibilities	Years for earnings to double in past
Comment on future	Years for market price to double in past

PERIODIC RE-CHECKS

Date	Stock Price	DJIA	Comment	Action taken, if any

COMPLETED TRANSACTIONS

Date closed	Period of time held	Profit or loss

Reason for profit or loss